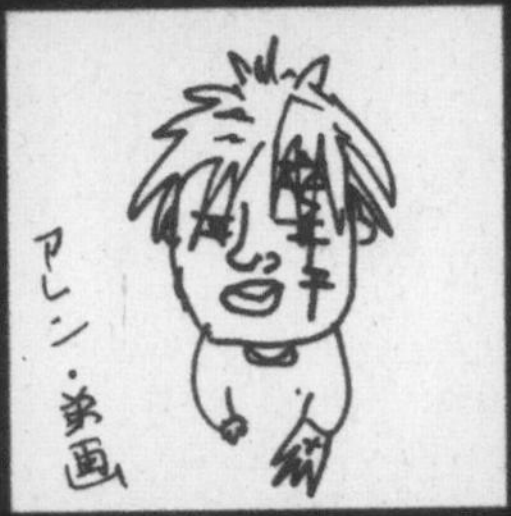
アレン・弟画

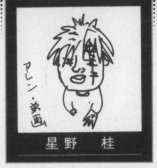

星野　桂

This is a picture of Allen that my little brother drew. We had a big laugh about it and decided to see which of us could draw another manga artist's characters better. The last character we competed on was Goku, and I swear I won!!

—Katsura Hoshino

Shiga Prefecture native Katsura Hoshino's hit manga series *D.Gray-man* has been serialized in *Weekly Shonen Jump* since 2004. Katsura's debut manga, "Continue," appeared for the first time in *Weekly Shonen Jump* in 2003.

Katsura adores cats.

D.GRAY-MAN
VOL. 10
The SHONEN JUMP ADVANCED
Manga Edition

STORY AND ART BY
KATSURA HOSHINO

English Adaptation/Lance Caselman
Translation/Toshifumi Yoshida
Touch-up Art & Lettering/Kelle Han
Design/Matt Hinrichs
Editor/Gary Leach

VP, Production/Alvin Lu
VP, Publishing Licensing/Rika Inouye
VP, Sales & Product Marketing/Gonzalo Ferreyra
VP, Creative/Linda Espinosa
Publisher/Hyoe Narita

D.GRAY-MAN © 2004 by Katsura Hoshino. All rights reserved.
First published in Japan in 2004 by SHUEISHA Inc., Tokyo. English translation rights arranged by SHUEISHA Inc. The stories, characters and incidents mentioned in this publication are entirely fictional.

Printed in the U.S.A.

Published by VIZ Media, LLC
P.O. Box 77010
San Francisco, CA 94107

SHONEN JUMP ADVANCED Manga Edition
10 9 8 7 6 5 4 3 2
First printing, August 2008
Second printing, March 2009

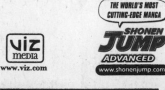

THE WORLD'S MOST
CUTTING-EDGE MANGA

www.viz.com

(www.shonenjump.com)

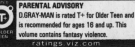

PARENTAL ADVISORY
D.GRAY-MAN is rated T+ for Older Teen and is recommended for ages 16 and up. This volume contains fantasy violence.
ratings.viz.com

SHONEN JUMP ADVANCED MANGA EDITION

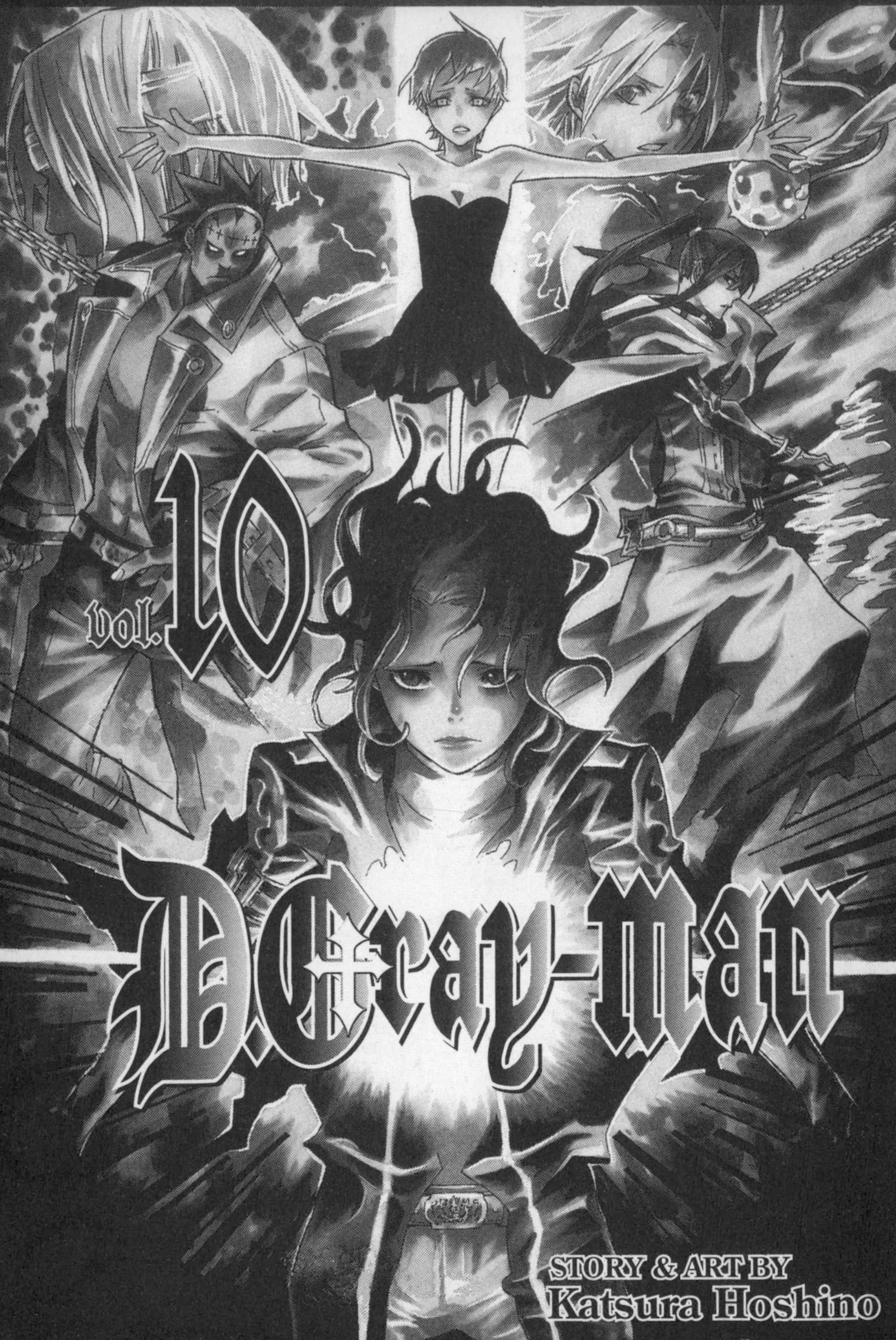
vol. 10
D.Gray-man
STORY & ART BY
Katsura Hoshino

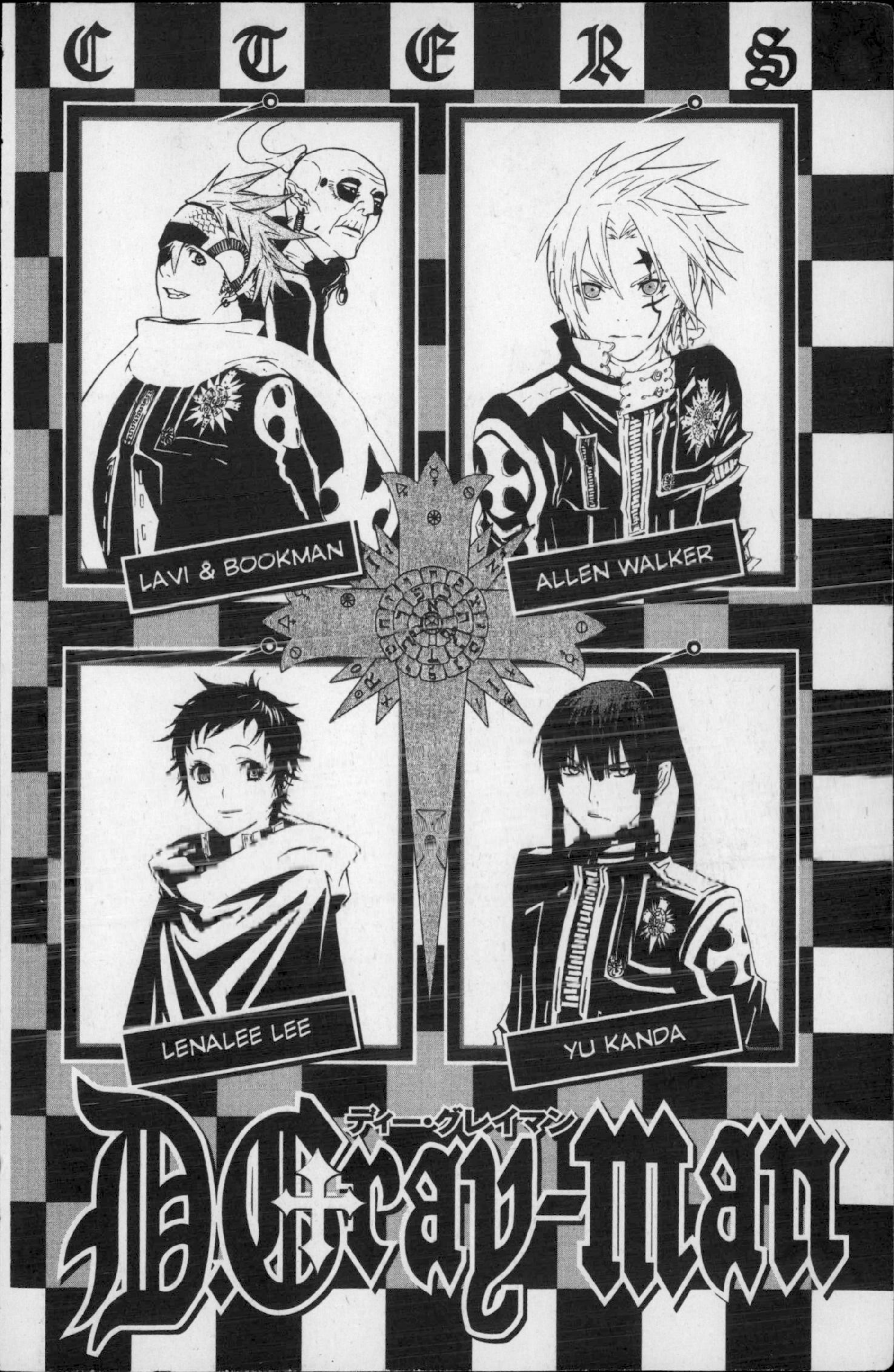
C T E R S
LAVI & BOOKMAN
ALLEN WALKER
LENALEE LEE
YU KANDA
ディー・グレイマン
D.Gray-man

D.GRAY-

V

CONTENTS

The 87th Night: Tiedoll's Entry 7

The 88th Night: The Villain Laughs 25

The 89th Night: Tragicomedy 43

The 90th Night: The Final Bell Has Yet to Toll 61

The 91st Night: A Key and Four Doors 79

The 92nd Night: Skin Boric's Room 97

The 93rd Night: Noah's Memory, Part 1 115

The 94th Night: Noah's Memory, Part 2 129

The 95th Night: Noah's Memory, Part 3 145

The 96th Night: Noah's Memory, Part 4 161

The 97th Night: Noah's Memory, Part 5 177

CHARA

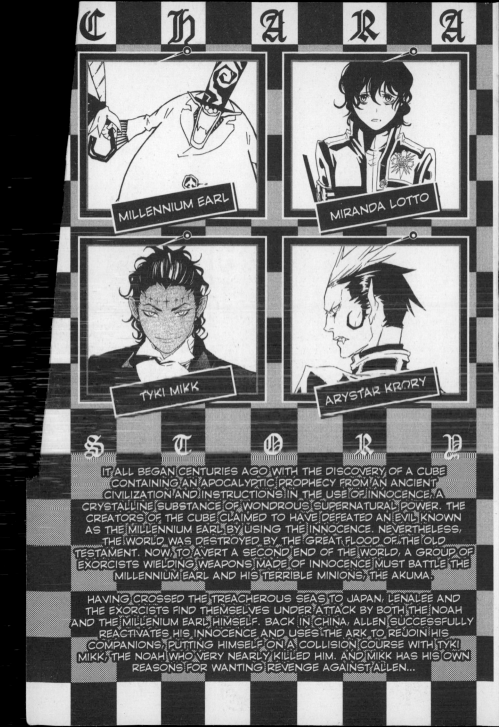

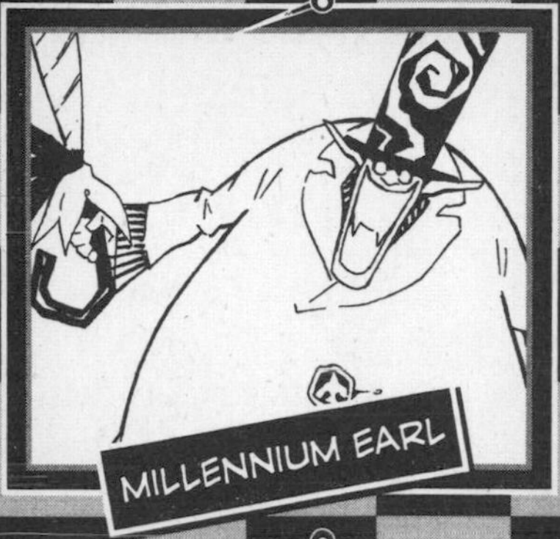
MILLENNIUM EARL

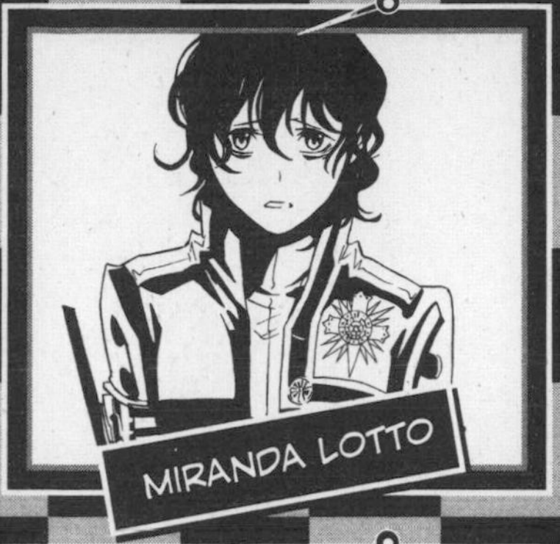
MIRANDA LOTTO

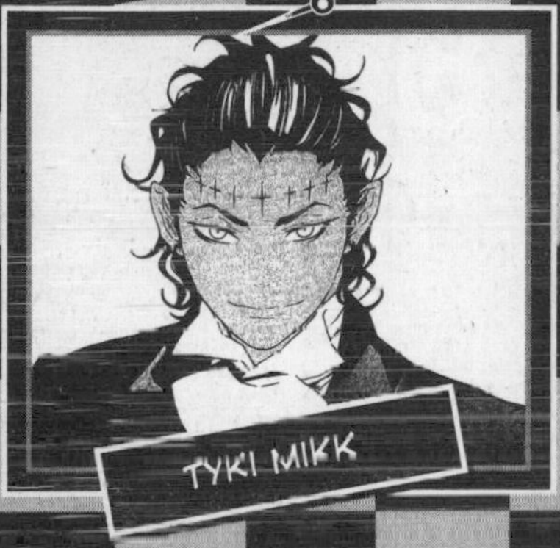
TYKI MIKK

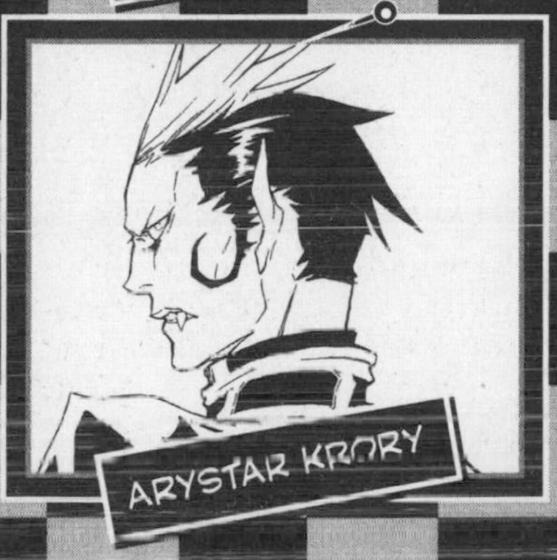
ARYSTAR KRORY

STORY

IT ALL BEGAN CENTURIES AGO WITH THE DISCOVERY OF A CUBE CONTAINING AN APOCALYPTIC PROPHECY FROM AN ANCIENT CIVILIZATION AND INSTRUCTIONS IN THE USE OF INNOCENCE, A CRYSTALLINE SUBSTANCE OF WONDROUS SUPERNATURAL POWER. THE CREATORS OF THE CUBE CLAIMED TO HAVE DEFEATED AN EVIL KNOWN AS THE MILLENNIUM EARL BY USING THE INNOCENCE. NEVERTHELESS, THE WORLD WAS DESTROYED BY THE GREAT FLOOD OF THE OLD TESTAMENT. NOW, TO AVERT A SECOND END OF THE WORLD, A GROUP OF EXORCISTS WIELDING WEAPONS MADE OF INNOCENCE MUST BATTLE THE MILLENNIUM EARL AND HIS TERRIBLE MINIONS, THE AKUMA.

HAVING CROSSED THE TREACHEROUS SEAS TO JAPAN, LENALEE AND THE EXORCISTS FIND THEMSELVES UNDER ATTACK BY BOTH THE NOAH AND THE MILLENIUM EARL HIMSELF. BACK IN CHINA, ALLEN SUCCESSFULLY REACTIVATES HIS INNOCENCE AND USES THE ARK TO REJOIN HIS COMPANIONS, PUTTING HIMSELF ON A COLLISION COURSE WITH TYKI MIKK, THE NOAH WHO VERY NEARLY KILLED HIM. AND MIKK HAS HIS OWN REASONS FOR WANTING REVENGE AGAINST ALLEN...

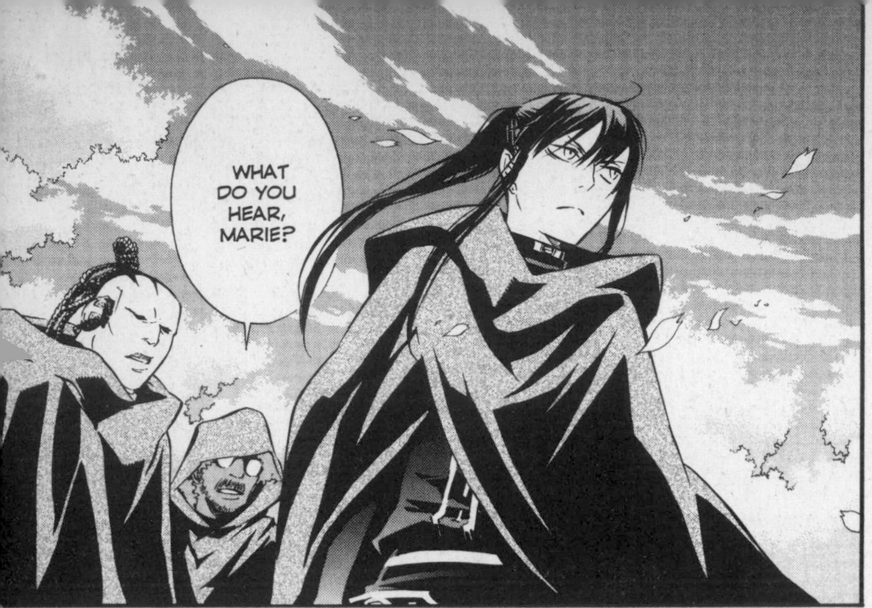
WHAT DO YOU HEAR, MARIE?

THE 87TH NIGHT: TIEDOLL'S ENTRY

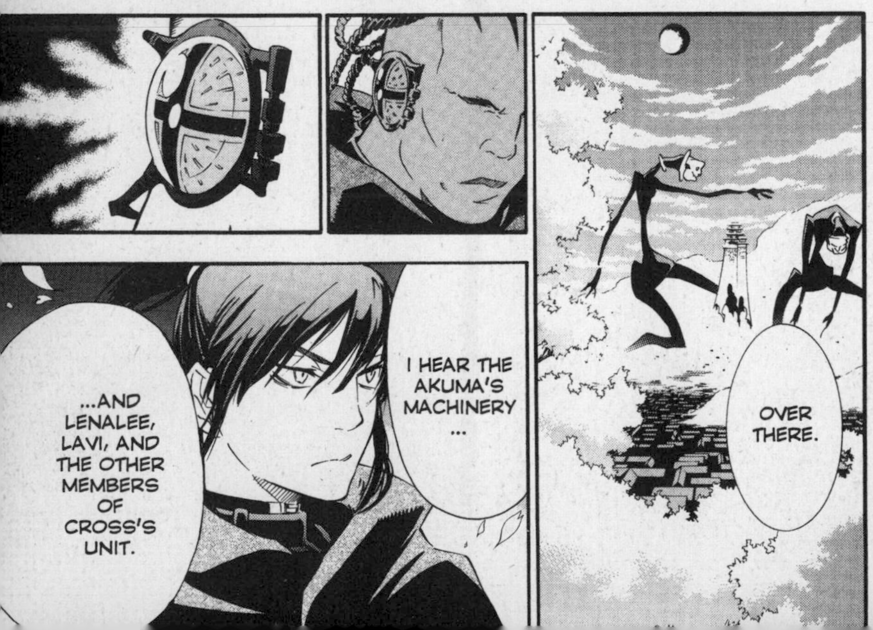
OVER THERE.
I HEAR THE AKUMA'S MACHINERY ...
...AND LENALEE, LAVI, AND THE OTHER MEMBERS OF CROSS'S UNIT.

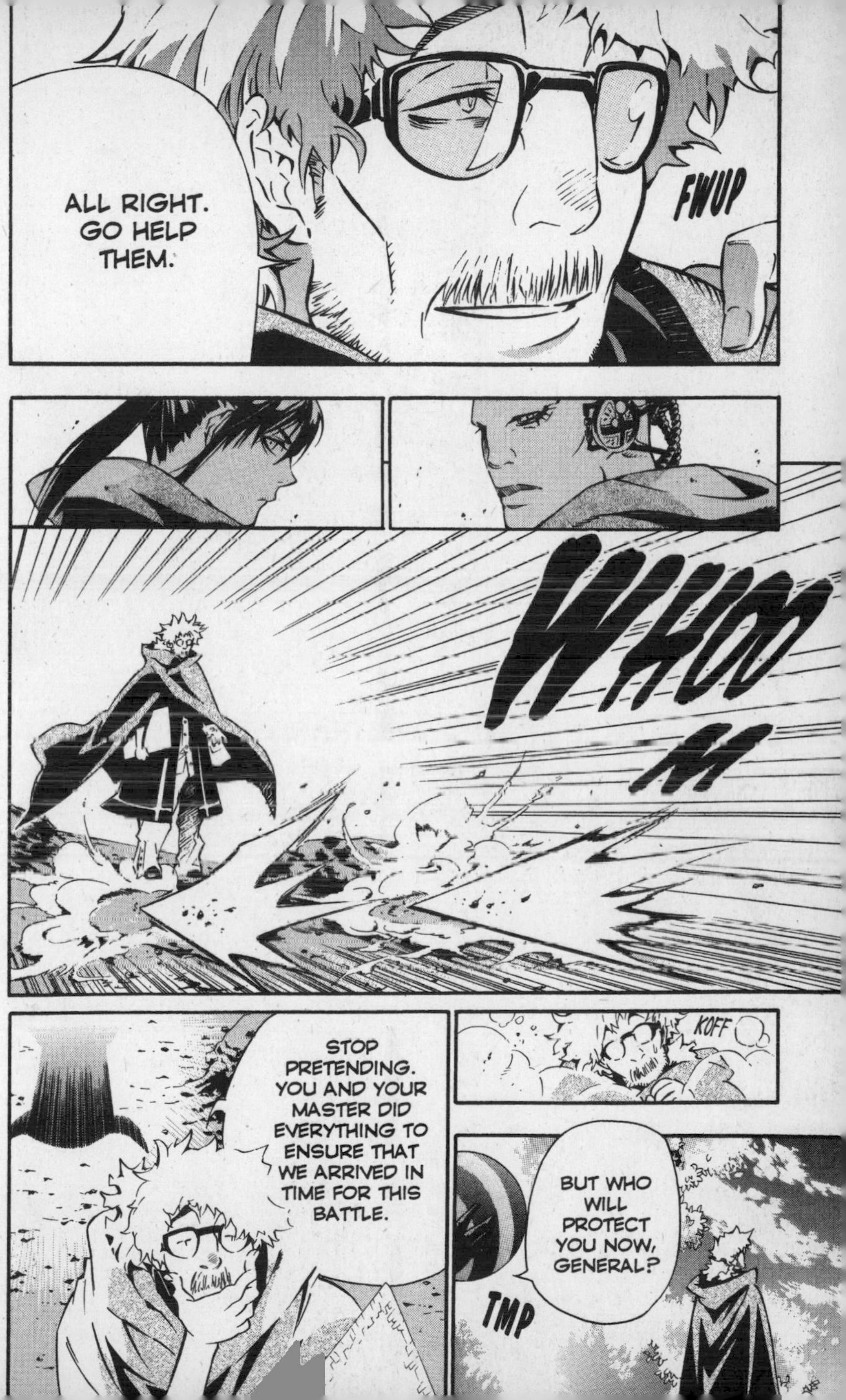
FWUP
ALL RIGHT. GO HELP THEM.
WHOOM
M
KOFF
BUT WHO WILL PROTECT YOU NOW, GENERAL?
TMP
STOP PRETENDING. YOU AND YOUR MASTER DID EVERYTHING TO ENSURE THAT WE ARRIVED IN TIME FOR THIS BATTLE.

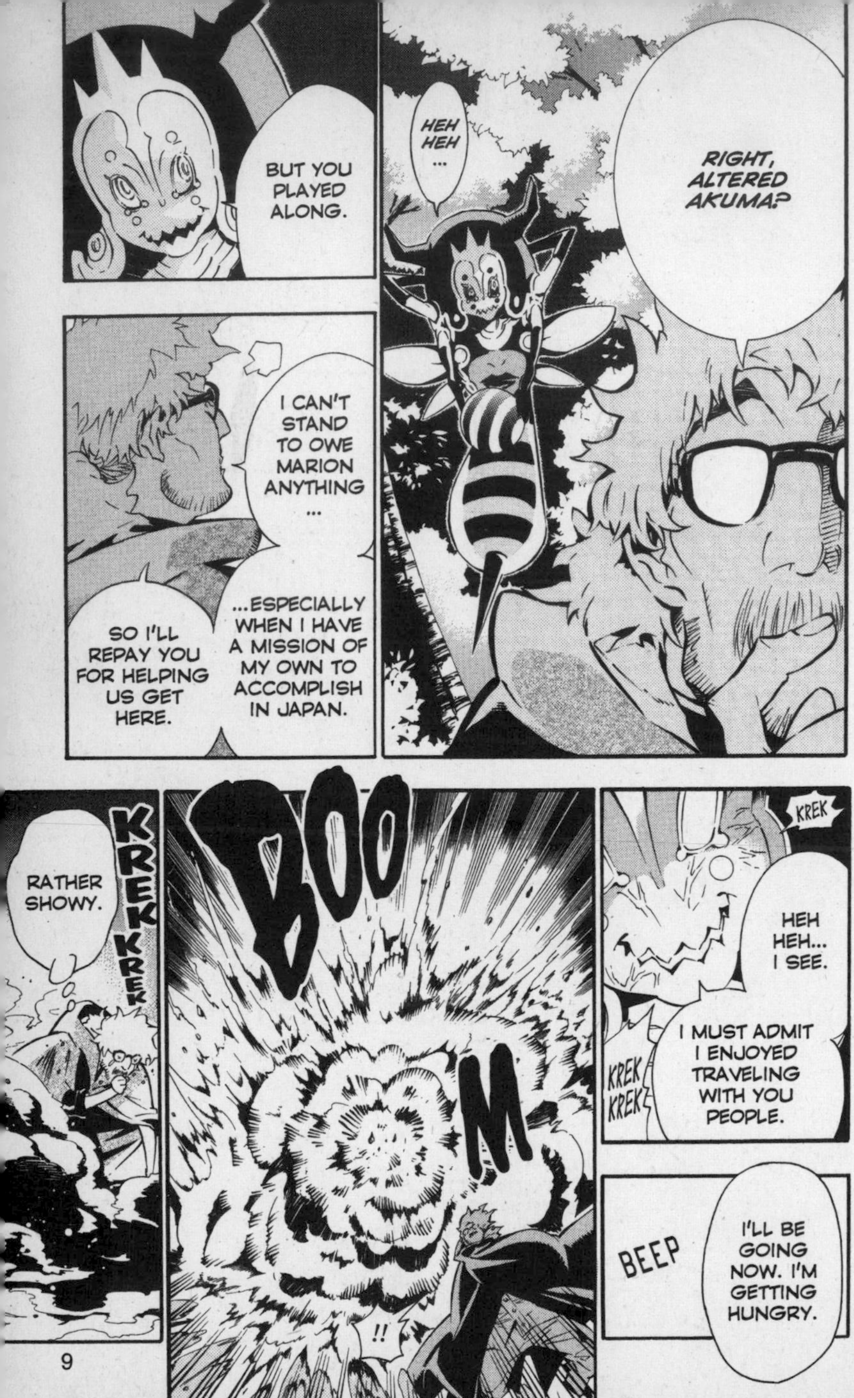
RIGHT, ALTERED AKUMA?
HEH HEH ...
BUT YOU PLAYED ALONG.
I CAN'T STAND TO OWE MARION ANYTHING ...
...ESPECIALLY WHEN I HAVE A MISSION OF MY OWN TO ACCOMPLISH IN JAPAN.
SO I'LL REPAY YOU FOR HELPING US GET HERE.
KREK
HEH HEH... I SEE.
I MUST ADMIT I ENJOYED TRAVELING WITH YOU PEOPLE.
KREK KREK
BEEP
I'LL BE GOING NOW. I'M GETTING HUNGRY.
BOOOM
!!
KREK KREK KREK
RATHER SHOWY.

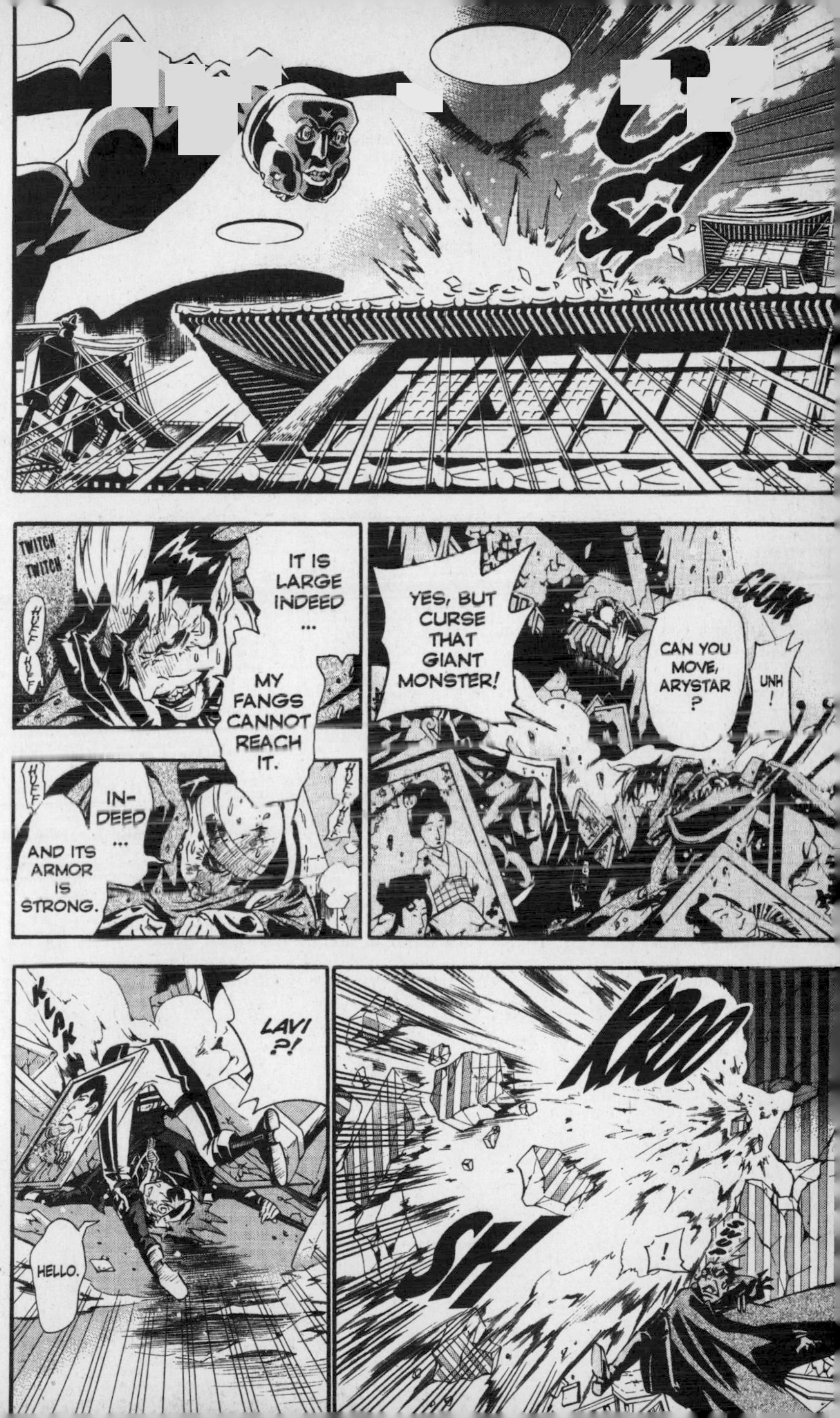
CAN YOU MOVE, ARYSTAR?
UNH!
YES, BUT CURSE THAT GIANT MONSTER!
IT IS LARGE INDEED ...
MY FANGS CANNOT REACH IT.
TWITCH TWITCH
HUFF HUFF
HUFF HUFF
IN-DEED ...
AND ITS ARMOR IS STRONG.
SH
!
LAVI ?!
HELLO.

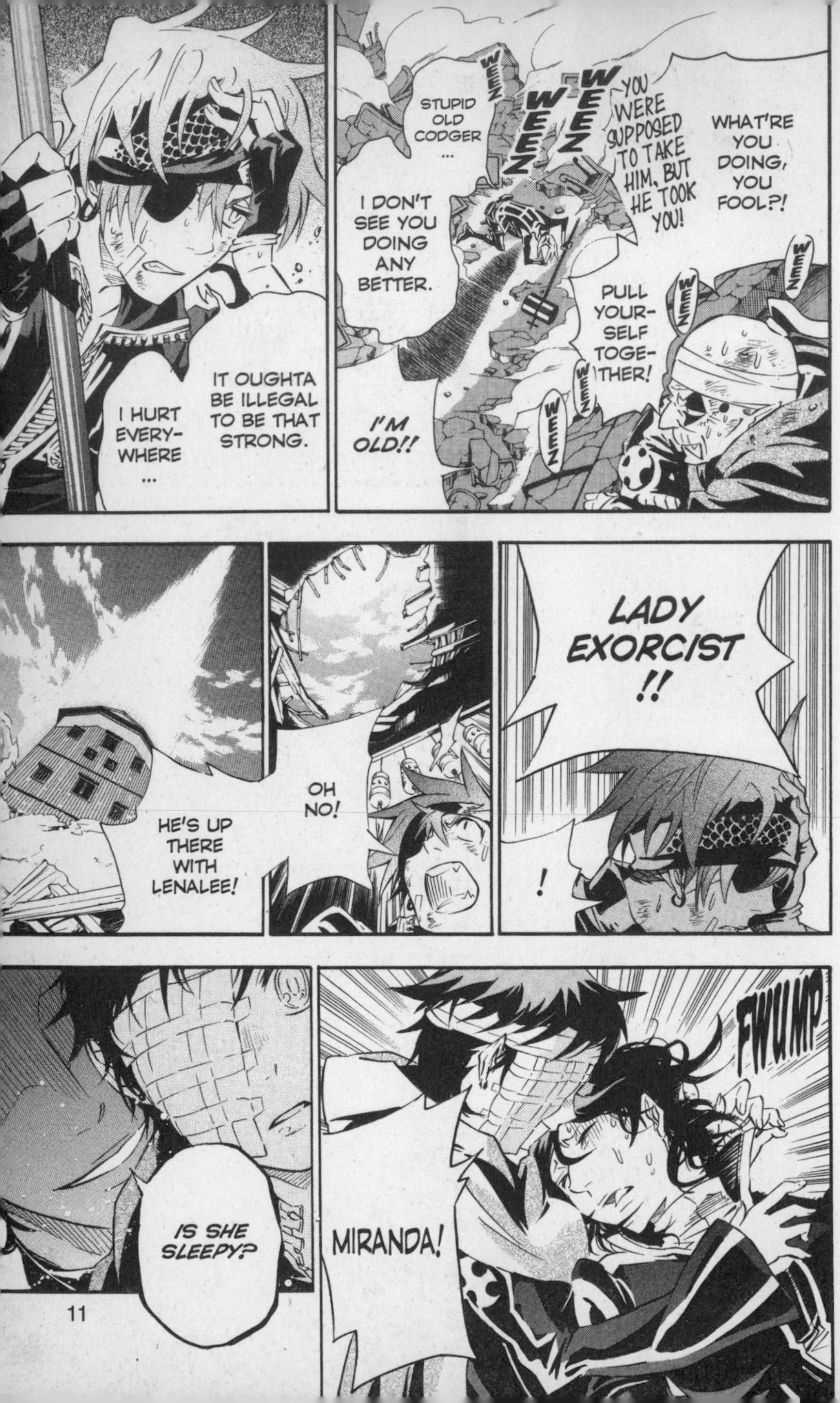
WHAT'RE YOU DOING, YOU FOOL?!
YOU WERE SUPPOSED TO TAKE HIM, BUT HE TOOK YOU!
WEEZ WEEZ WEEZ
STUPID OLD CODGER ...
WEEZ WEEZ
PULL YOURSELF TOGETHER!
I DON'T SEE YOU DOING ANY BETTER.
WEEZ WEEZ
I'M OLD!!
IT OUGHTA BE ILLEGAL TO BE THAT STRONG.
I HURT EVERYWHERE ...
LADY EXORCIST !!
!
OH NO!
HE'S UP THERE WITH LENALEE!
FWUMP
MIRANDA!
IS SHE SLEEPY?

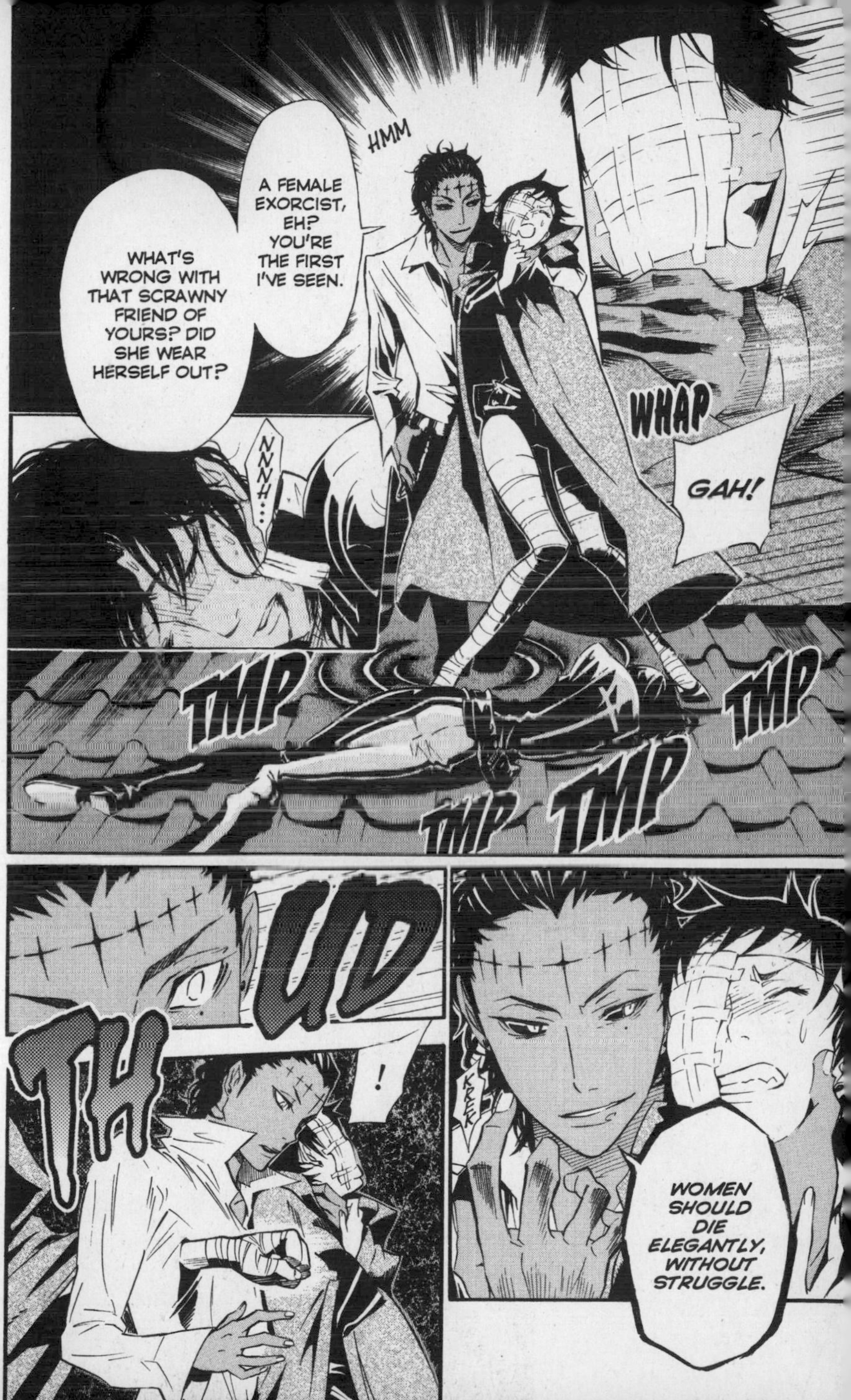
HMM
A FEMALE EXORCIST, EH? YOU'RE THE FIRST I'VE SEEN.
WHAT'S WRONG WITH THAT SCRAWNY FRIEND OF YOURS? DID SHE WEAR HERSELF OUT?
WHAP
GAH!
NNNH...
TMP
TMP
TMP
TMP
KREEK
WOMEN SHOULD DIE ELEGANTLY, WITHOUT STRUGGLE.
THUD
!

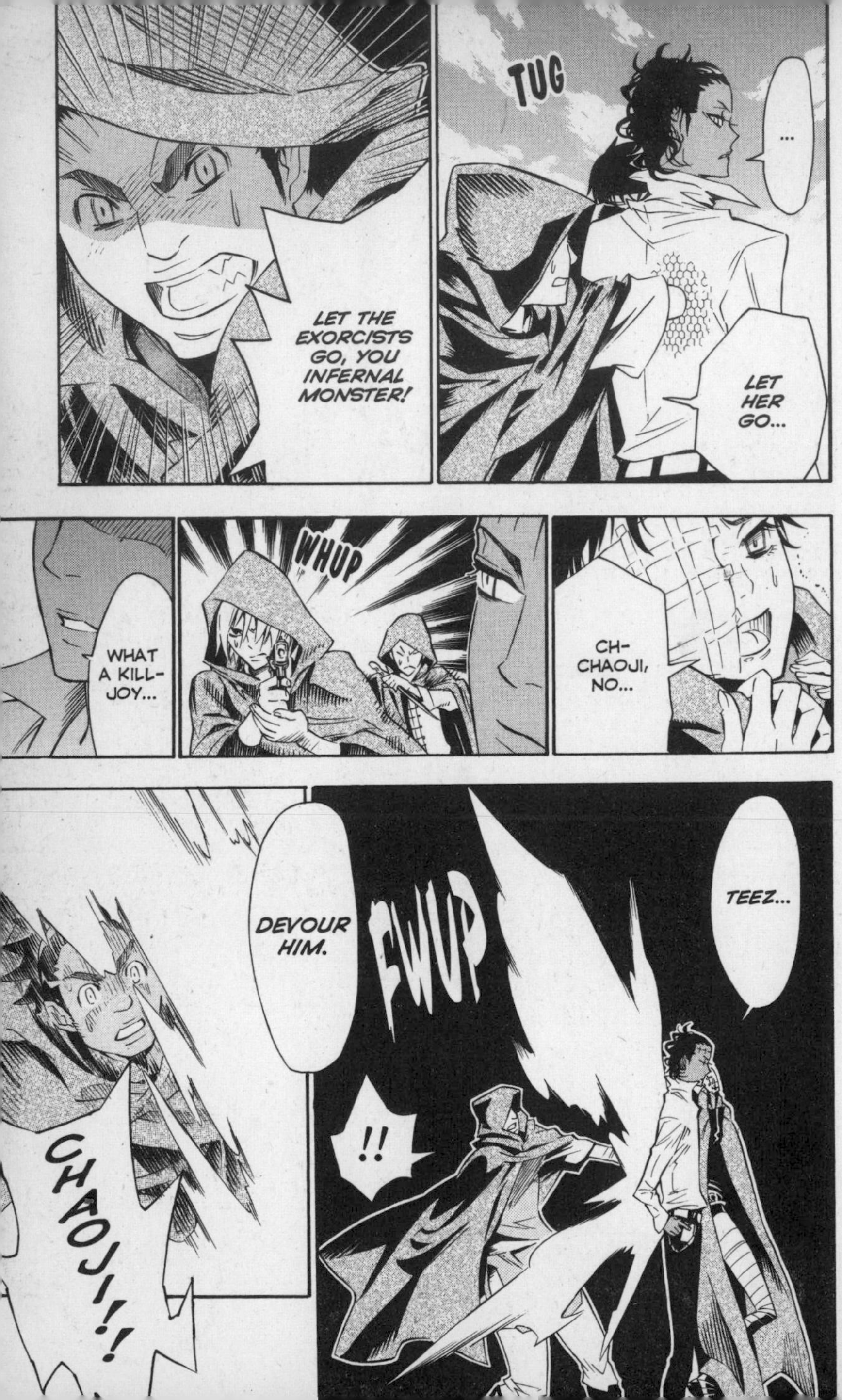
...
TUG
LET HER GO...
LET THE EXORCISTS GO, YOU INFERNAL MONSTER!
CH-CHAOJI, NO...
WHUP
WHAT A KILL-JOY...
TEEZ...
DEVOUR HIM.
FWUP
!!
CHAOJI!!!

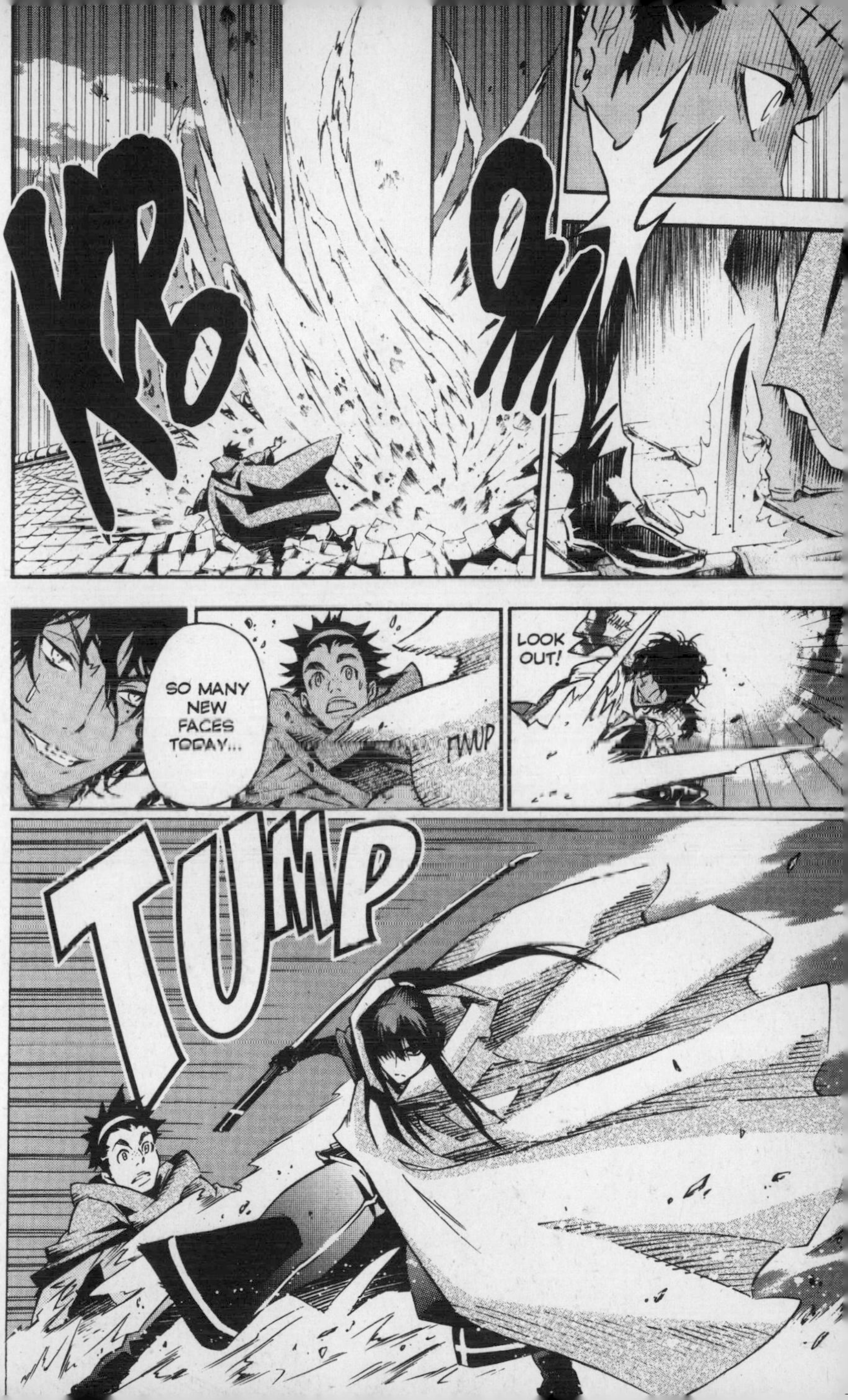
LOOK OUT!
SO MANY NEW FACES TODAY...
FWUP
TUMP

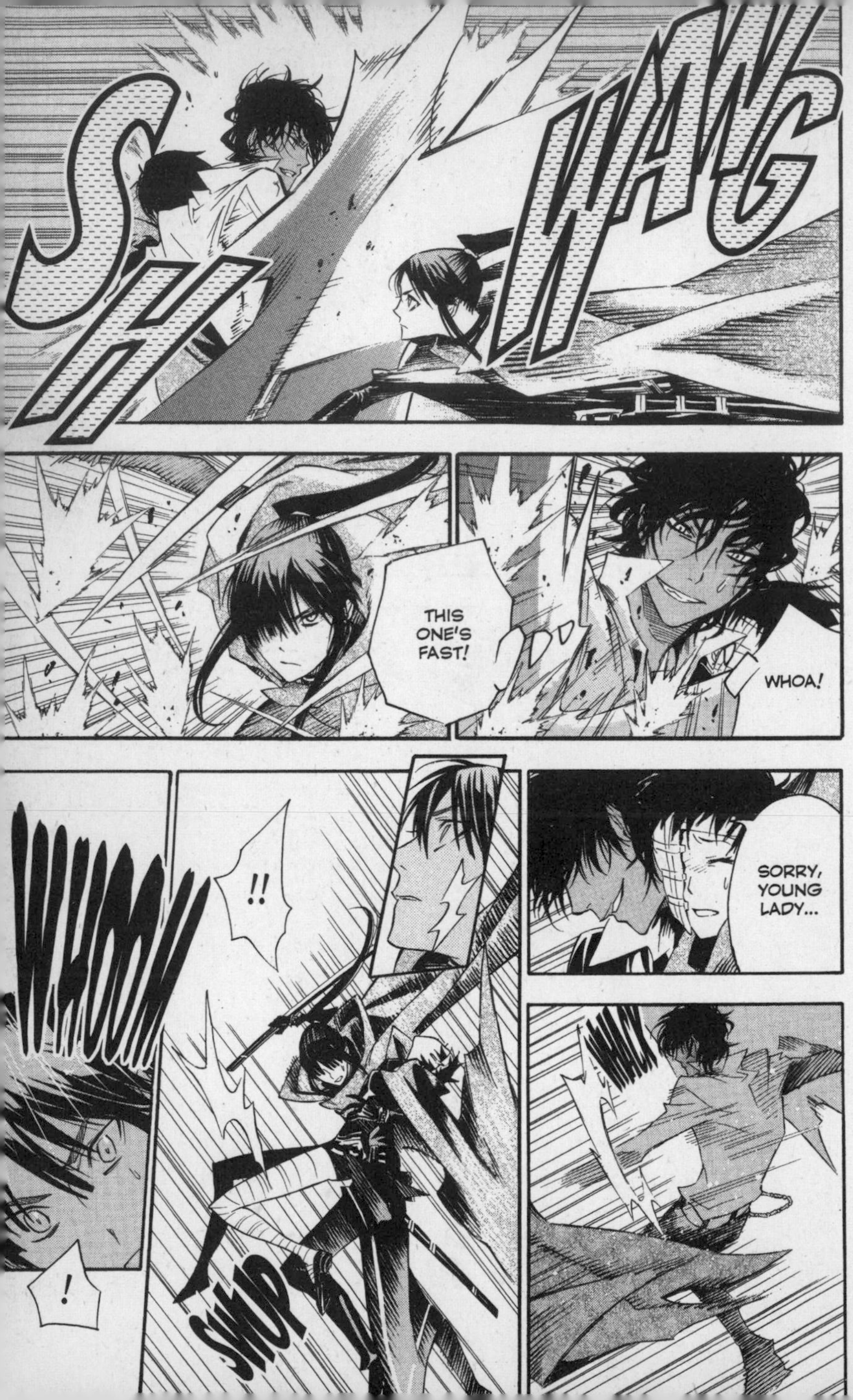
SHWANG
WHOA!
THIS ONE'S FAST!
SORRY, YOUNG LADY...
WHACK
!!
SWIP
WHOOM
!

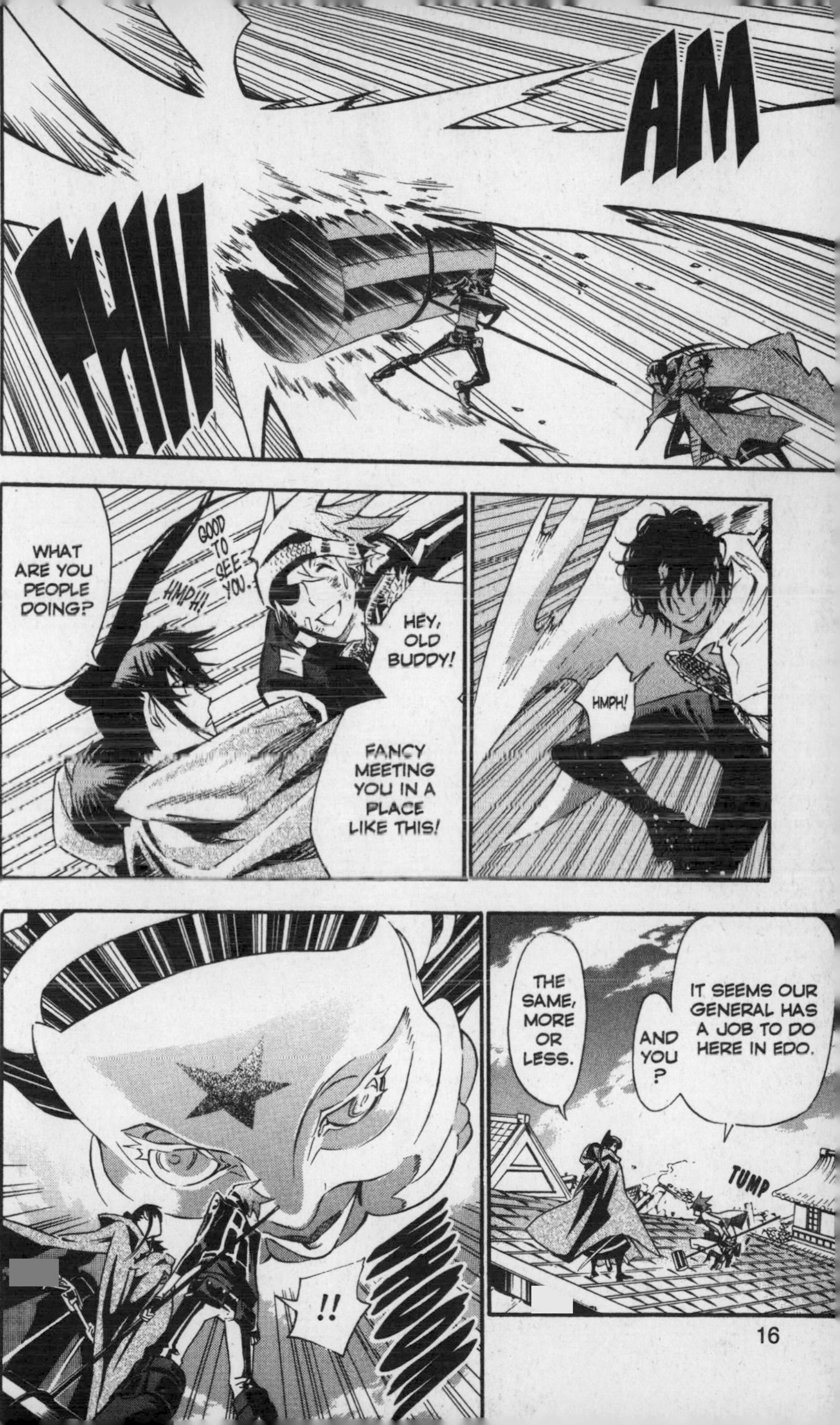
THW
AM
HMPH!
HEY, OLD BUDDY!
FANCY MEETING YOU IN A PLACE LIKE THIS!
GOOD TO SEE YOU.
HMPH!!
WHAT ARE YOU PEOPLE DOING?
IT SEEMS OUR GENERAL HAS A JOB TO DO HERE IN EDO.
AND YOU?
THE SAME, MORE OR LESS.
TUMP
!!

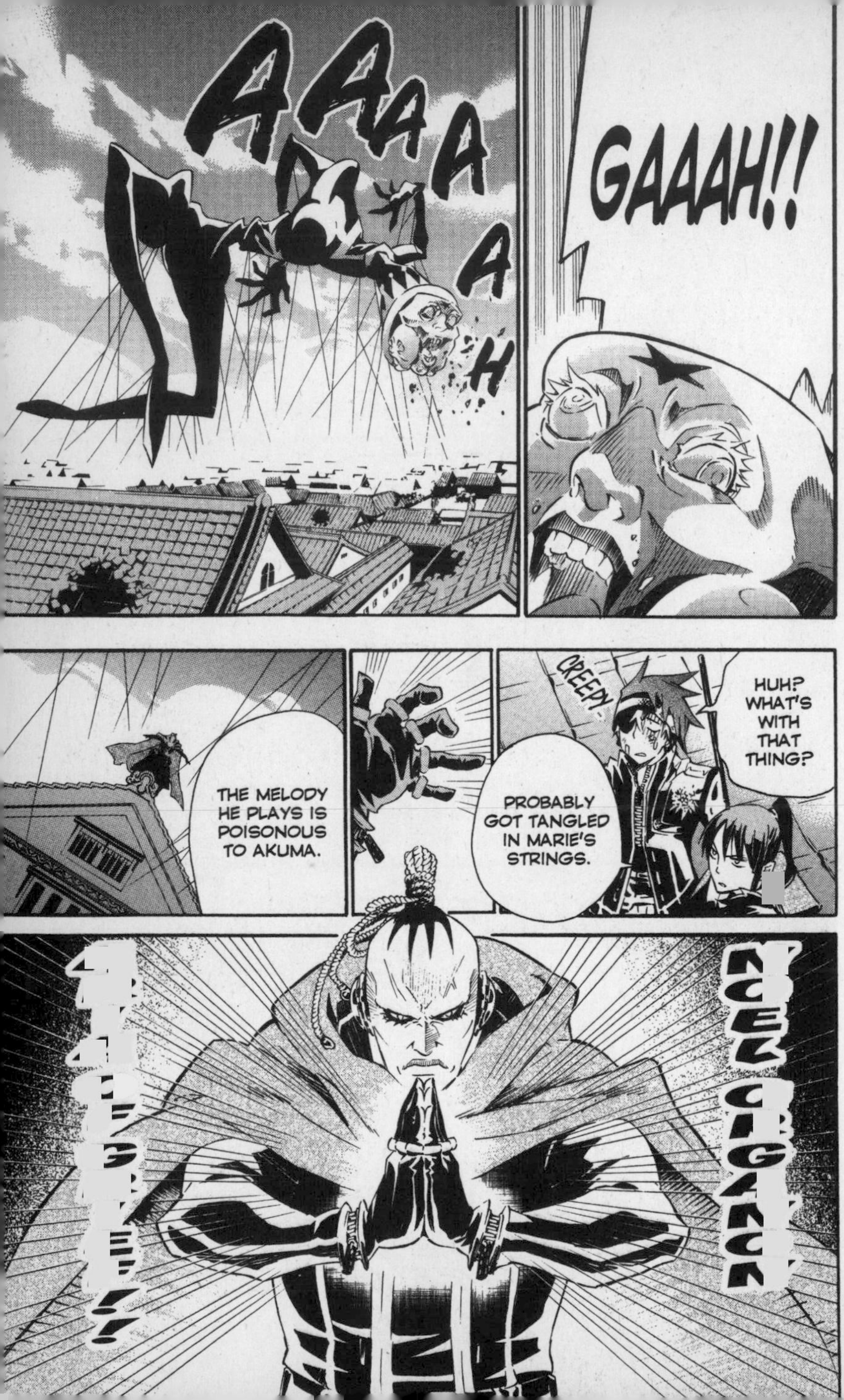
GAAAH!!
AAAAAH
HUH? WHAT'S WITH THAT THING?
CREEPY
PROBABLY GOT TANGLED IN MARIE'S STRINGS.
THE MELODY HE PLAYS IS POISONOUS TO AKUMA.

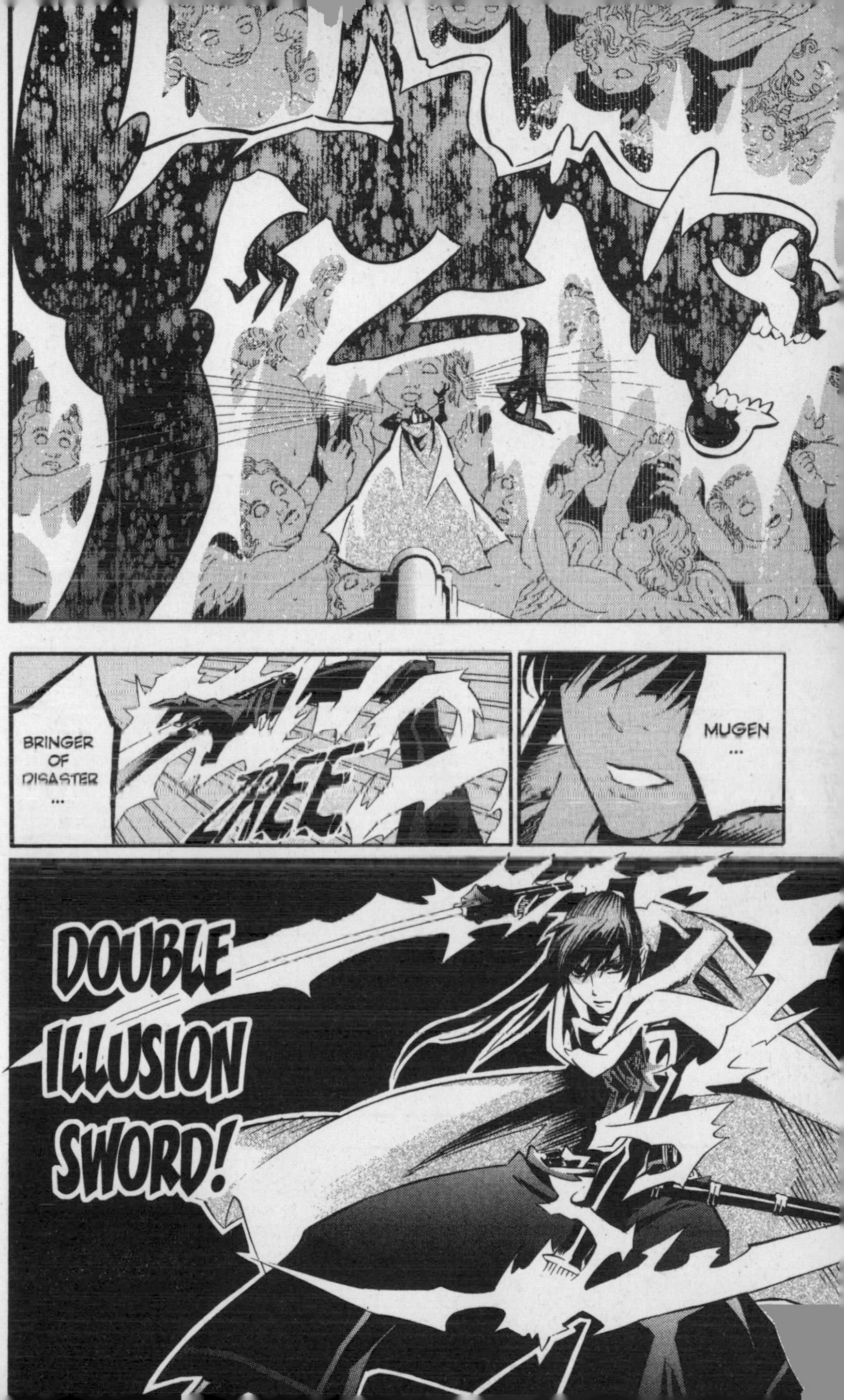
MUGEN
...
BRINGER OF DISASTER
...
DOUBLE ILLUSION SWORD!

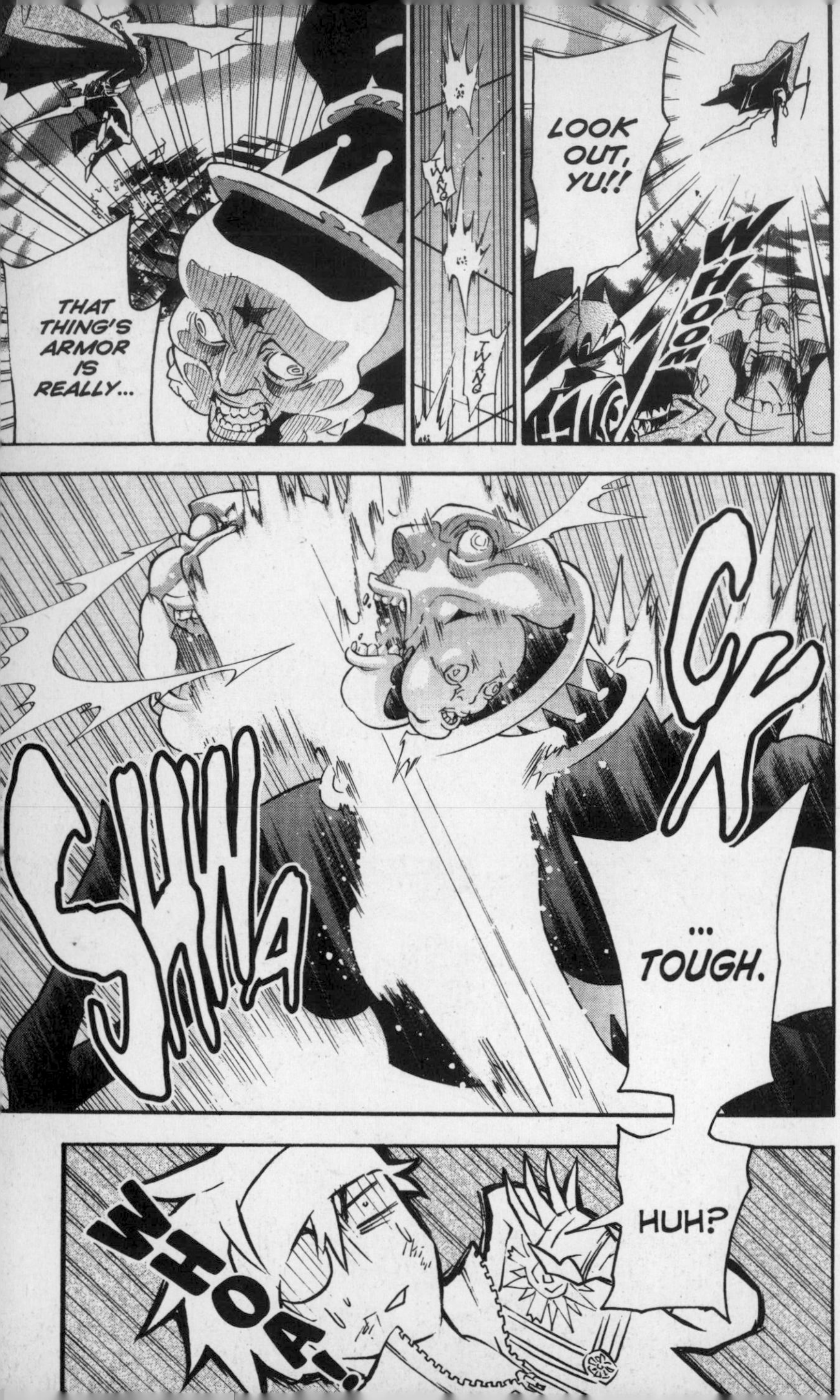
LOOK OUT, YU!!
WHOOOM
TWANG
TWANG
THAT THING'S ARMOR IS REALLY...
... TOUGH.
HUH?
WHOA!!

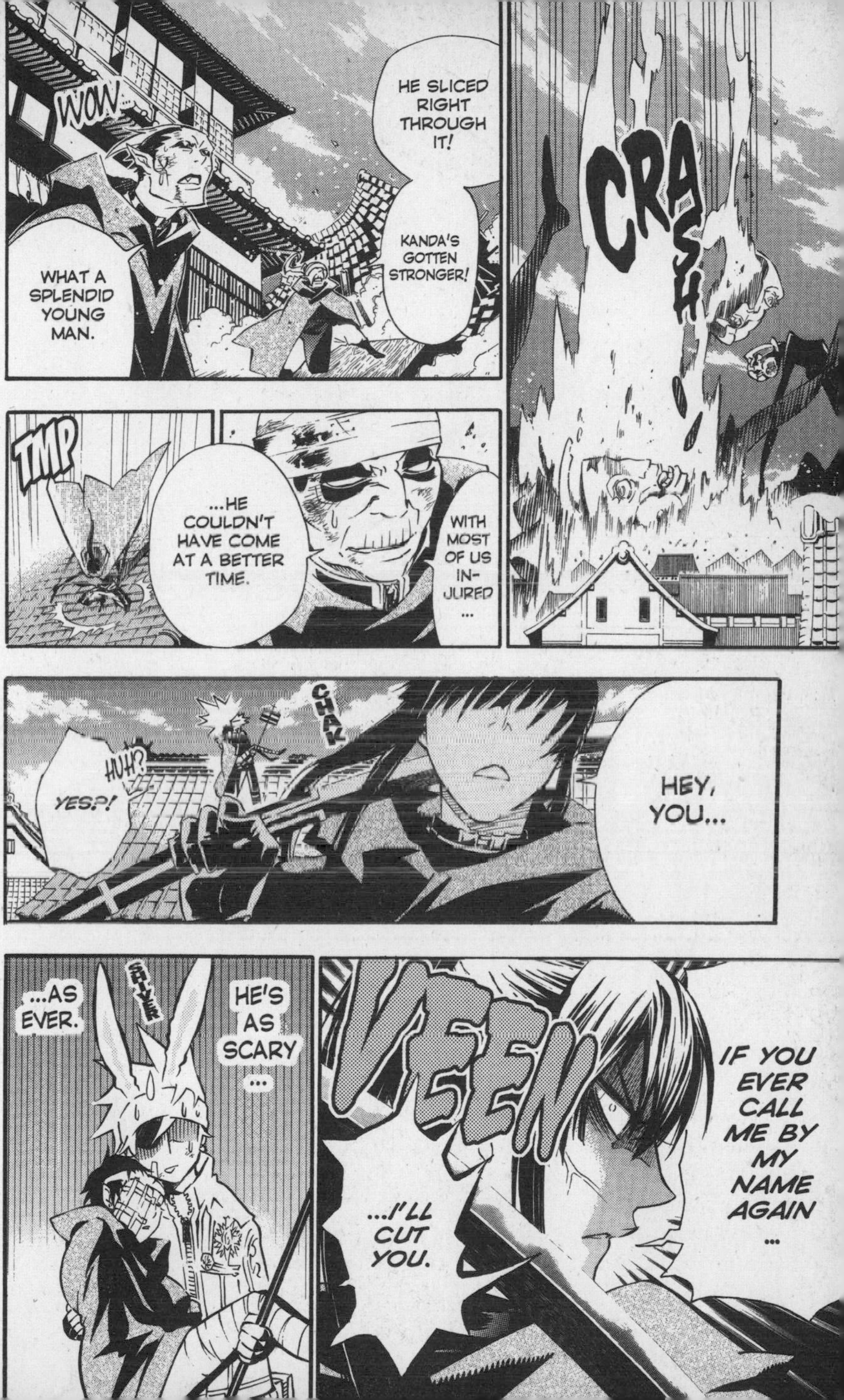
CRASH
HE SLICED RIGHT THROUGH IT!
KANDA'S GOTTEN STRONGER!
WOW...
WHAT A SPLENDID YOUNG MAN.
WITH MOST OF US IN-JURED...
...HE COULDN'T HAVE COME AT A BETTER TIME.
TMP
HEY, YOU...
CHAK
HUH?
YES?!
IF YOU EVER CALL ME BY MY NAME AGAIN...
VEEN
...I'LL CUT YOU.
SHIVER
HE'S AS SCARY...
...AS EVER.

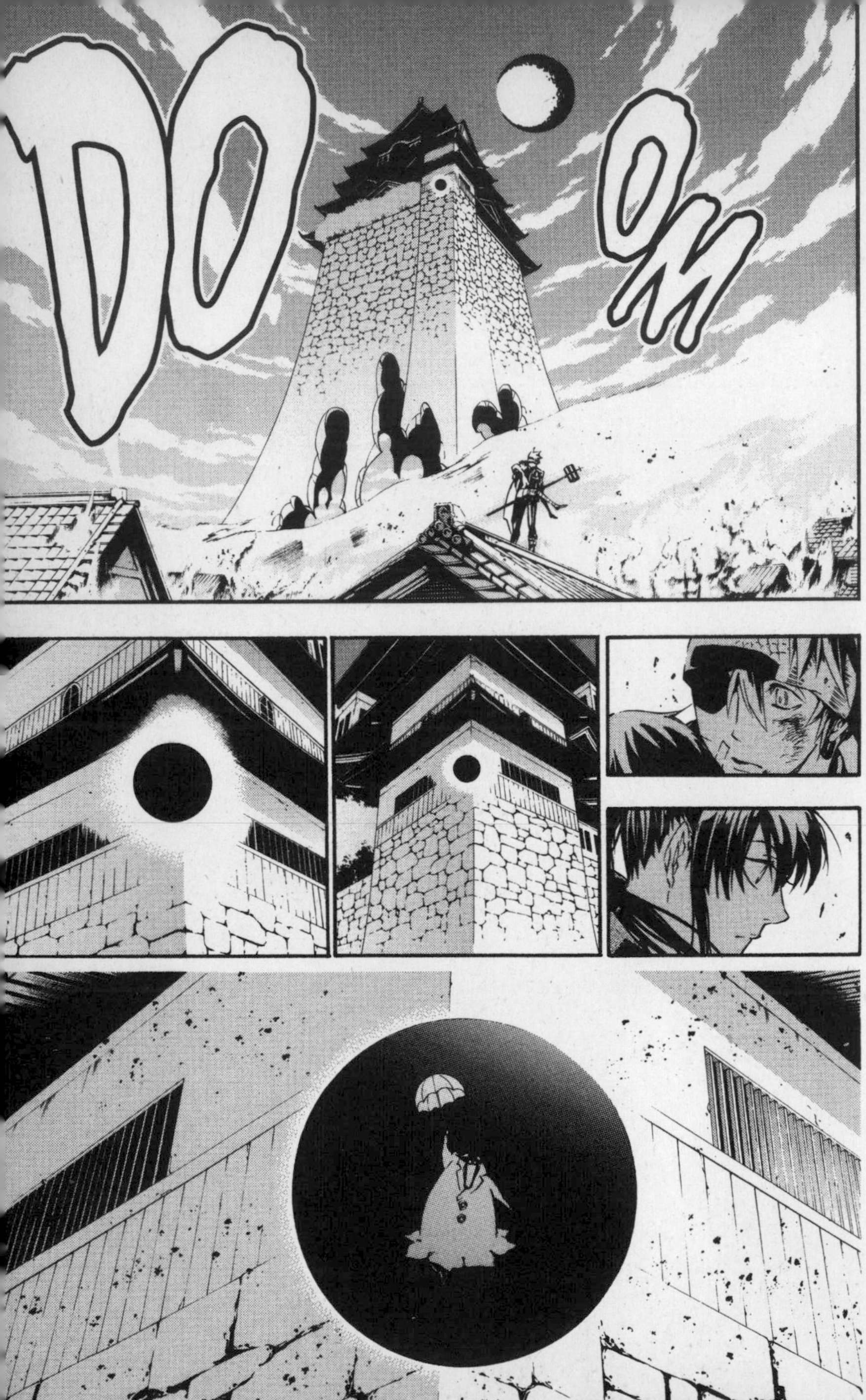
DOOOM

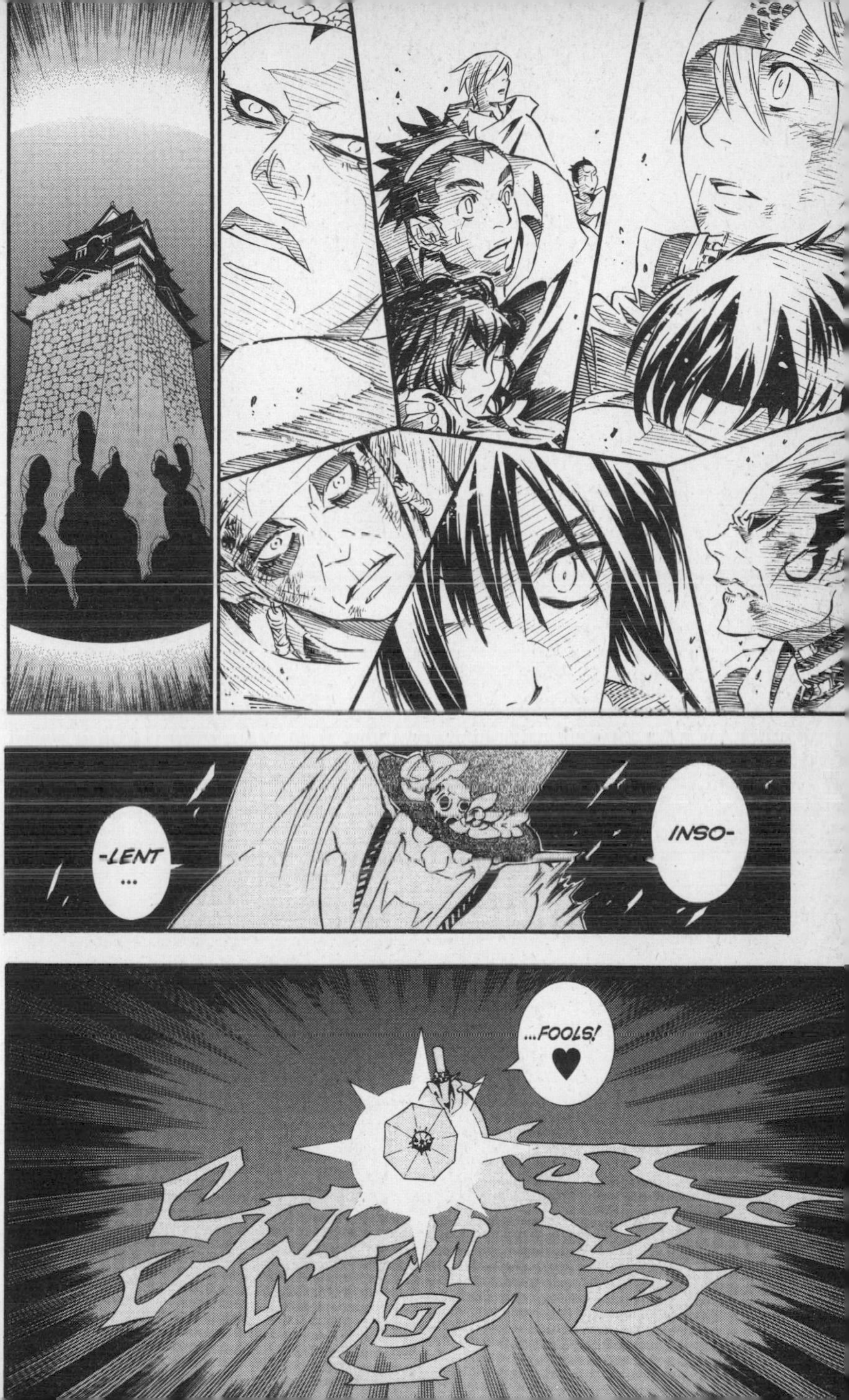
INSO-
-LENT ...
...FOOLS! ♥

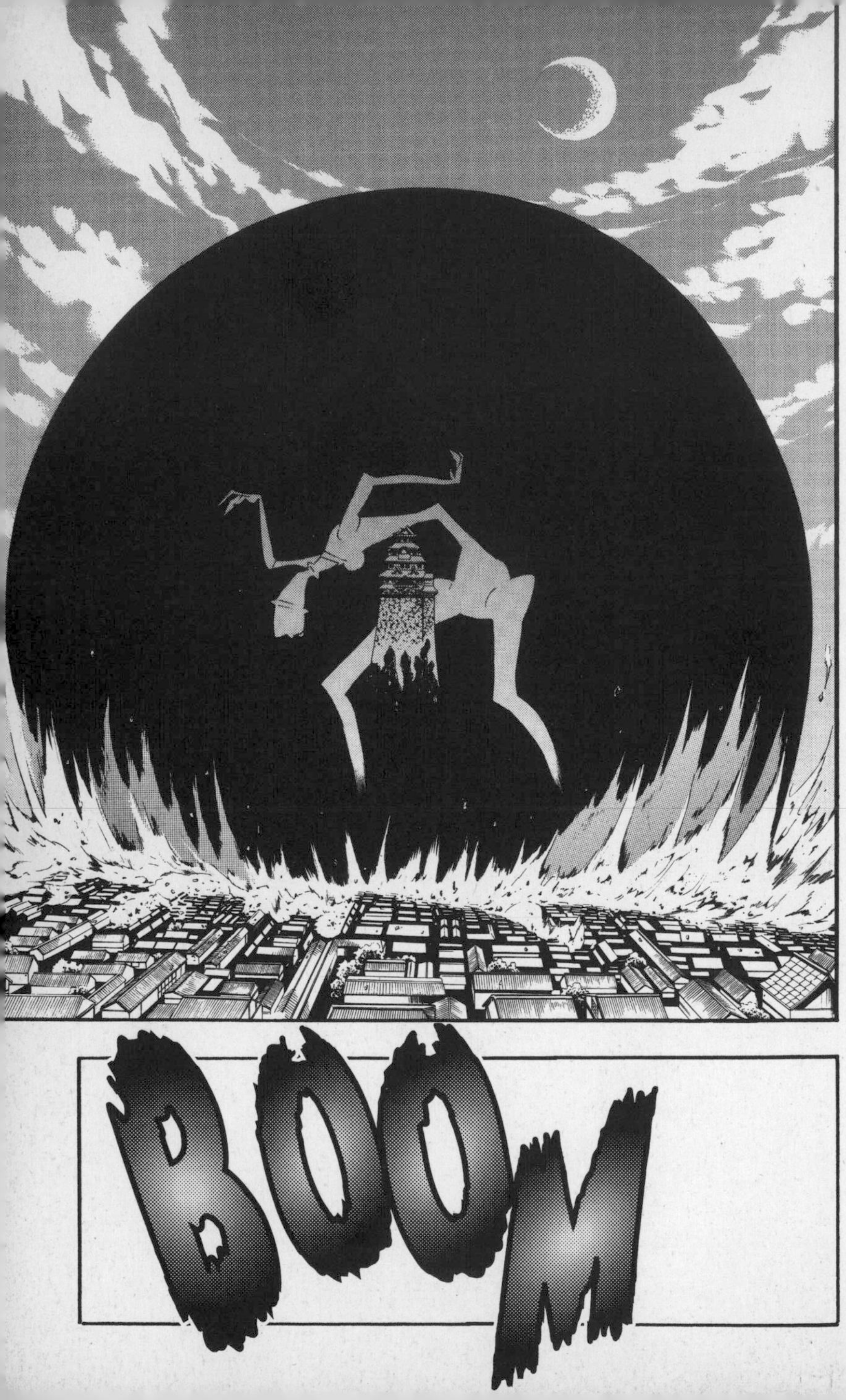
BOOM

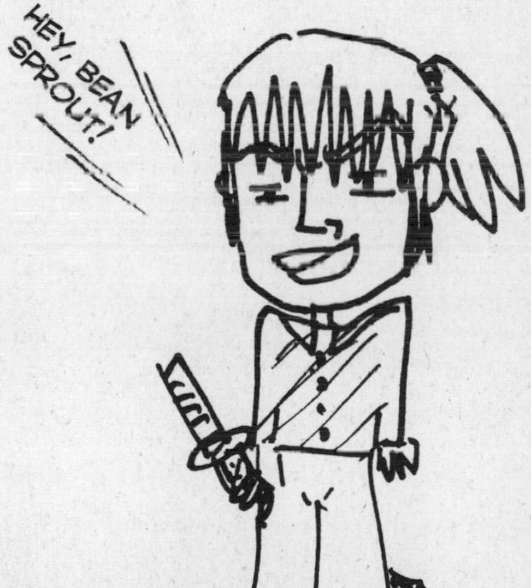
HEY, BEAN SPROUT!

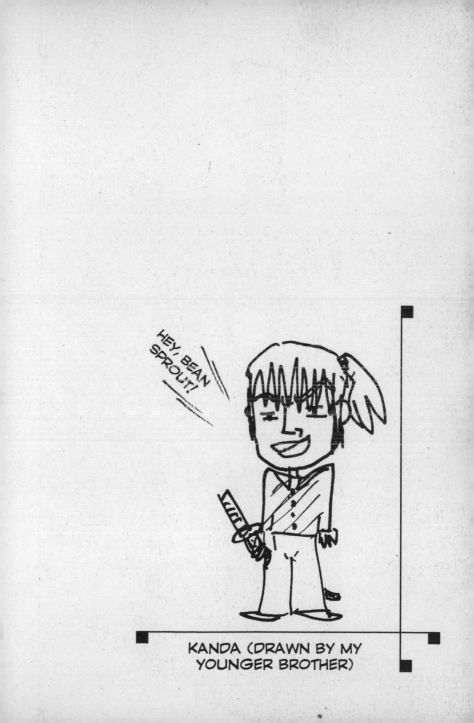

KANDA (DRAWN BY MY YOUNGER BROTHER)

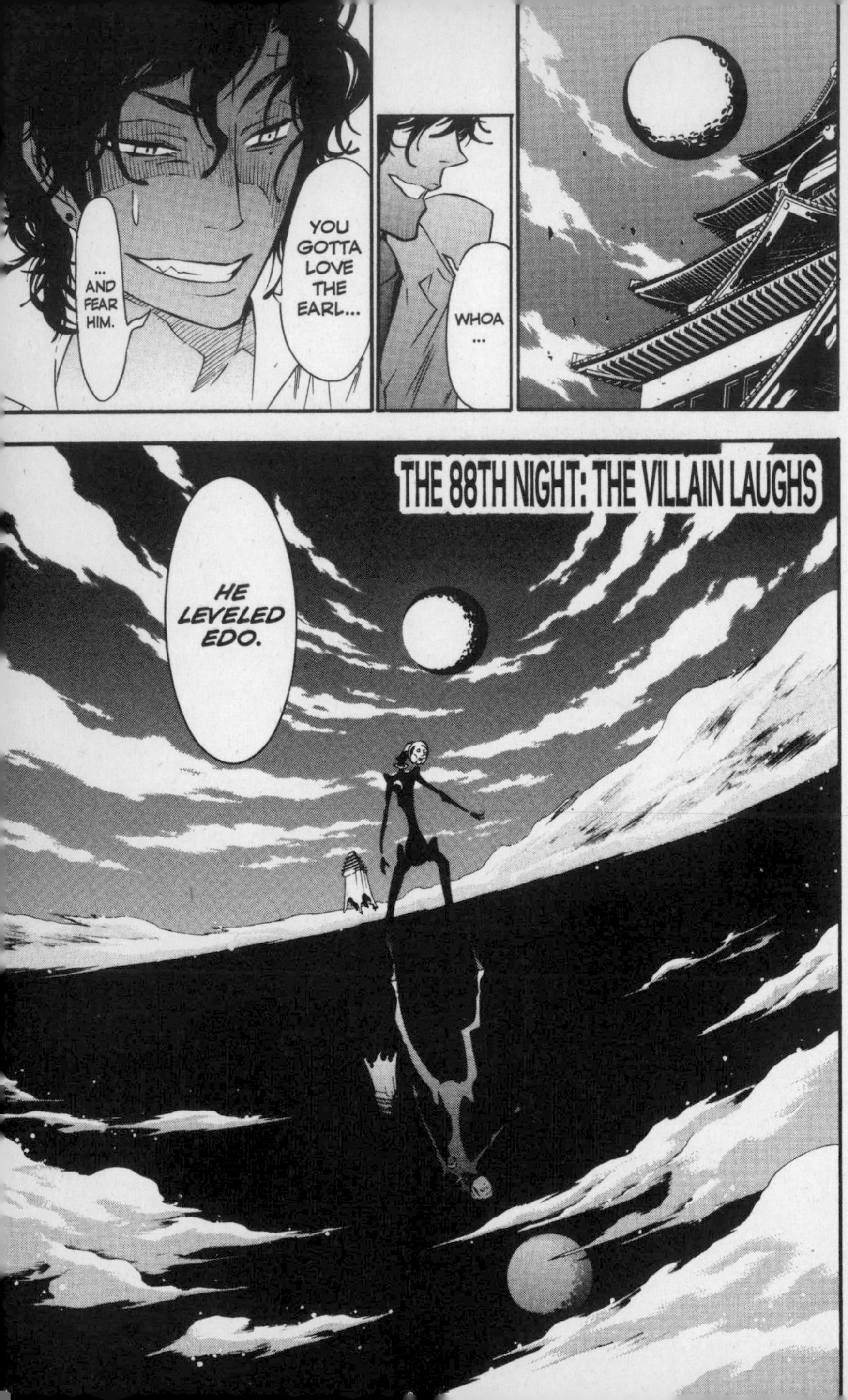
WHOA ...
YOU GOTTA LOVE THE EARL...
... AND FEAR HIM.
THE 88TH NIGHT: THE VILLAIN LAUGHS
HE LEVELED EDO.

THE 88TH NIGHT: THE VILLAIN LAUGHS

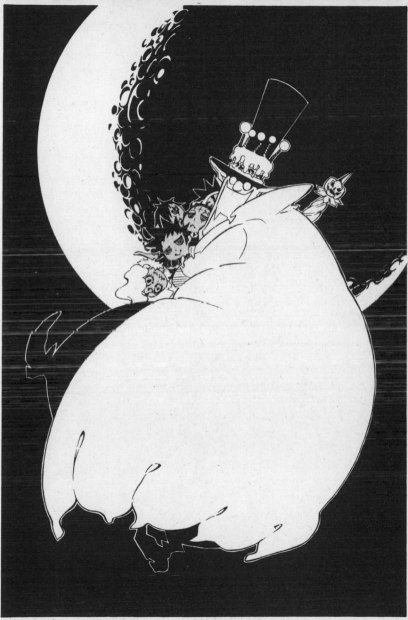

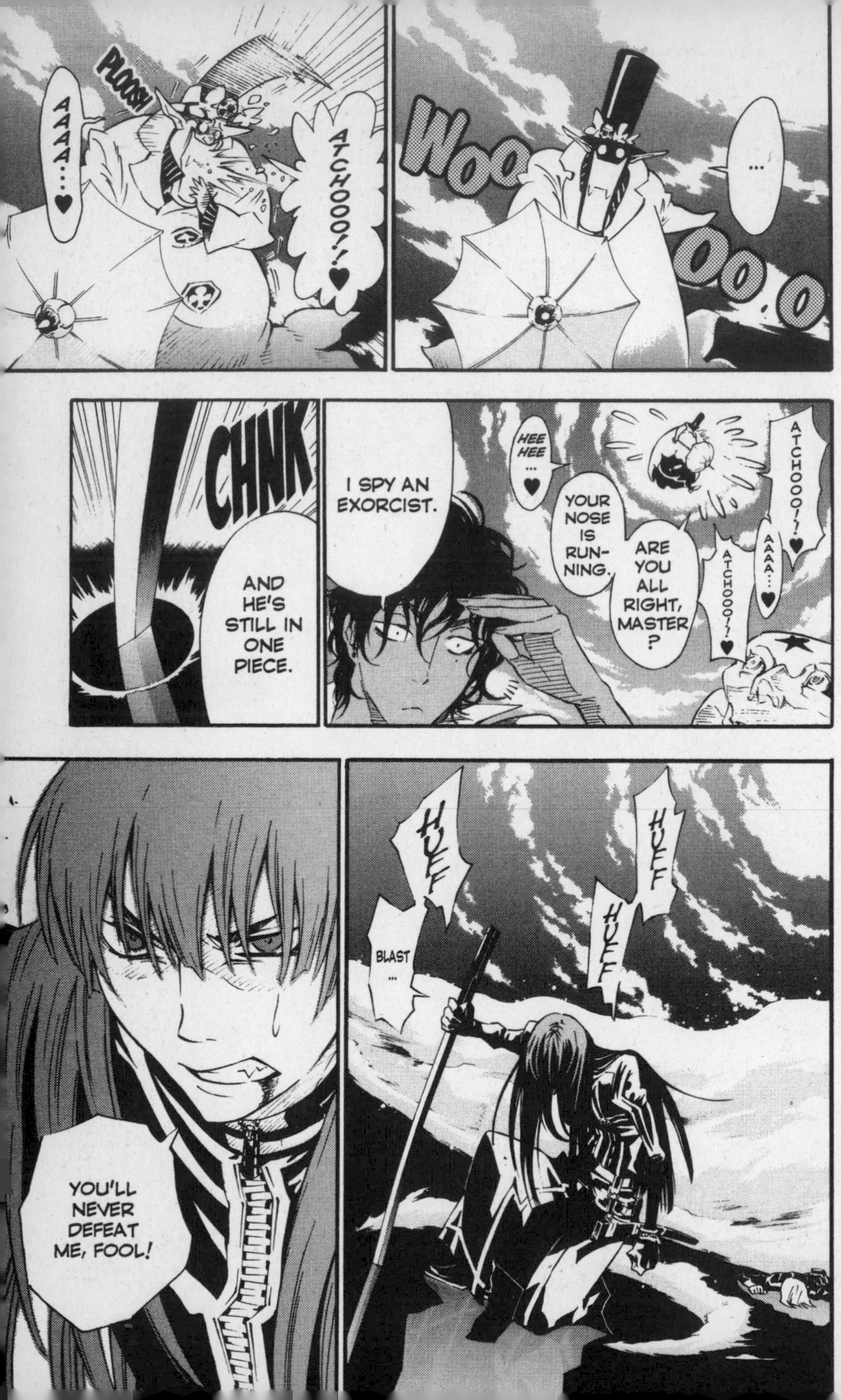
...
WOOOOOO.O
ATCHOOO!!♥
PLOOSH
AAAA...♥
ATCHOOO!!♥
AAAA...♥
ATCHOOO!!♥
ARE YOU ALL RIGHT, MASTER?
YOUR NOSE IS RUNNING.
HEE HEE...♥
I SPY AN EXORCIST.
CHNK
AND HE'S STILL IN ONE PIECE.
HUFF
HUFF
HUFF
BLAST...
YOU'LL NEVER DEFEAT ME, FOOL!

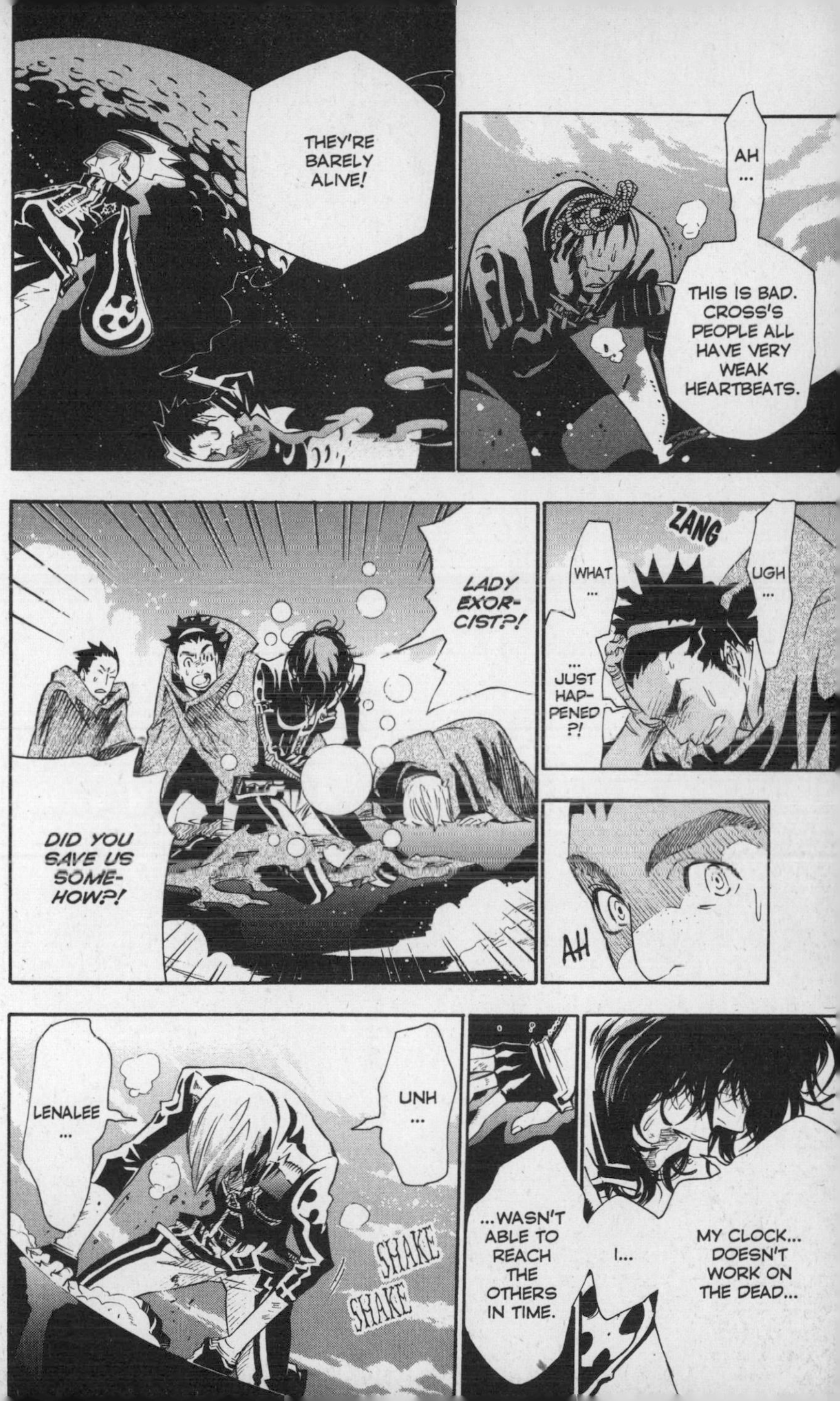
AH ...
THIS IS BAD. CROSS'S PEOPLE ALL HAVE VERY WEAK HEARTBEATS.
THEY'RE BARELY ALIVE!
ZANG
UGH ...
WHAT ...
... JUST HAPPENED ?!
AH
LADY EXORCIST?!
DID YOU SAVE US SOME-HOW?!
MY CLOCK... DOESN'T WORK ON THE DEAD...
I...
...WASN'T ABLE TO REACH THE OTHERS IN TIME.
UNH ...
LENALEE ...
SHAKE
SHAKE

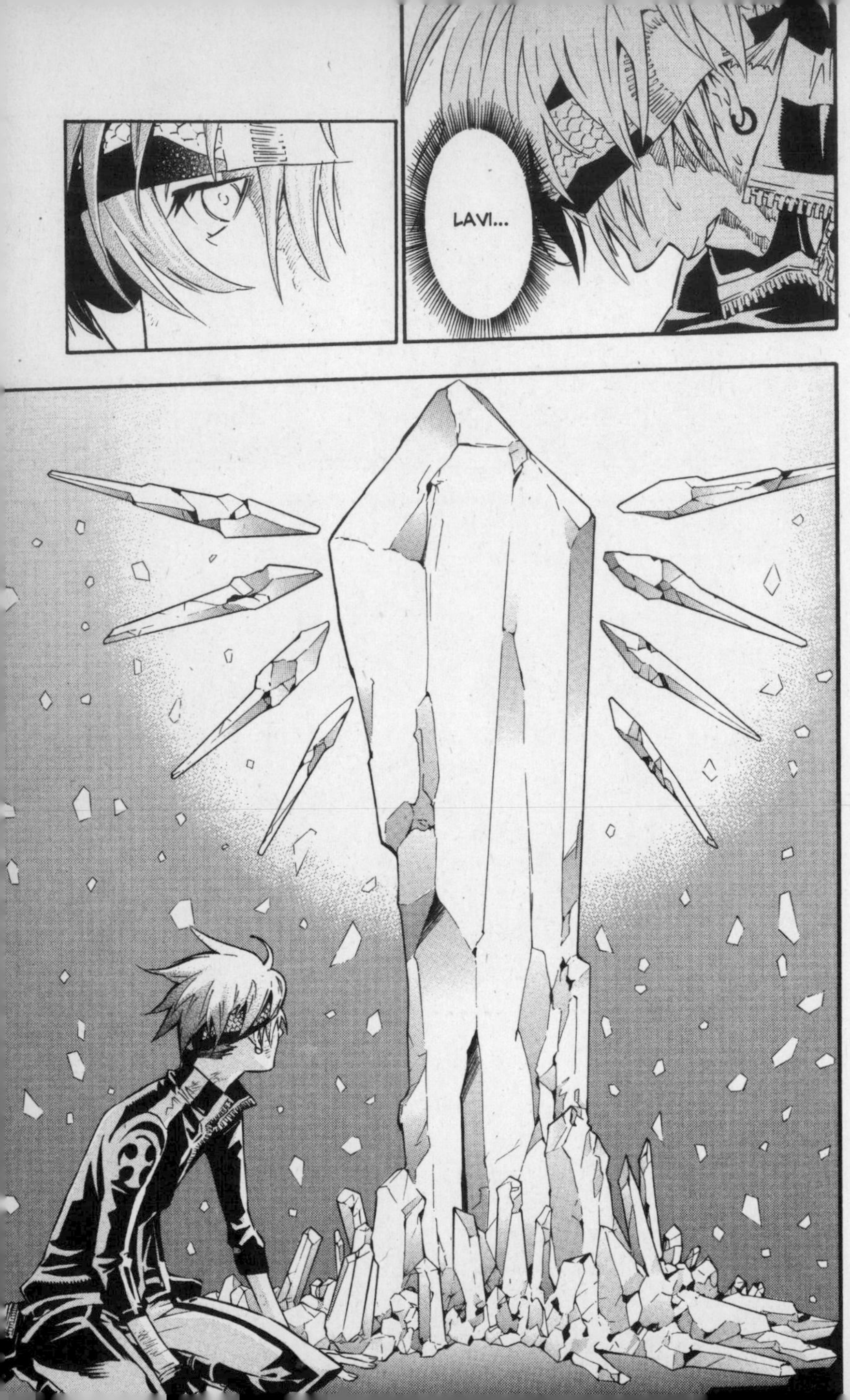
LAVI...

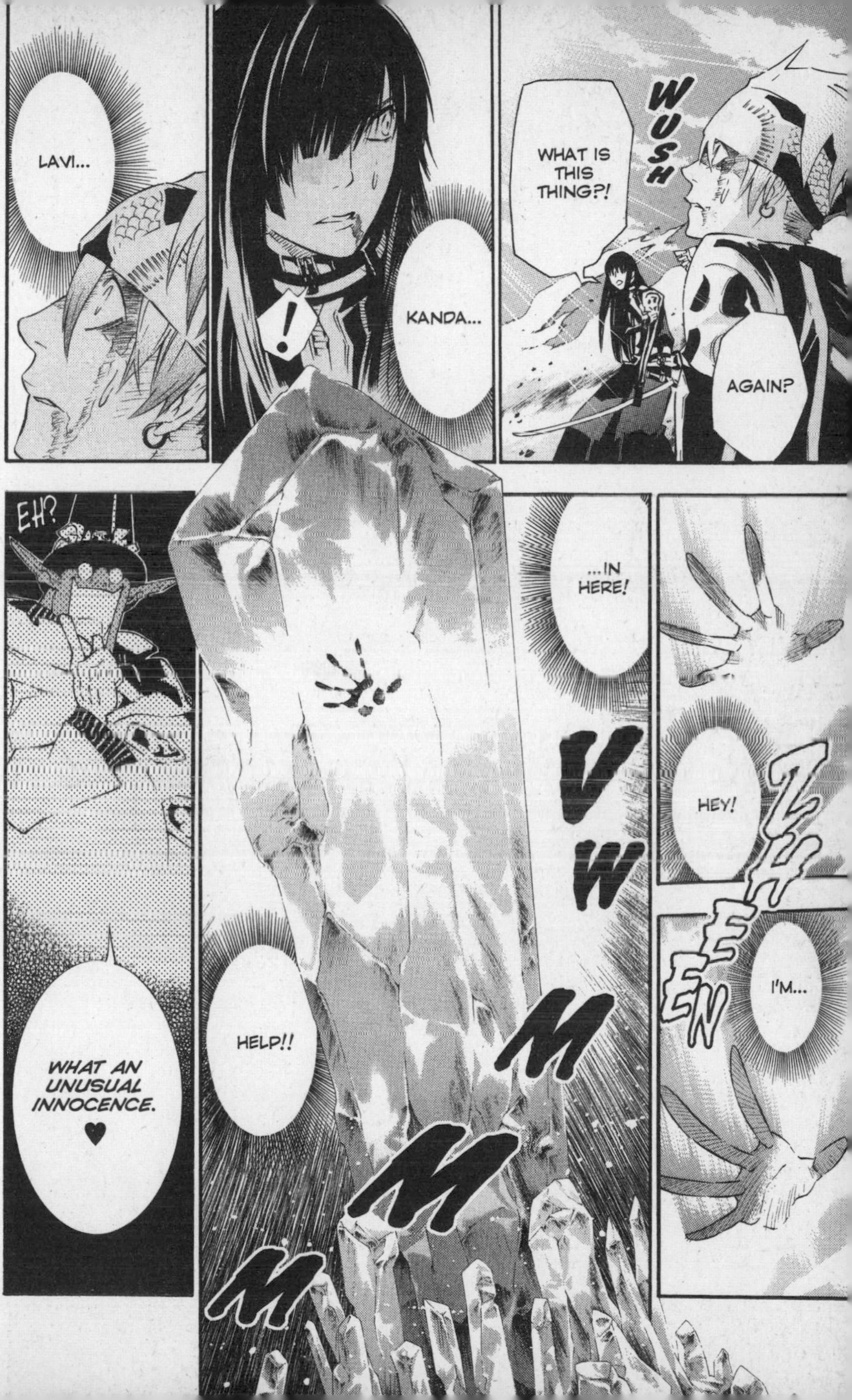
WUSH
WHAT IS THIS THING?!
AGAIN?
!
KANDA...
LAVI...
HEY!
ZHEEEN
I'M...
...IN HERE!
VWMMM
HELP!!
EH?
WHAT AN UNUSUAL INNOCENCE. ♥

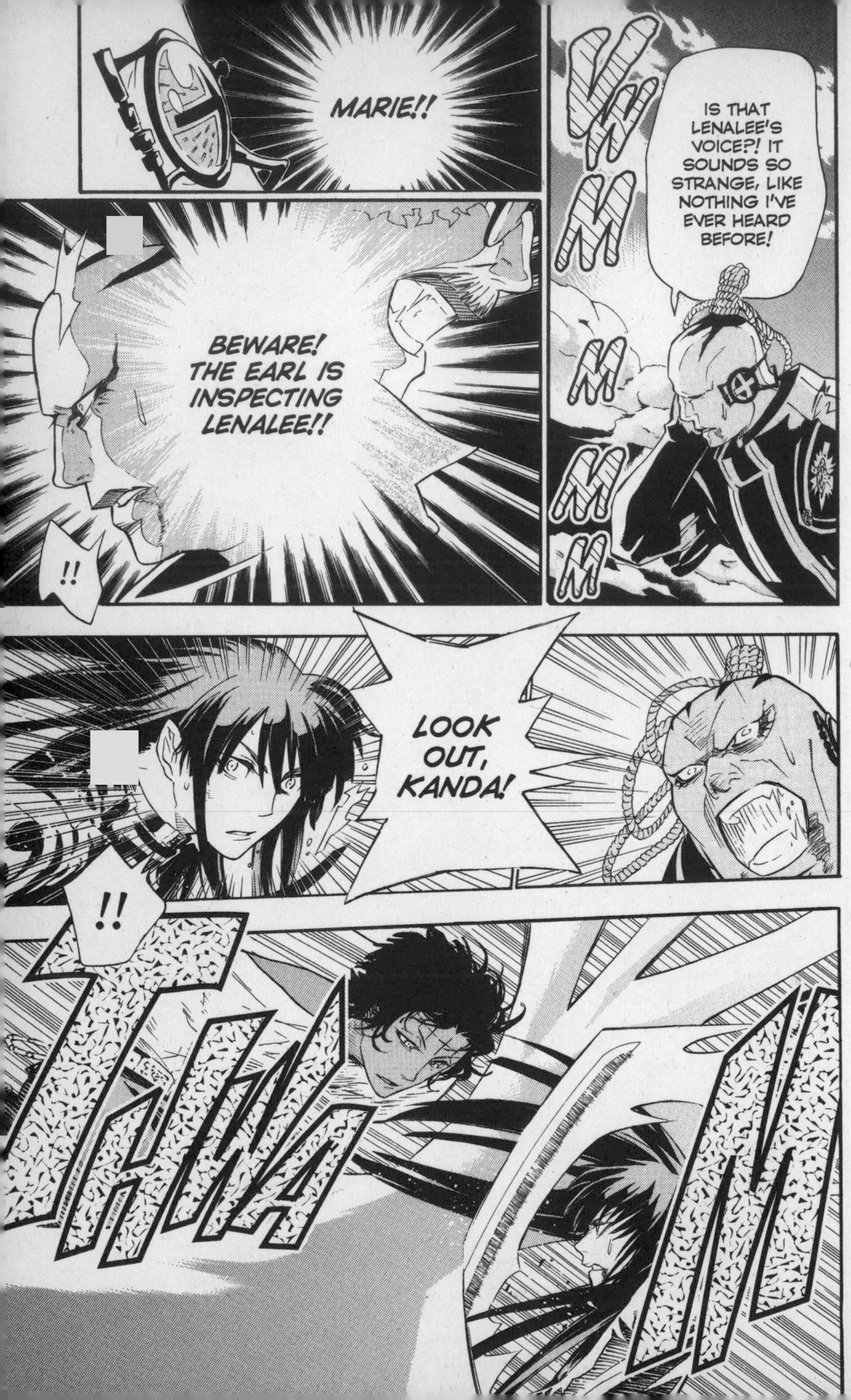
IS THAT LENALEE'S VOICE?! IT SOUNDS SO STRANGE, LIKE NOTHING I'VE EVER HEARD BEFORE!
MARIE!!
BEWARE! THE EARL IS INSPECTING LENALEE!!
!!
LOOK OUT, KANDA!
!!

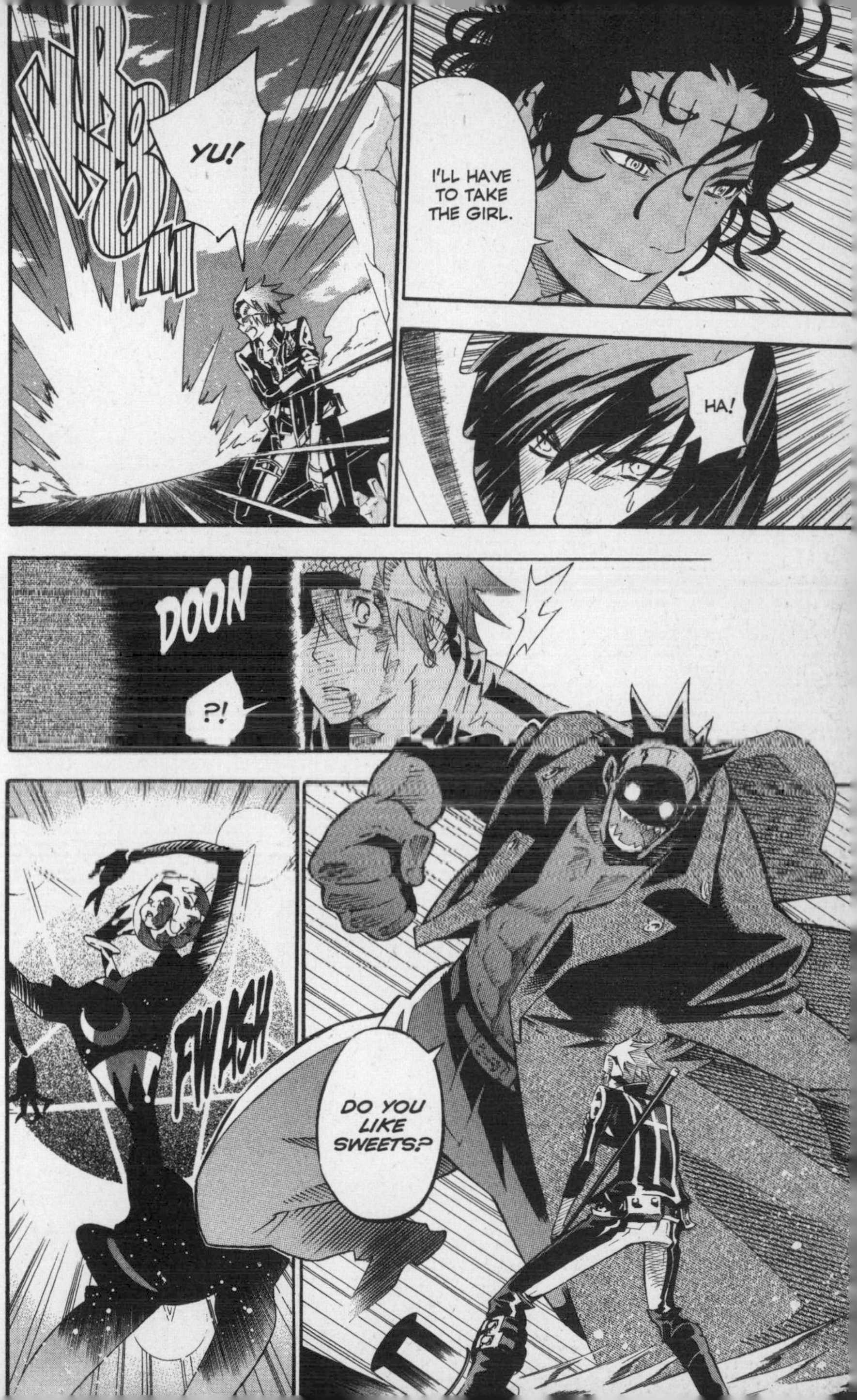

I'LL HAVE TO TAKE THE GIRL.
HA!
YU!
BOOM
DOON
?!
DO YOU LIKE SWEETS?
FWASH

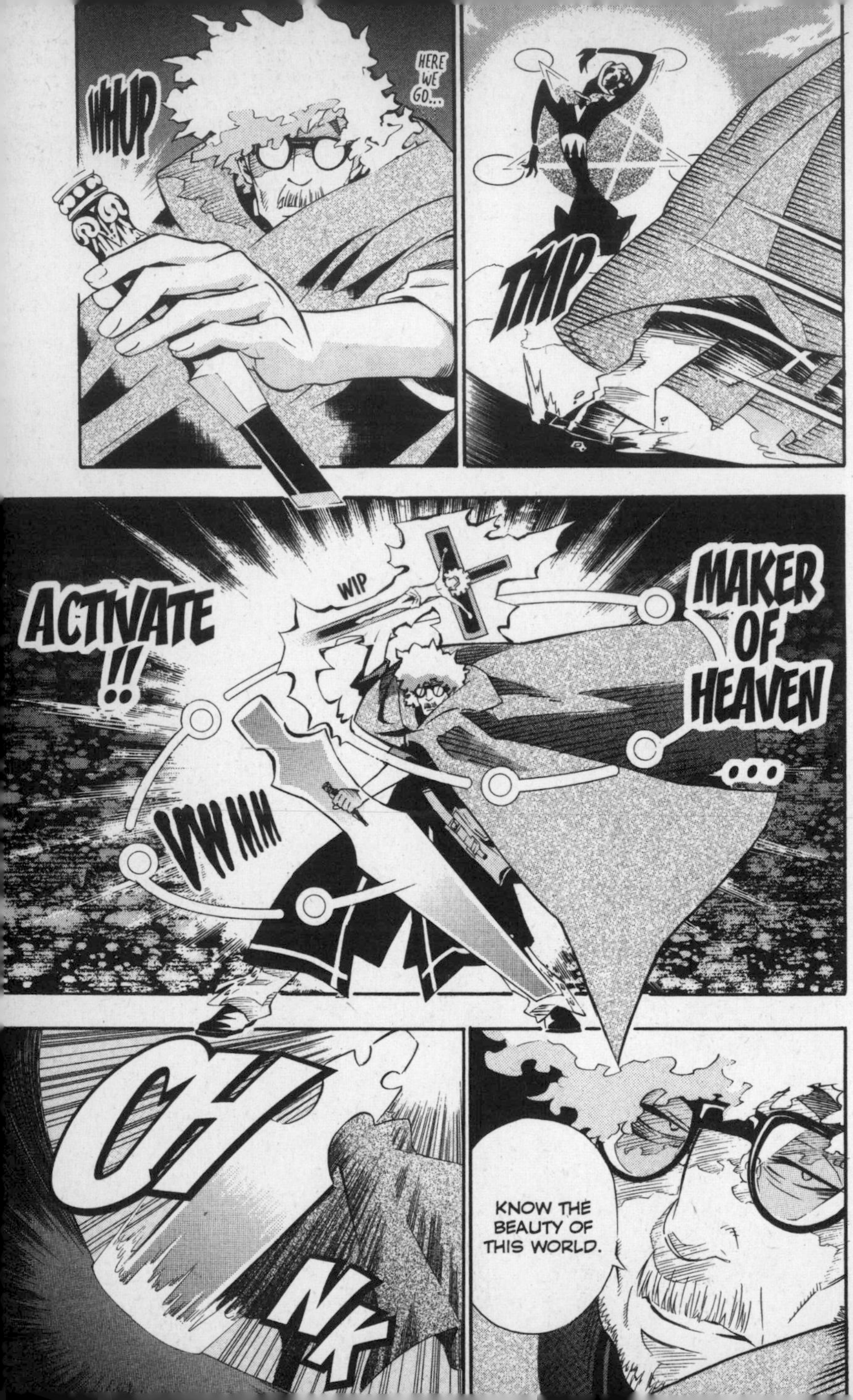
TMP
HERE WE GO...
WHUP
MAKER OF HEAVEN
WIP
ACTIVATE!!
...
VWMM
KNOW THE BEAUTY OF THIS WORLD.
CHINK

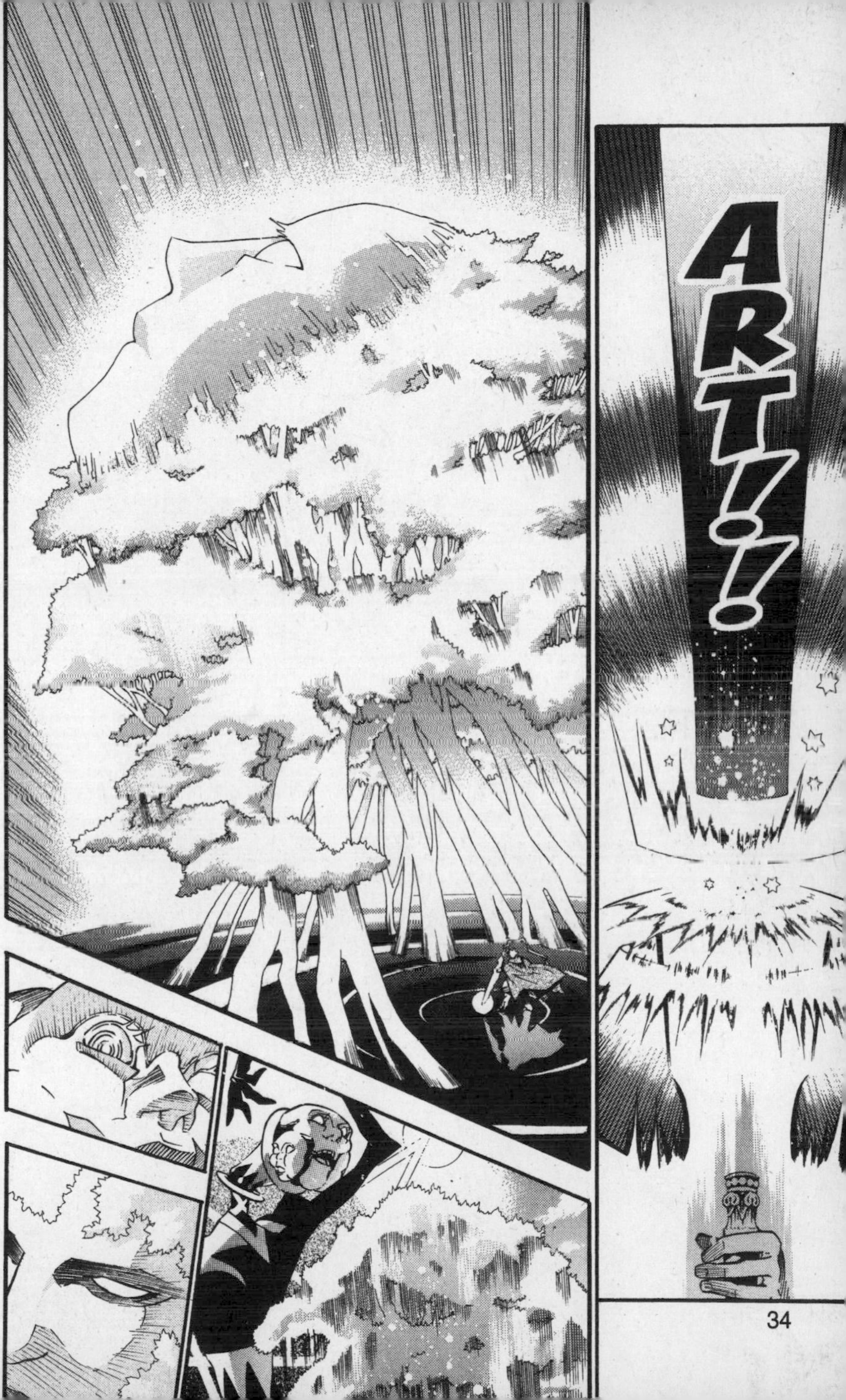
ARTIIO!

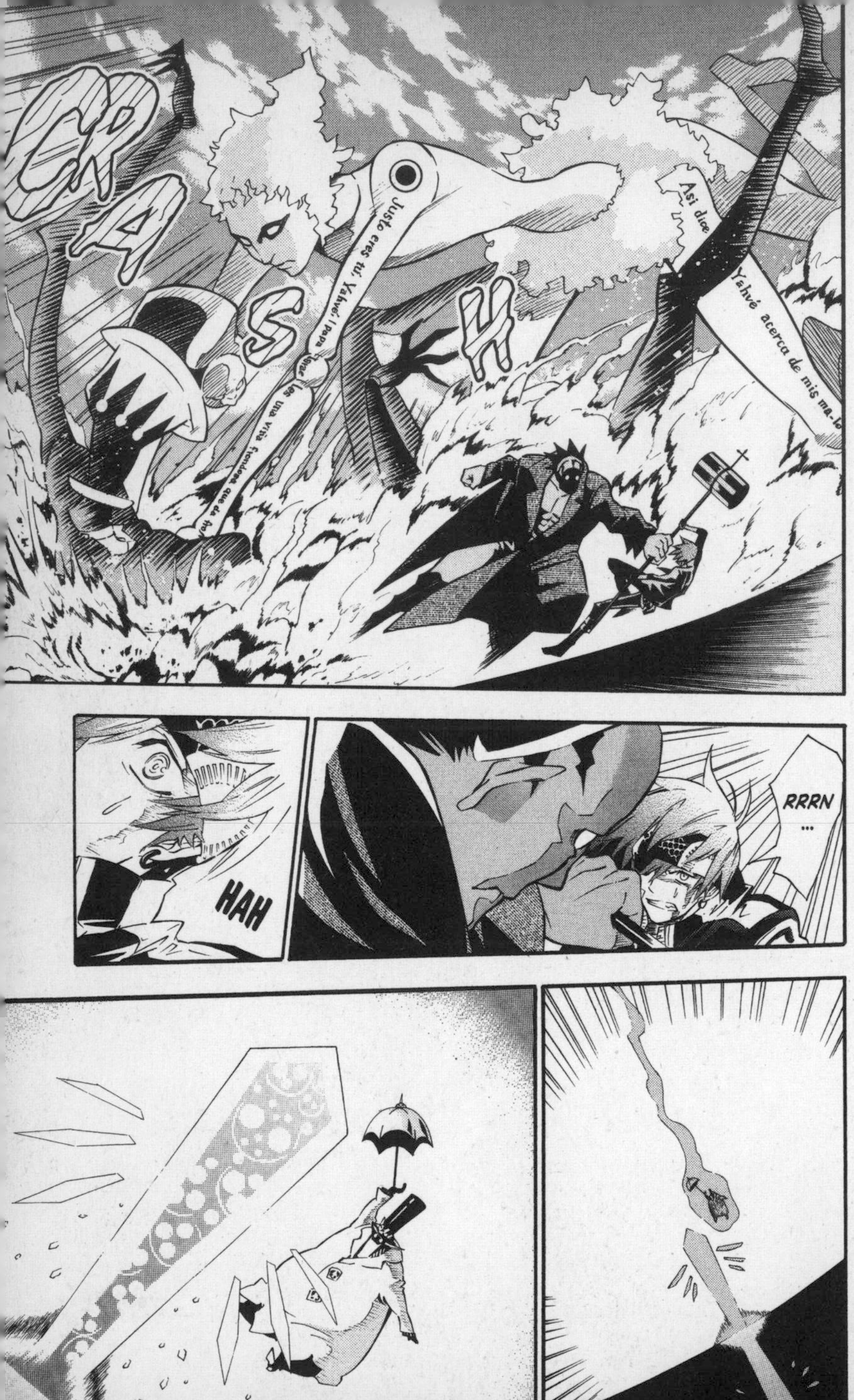
Así dice
Yahvé acerca de mis ma-
Justo eres tú, Yahvé. ¡Papa
les una viña frondosa que da
CRASH
RRRN
...
HAH

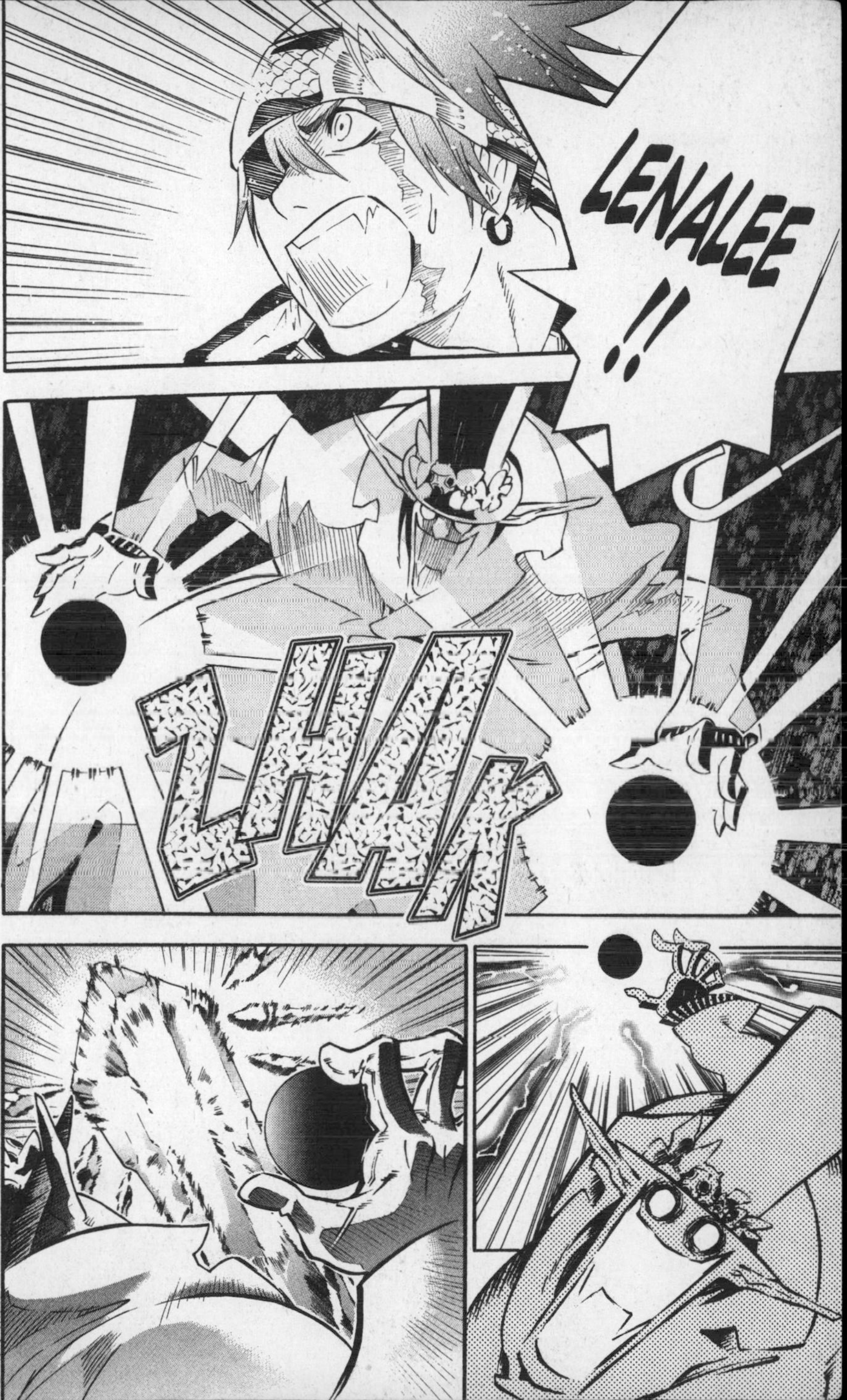
LENALEE !!
ZWAK

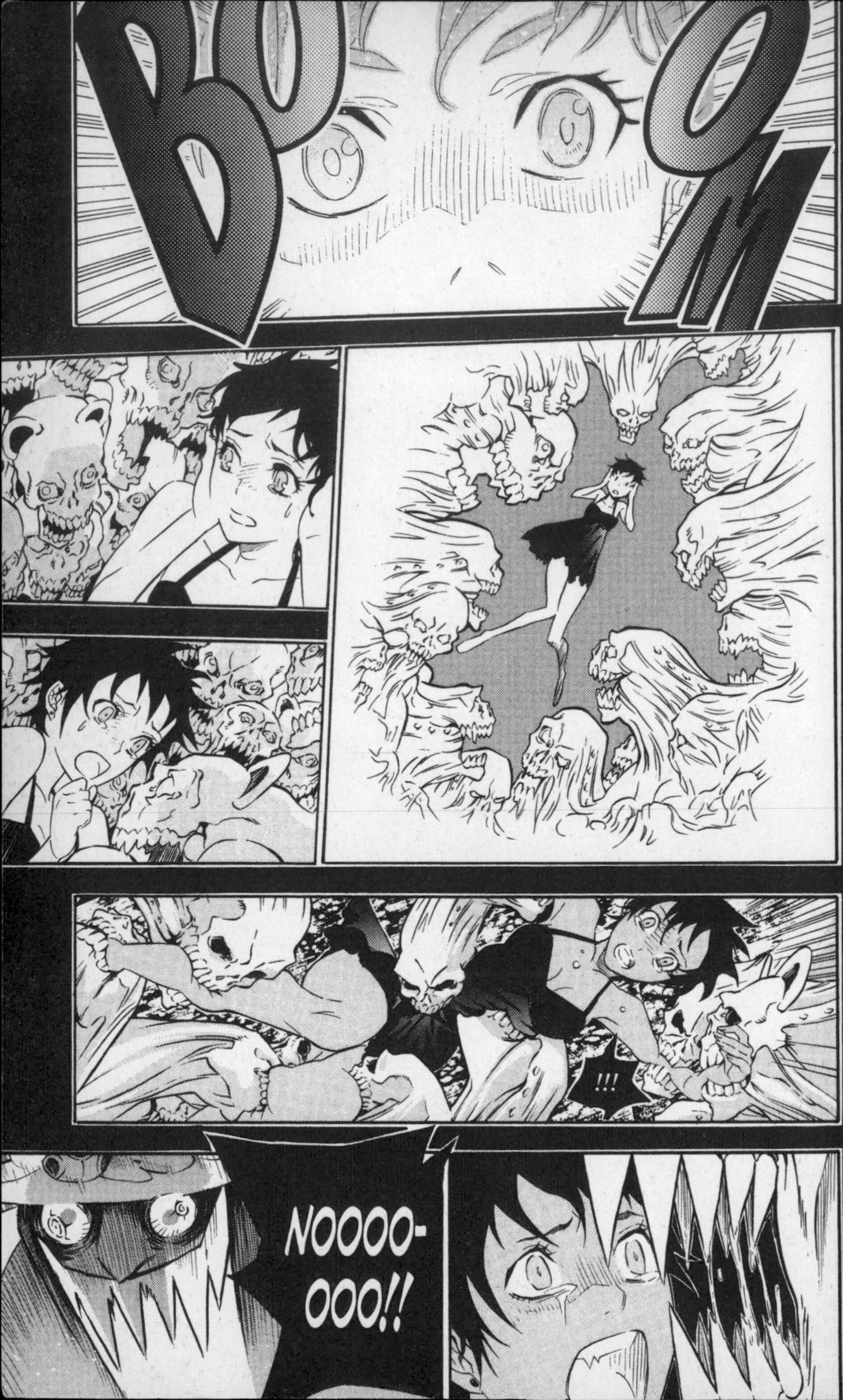
BOOM
!!!
NOOOO-
OOO!!

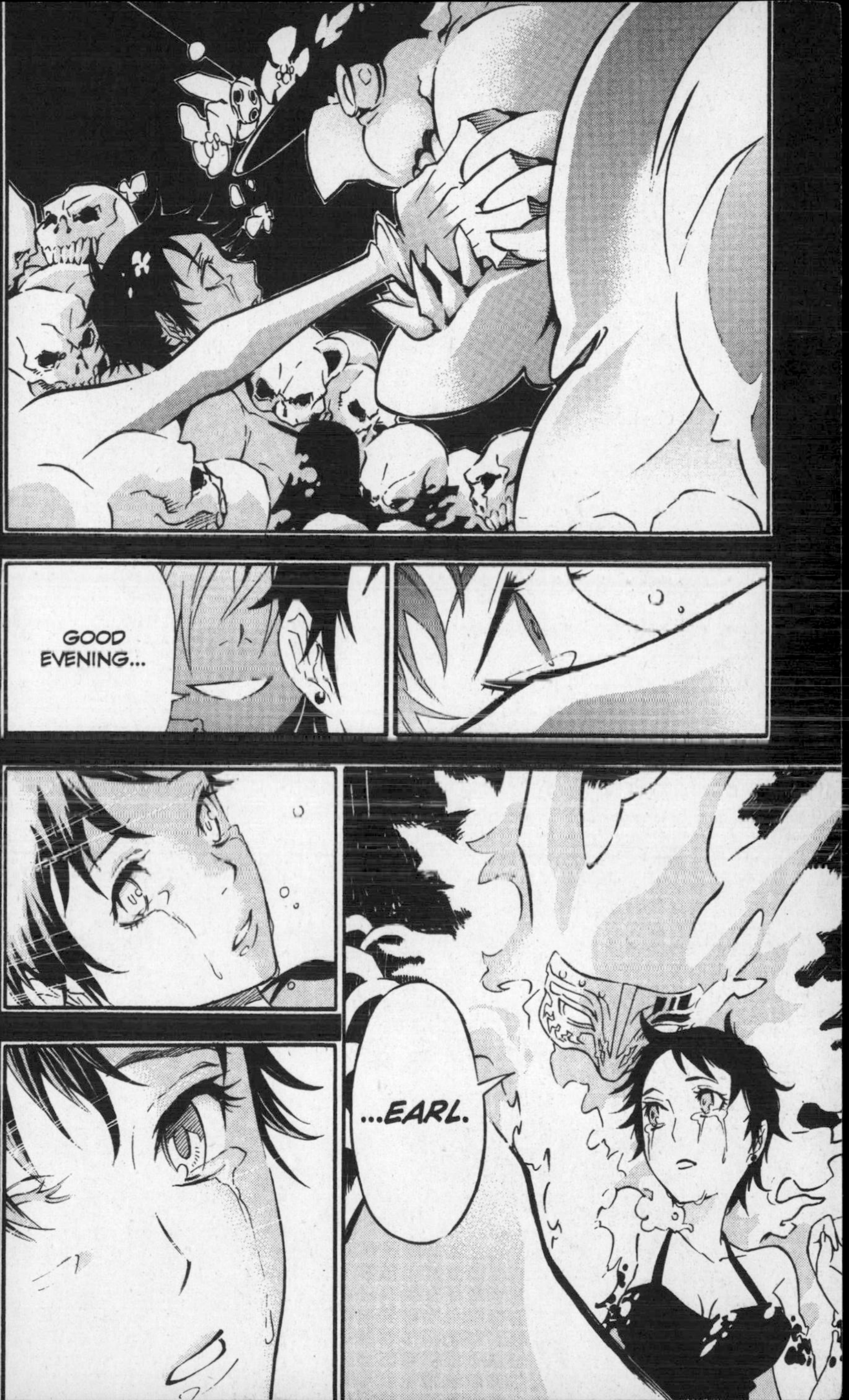
GOOD EVENING...
...EARL.

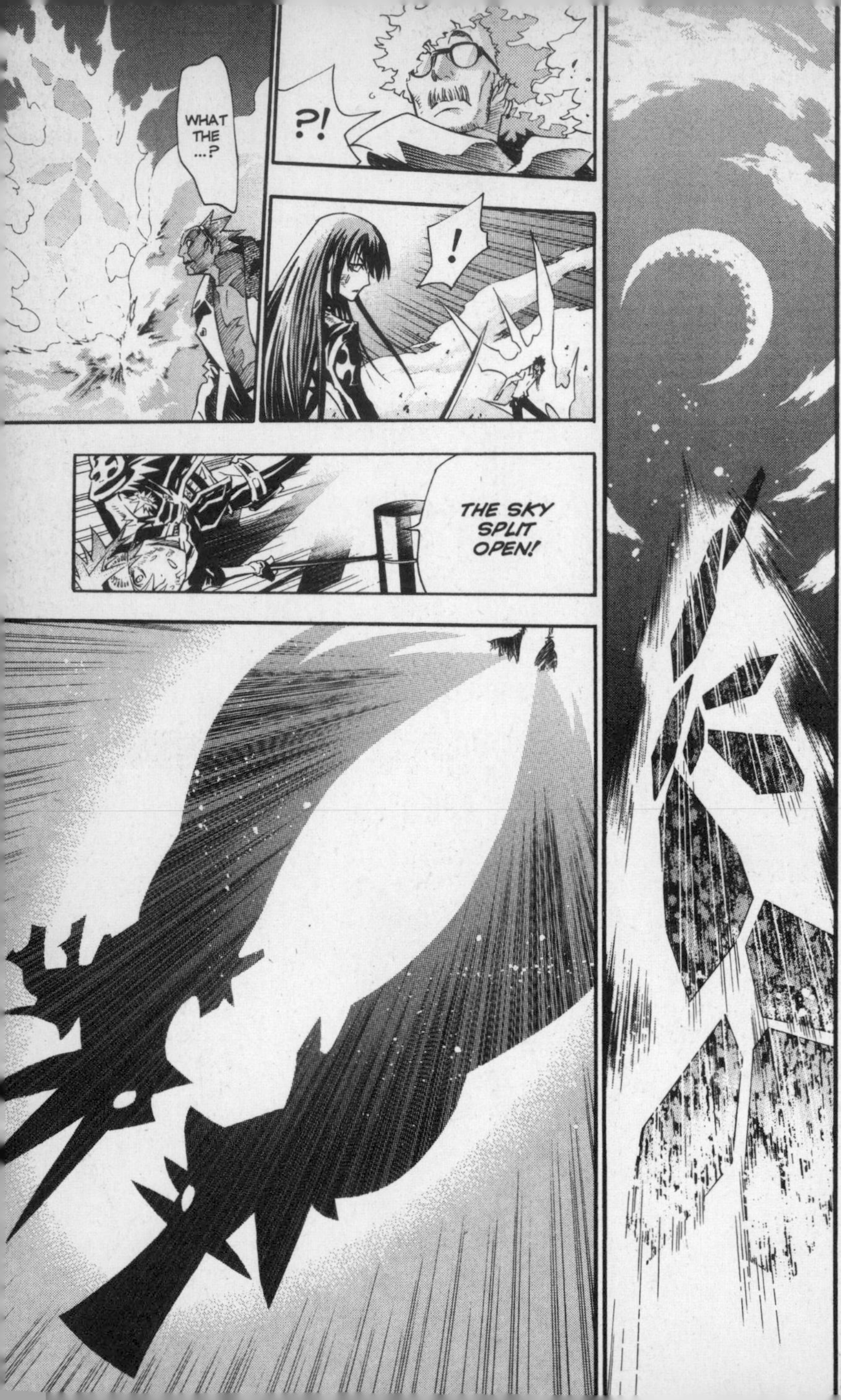

?!
!
WHAT THE ...?
THE SKY SPLIT OPEN!

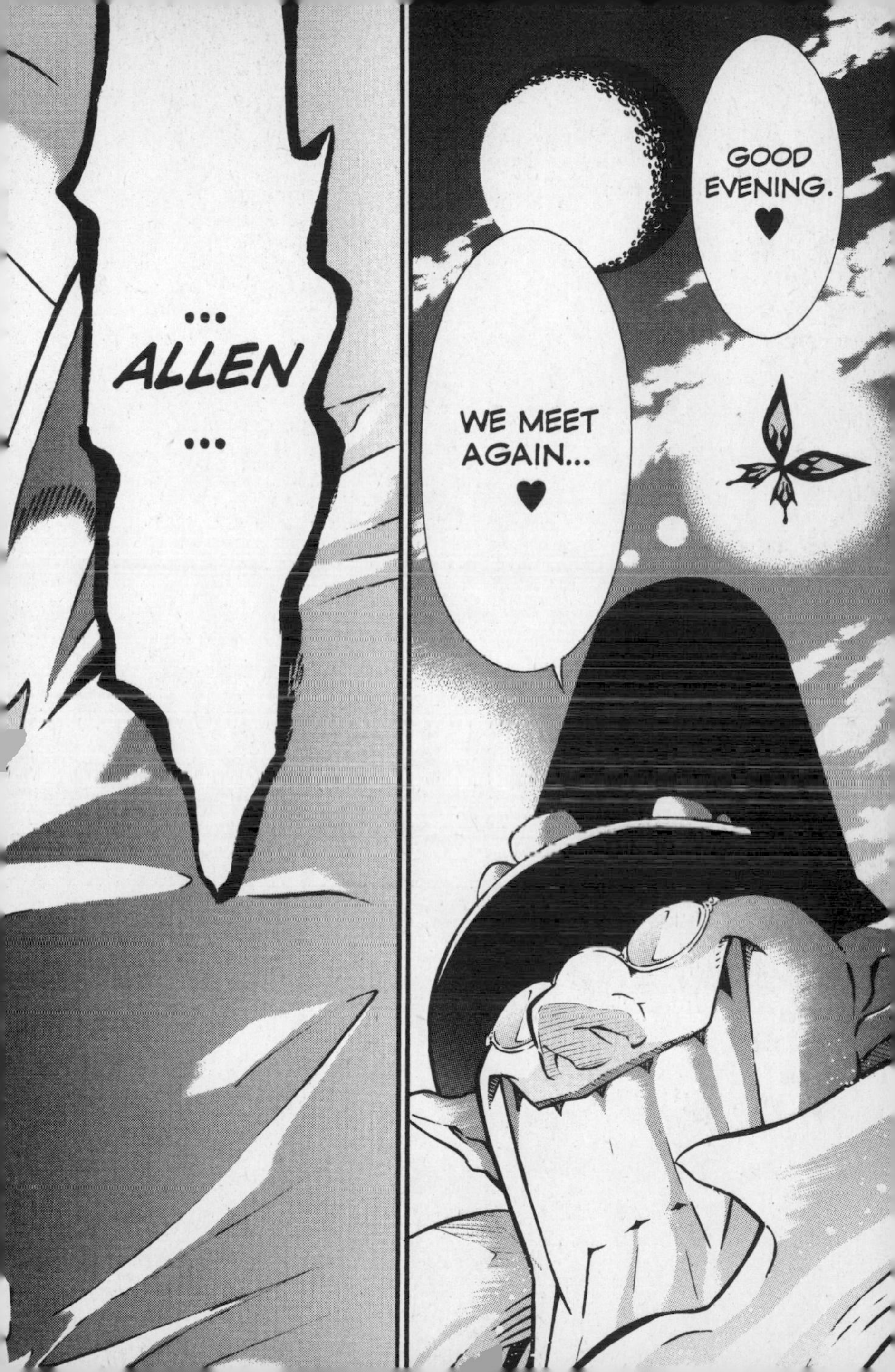
GOOD EVENING. ♥
WE MEET AGAIN... ♥
...ALLEN...

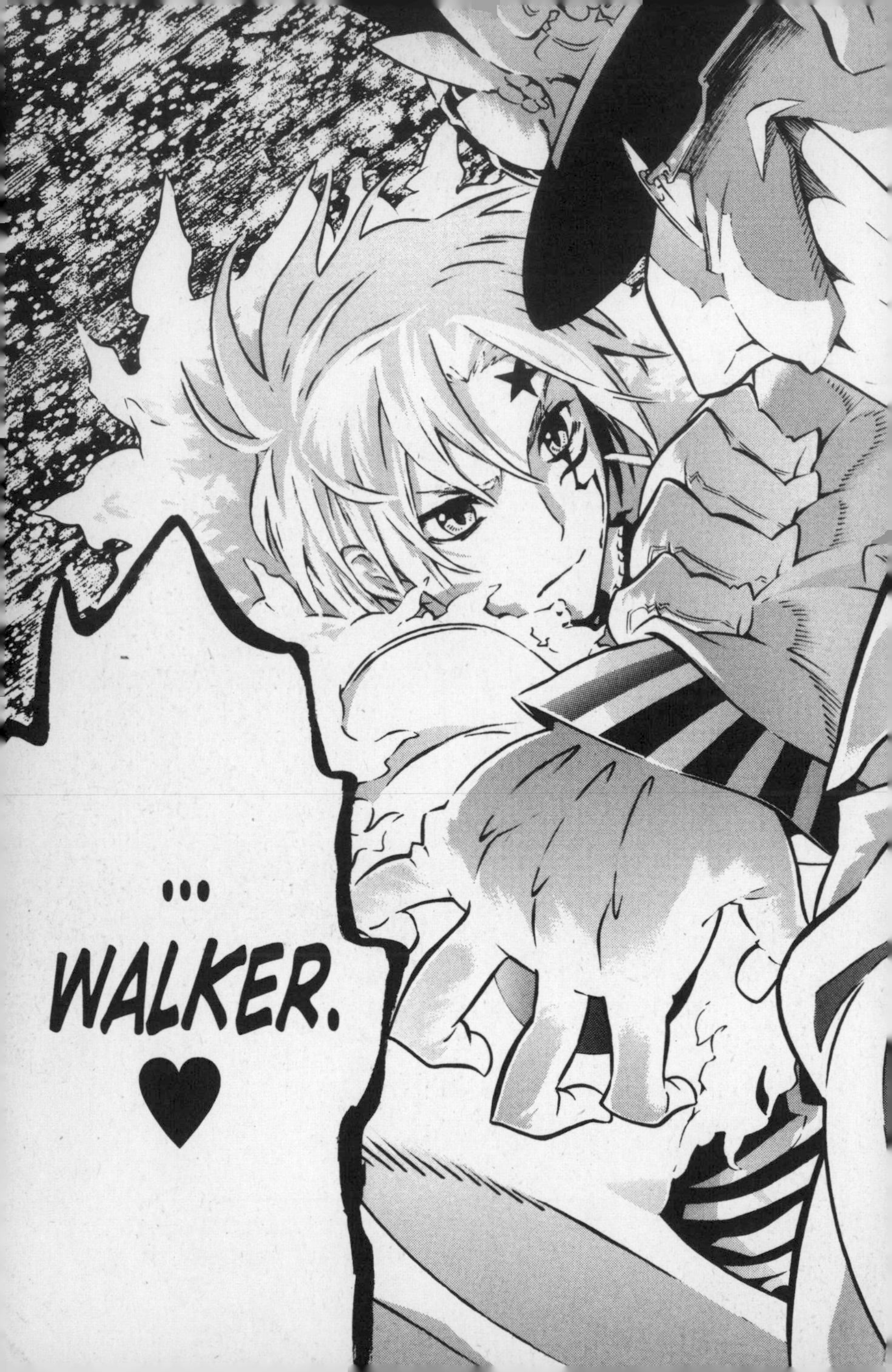
...WALKER. ♥

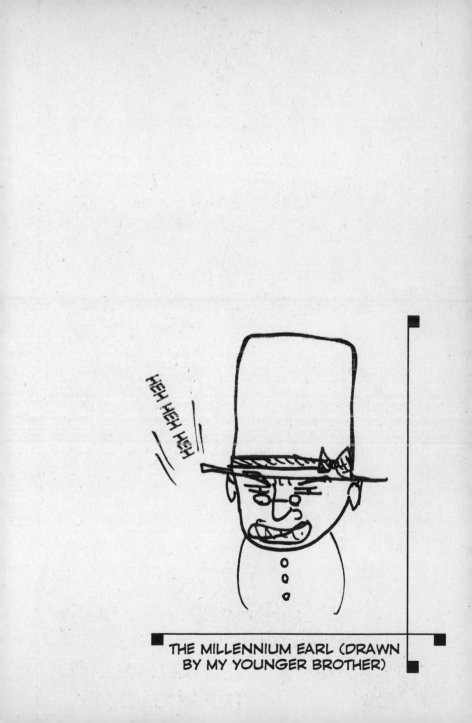

HEH HEH HEH

THE MILLENNIUM EARL (DRAWN
BY MY YOUNGER BROTHER)

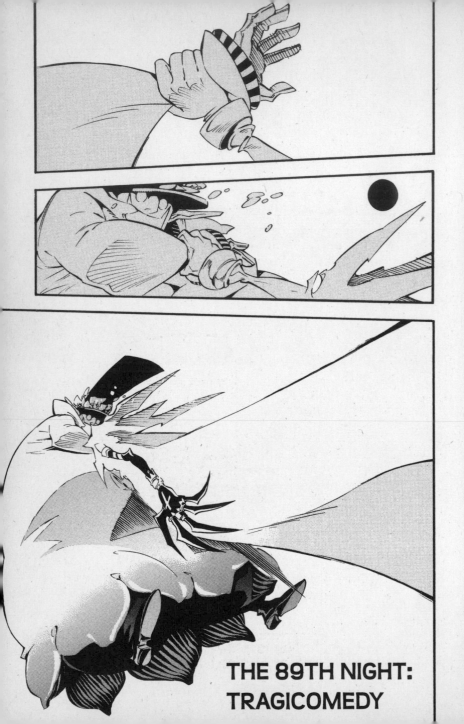

THE 89TH NIGHT: TRAGICOMEDY

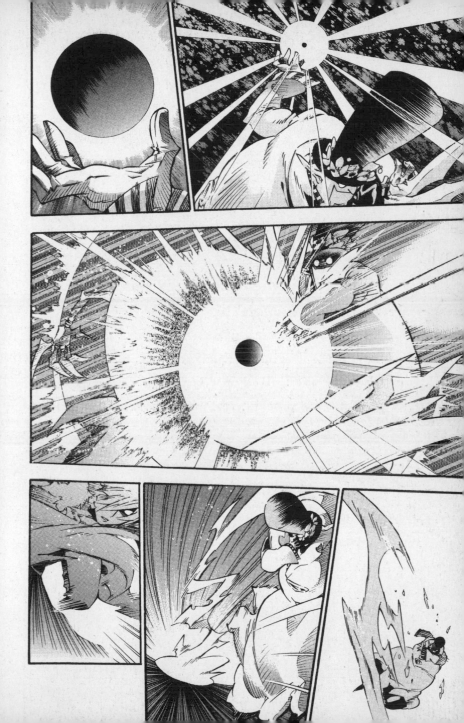

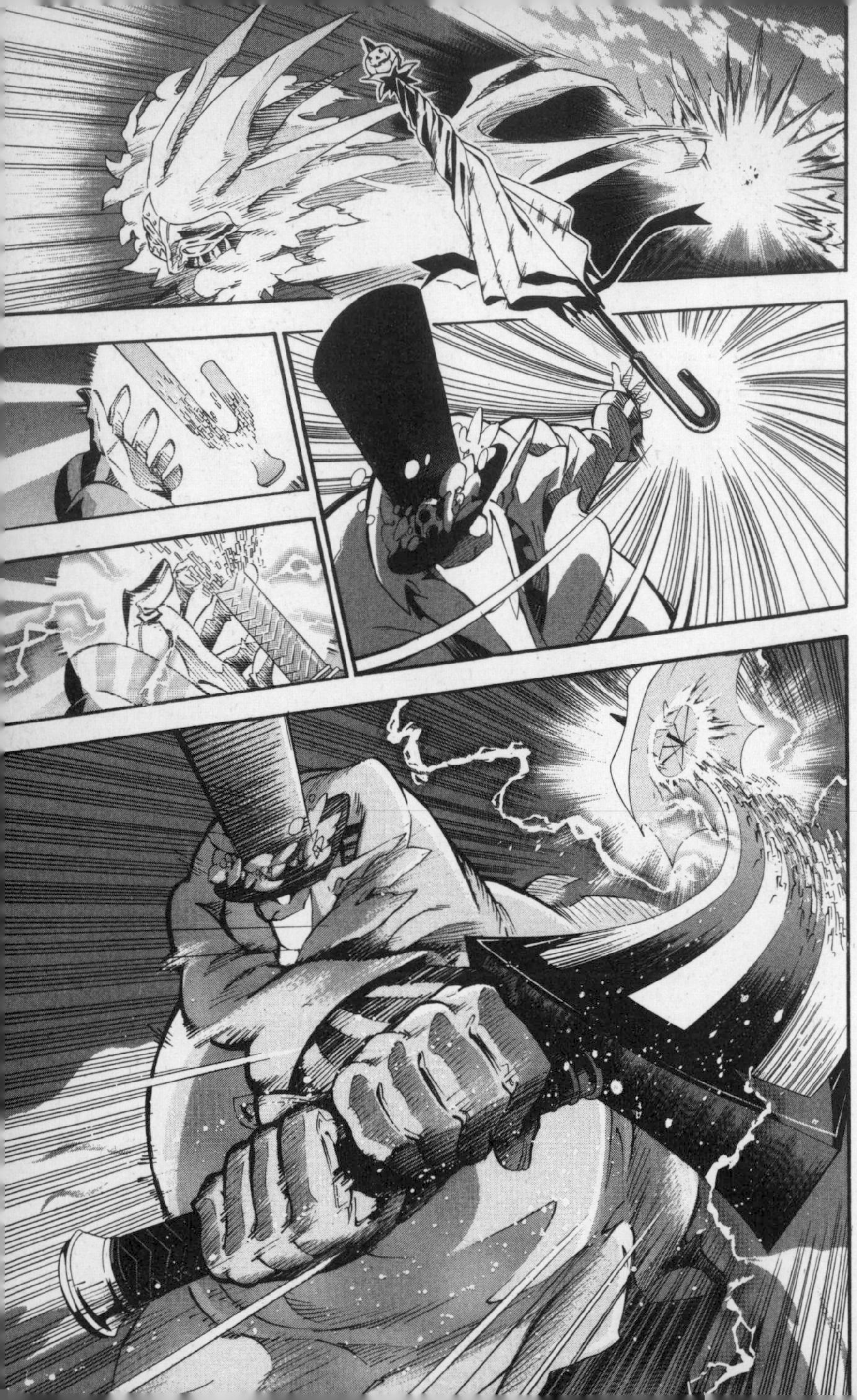

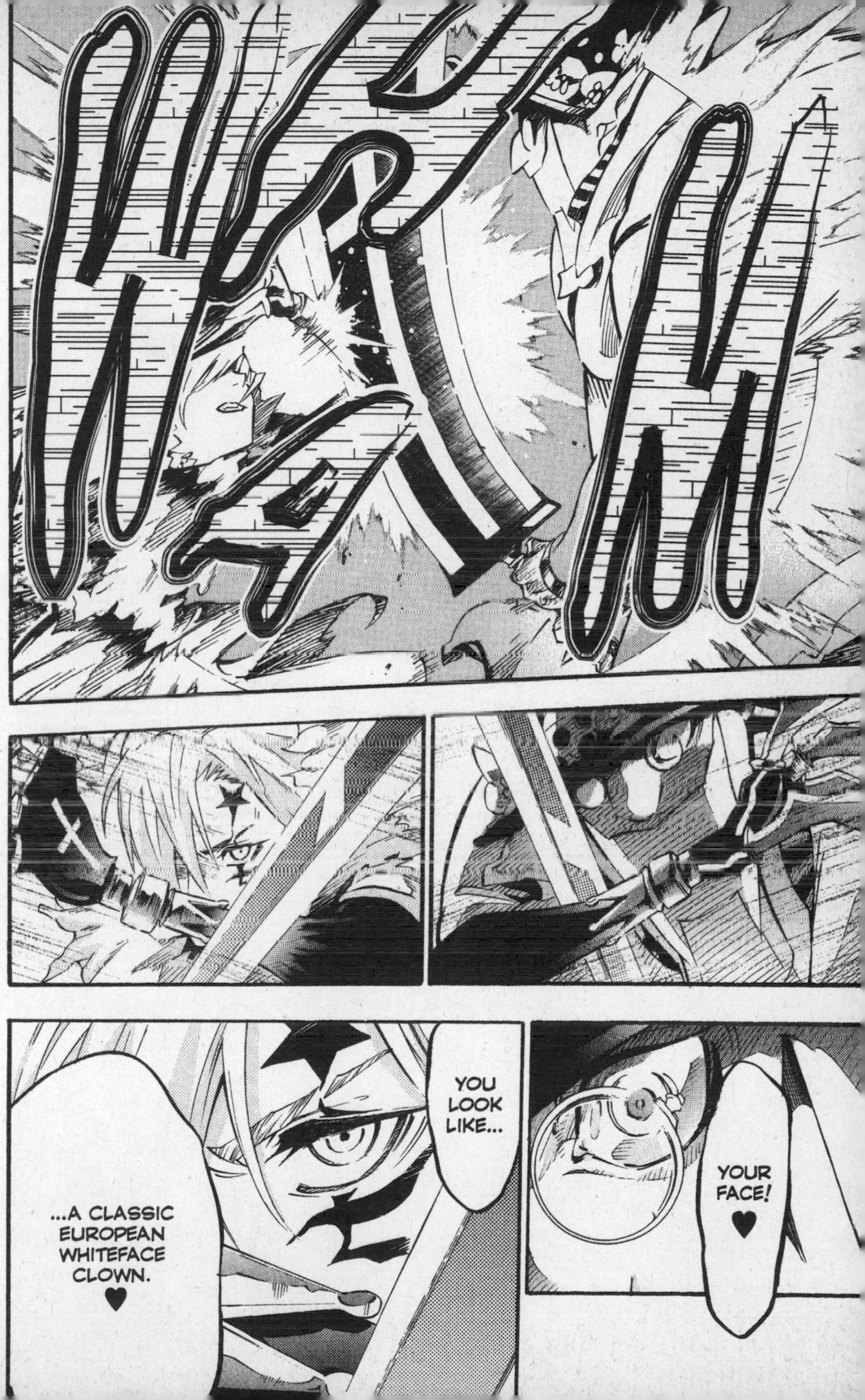
YOU LOOK LIKE...
YOUR FACE! ♥
...A CLASSIC EUROPEAN WHITEFACE CLOWN. ♥

THE 89TH NIGHT: TRAGICOMEDY

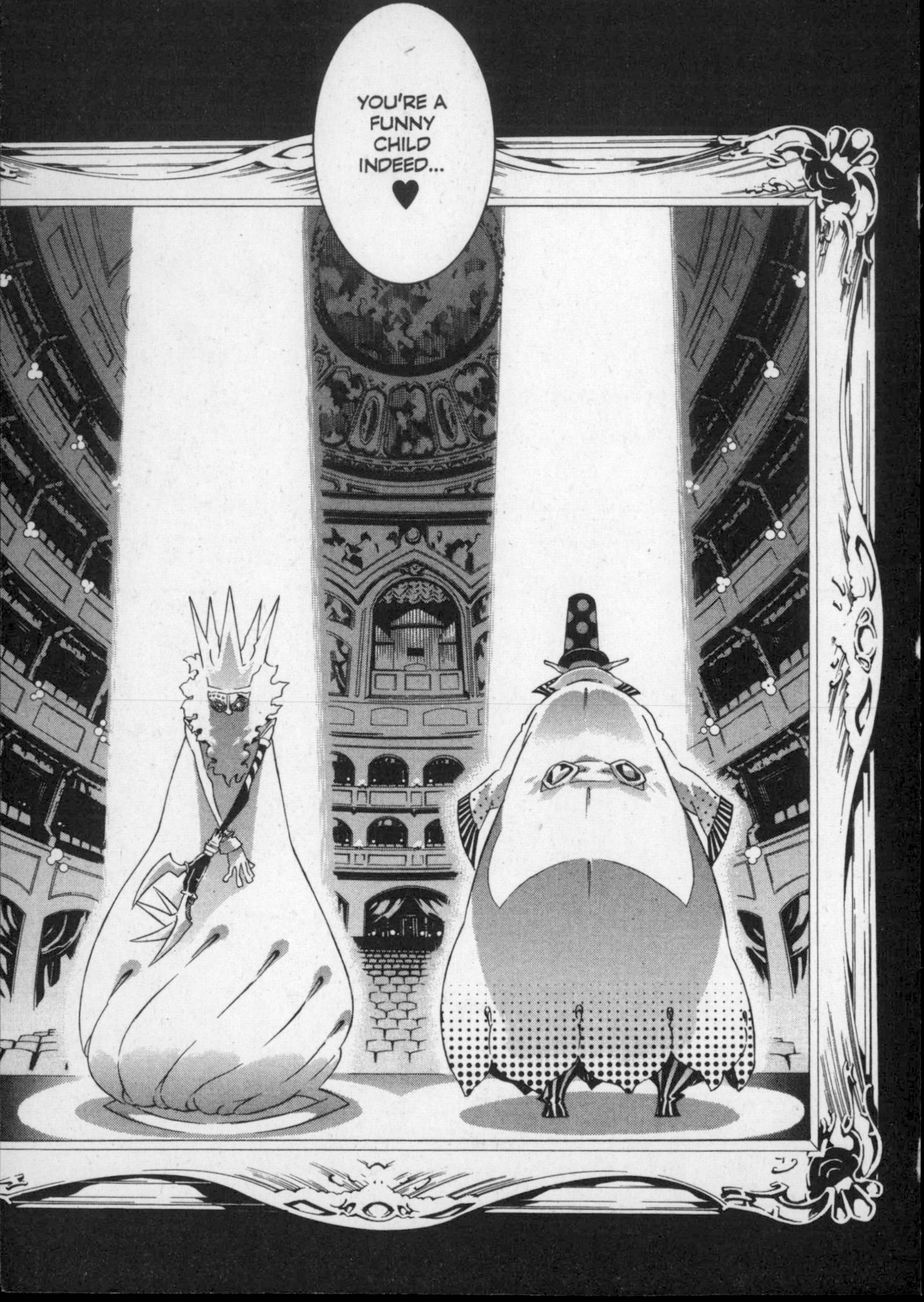
YOU'RE A FUNNY CHILD INDEED... ♥

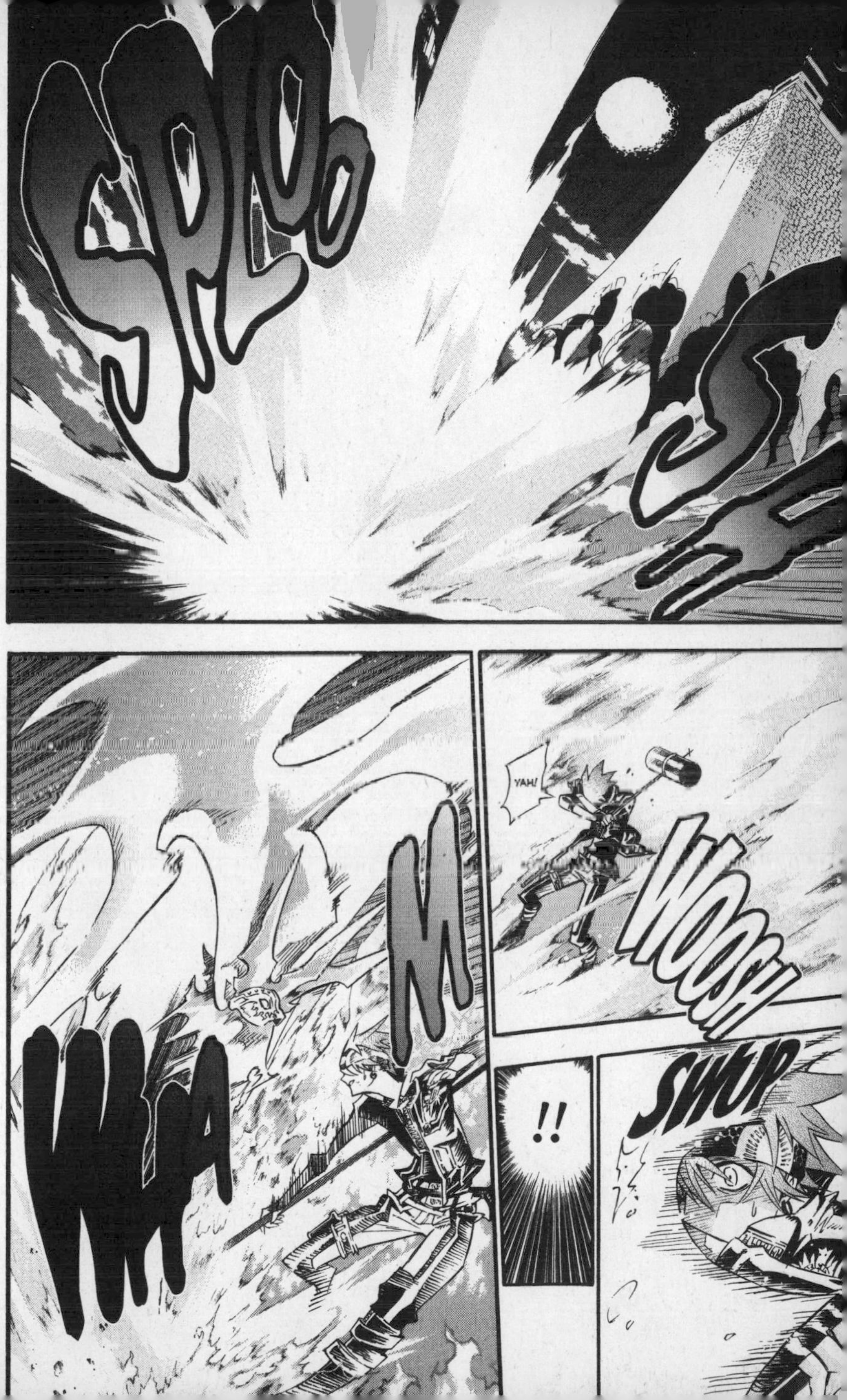
SPLOO
YAH!
WOOSH
SWIP
!!
M
WHA

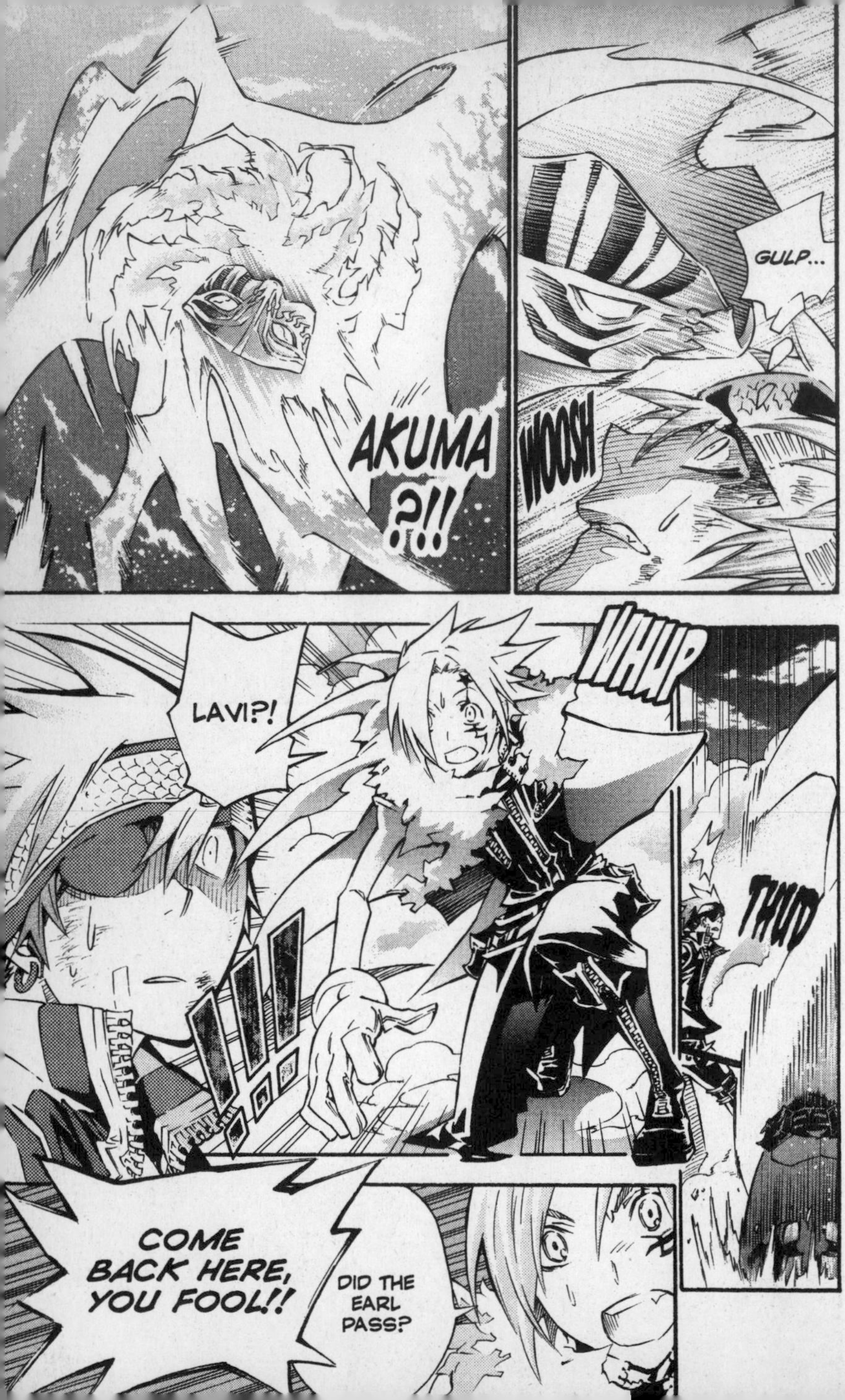
GULP...
WOOSH
AKUMA ?!!
WHUP
THUD
LAVI?!
DID THE EARL PASS?
COME BACK HERE, YOU FOOL!!

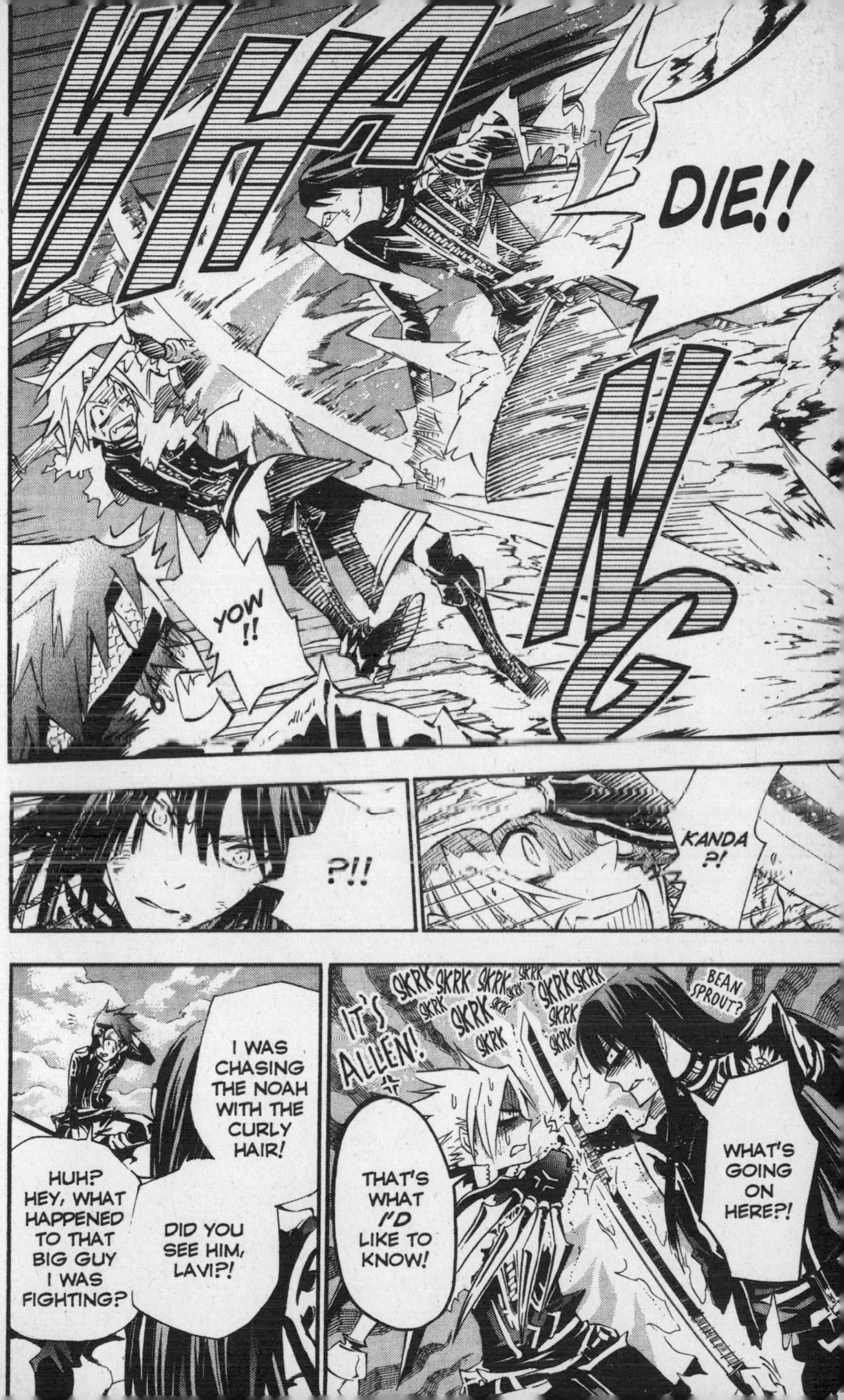
DIE!!
WHANG
YOW!!
KANDA?!
?!!
BEAN SPROUT?
WHAT'S GOING ON HERE?!
SKRK SKRK SKRK SKRK SKRK SKRK SKRK SKRK SKRK SKRK SKRK SKRK
IT'S ALLEN!
THAT'S WHAT I'D LIKE TO KNOW!
I WAS CHASING THE NOAH WITH THE CURLY HAIR!
DID YOU SEE HIM, LAVI?!
HUH? HEY, WHAT HAPPENED TO THAT BIG GUY I WAS FIGHTING?

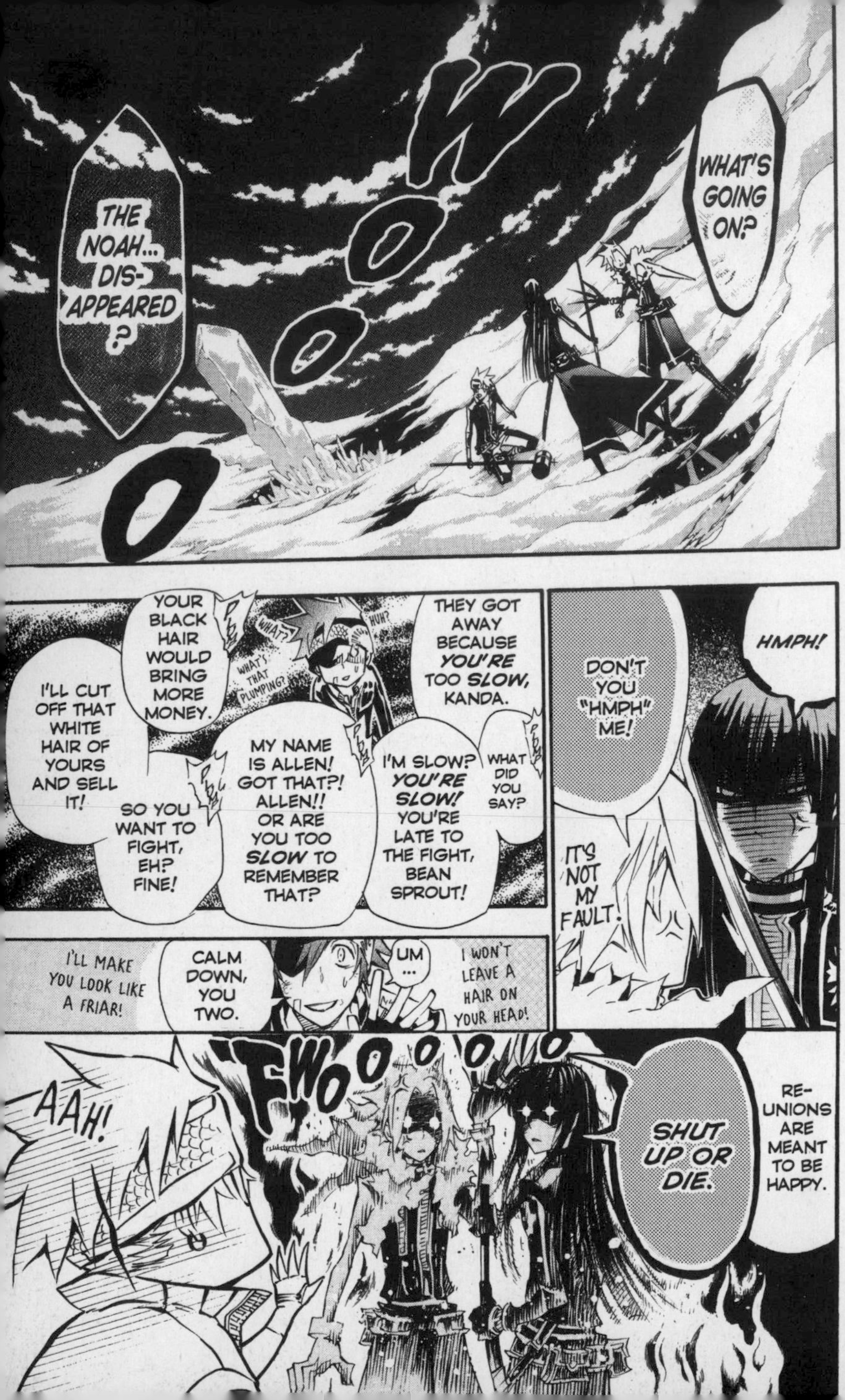
WHAT'S GOING ON?
WOOO
THE NOAH... DIS-APPEARED?
O
HMPH!
DON'T YOU "HMPH" ME!
IT'S NOT MY FAULT.
THEY GOT AWAY BECAUSE YOU'RE TOO SLOW, KANDA.
HUH?
YOUR BLACK HAIR WOULD BRING MORE MONEY.
WHAT?
WHAT'S THAT PLUMPING?
WHAT DID YOU SAY?
I'M SLOW? YOU'RE SLOW! YOU'RE LATE TO THE FIGHT, BEAN SPROUT!
MY NAME IS ALLEN! GOT THAT?! ALLEN!! OR ARE YOU TOO SLOW TO REMEMBER THAT?
I'LL CUT OFF THAT WHITE HAIR OF YOURS AND SELL IT!
SO YOU WANT TO FIGHT, EH? FINE!
I WON'T LEAVE A HAIR ON YOUR HEAD!
UM ...
CALM DOWN, YOU TWO.
I'LL MAKE YOU LOOK LIKE A FRIAR!
RE-UNIONS ARE MEANT TO BE HAPPY.
SHUT UP OR DIE.
FWOOOOOO
AAH!

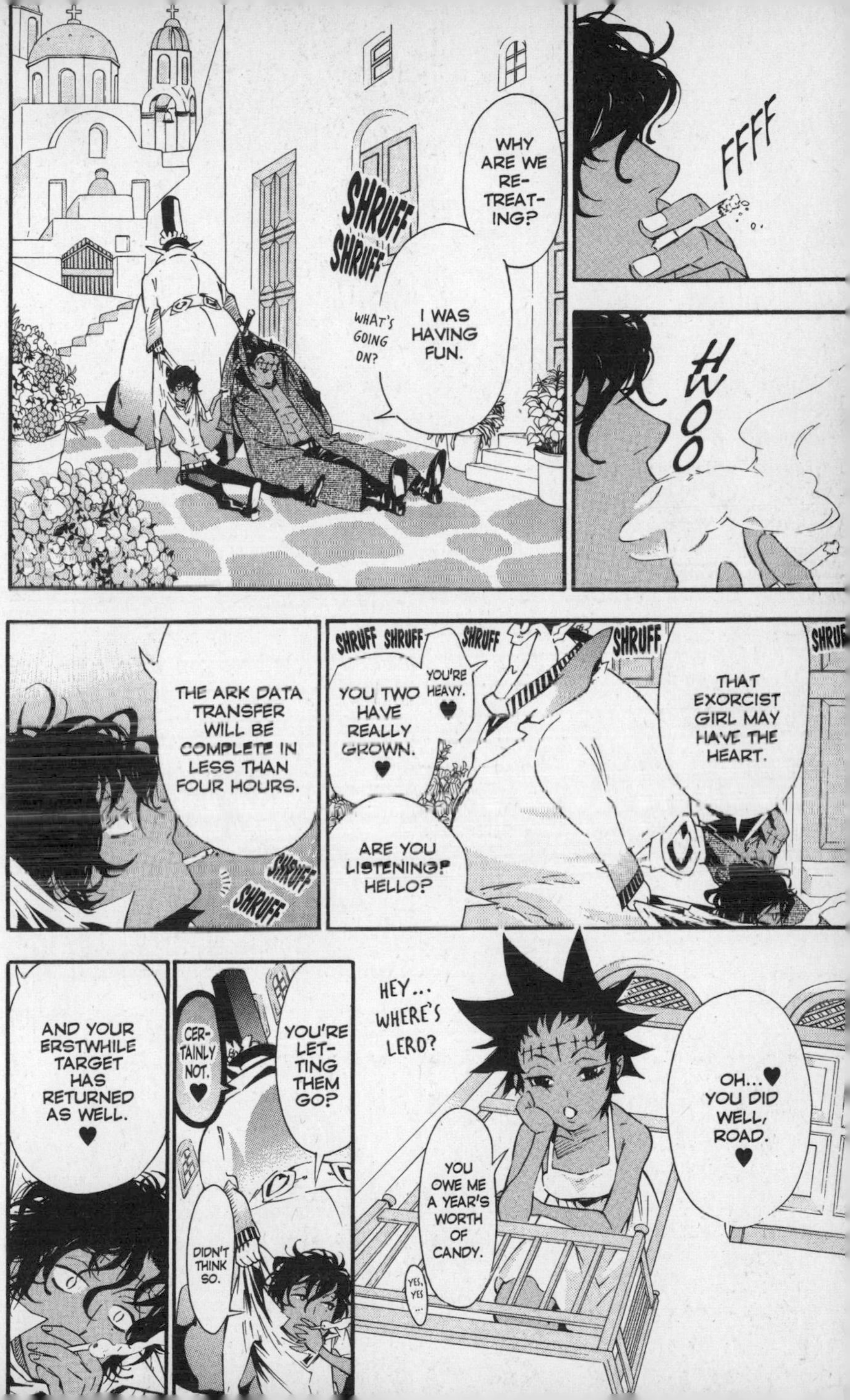
FFFF
HWOOO
WHY ARE WE RE-TREAT-ING?
I WAS HAVING FUN.
WHAT'S GOING ON?
SHRUFF SHRUFF
SHRUFF
THAT EXORCIST GIRL MAY HAVE THE HEART.
SHRUFF
SHRUFF SHRUFF
SHRUFF
YOU'RE HEAVY. ♥
YOU TWO HAVE REALLY GROWN. ♥
ARE YOU LISTENING? HELLO?
THE ARK DATA TRANSFER WILL BE COMPLETE IN LESS THAN FOUR HOURS.
SHRUFF SHRUFF
OH...♥ YOU DID WELL, ROAD. ♥
HEY... WHERE'S LERO?
YOU OWE ME A YEAR'S WORTH OF CANDY.
YES, YES...
YOU'RE LET-TING THEM GO?
CER-TAINLY NOT. ♥
DIDN'T THINK SO.
AND YOUR ERSTWHILE TARGET HAS RETURNED AS WELL. ♥

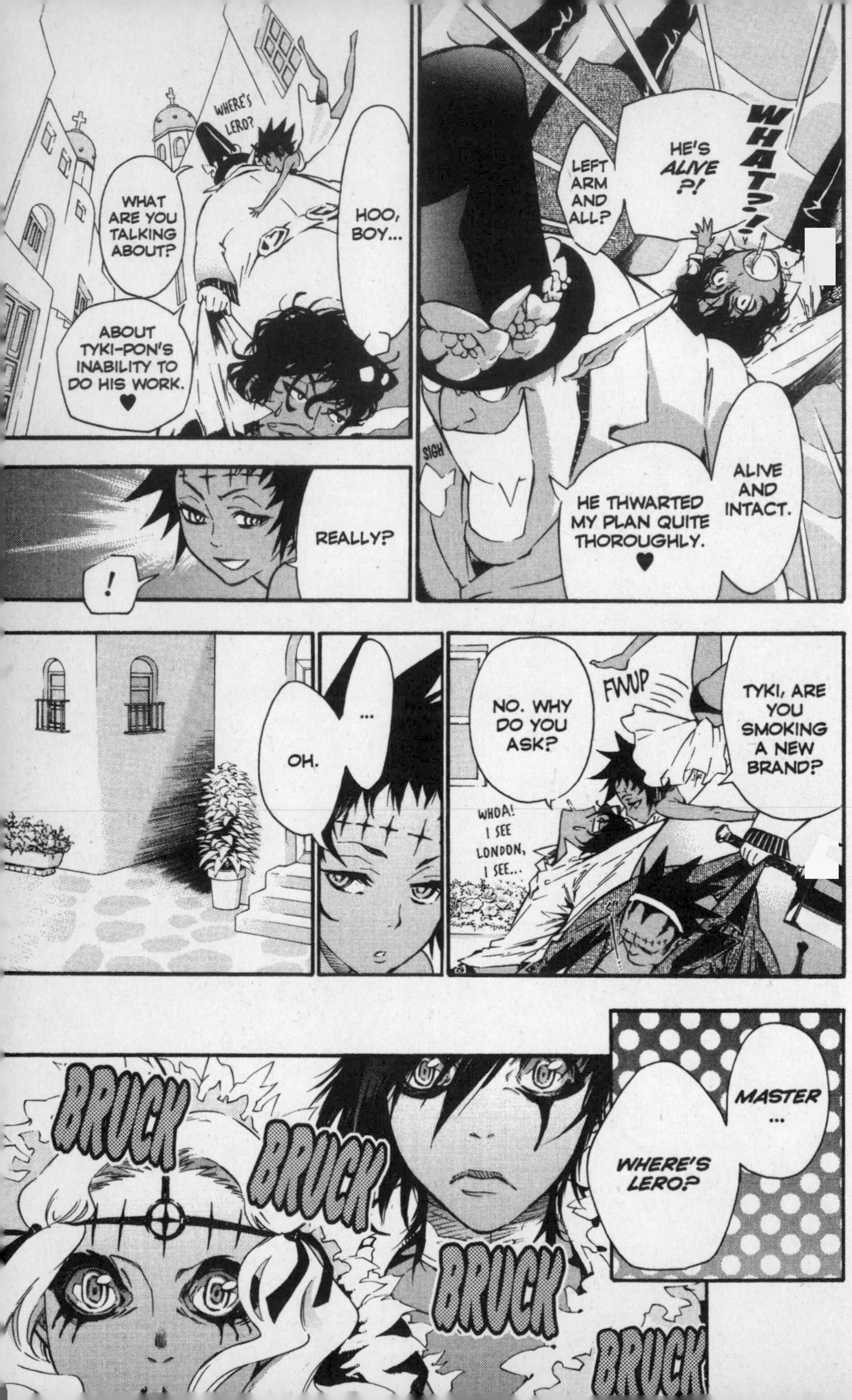

WHAT?!
HE'S ALIVE?!
LEFT ARM AND ALL?
ALIVE AND INTACT.
HE THWARTED MY PLAN QUITE THOROUGHLY. ♥
SIGH
HOO, BOY...
WHERE'S LERO?
WHAT ARE YOU TALKING ABOUT?
ABOUT TYKI-PON'S INABILITY TO DO HIS WORK. ♥
REALLY?
!
TYKI, ARE YOU SMOKING A NEW BRAND?
FWUP
NO. WHY DO YOU ASK?
WHOA! I SEE LONDON, I SEE...
...
OH.
MASTER ...
WHERE'S LERO?
BRUCK
BRUCK
BRUCK
BRUCK

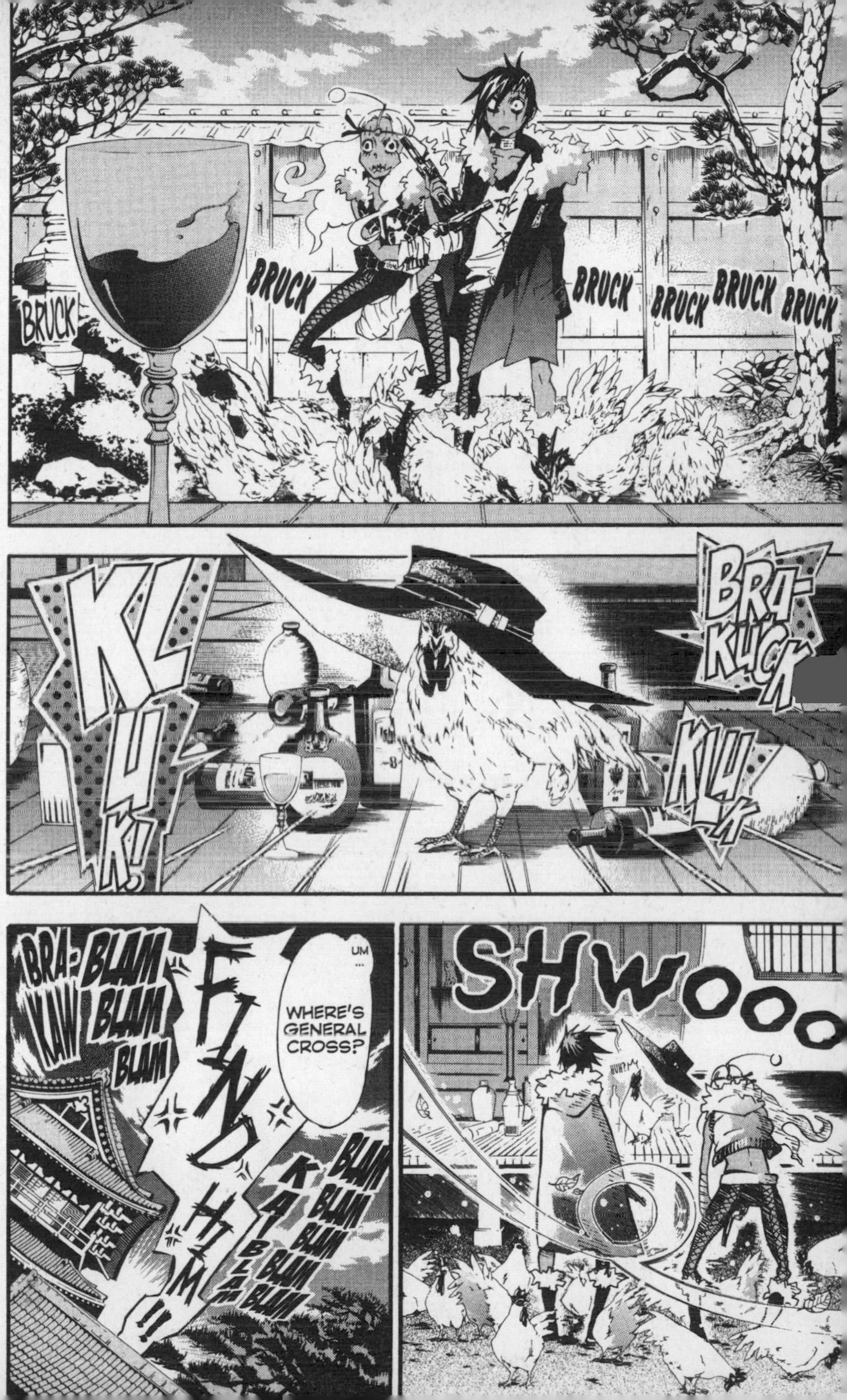
BRUCK
BRUCK
BRUCK
BRUCK
BRUCK
BRUCK
BRA-KUCK
KLUK
KLUK!
SHWOOO
HUH?
UM...
WHERE'S GENERAL CROSS?
FIND HIM!!
BLAM BLAM BLAM BLAM BLAM BLAM
KA-BLAM
BRA-KAW
BLAM BLAM BLAM

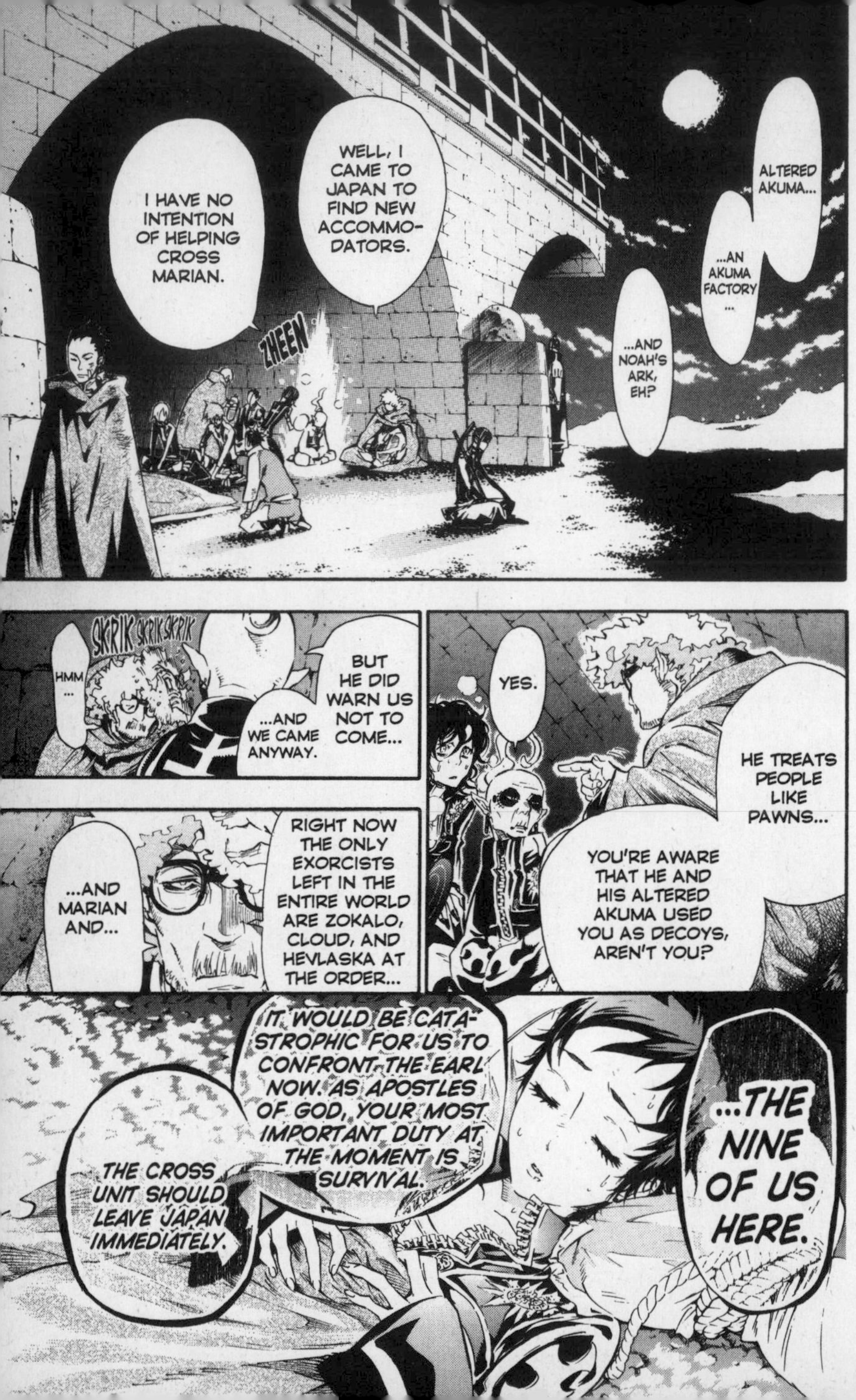
ALTERED AKUMA...
...AN AKUMA FACTORY ...
...AND NOAH'S ARK, EH?
WELL, I CAME TO JAPAN TO FIND NEW ACCOMMODATORS.
I HAVE NO INTENTION OF HELPING CROSS MARIAN.
ZHEEN
HE TREATS PEOPLE LIKE PAWNS...
YOU'RE AWARE THAT HE AND HIS ALTERED AKUMA USED YOU AS DECOYS, AREN'T YOU?
YES.
SKRIK SKRIK SKRIK
BUT HE DID WARN US NOT TO COME...
...AND WE CAME ANYWAY.
HMM...
RIGHT NOW THE ONLY EXORCISTS LEFT IN THE ENTIRE WORLD ARE ZOKALO, CLOUD, AND HEVLASKA AT THE ORDER...
...AND MARIAN AND...
...THE NINE OF US HERE.
IT WOULD BE CATASTROPHIC FOR US TO CONFRONT THE EARL NOW. AS APOSTLES OF GOD, YOUR MOST IMPORTANT DUTY AT THE MOMENT IS SURVIVAL.
THE CROSS UNIT SHOULD LEAVE JAPAN IMMEDIATELY.

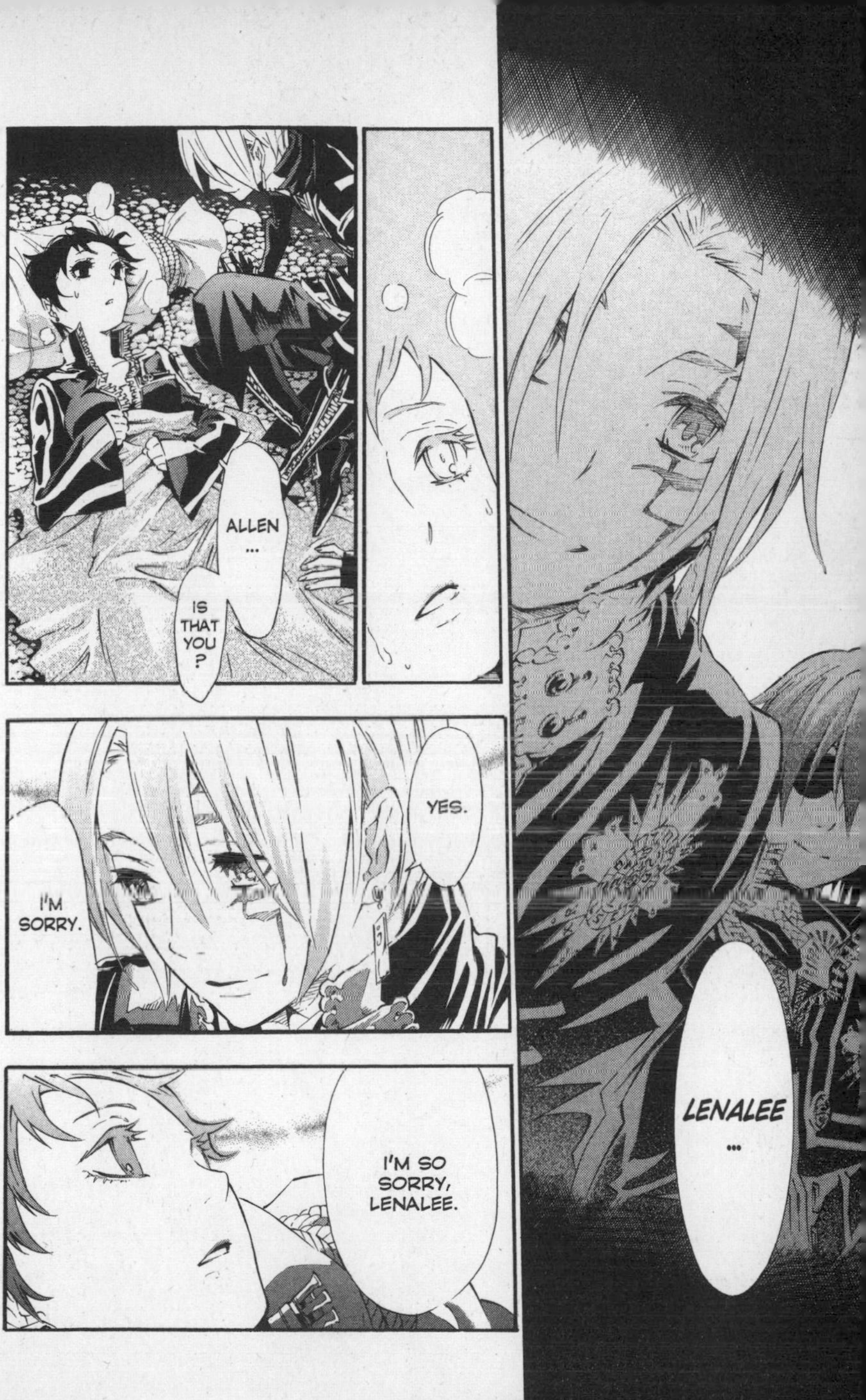
LENALEE ...
ALLEN ...
IS THAT YOU ?
YES.
I'M SORRY.
I'M SO SORRY, LENALEE.

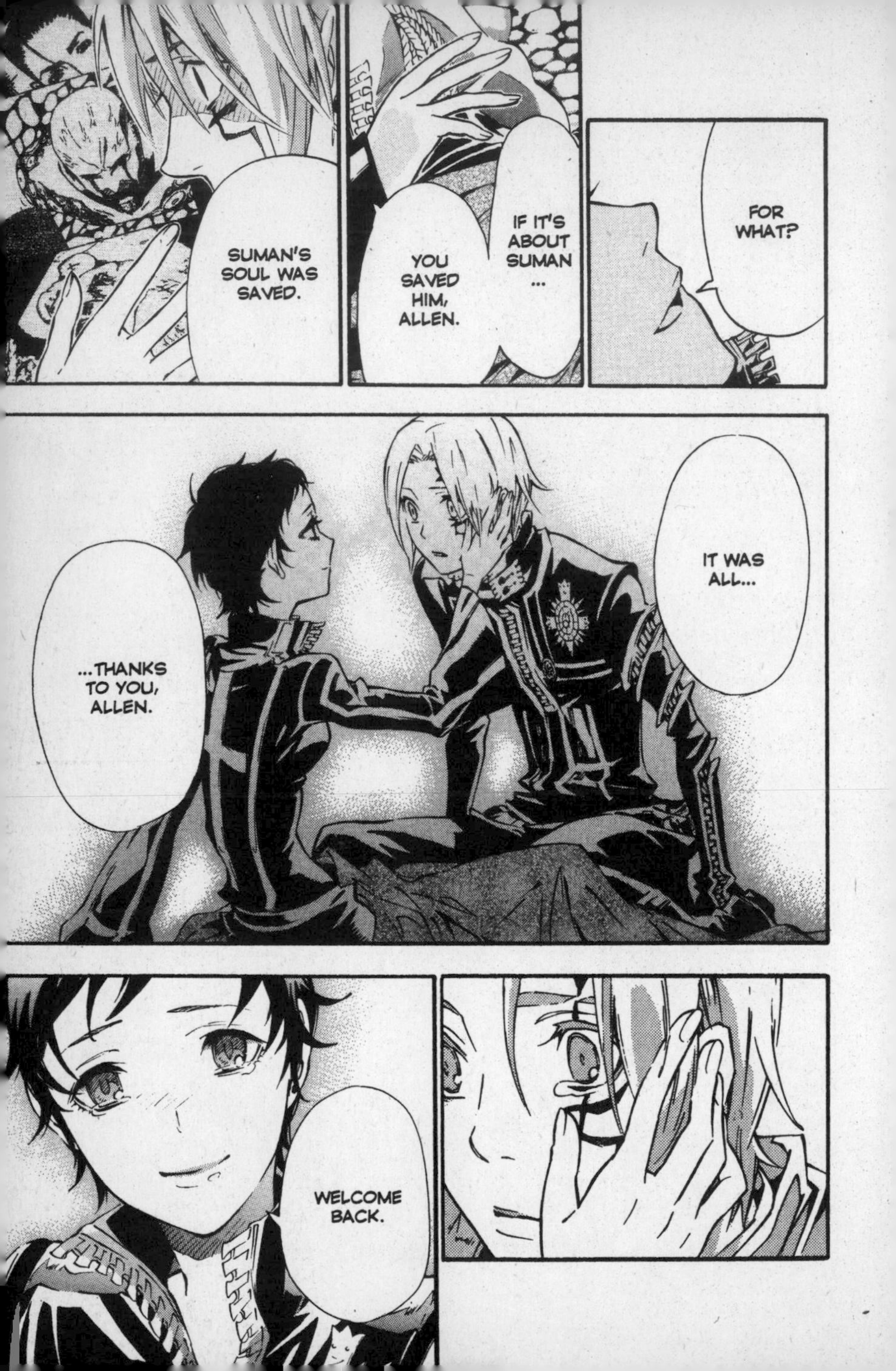
FOR WHAT?
IF IT'S ABOUT SUMAN ...
YOU SAVED HIM, ALLEN.
SUMAN'S SOUL WAS SAVED.
IT WAS ALL...
...THANKS TO YOU, ALLEN.
WELCOME BACK.

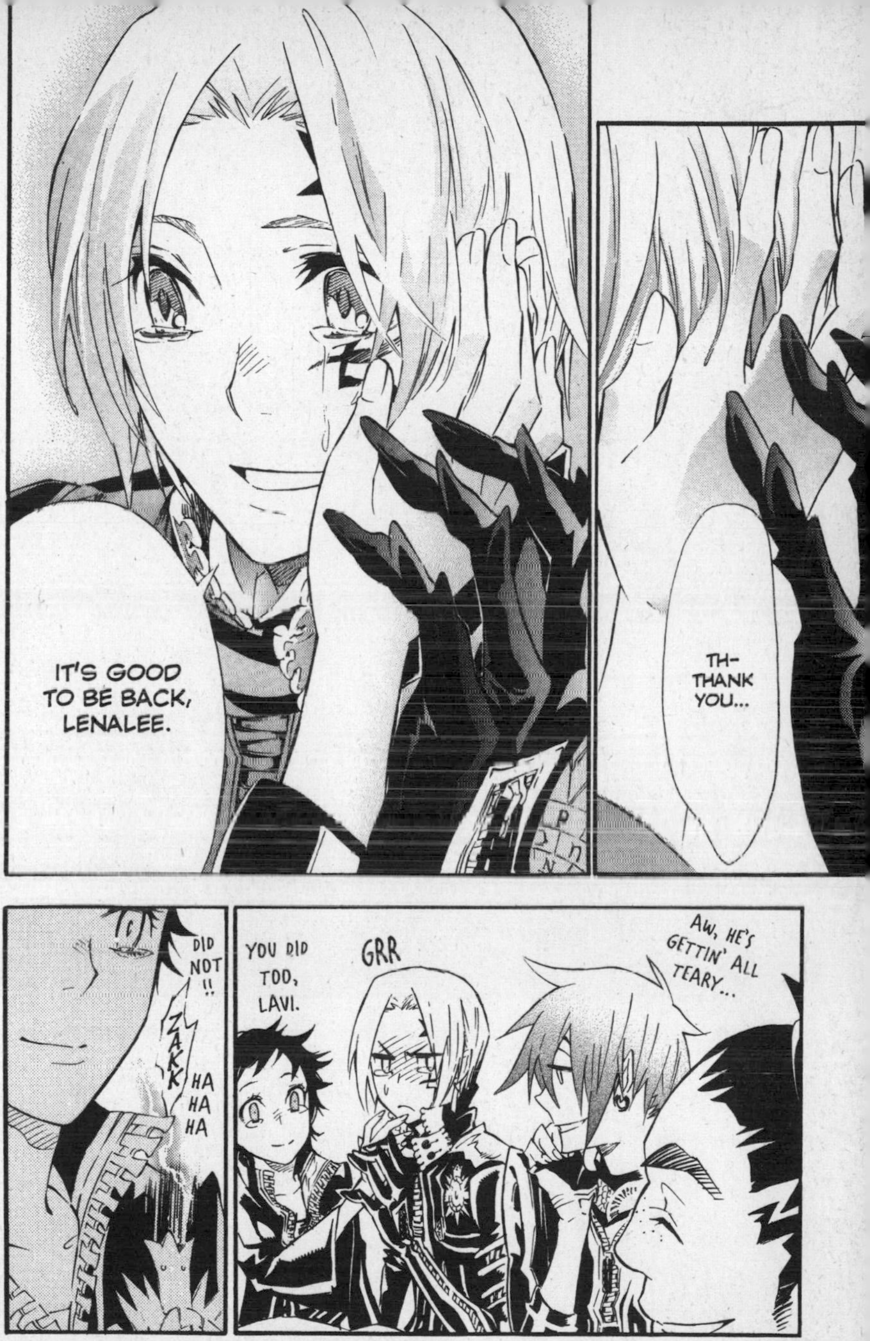
TH- THANK YOU...
IT'S GOOD TO BE BACK, LENALEE.
AW, HE'S GETTIN' ALL TEARY...
GRR
YOU DID TOO, LAVI.
DID NOT !!
ZAKK
HA HA HA HA

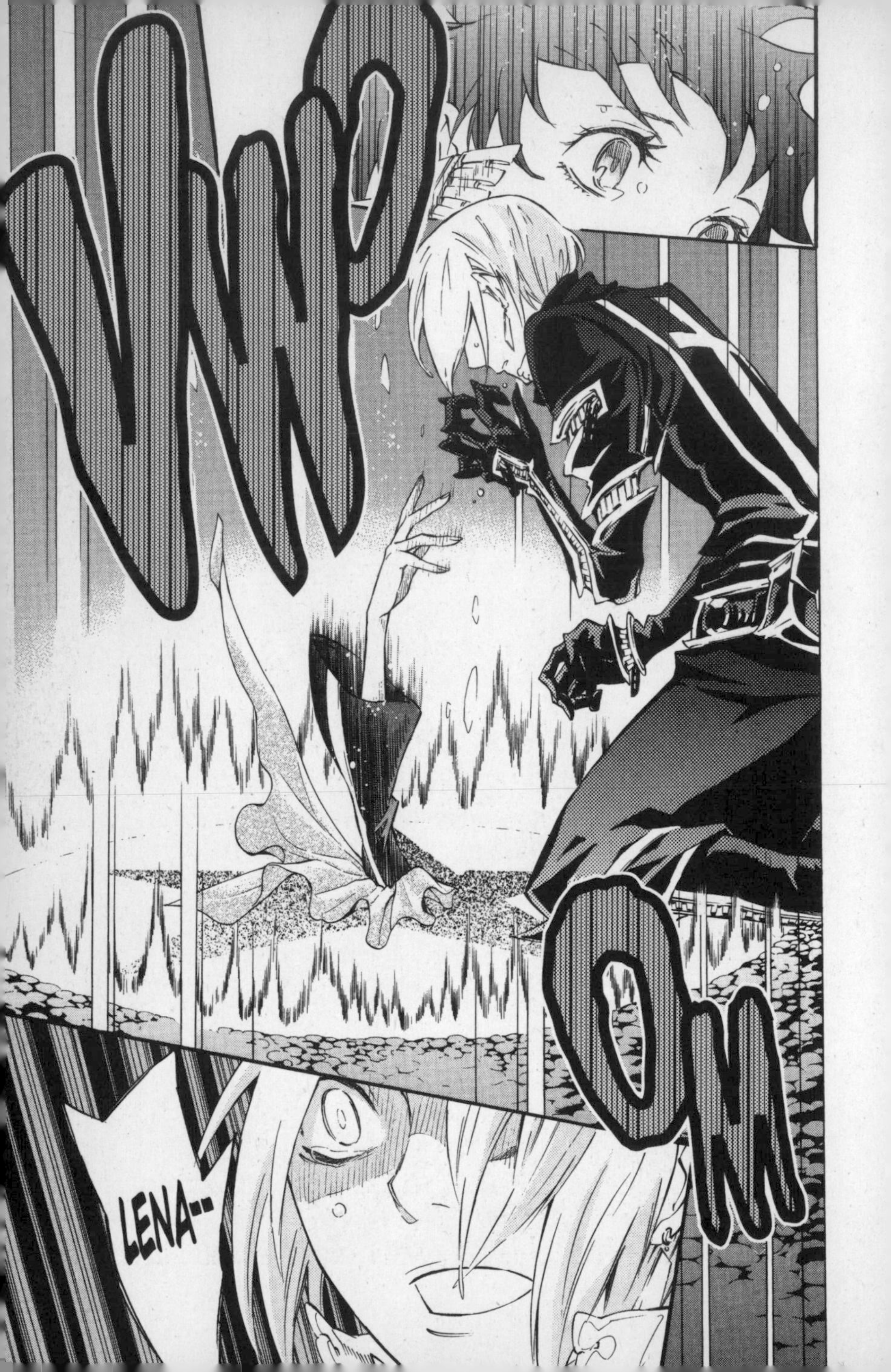
LENA...

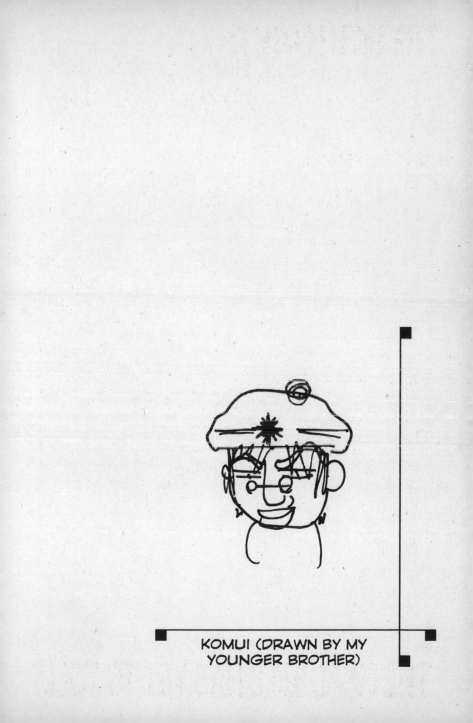

KOMUI (DRAWN BY MY
YOUNGER BROTHER)

THE 90TH NIGHT:

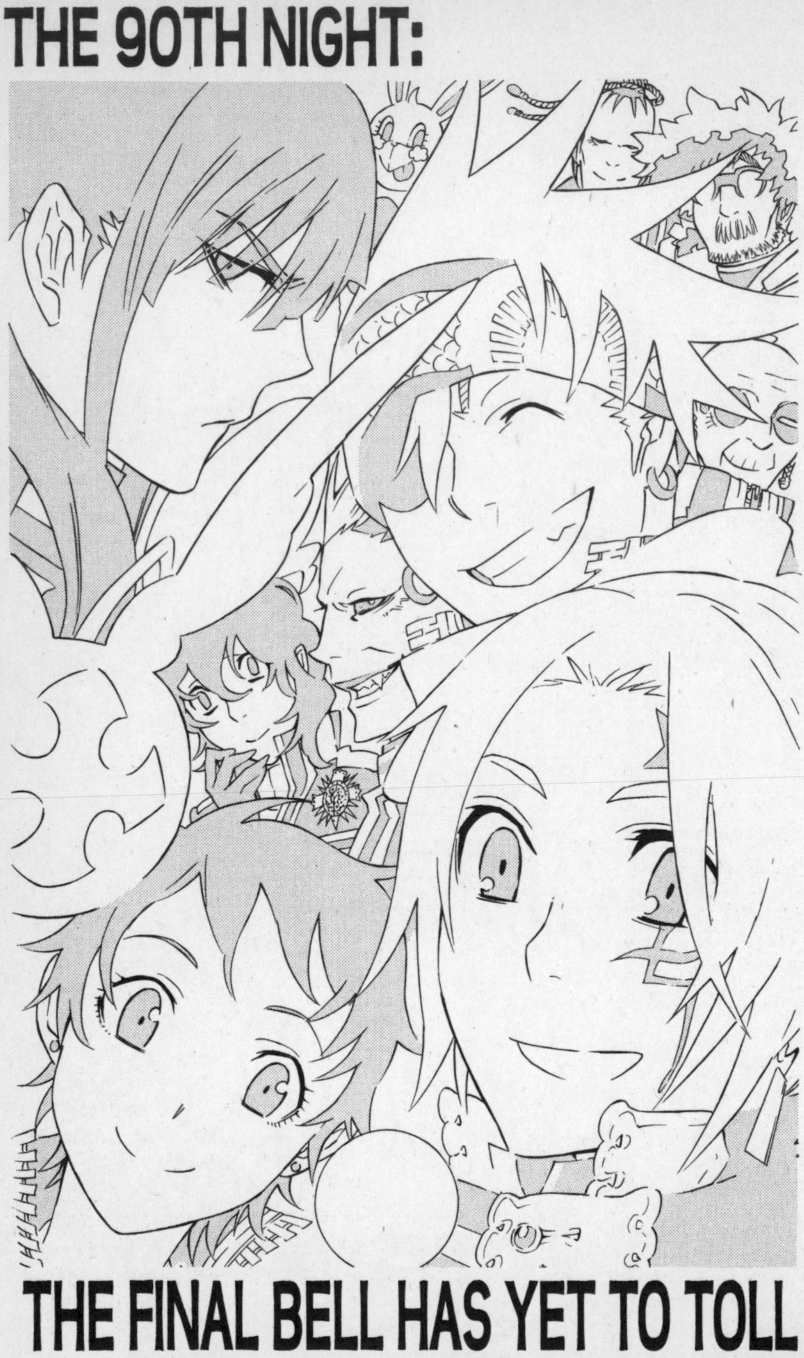

THE FINAL BELL HAS YET TO TOLL

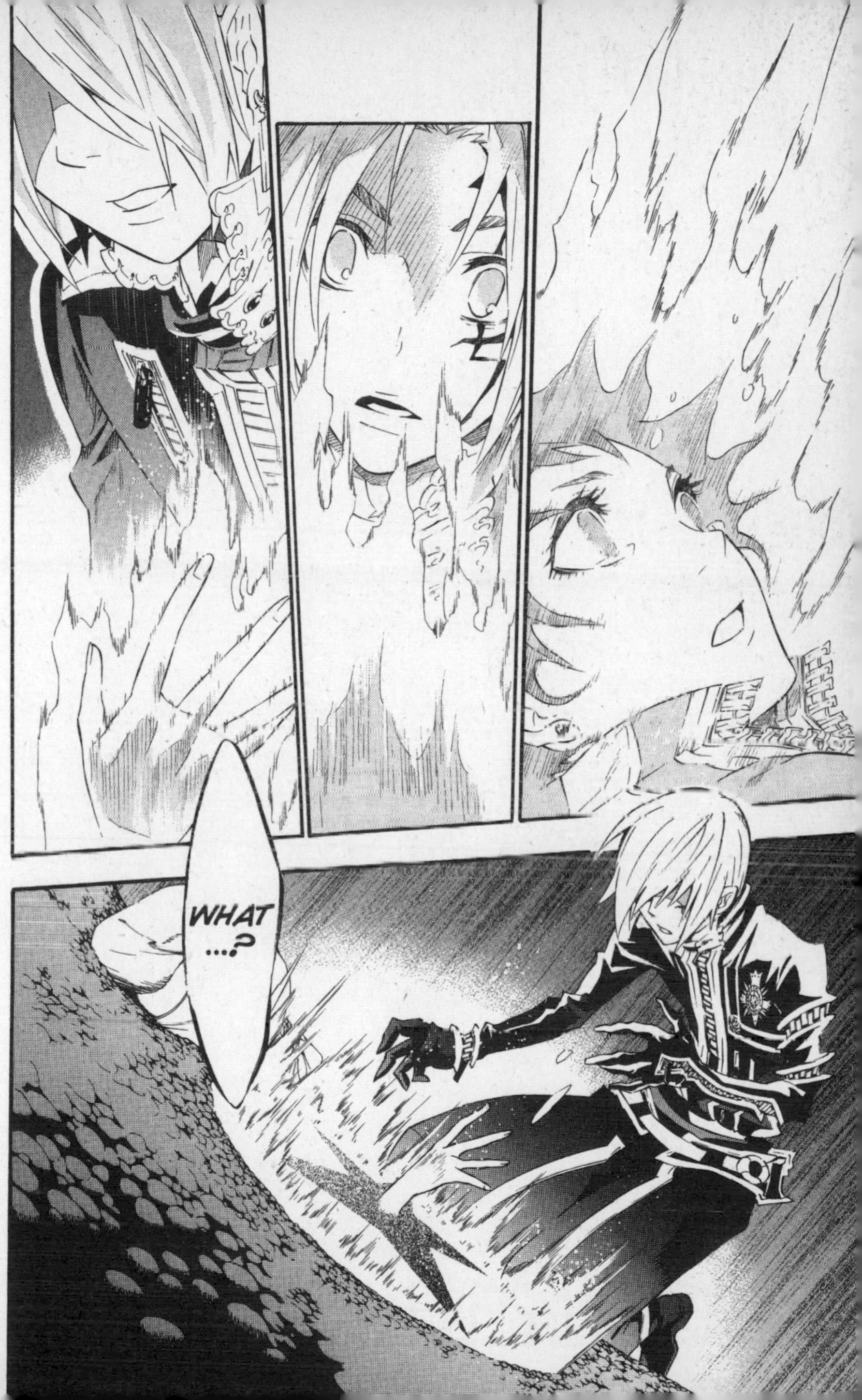
WHAT ...?

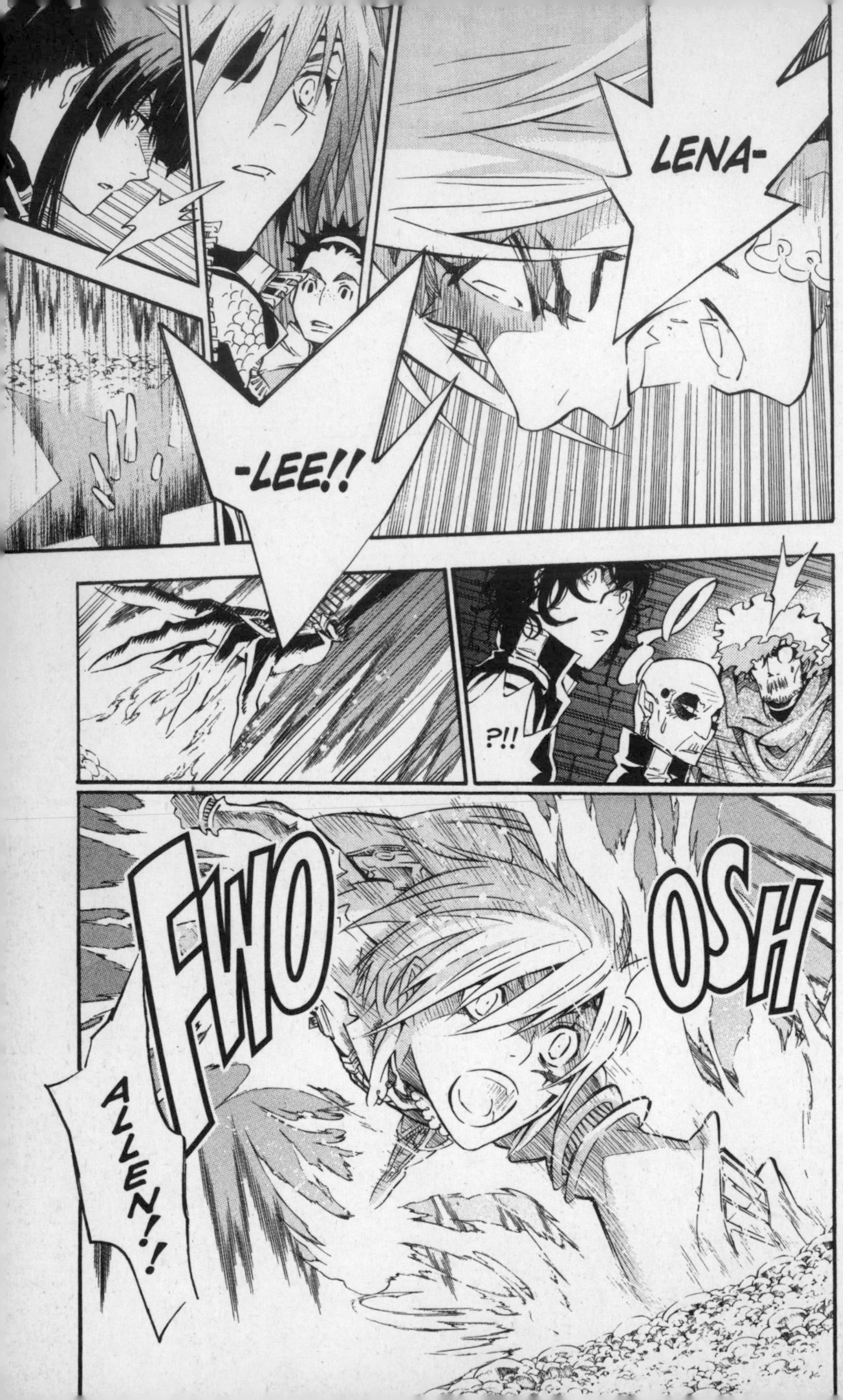
LENA-
-LEE!!
?!!
FWOOSH
ALLEN!!

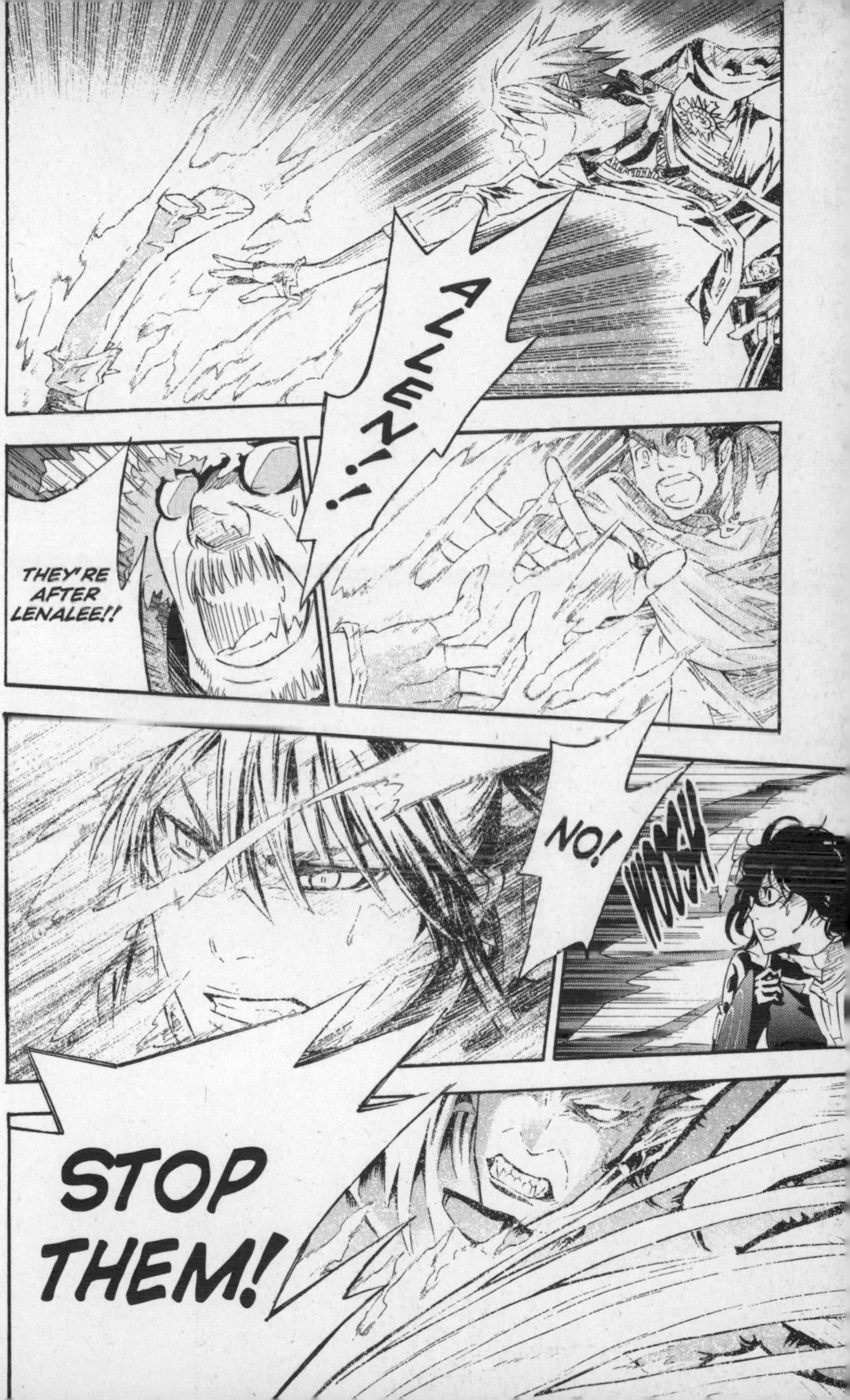
ALLEN!!
THEY'RE AFTER LENALEE!!
NO!
STOP THEM!

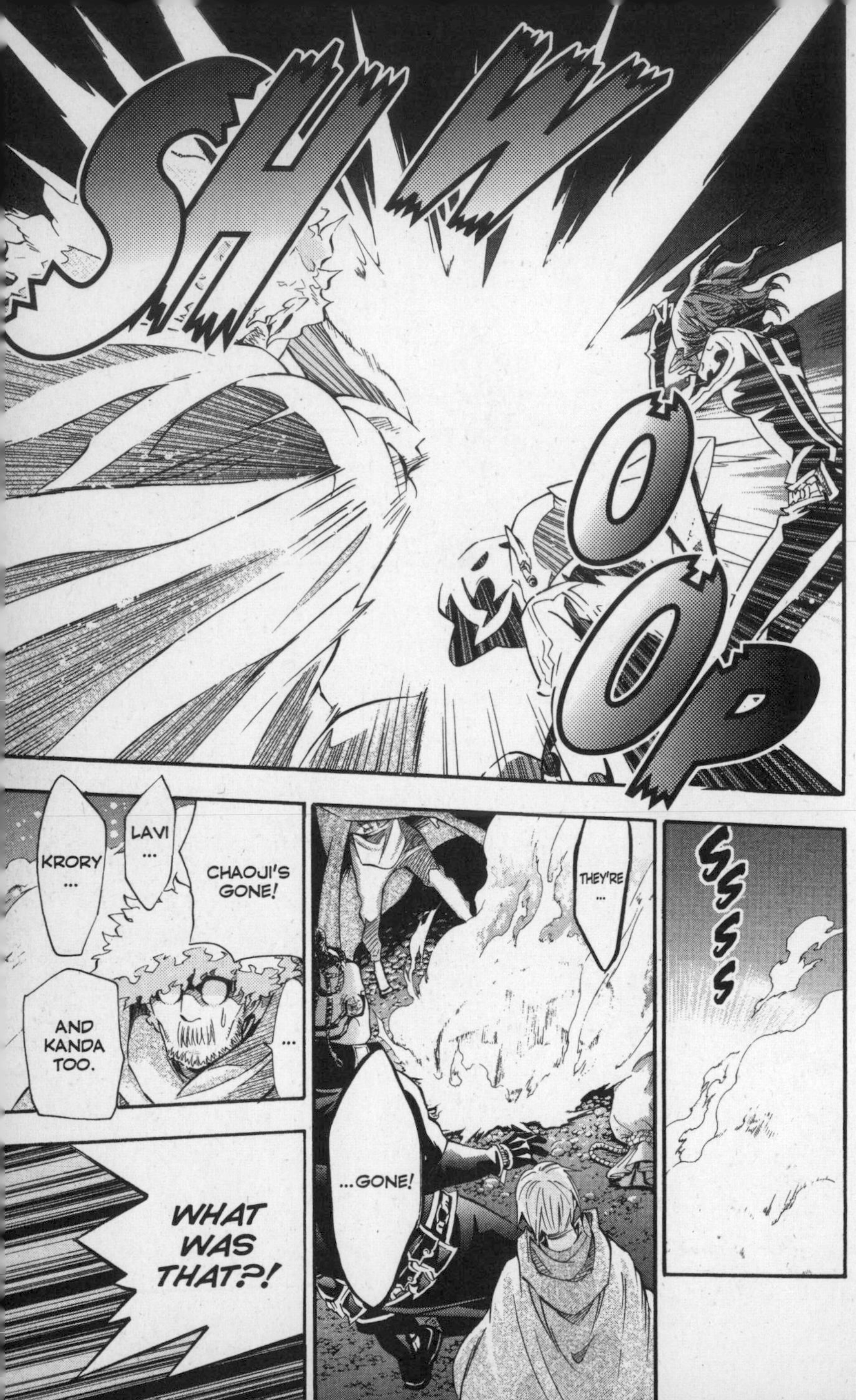
SHHHOOP
SSSS
THEY'RE ...
...GONE!
LAVI ...
KRORY ...
CHAOJI'S GONE!
AND KANDA TOO.
...
WHAT WAS THAT?!

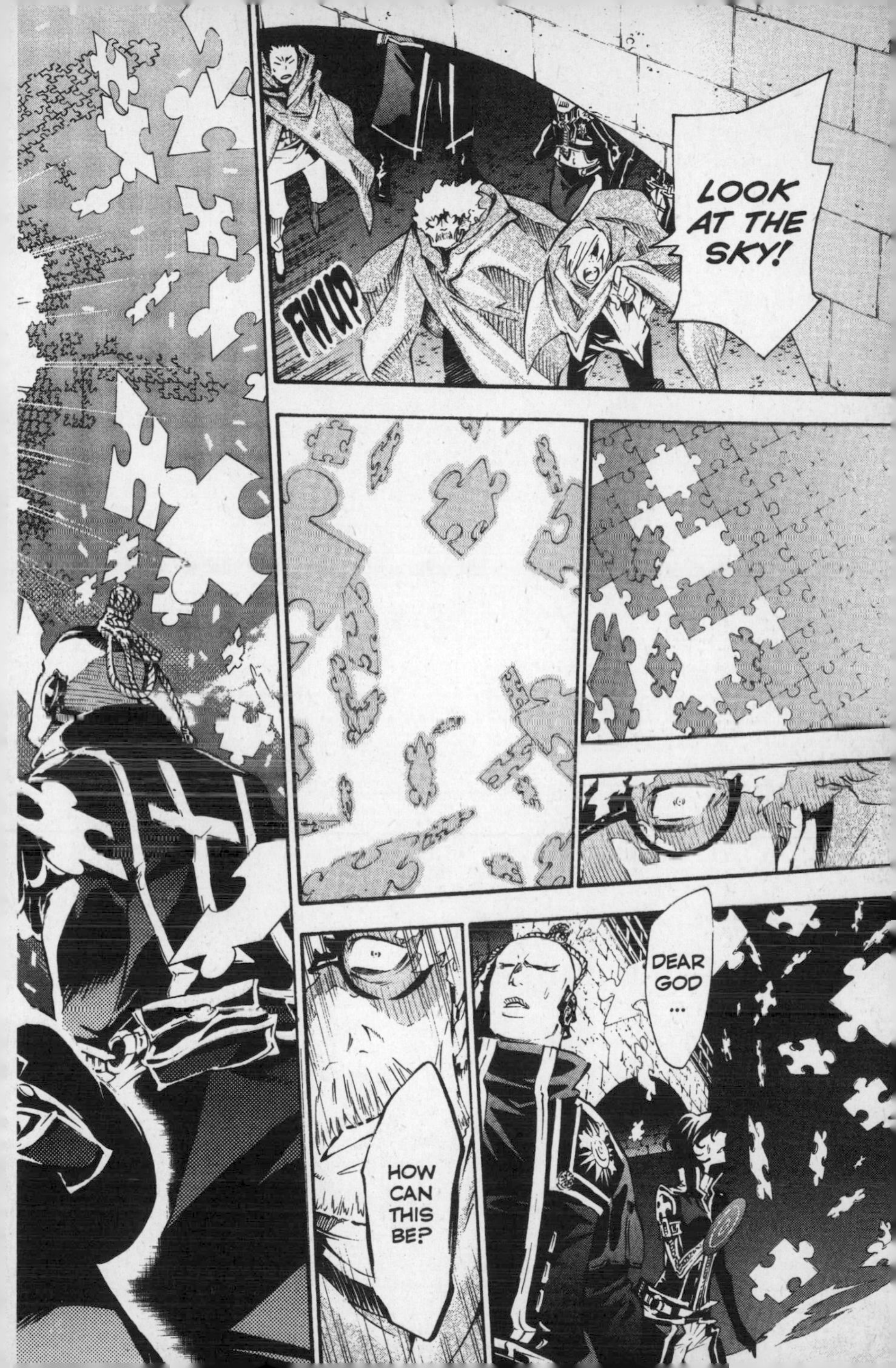
LOOK AT THE SKY!
FWUP
DEAR GOD ...
HOW CAN THIS BE?

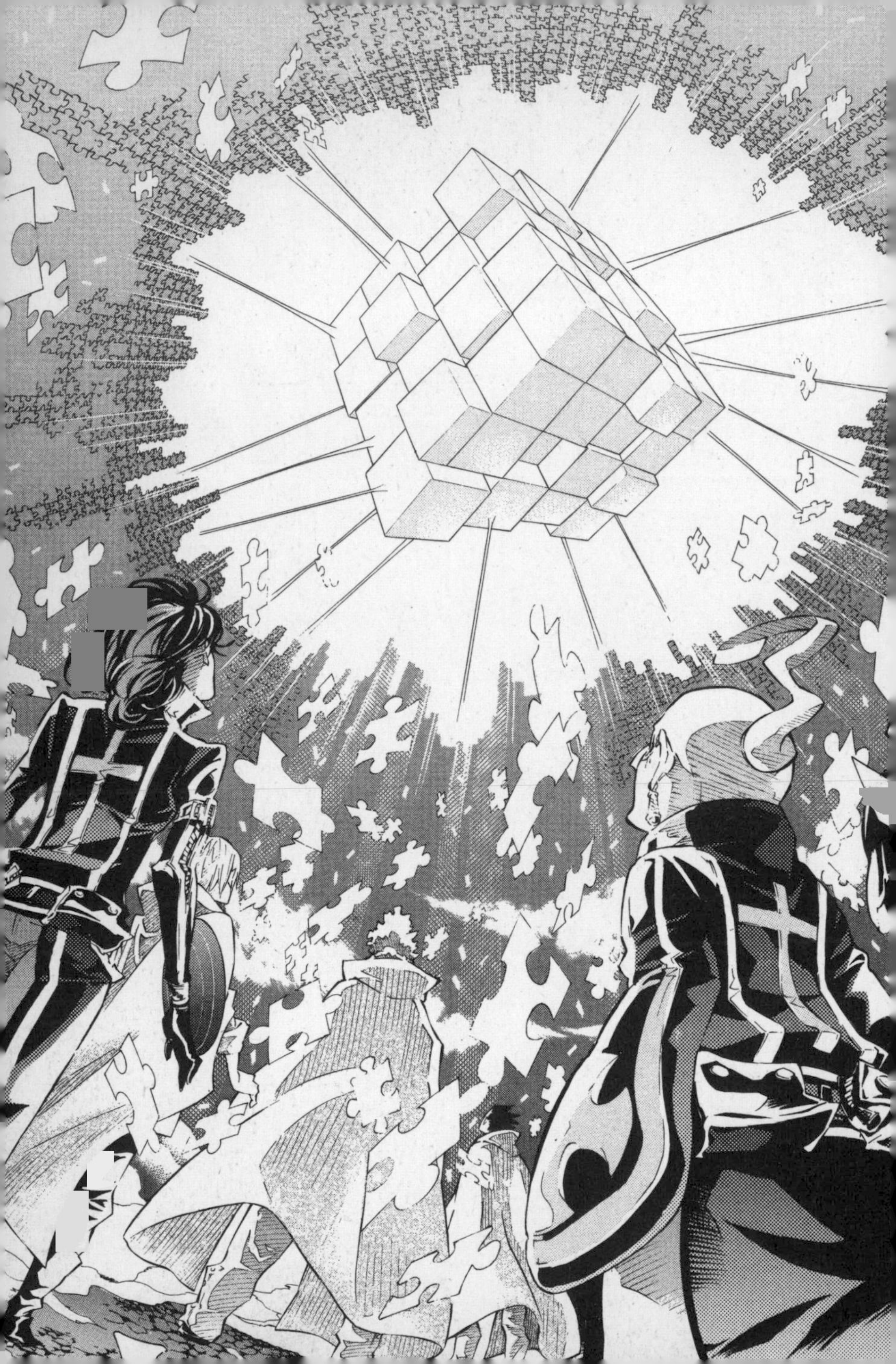

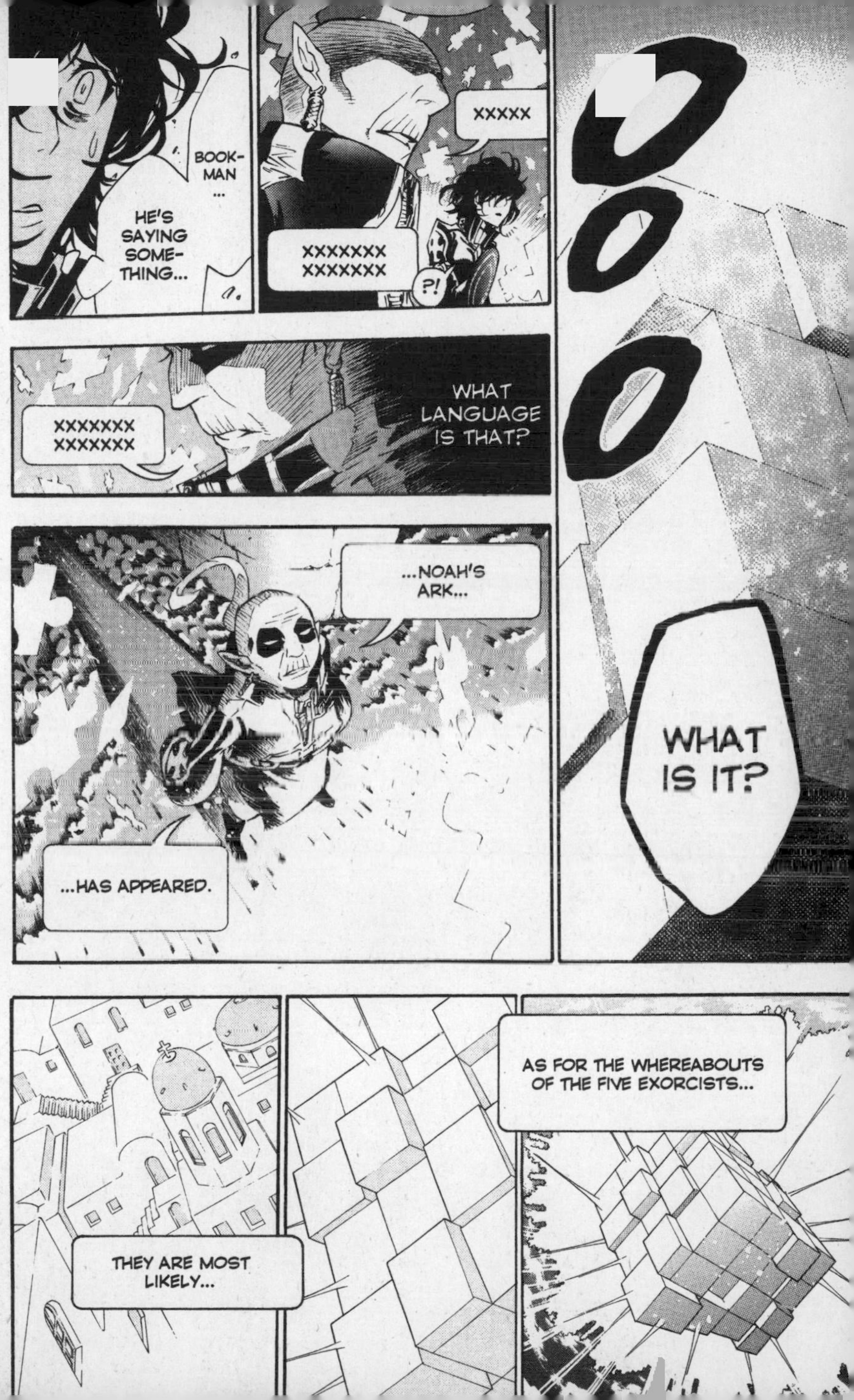
OOO
WHAT IS IT?
XXXXX
XXXXXXX XXXXXXX
?!
BOOK-MAN...
HE'S SAYING SOME-THING...
WHAT LANGUAGE IS THAT?
XXXXXXX XXXXXXX
...NOAH'S ARK...
...HAS APPEARED.
AS FOR THE WHEREABOUTS OF THE FIVE EXORCISTS...
THEY ARE MOST LIKELY...

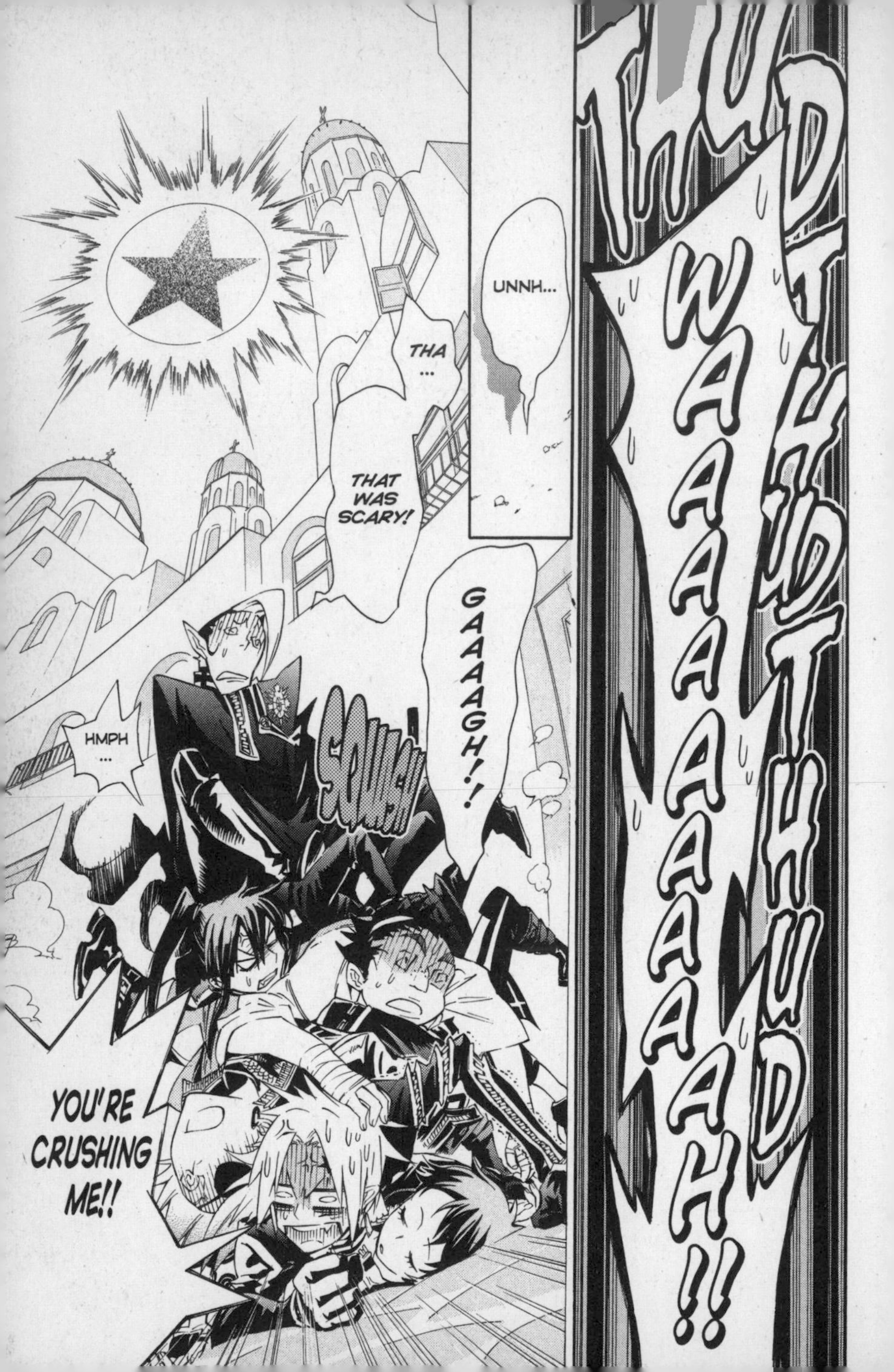
THUD THUD THUD
WAAAAAAAAAH!!
UNNH...
THA...
THAT WAS SCARY!
GAAAAAGH!!
SQUISH
HMPH...
YOU'RE CRUSHING ME!!

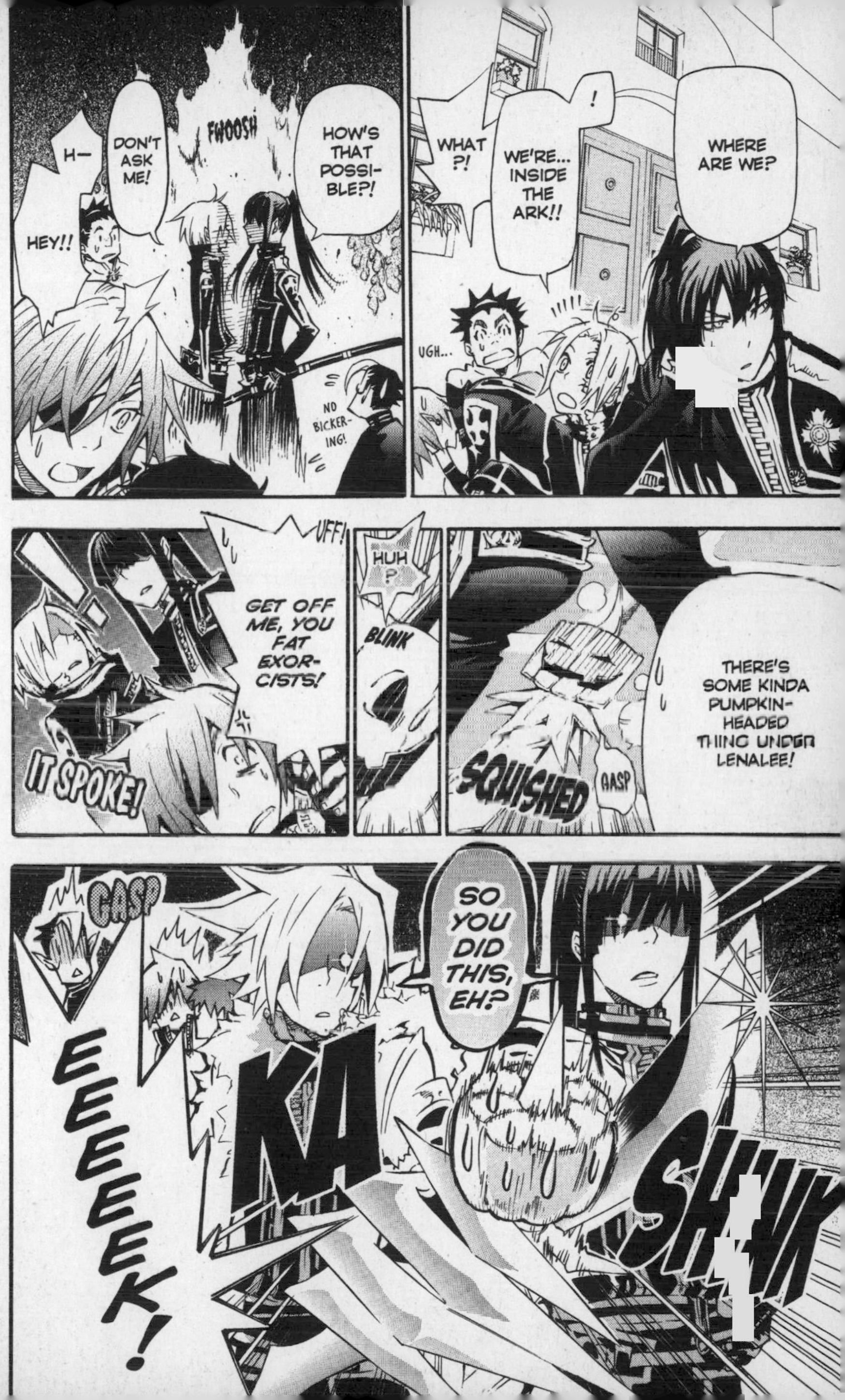
WHERE ARE WE?
!
WE'RE... INSIDE THE ARK!!
WHAT ?!
UGH...
HOW'S THAT POSSI-BLE?!
FWOOSH
DON'T ASK ME!
H—
HEY!!
NO BICKER-ING!
THERE'S SOME KINDA PUMPKIN-HEADED THING UNDER LENALEE!
GASP
SQUISHED
HUH ?
BLINK
UFF!
GET OFF ME, YOU FAT EXOR-CISTS!
IT SPOKE!
SO YOU DID THIS, EH?
SHINK
KA
GASP
EEEEEK!

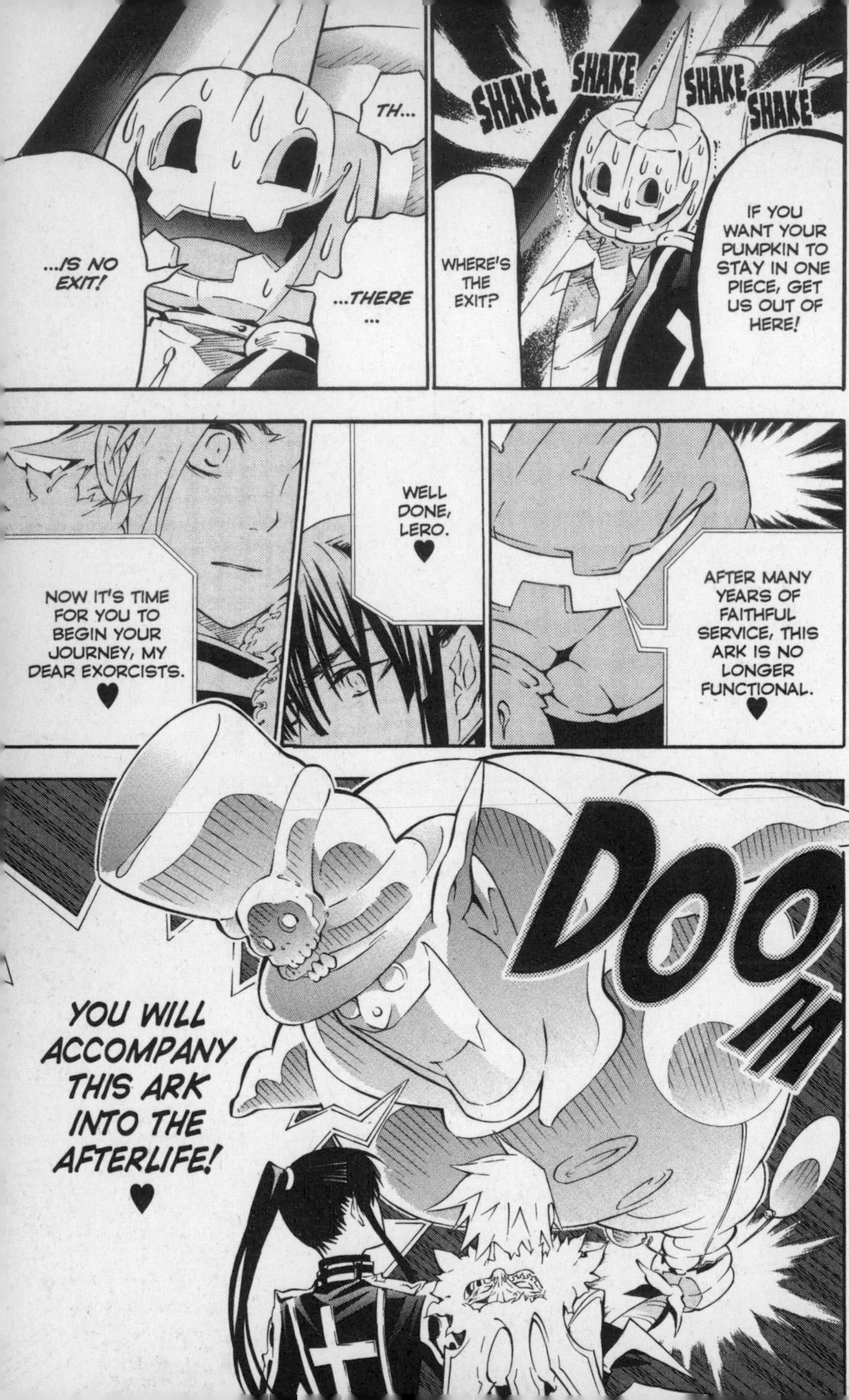
SHAKE
SHAKE
SHAKE
SHAKE
IF YOU WANT YOUR PUMPKIN TO STAY IN ONE PIECE, GET US OUT OF HERE!
WHERE'S THE EXIT?
TH...
...THERE ...
...IS NO EXIT!
AFTER MANY YEARS OF FAITHFUL SERVICE, THIS ARK IS NO LONGER FUNCTIONAL. ♥
WELL DONE, LERO. ♥
NOW IT'S TIME FOR YOU TO BEGIN YOUR JOURNEY, MY DEAR EXORCISTS. ♥
DOOM
YOU WILL ACCOMPANY THIS ARK INTO THE AFTERLIFE! ♥

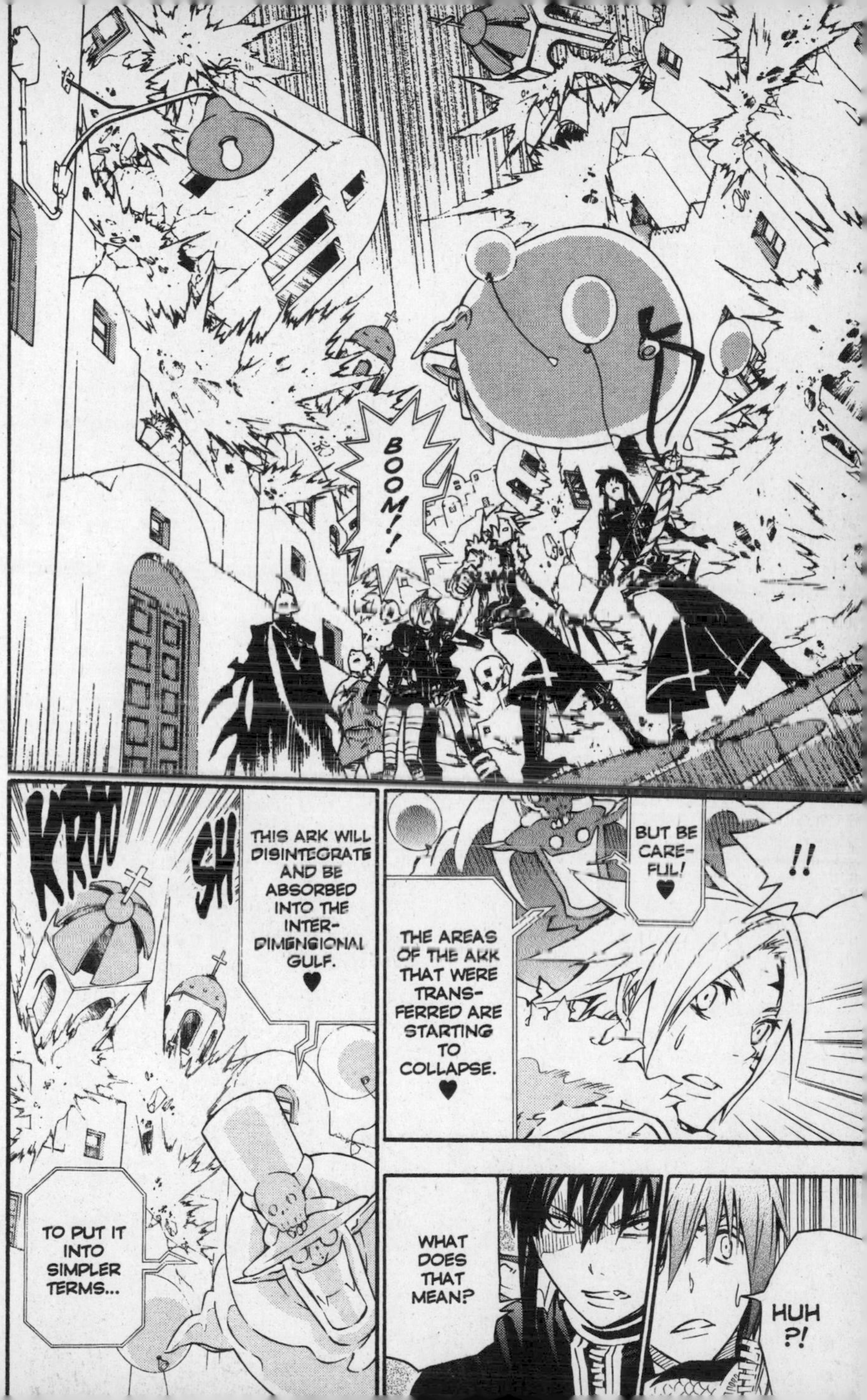
BOOM!!
BUT BE CARE-FUL! ♥
THE AREAS OF THE ARK THAT WERE TRANS-FERRED ARE STARTING TO COLLAPSE. ♥
!!
HUH?!
WHAT DOES THAT MEAN?
THIS ARK WILL DISINTEGRATE AND BE ABSORBED INTO THE INTER-DIMENSIONAL GULF. ♥
TO PUT IT INTO SIMPLER TERMS...

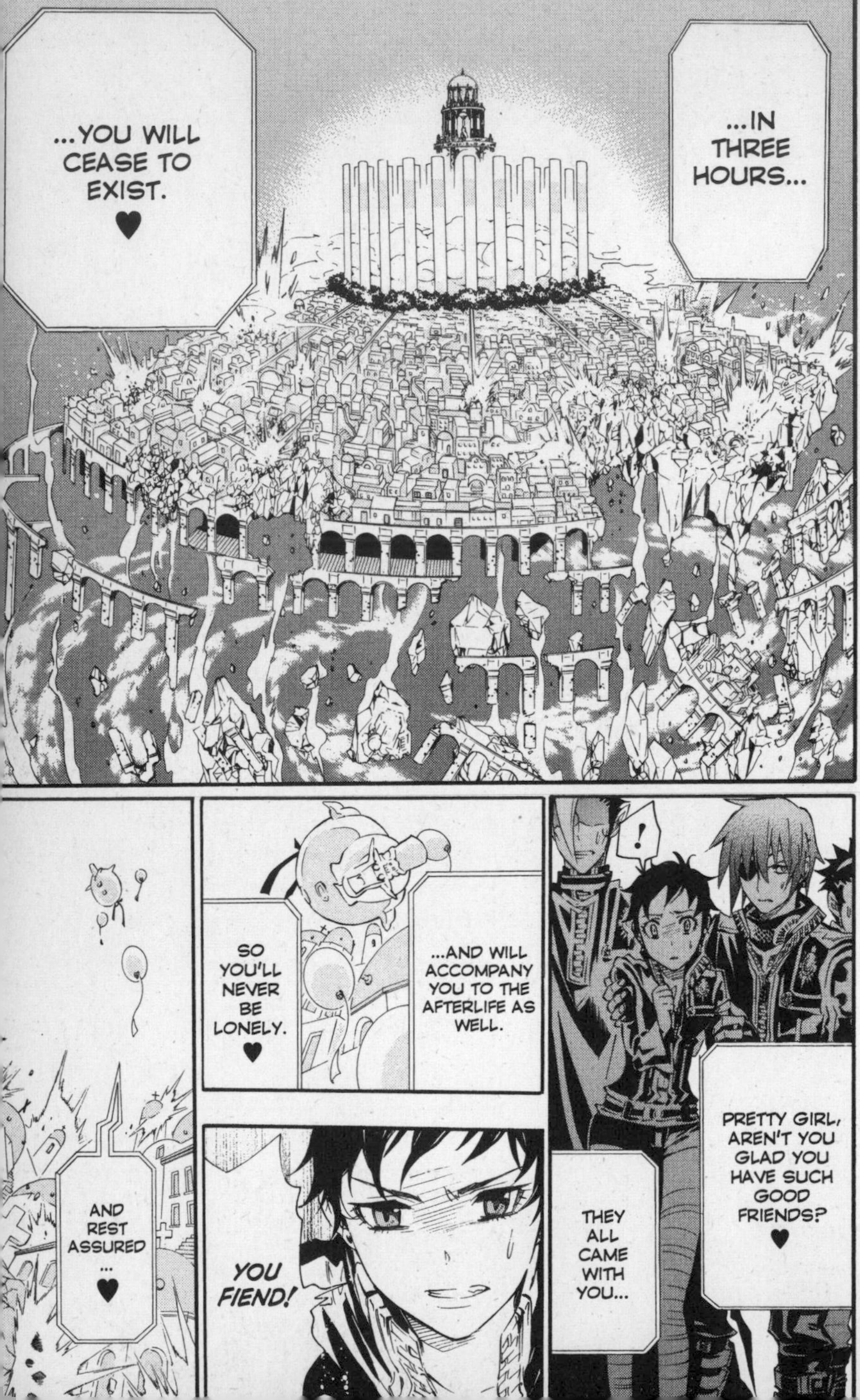
...IN THREE HOURS...
...YOU WILL CEASE TO EXIST. ♥
!
PRETTY GIRL, AREN'T YOU GLAD YOU HAVE SUCH GOOD FRIENDS? ♥
THEY ALL CAME WITH YOU...
...AND WILL ACCOMPANY YOU TO THE AFTERLIFE AS WELL.
SO YOU'LL NEVER BE LONELY. ♥
YOU FIEND!
AND REST ASSURED ... ♥

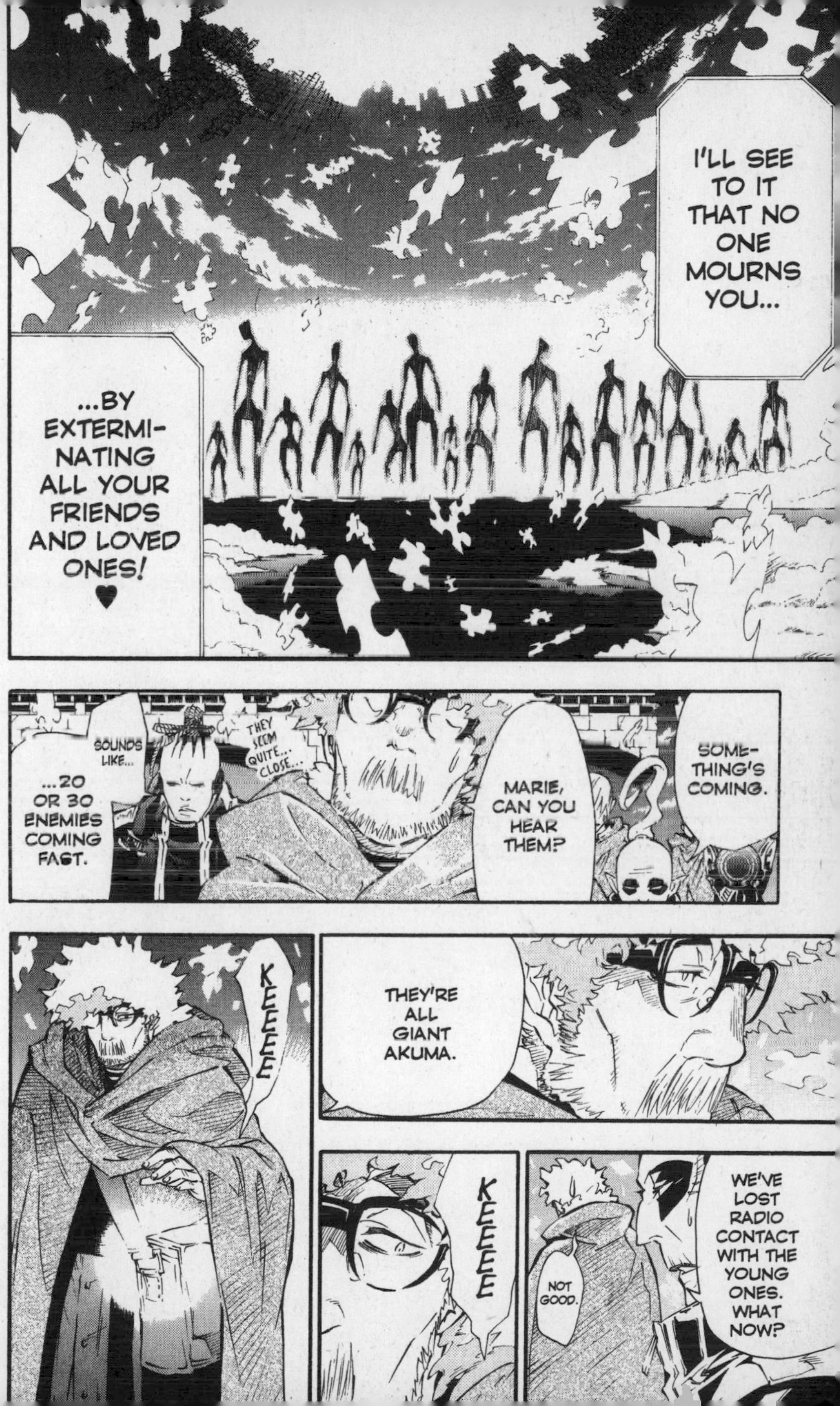
I'LL SEE TO IT THAT NO ONE MOURNS YOU...
...BY EXTERMI-NATING ALL YOUR FRIENDS AND LOVED ONES! ♥
SOME-THING'S COMING.
MARIE, CAN YOU HEAR THEM?
THEY SEEM QUITE... CLOSE...
SOUNDS LIKE...
...20 OR 30 ENEMIES COMING FAST.
THEY'RE ALL GIANT AKUMA.
WE'VE LOST RADIO CONTACT WITH THE YOUNG ONES. WHAT NOW?
NOT GOOD.
KEEEE
KEEEE

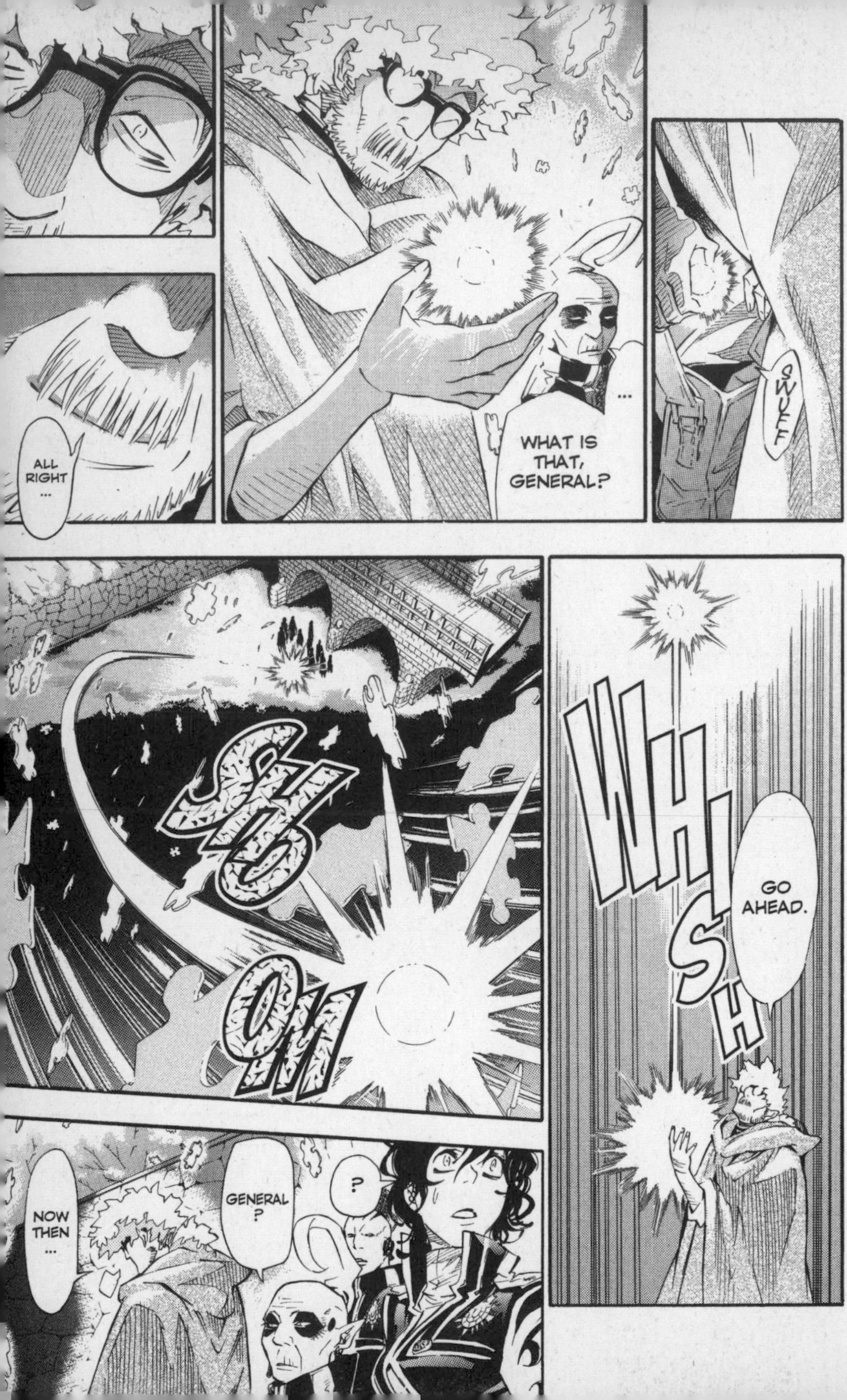
SWUFF
...
WHAT IS THAT, GENERAL?
ALL RIGHT ...
GO AHEAD.
WHISH
SHOOM
?
GENERAL ?
NOW THEN ...

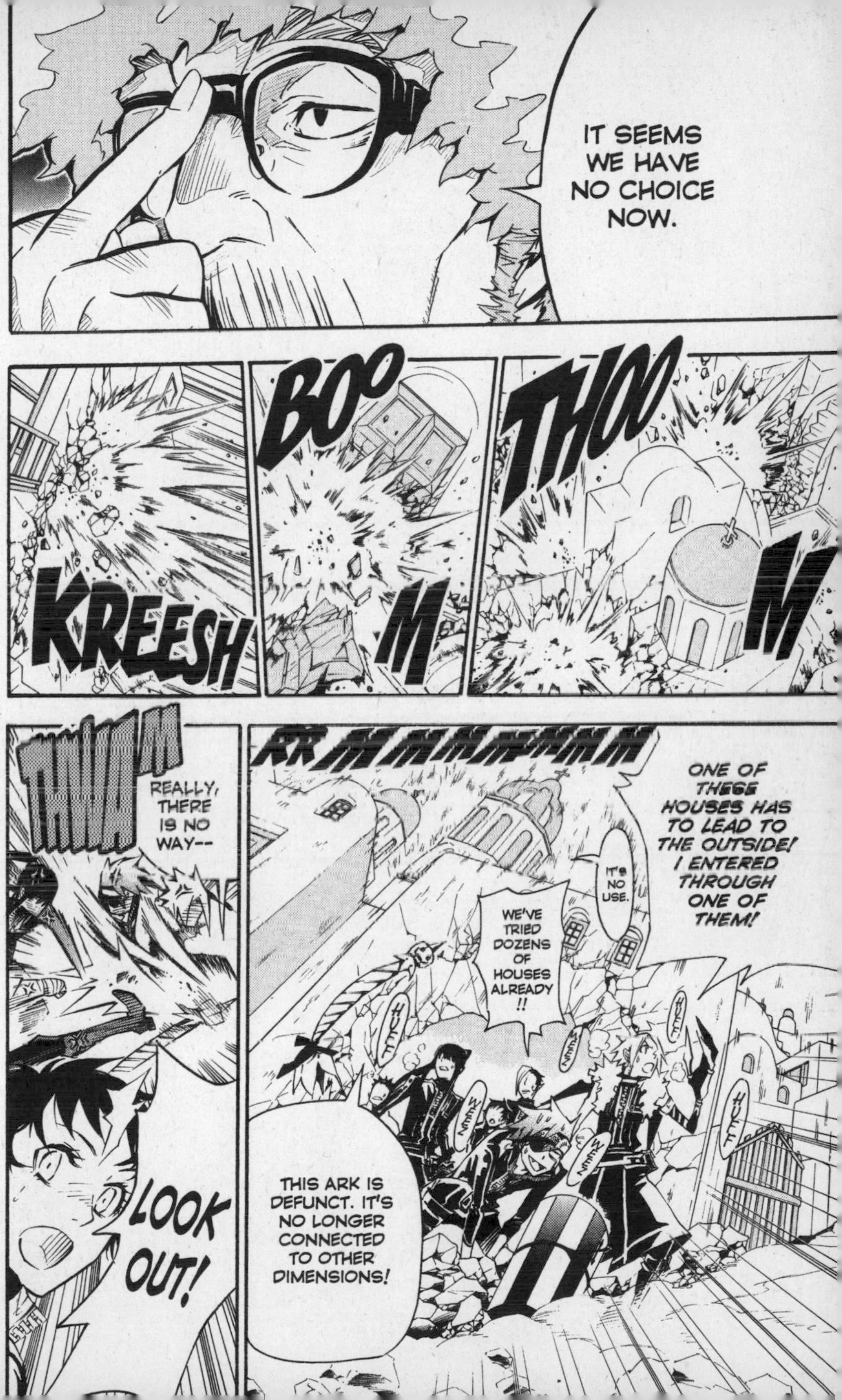
IT SEEMS WE HAVE NO CHOICE NOW.
THOOM
BOOM
KREESH
ONE OF THESE HOUSES HAS TO LEAD TO THE OUTSIDE! I ENTERED THROUGH ONE OF THEM!
IT'S NO USE.
WE'VE TRIED DOZENS OF HOUSES ALREADY!!
HUFF
HUFF
HUFF
THIS ARK IS DEFUNCT. IT'S NO LONGER CONNECTED TO OTHER DIMENSIONS!
THWAM
REALLY, THERE IS NO WAY--
LOOK OUT!

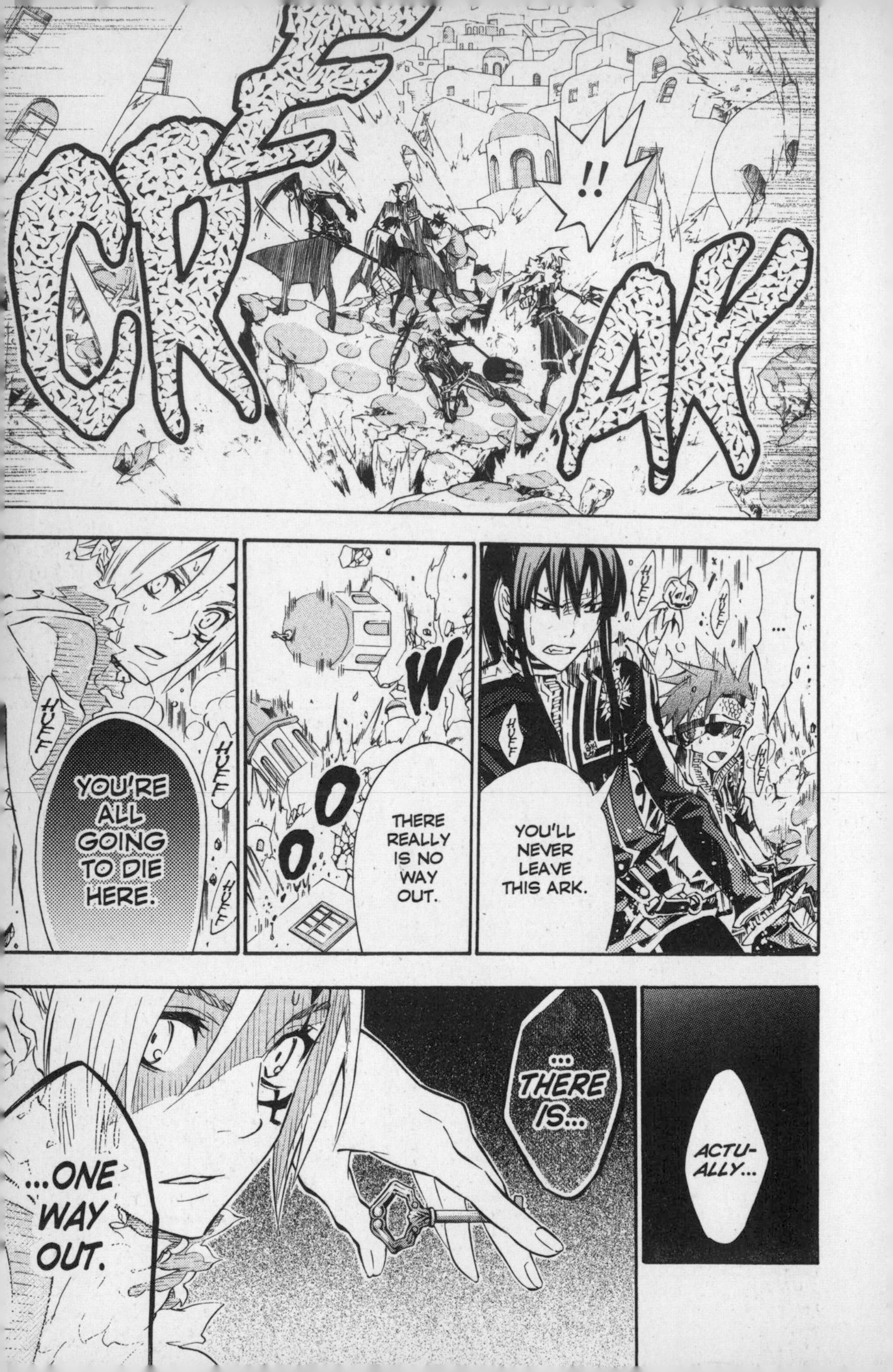
CRAAK
!!
HUFF
HUFF
...
HUFF
YOU'LL NEVER LEAVE THIS ARK.
WOO
THERE REALLY IS NO WAY OUT.
HUFF
HUFF
HUFF
YOU'RE ALL GOING TO DIE HERE.
ACTU-ALLY...
...THERE IS...
...ONE WAY OUT.

KOMUI'S DISCUSSION ROOM (EVEN THOUGH KOMUI NEVER SEEMS TO SHOW UP FOR IT), VOL.1☆

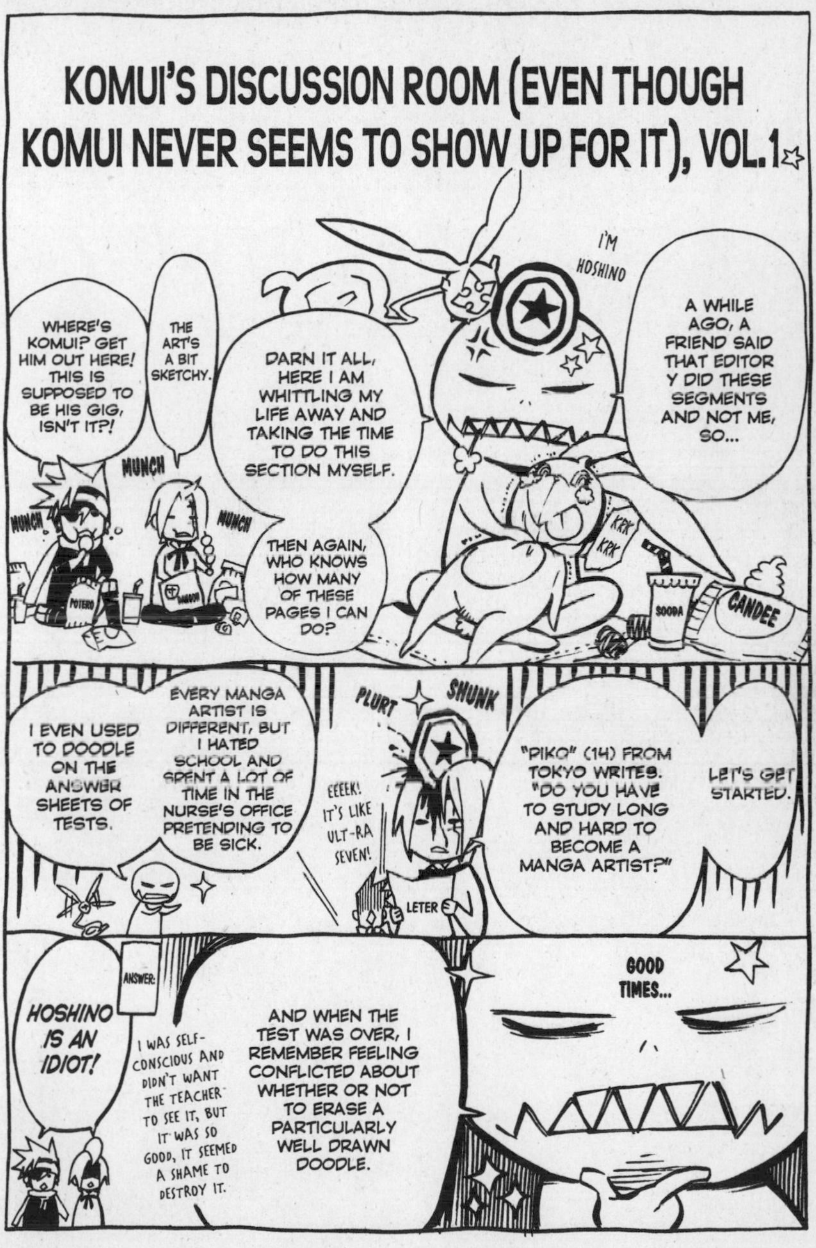
I'M HOSHINO
A WHILE AGO, A FRIEND SAID THAT EDITOR Y DID THESE SEGMENTS AND NOT ME, SO...
DARN IT ALL, HERE I AM WHITTLING MY LIFE AWAY AND TAKING THE TIME TO DO THIS SECTION MYSELF.
THEN AGAIN, WHO KNOWS HOW MANY OF THESE PAGES I CAN DO?
KRK KRK
CANDEE
SOODA
THE ART'S A BIT SKETCHY.
WHERE'S KOMUI? GET HIM OUT HERE! THIS IS SUPPOSED TO BE HIS GIG, ISN'T IT?!
MUNCH
MUNCH
MUNCH
POTERO
LET'S GET STARTED.
"PIKO" (14) FROM TOKYO WRITES. "DO YOU HAVE TO STUDY LONG AND HARD TO BECOME A MANGA ARTIST?"
SHUNK
PLURT
EEEEK! IT'S LIKE ULT-RA SEVEN!
LETER
EVERY MANGA ARTIST IS DIFFERENT, BUT I HATED SCHOOL AND SPENT A LOT OF TIME IN THE NURSE'S OFFICE PRETENDING TO BE SICK.
I EVEN USED TO DOODLE ON THE ANSWER SHEETS OF TESTS.
GOOD TIMES...
AND WHEN THE TEST WAS OVER, I REMEMBER FEELING CONFLICTED ABOUT WHETHER OR NOT TO ERASE A PARTICULARLY WELL DRAWN DOODLE.
I WAS SELF-CONSCIOUS AND DIDN'T WANT THE TEACHER TO SEE IT, BUT IT WAS SO GOOD, IT SEEMED A SHAME TO DESTROY IT.
ANSWER:
HOSHINO IS AN IDIOT!

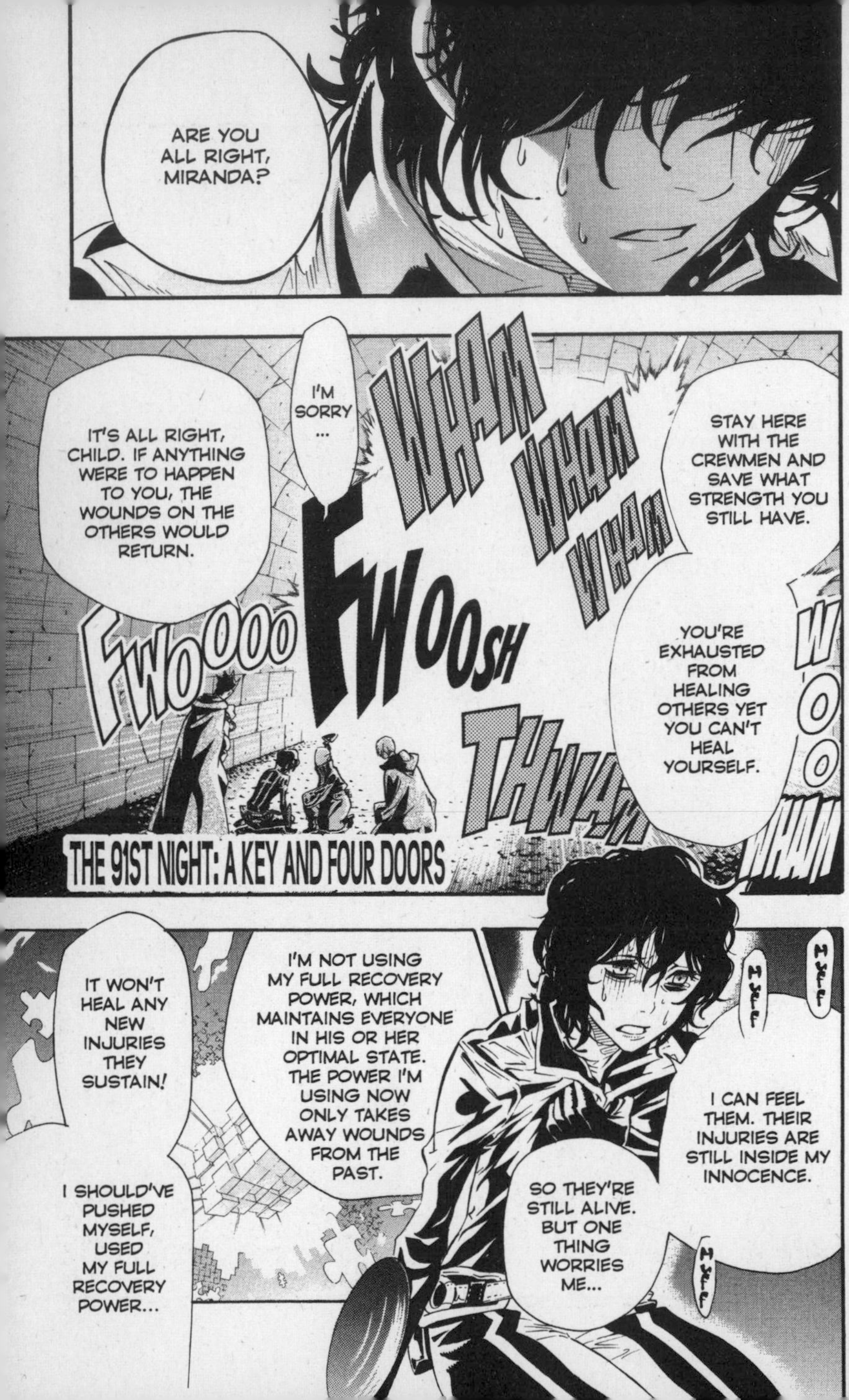
ARE YOU ALL RIGHT, MIRANDA?
STAY HERE WITH THE CREWMEN AND SAVE WHAT STRENGTH YOU STILL HAVE.
YOU'RE EXHAUSTED FROM HEALING OTHERS YET YOU CAN'T HEAL YOURSELF.
WHAM
WHAM
WHAM
THWAM
FWOOSH
I'M SORRY...
IT'S ALL RIGHT, CHILD. IF ANYTHING WERE TO HAPPEN TO YOU, THE WOUNDS ON THE OTHERS WOULD RETURN.
FWOOOO
THE 91ST NIGHT: A KEY AND FOUR DOORS
I CAN FEEL THEM. THEIR INJURIES ARE STILL INSIDE MY INNOCENCE.
SO THEY'RE STILL ALIVE. BUT ONE THING WORRIES ME...
I'M NOT USING MY FULL RECOVERY POWER, WHICH MAINTAINS EVERYONE IN HIS OR HER OPTIMAL STATE. THE POWER I'M USING NOW ONLY TAKES AWAY WOUNDS FROM THE PAST.
IT WON'T HEAL ANY NEW INJURIES THEY SUSTAIN!
I SHOULD'VE PUSHED MYSELF, USED MY FULL RECOVERY POWER...

THE 91ST NIGHT: A KEY AND FOUR DOORS

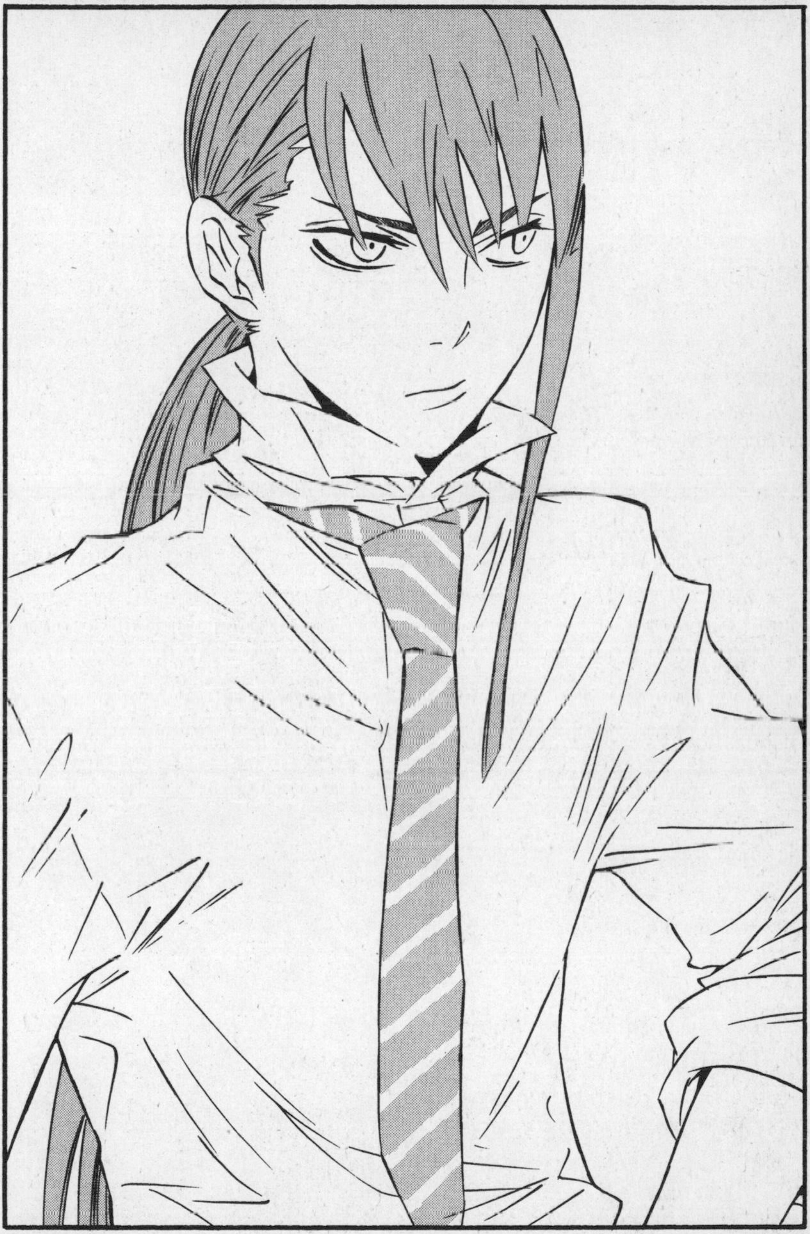

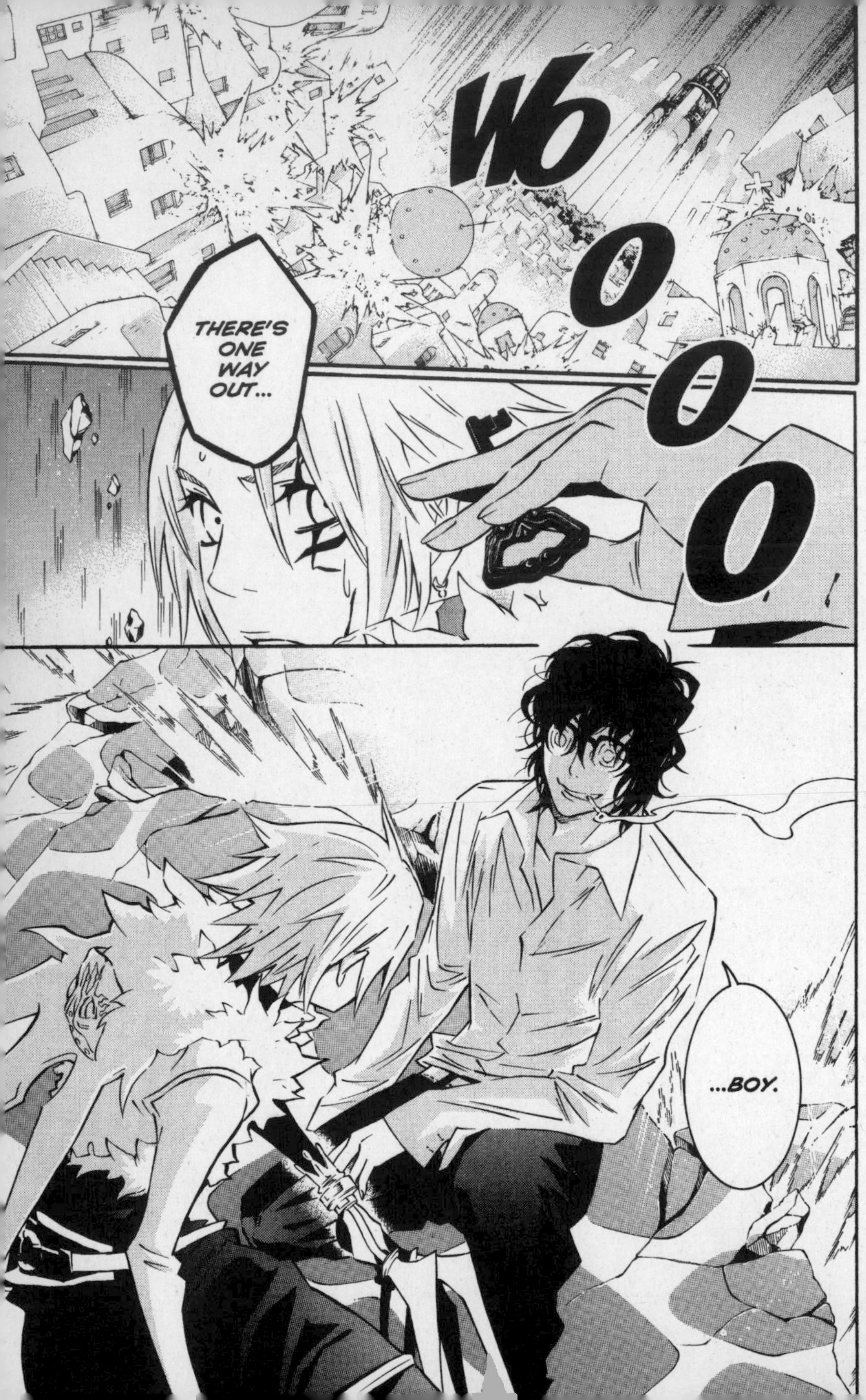
WOOOO
THERE'S ONE WAY OUT...
...BOY.

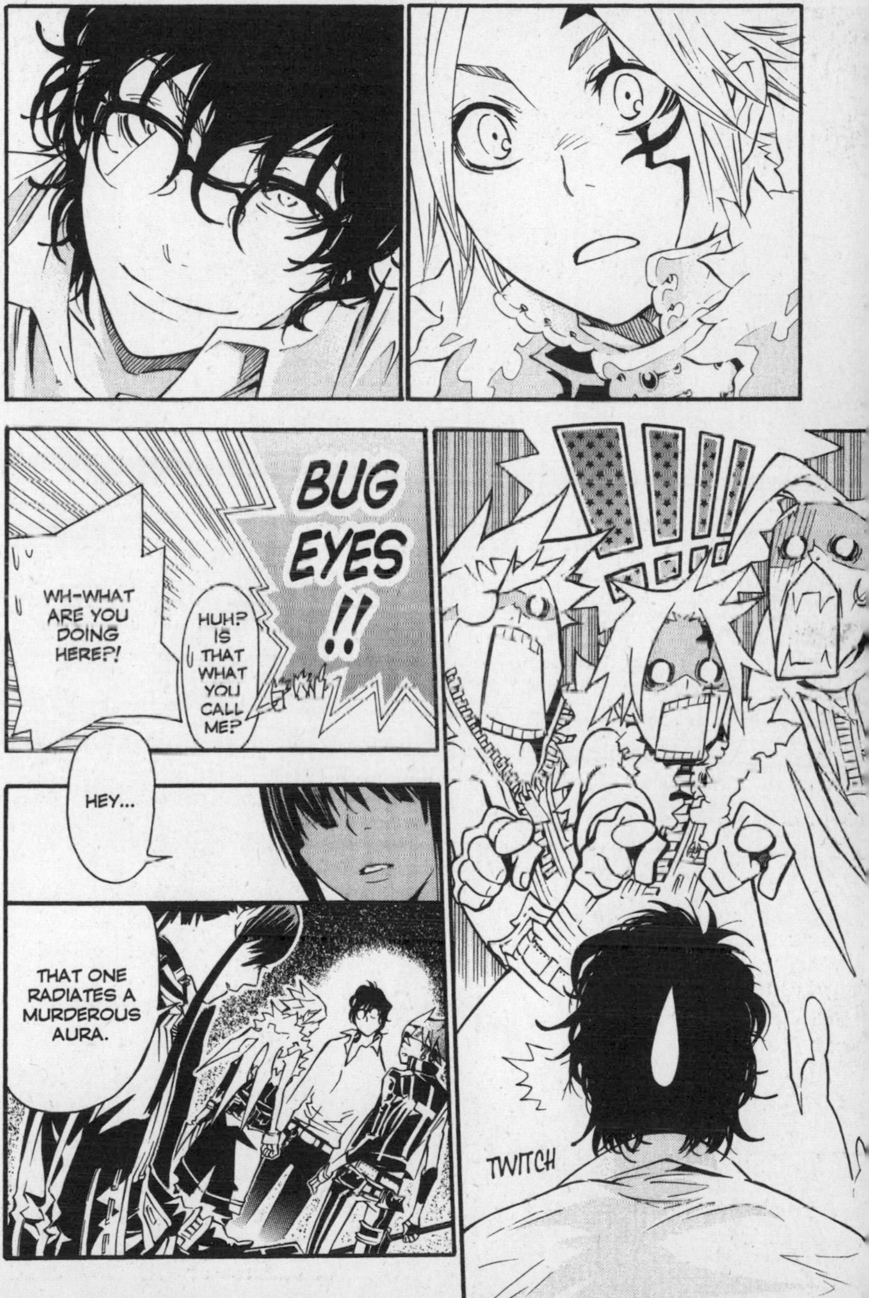
TWITCH
BUG EYES!!
HUH? IS THAT WHAT YOU CALL ME?
WH-WHAT ARE YOU DOING HERE?!
HEY...
THAT ONE RADIATES A MURDEROUS AURA.

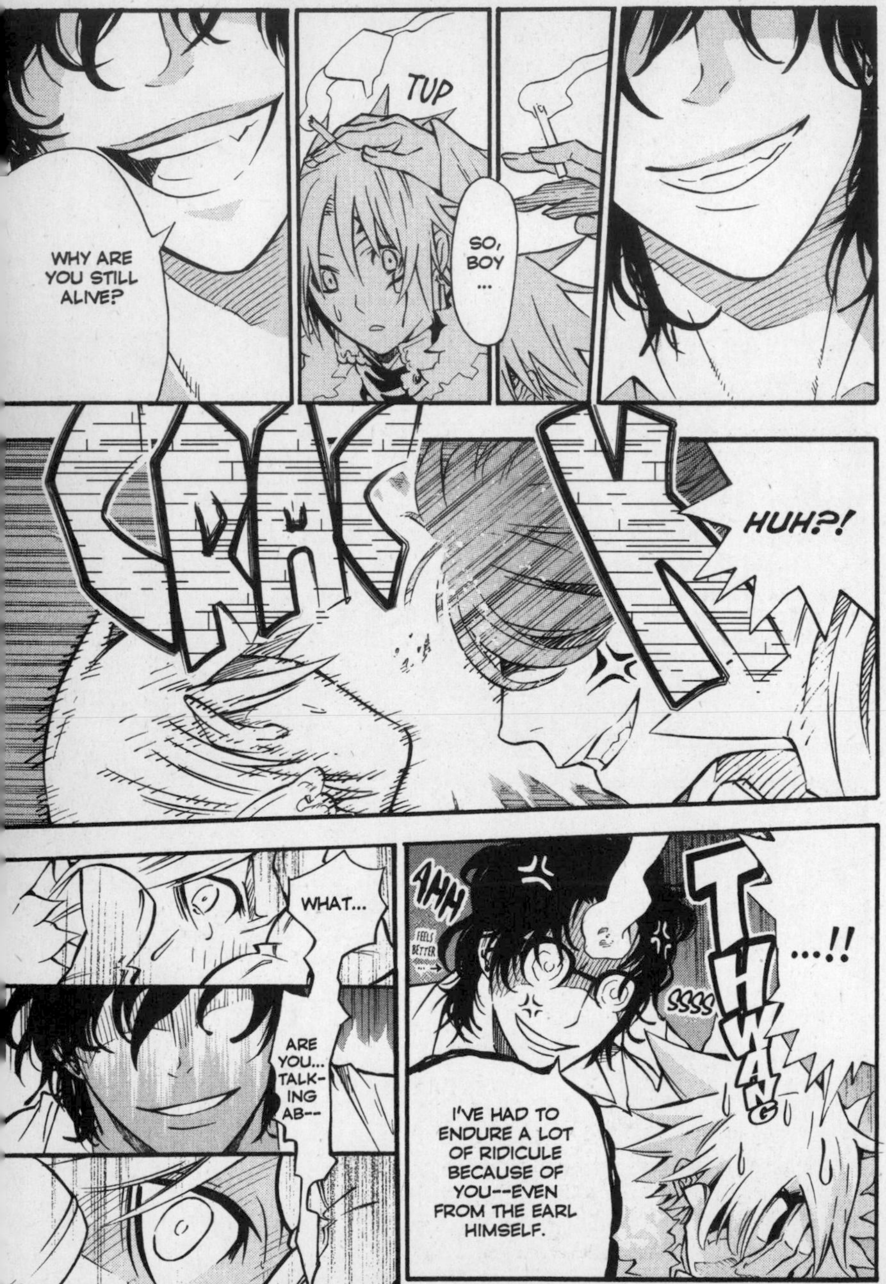

SO, BOY ...
TUP
WHY ARE YOU STILL ALIVE?
HUH?!
...!!
THWANG
SSSS
AHH
FEELS BETTER
I'VE HAD TO ENDURE A LOT OF RIDICULE BECAUSE OF YOU--EVEN FROM THE EARL HIMSELF.
WHAT...
ARE YOU... TALKING AB--

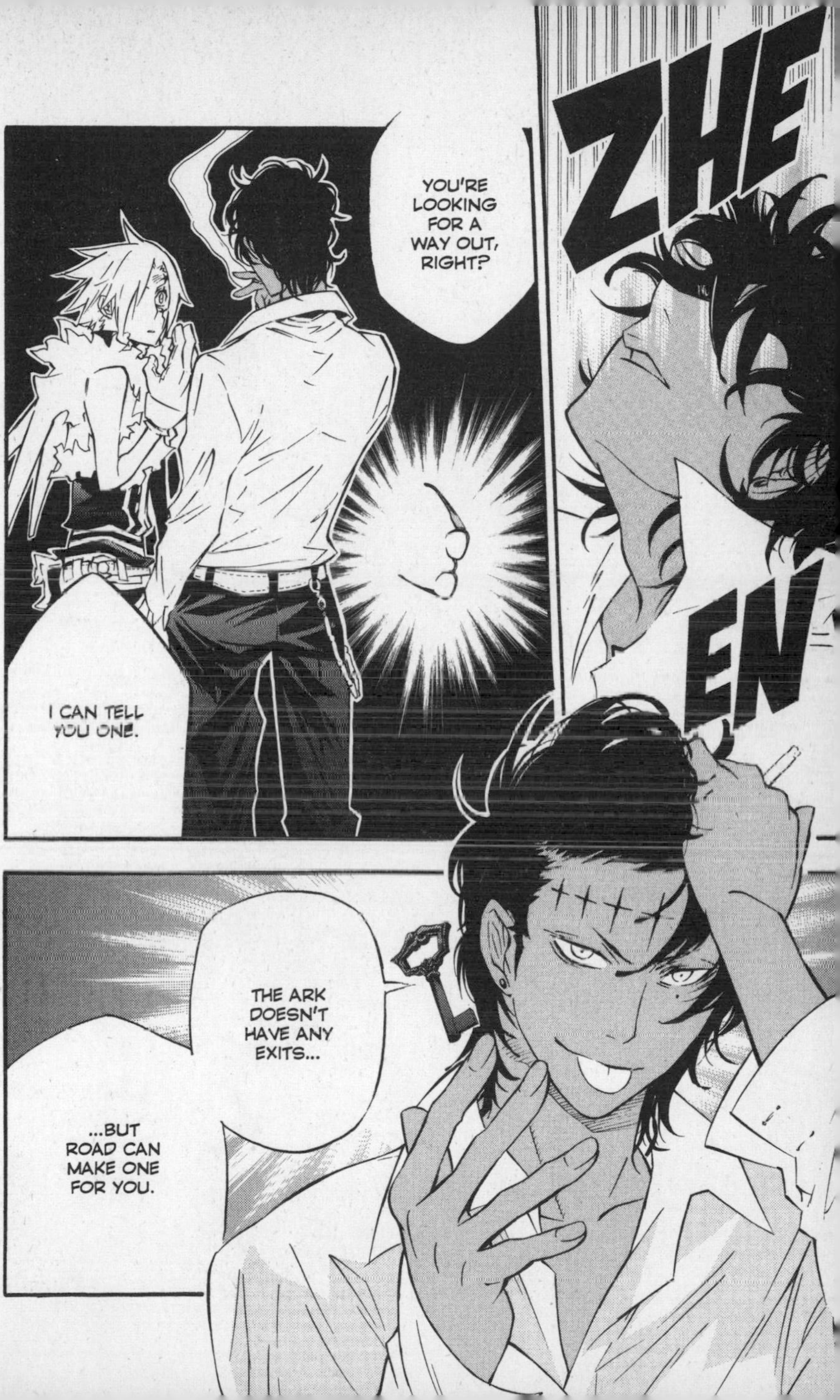
ZHE
EN
YOU'RE LOOKING FOR A WAY OUT, RIGHT?
I CAN TELL YOU ONE.
THE ARK DOESN'T HAVE ANY EXITS...
...BUT ROAD CAN MAKE ONE FOR YOU.

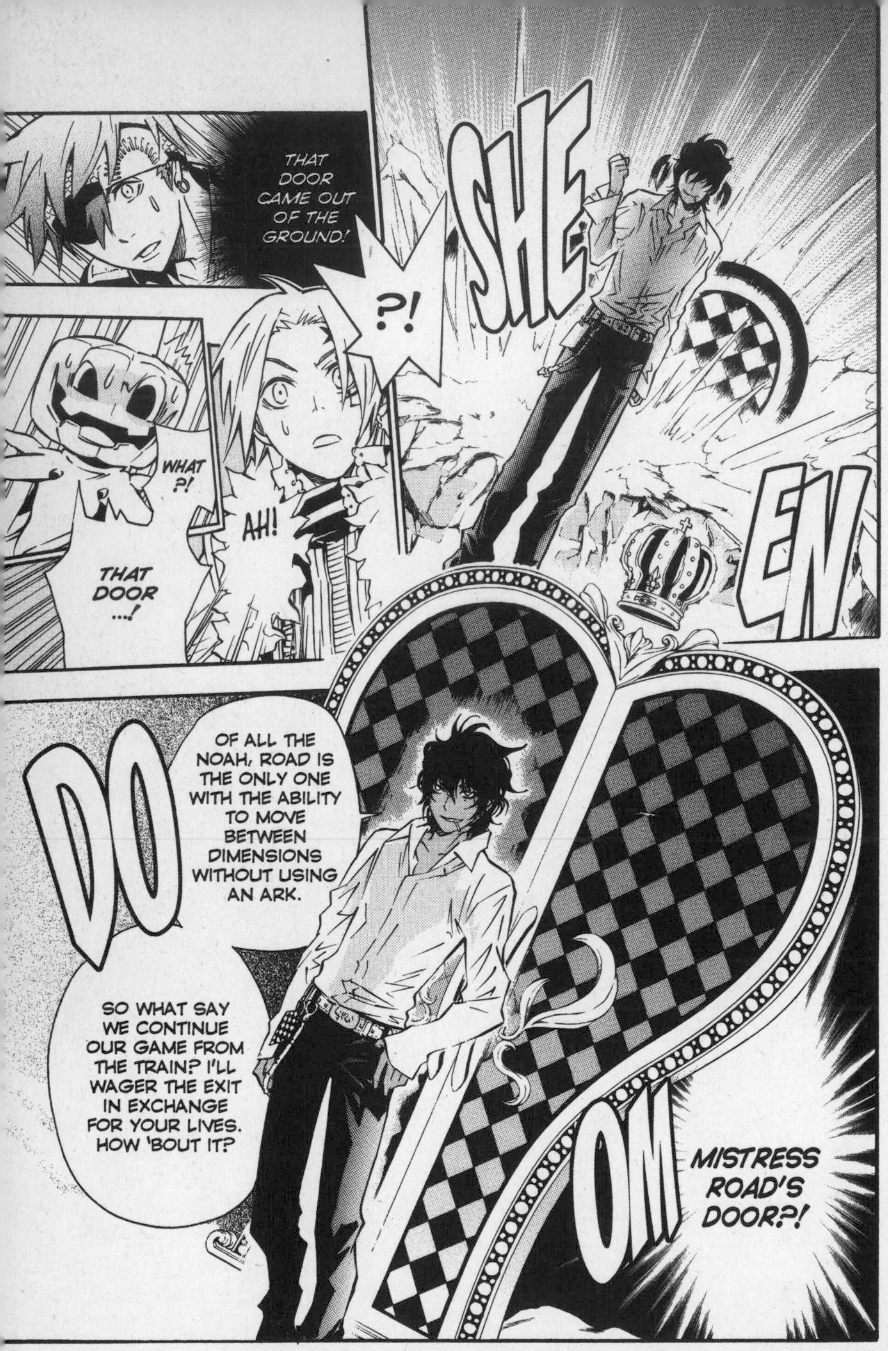
SHE
EN
THAT DOOR CAME OUT OF THE GROUND!
?!
AH!
WHAT ?!
THAT DOOR ...!
DO
OM
MISTRESS ROAD'S DOOR?!
OF ALL THE NOAH, ROAD IS THE ONLY ONE WITH THE ABILITY TO MOVE BETWEEN DIMENSIONS WITHOUT USING AN ARK.
SO WHAT SAY WE CONTINUE OUR GAME FROM THE TRAIN? I'LL WAGER THE EXIT IN EXCHANGE FOR YOUR LIVES. HOW 'BOUT IT?

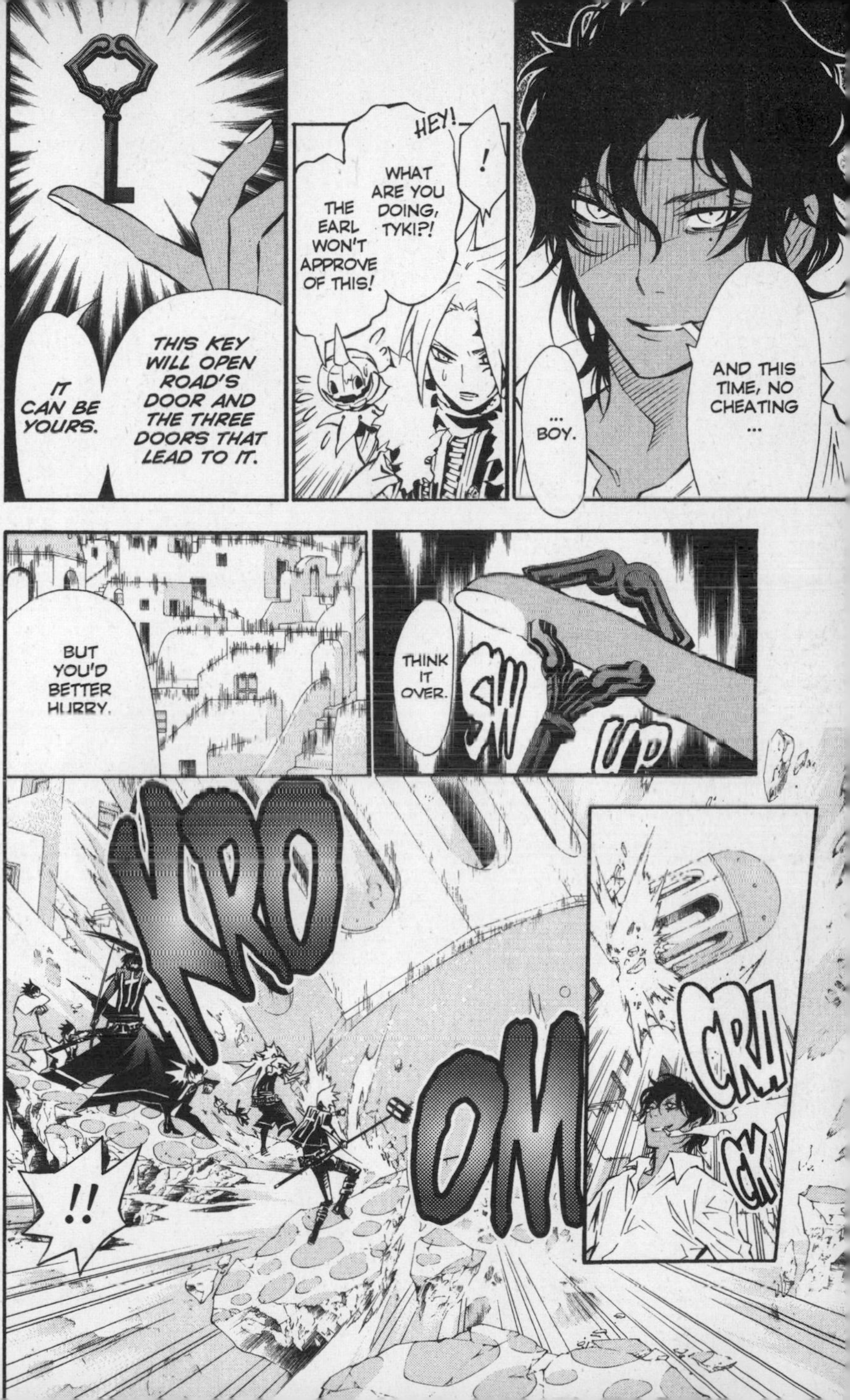
AND THIS TIME, NO CHEATING ...
... BOY.
HEY!
!
WHAT ARE YOU DOING, TYKI?!
THE EARL WON'T APPROVE OF THIS!
THIS KEY WILL OPEN ROAD'S DOOR AND THE THREE DOORS THAT LEAD TO IT.
IT CAN BE YOURS.
THINK IT OVER.
SHUP
BUT YOU'D BETTER HURRY.
CRACK
KROOM
!!

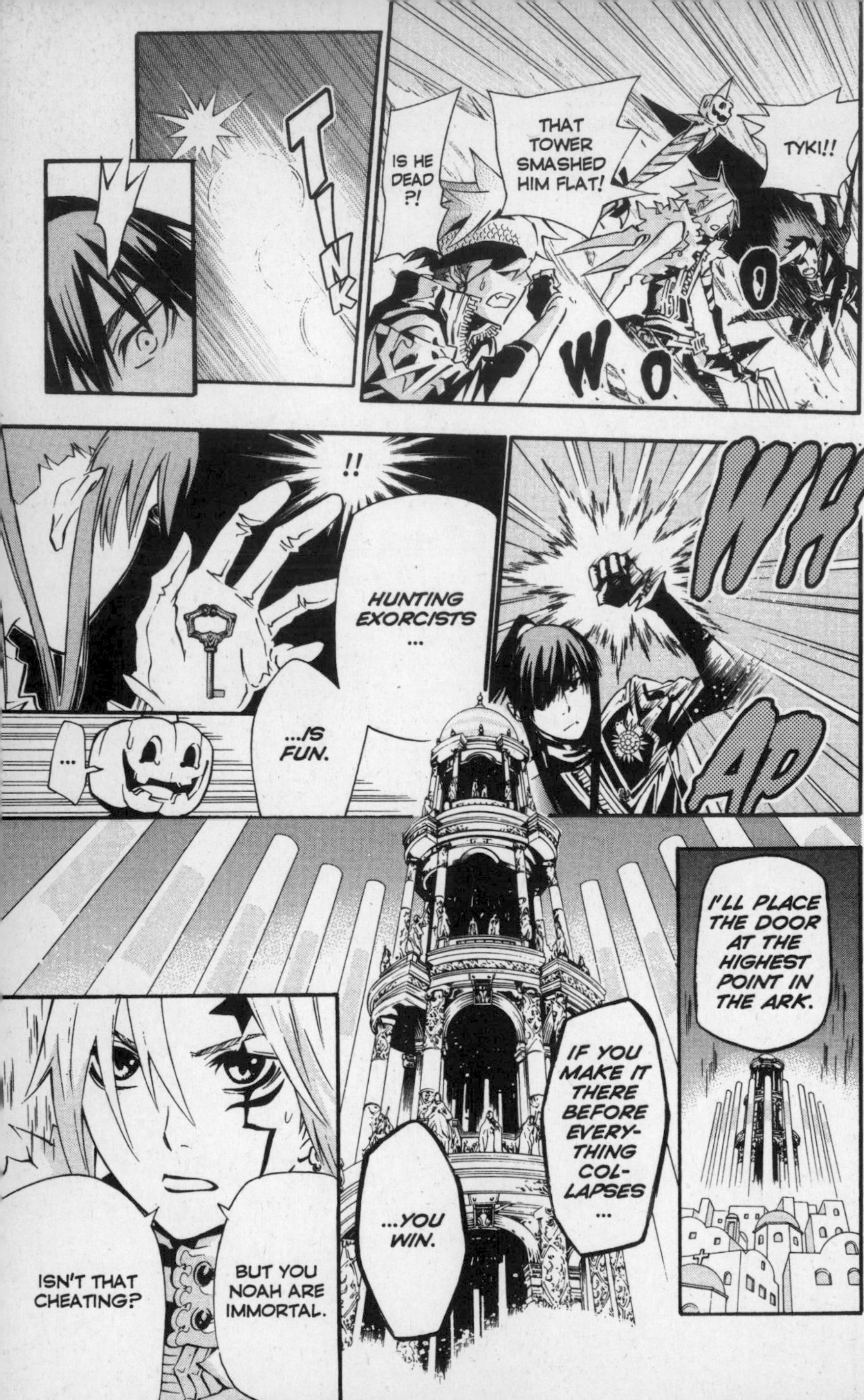
TYKI!!
THAT TOWER SMASHED HIM FLAT!
IS HE DEAD?!
WOO
TINK
WHAP
!!
HUNTING EXORCISTS...
...IS FUN.
...
I'LL PLACE THE DOOR AT THE HIGHEST POINT IN THE ARK.
IF YOU MAKE IT THERE BEFORE EVERY-THING COL-LAPSES...
...YOU WIN.
BUT YOU NOAH ARE IMMORTAL.
ISN'T THAT CHEATING?

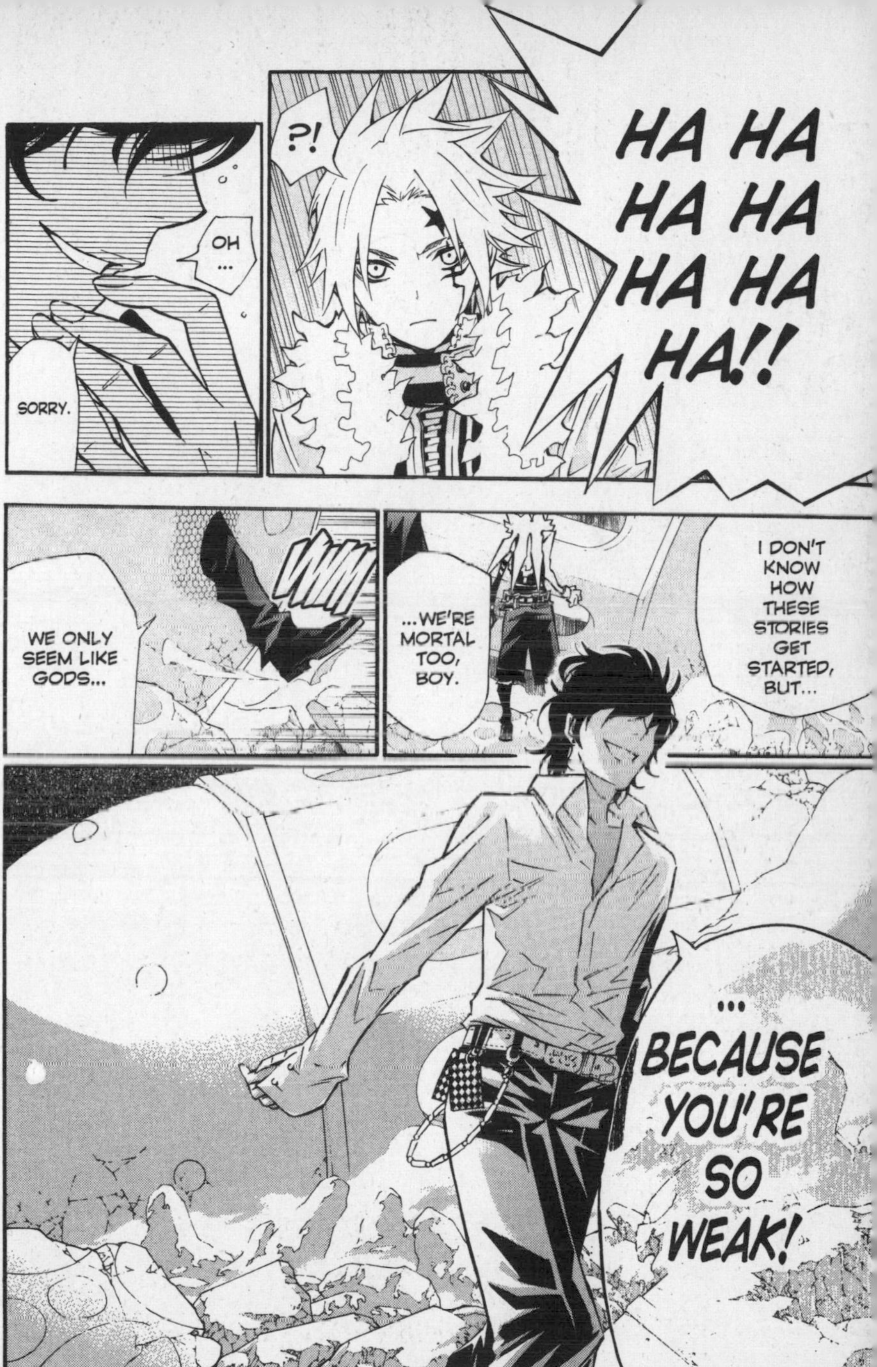
HA HA HA HA HA HA HA!!
?!
OH ...
SORRY.
I DON'T KNOW HOW THESE STORIES GET STARTED, BUT...
...WE'RE MORTAL TOO, BOY.
WE ONLY SEEM LIKE GODS...
... BECAUSE YOU'RE SO WEAK!

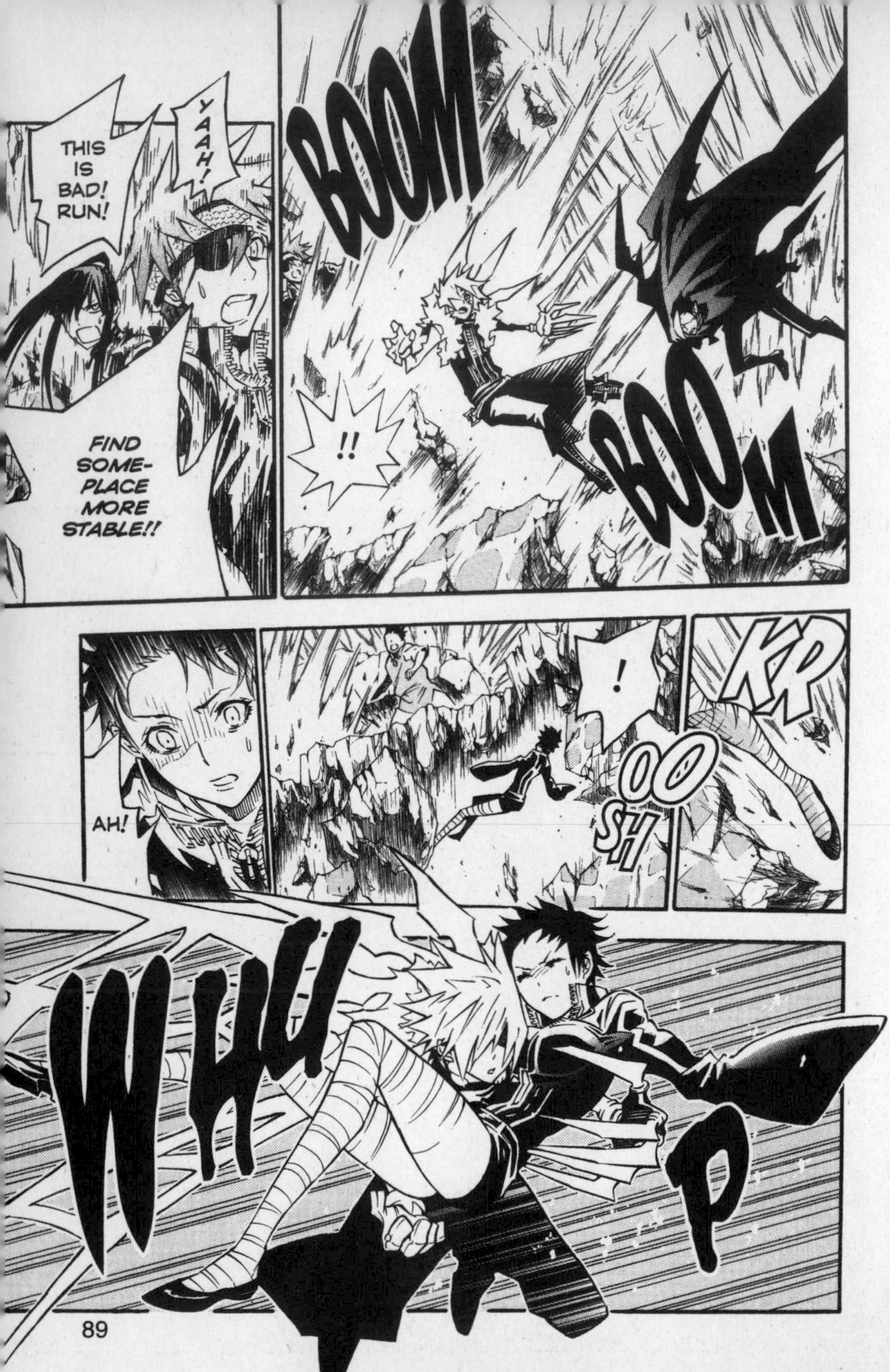
BOOM
BOOM
!!
YAAH!
THIS IS BAD! RUN!
FIND SOME-PLACE MORE STABLE!!
KR
OOSH
!
AH!
WHUP

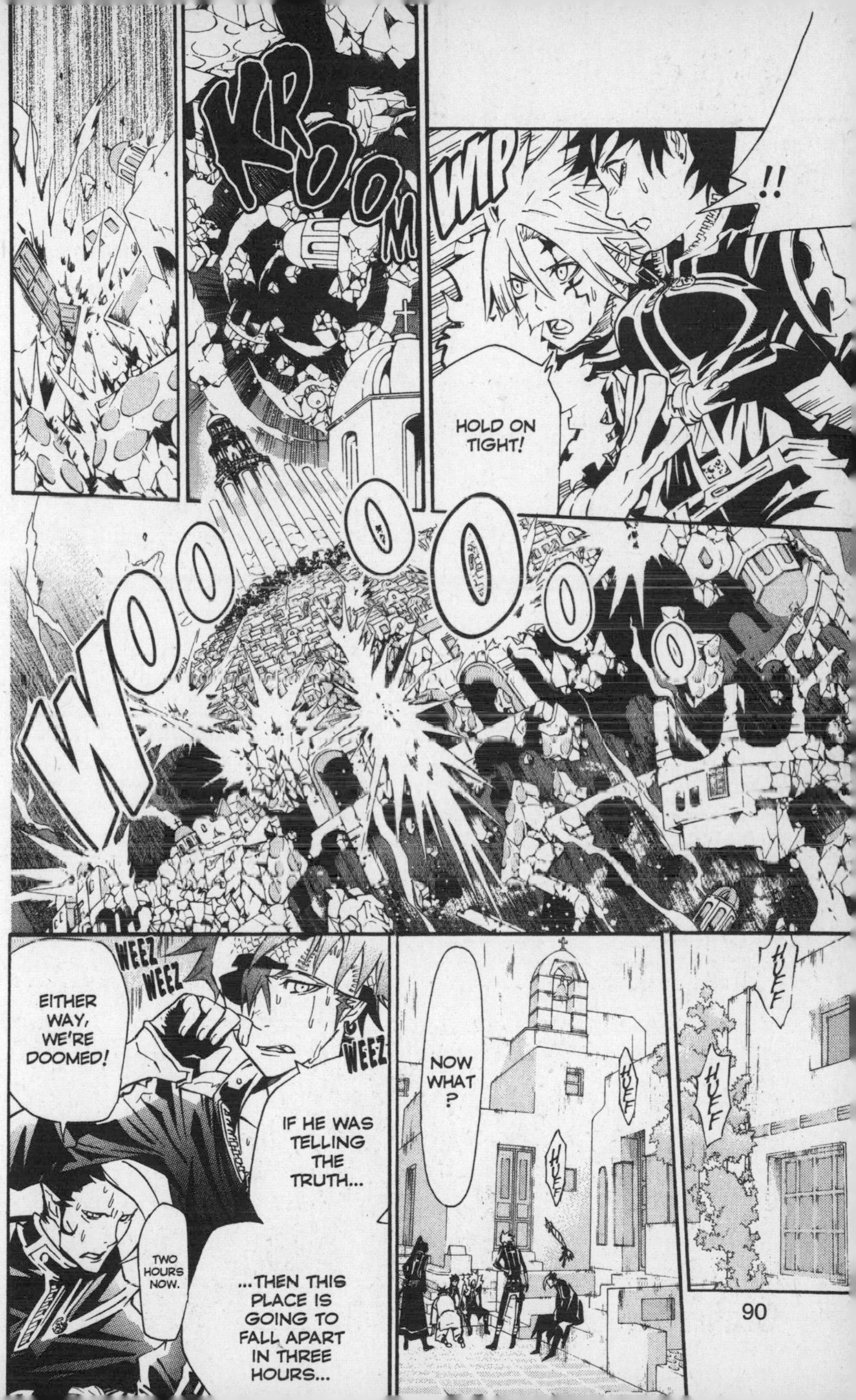
!!
WIP
HOLD ON TIGHT!
KROOOM
WOOOOOOOM
HUFF
HUFF
NOW WHAT?
HUFF
HUFF
WEEZ WEEZ
WEEZ
EITHER WAY, WE'RE DOOMED!
IF HE WAS TELLING THE TRUTH...
...THEN THIS PLACE IS GOING TO FALL APART IN THREE HOURS...
TWO HOURS NOW.

READ THIS WAY

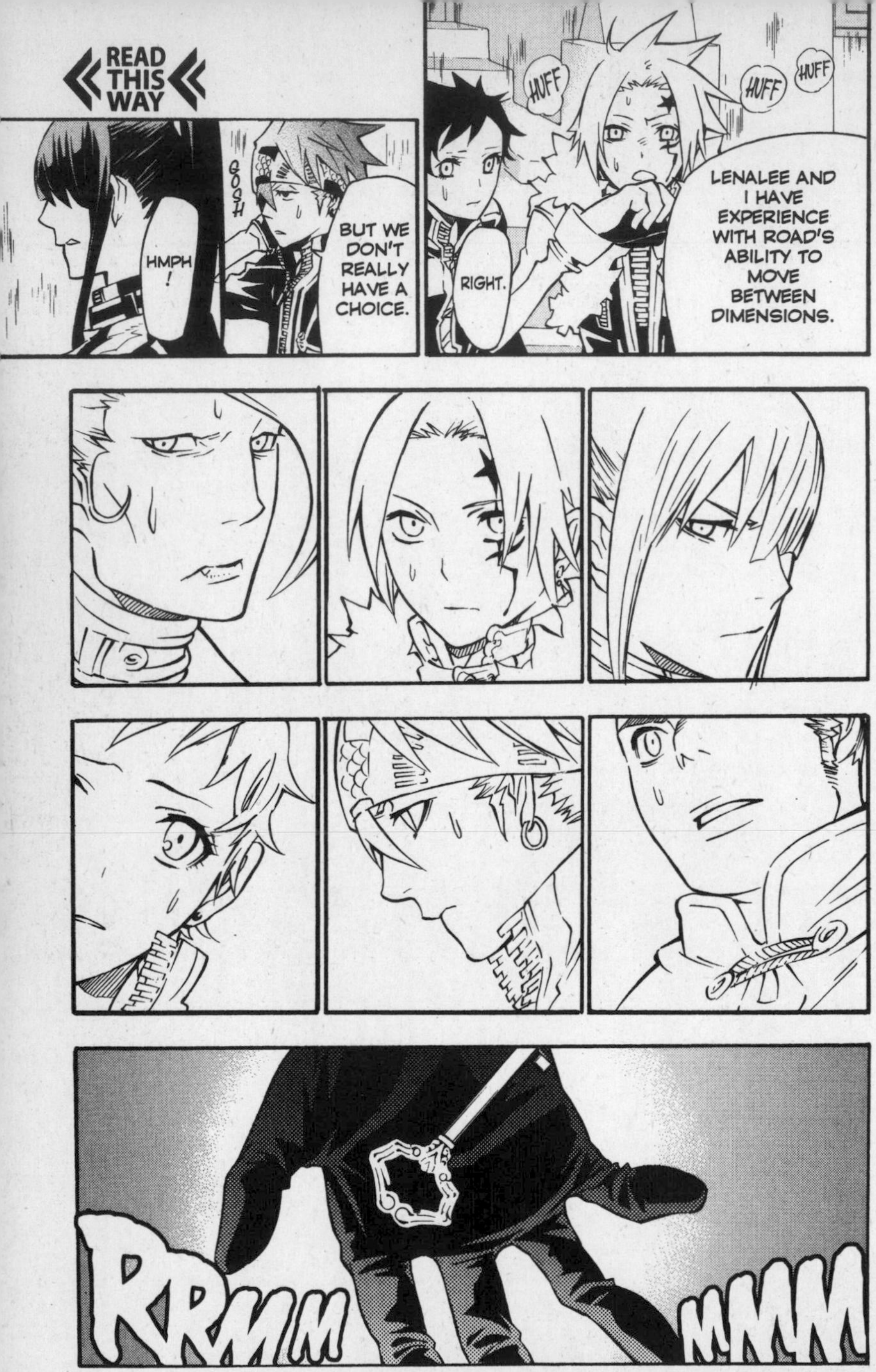
HUFF
HUFF
HUFF
LENALEE AND I HAVE EXPERIENCE WITH ROAD'S ABILITY TO MOVE BETWEEN DIMENSIONS.
RIGHT.
BUT WE DON'T REALLY HAVE A CHOICE.
GOSH
HMPH!
RRMM MMM

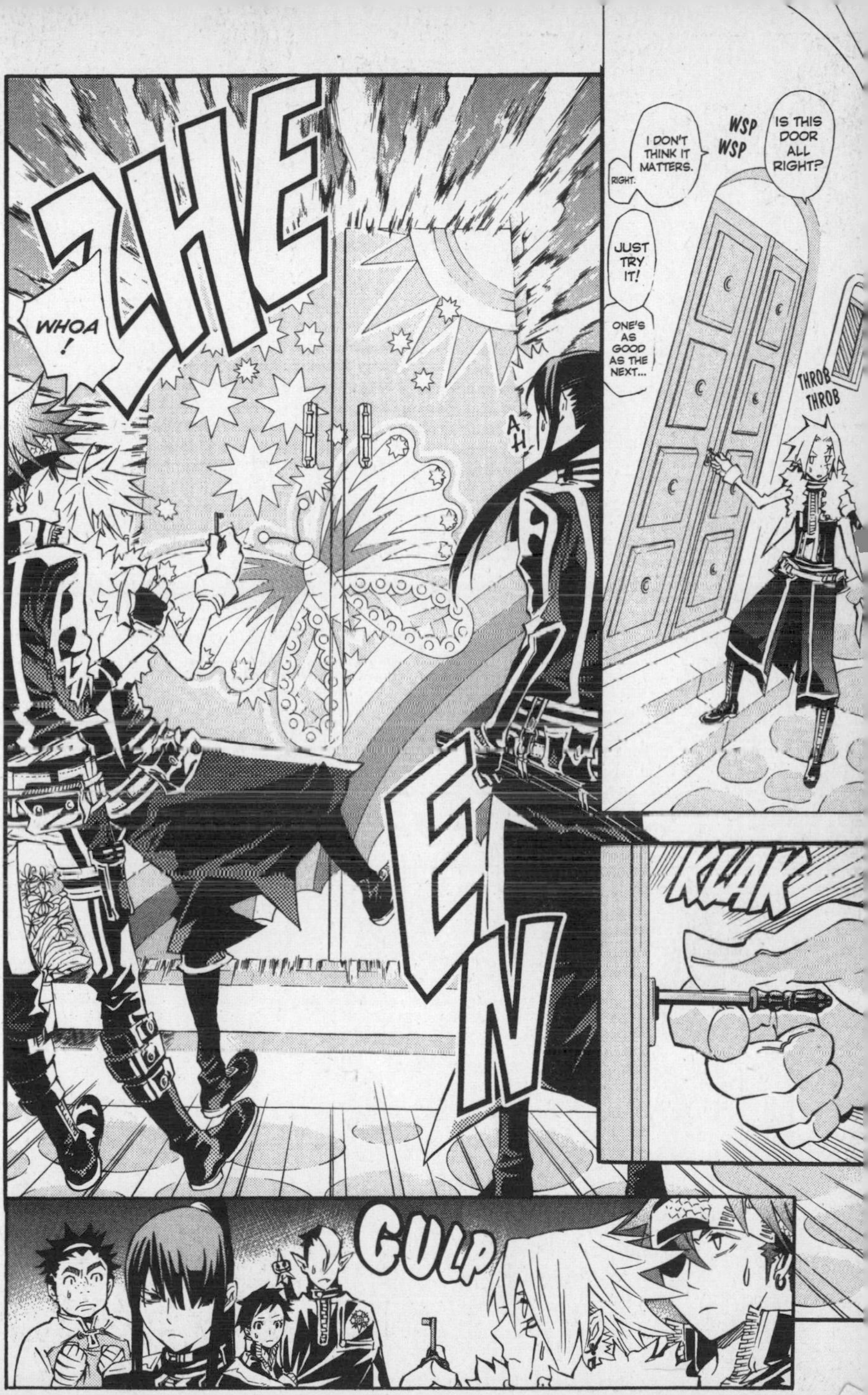
IS THIS DOOR ALL RIGHT?
WSP WSP
I DON'T THINK IT MATTERS.
RIGHT.
JUST TRY IT!
ONE'S AS GOOD AS THE NEXT...
THROB THROB
KLAK
ZHE
WHOA!
AH
EN
GULP

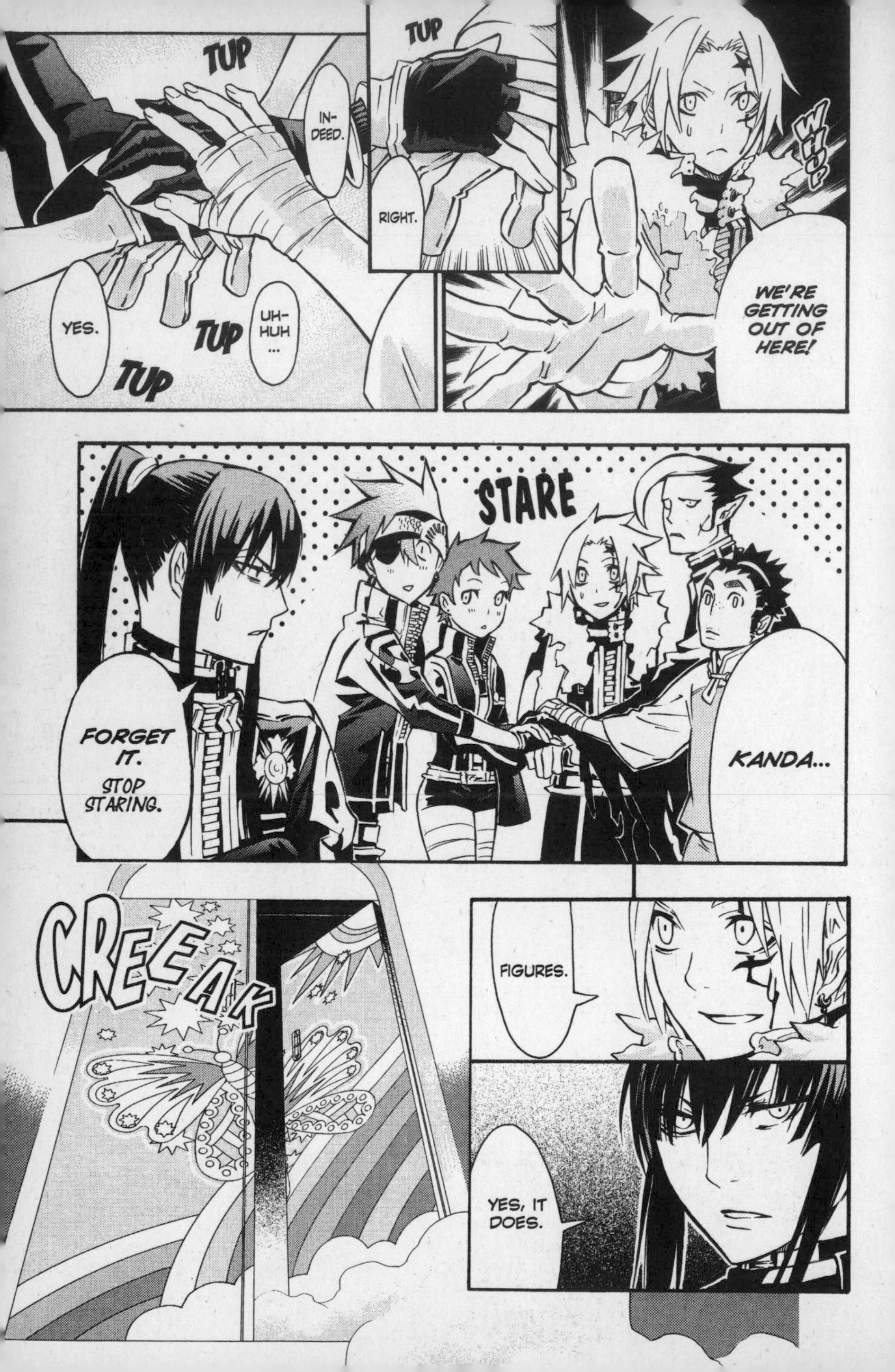
WHUP
WE'RE GETTING OUT OF HERE!
TUP
RIGHT.
TUP
IN-DEED.
UH-HUH ...
TUP
YES.
TUP
STARE
KANDA...
FORGET IT. STOP STARING.
FIGURES.
YES, IT DOES.
CREEAK

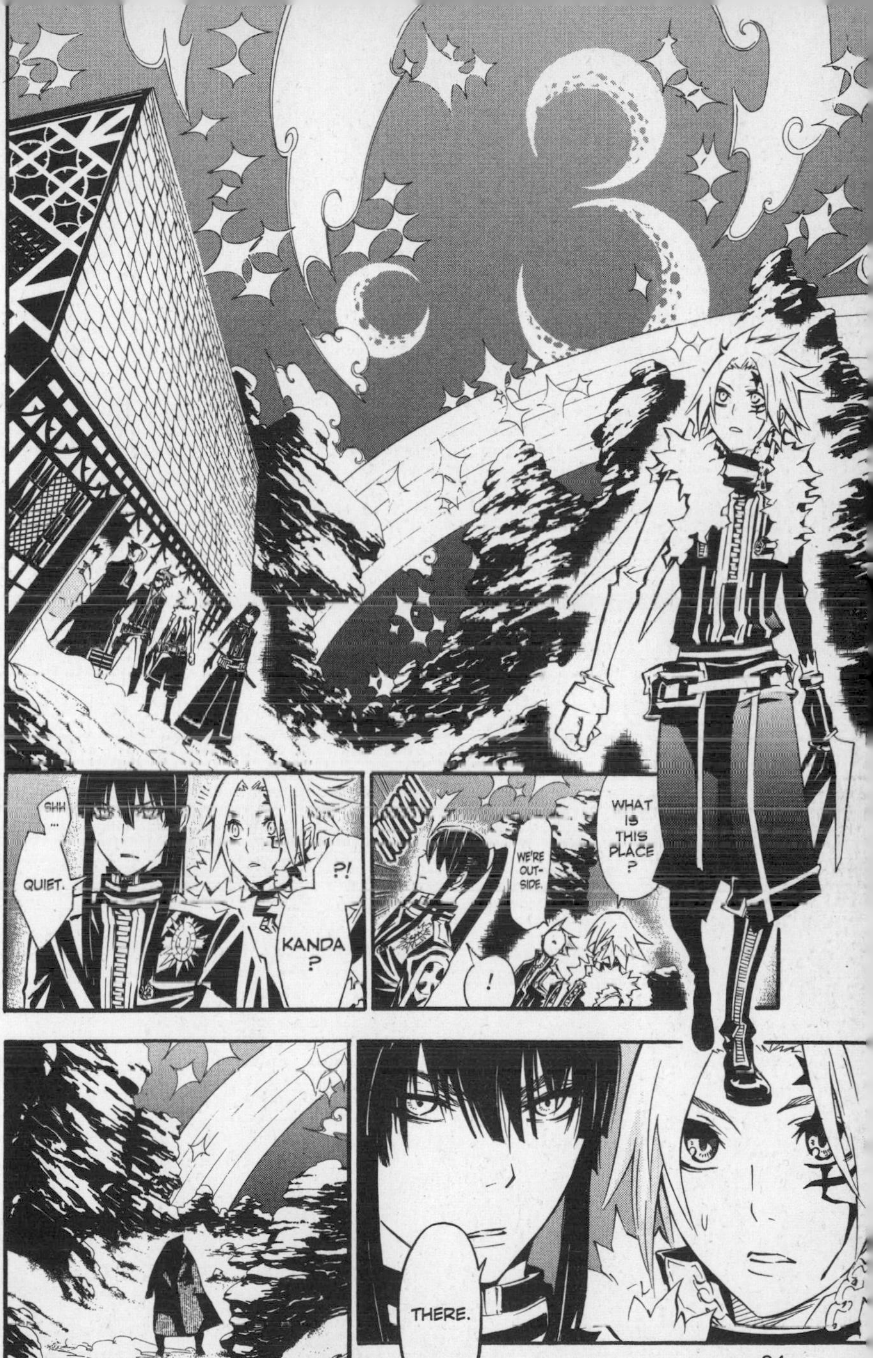
WHAT IS THIS PLACE?
TWITCH
WE'RE OUTSIDE.
!
SHH...
QUIET.
?!
KANDA?
THERE.

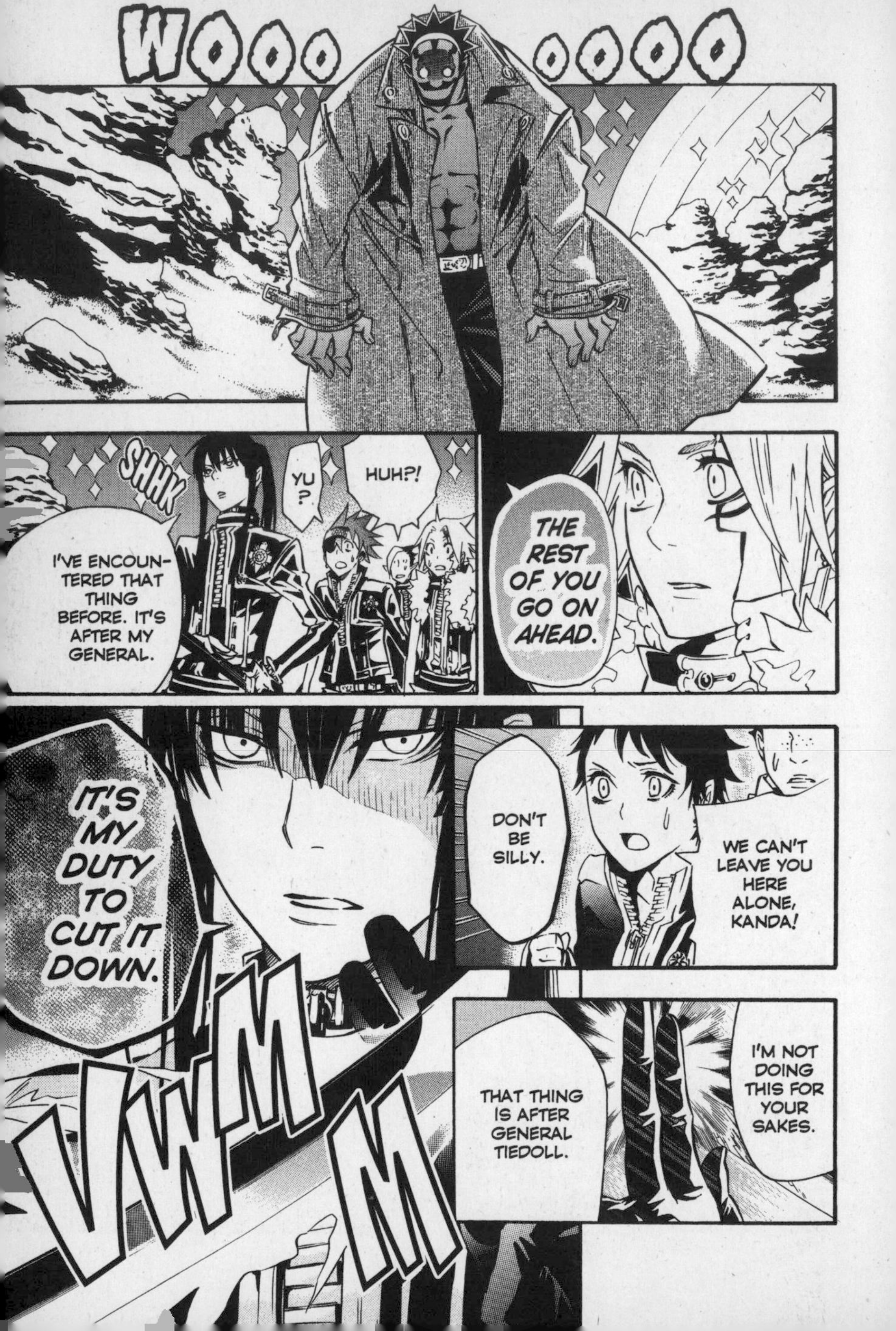
WOOO OOOO
THE REST OF YOU GO ON AHEAD.
HUH?!
YU ?
SHHK
I'VE ENCOUNTERED THAT THING BEFORE. IT'S AFTER MY GENERAL.
WE CAN'T LEAVE YOU HERE ALONE, KANDA!
DON'T BE SILLY.
I'M NOT DOING THIS FOR YOUR SAKES.
THAT THING IS AFTER GENERAL TIEDOLL.
IT'S MY DUTY TO CUT IT DOWN.
VWM
M

KOMUI'S DISCUSSION ROOM, VOL. 2

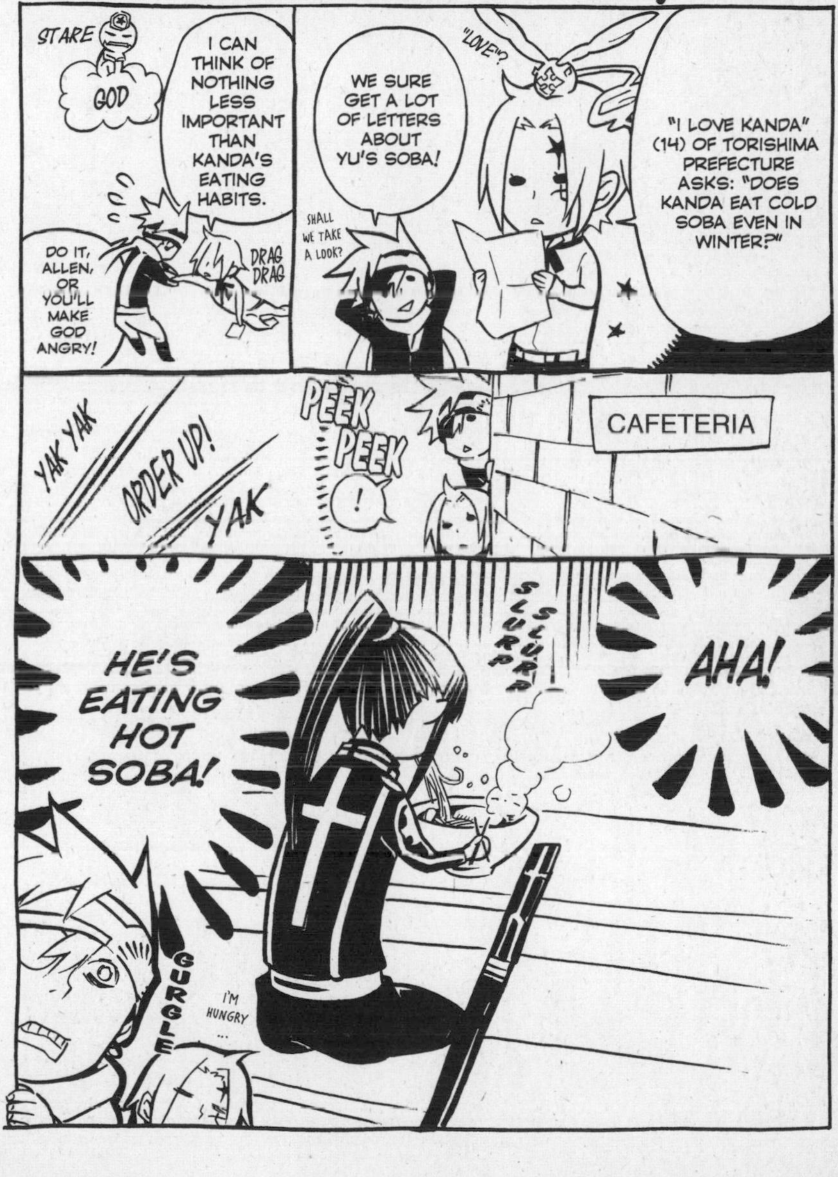
"I LOVE KANDA" (14) OF TORISHIMA PREFECTURE ASKS: "DOES KANDA EAT COLD SOBA EVEN IN WINTER?"
"LOVE"?
WE SURE GET A LOT OF LETTERS ABOUT YU'S SOBA!
SHALL WE TAKE A LOOK?
I CAN THINK OF NOTHING LESS IMPORTANT THAN KANDA'S EATING HABITS.
STARE
GOD
DRAG DRAG
DO IT, ALLEN, OR YOU'LL MAKE GOD ANGRY!
CAFETERIA
PEEK PEEK
!
YAK
ORDER UP!
YAK YAK
AHA!
SLURP SLURP
HE'S EATING HOT SOBA!
I'M HUNGRY...
GURGLE

THE 92ND NIGHT: SKIN BORIC'S ROOM

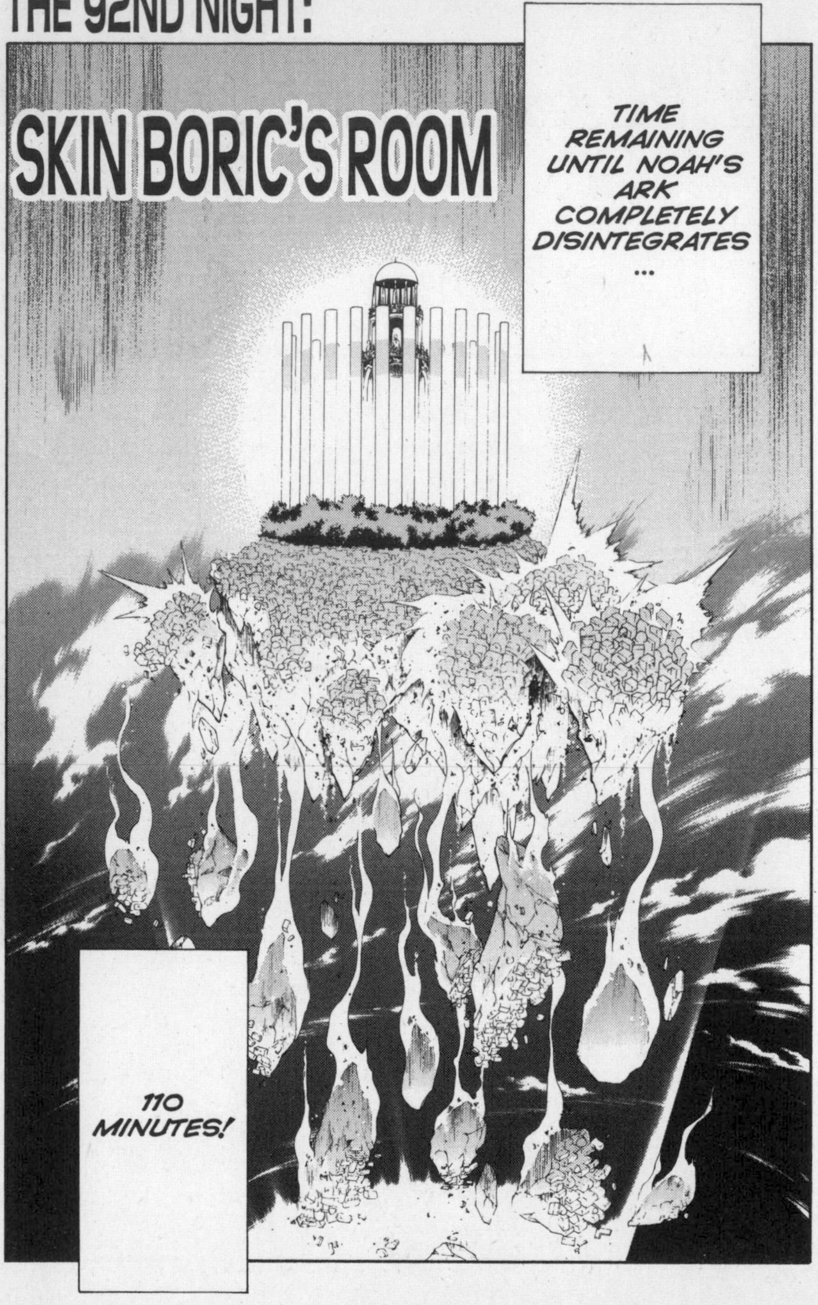
TIME REMAINING UNTIL NOAH'S ARK COMPLETELY DISINTEGRATES ...
110 MINUTES!

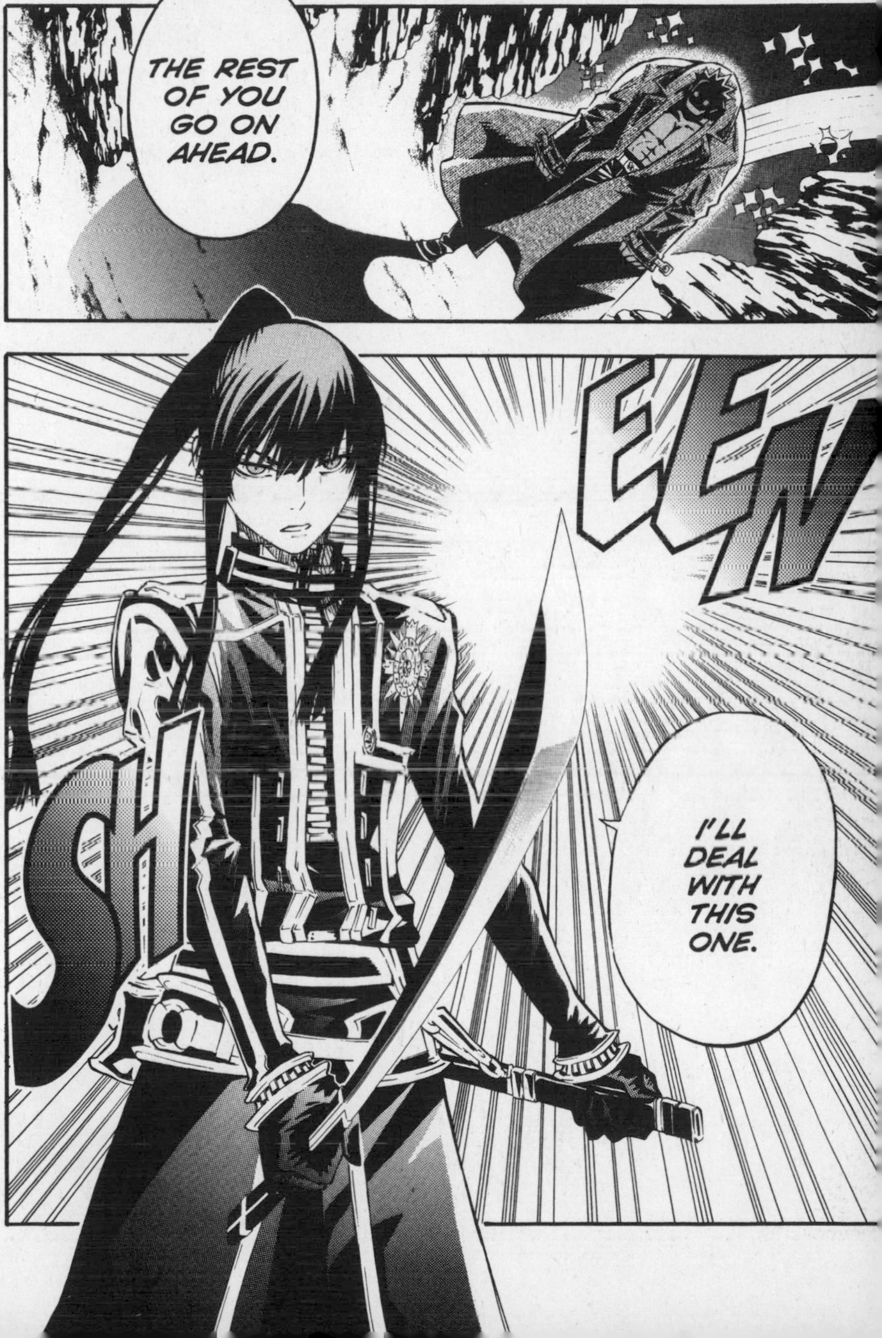
THE REST OF YOU GO ON AHEAD.
I'LL DEAL WITH THIS ONE.
SH
EEN

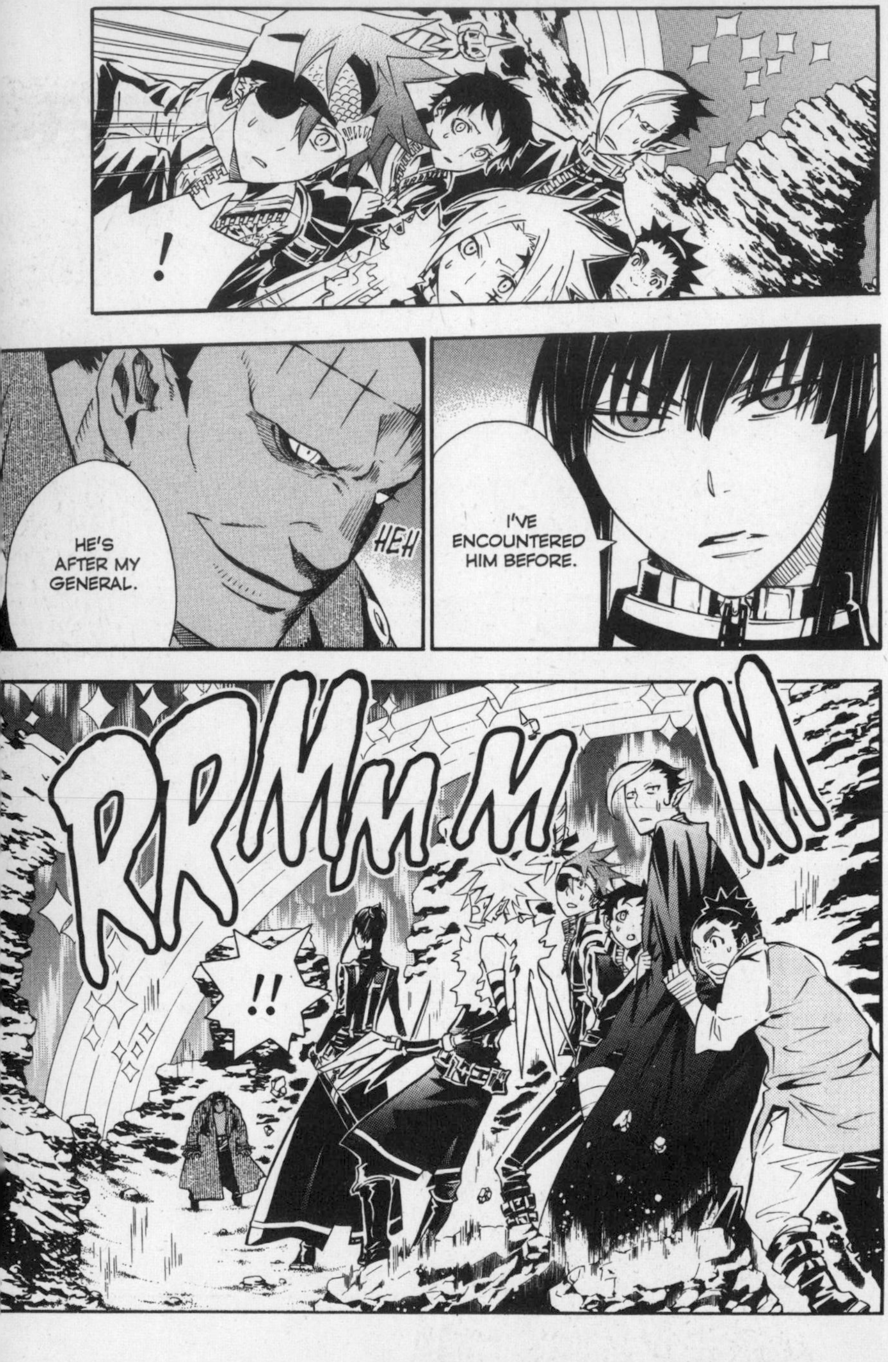
!
I'VE ENCOUNTERED HIM BEFORE.
HE'S AFTER MY GENERAL.
HEH
RRMMM M
!!

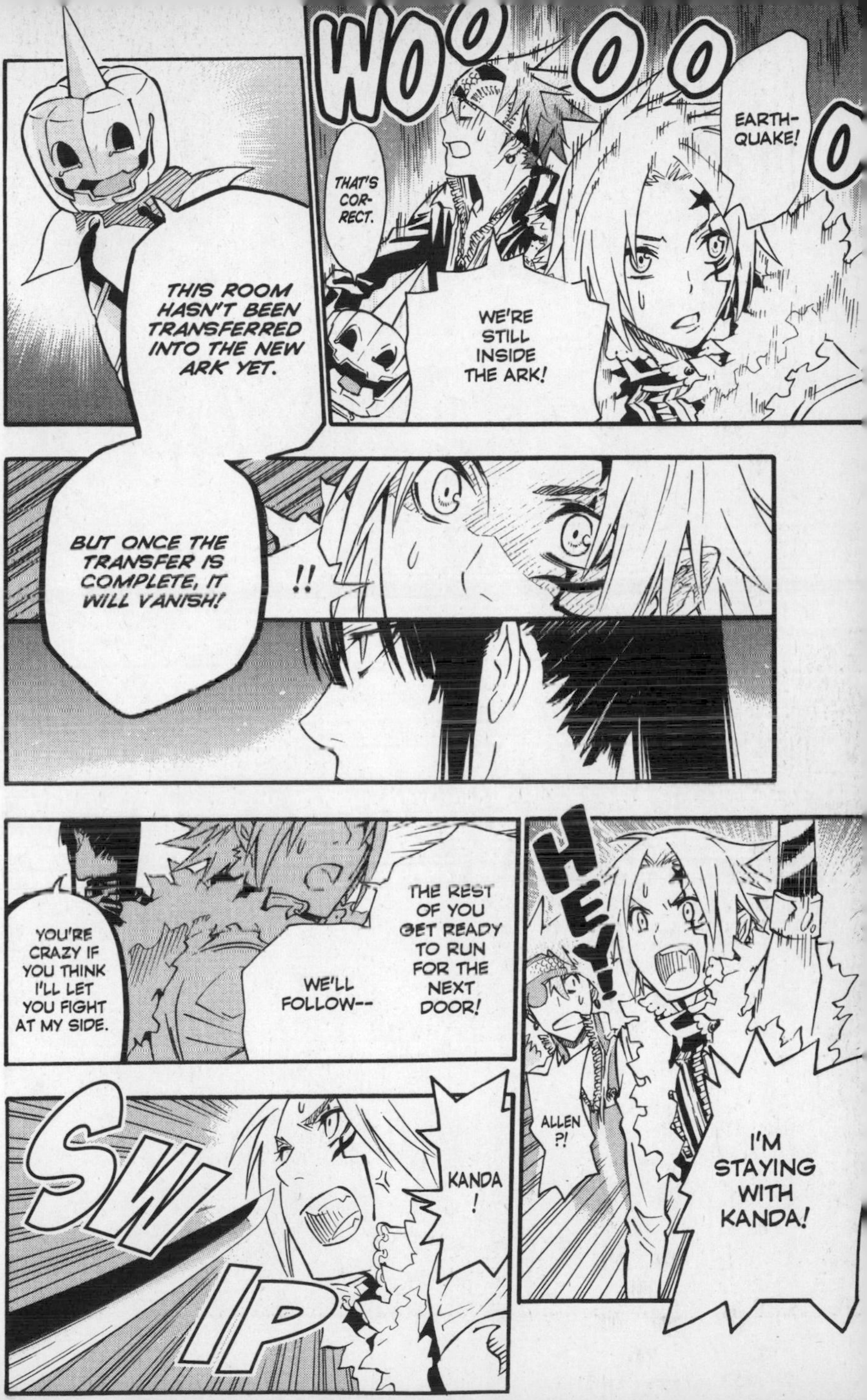
WOOOOOOO
EARTH-QUAKE!
WE'RE STILL INSIDE THE ARK!
THAT'S COR-RECT.
THIS ROOM HASN'T BEEN TRANSFERRED INTO THE NEW ARK YET.
BUT ONCE THE TRANSFER IS COMPLETE, IT WILL VANISH!
!!
HEY!
I'M STAYING WITH KANDA!
ALLEN ?!
THE REST OF YOU GET READY TO RUN FOR THE NEXT DOOR!
WE'LL FOLLOW--
YOU'RE CRAZY IF YOU THINK I'LL LET YOU FIGHT AT MY SIDE.
KANDA!
SWIP

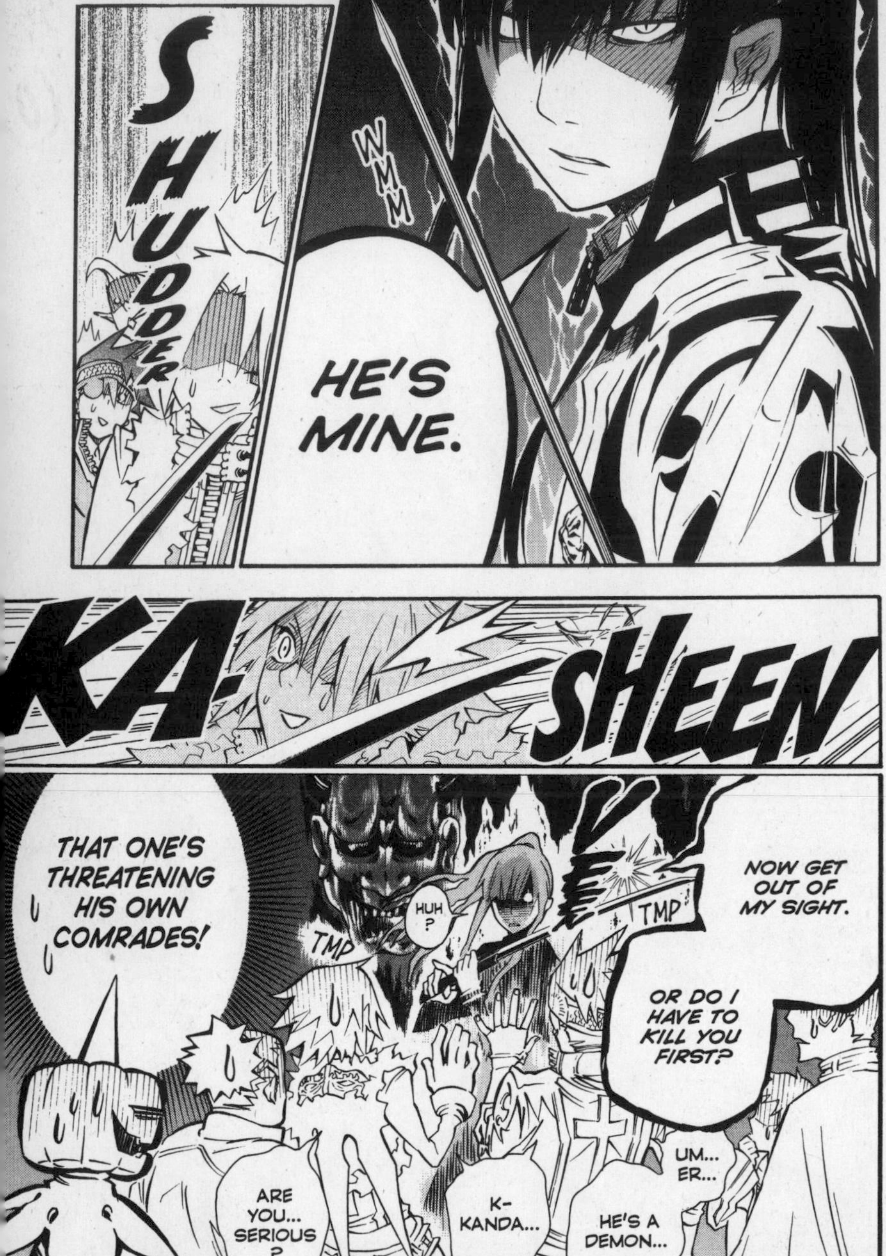
WMMM
HE'S MINE.
SHUDDER
KA-SHEEN
NOW GET OUT OF MY SIGHT.
OR DO I HAVE TO KILL YOU FIRST?
TMP
HUH ?
TMP
THAT ONE'S THREATENING HIS OWN COMRADES!
UM... ER...
HE'S A DEMON...
K-KANDA...
ARE YOU... SERIOUS ?

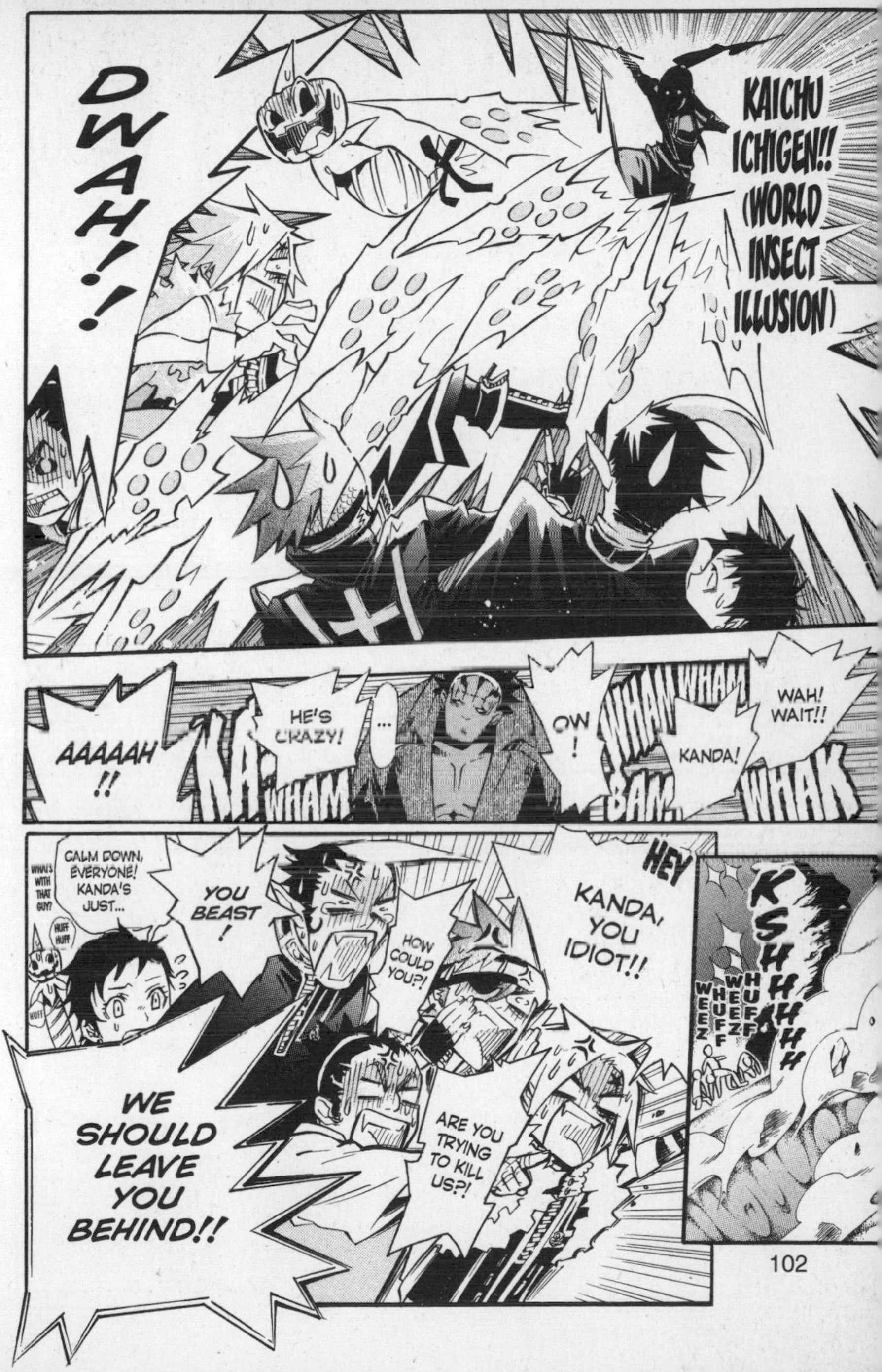
KAICHU ICHIGEN!! (WORLD INSECT ILLUSION)
DWAH!!
WAH! WAIT!!
WHAM WHAM
KANDA!
WHAK
BAM
OW!
...
HE'S CRAZY!
WHAM
AAAAAH!!
KSHHHHHHH
HUFF HUFF
WEEZ
HEY
KANDA, YOU IDIOT!!
HOW COULD YOU?!
YOU BEAST!
CALM DOWN, EVERYONE! KANDA'S JUST...
WHAT'S WITH THAT GUY?
HUFF HUFF
ARE YOU TRYING TO KILL US?!
WE SHOULD LEAVE YOU BEHIND!!

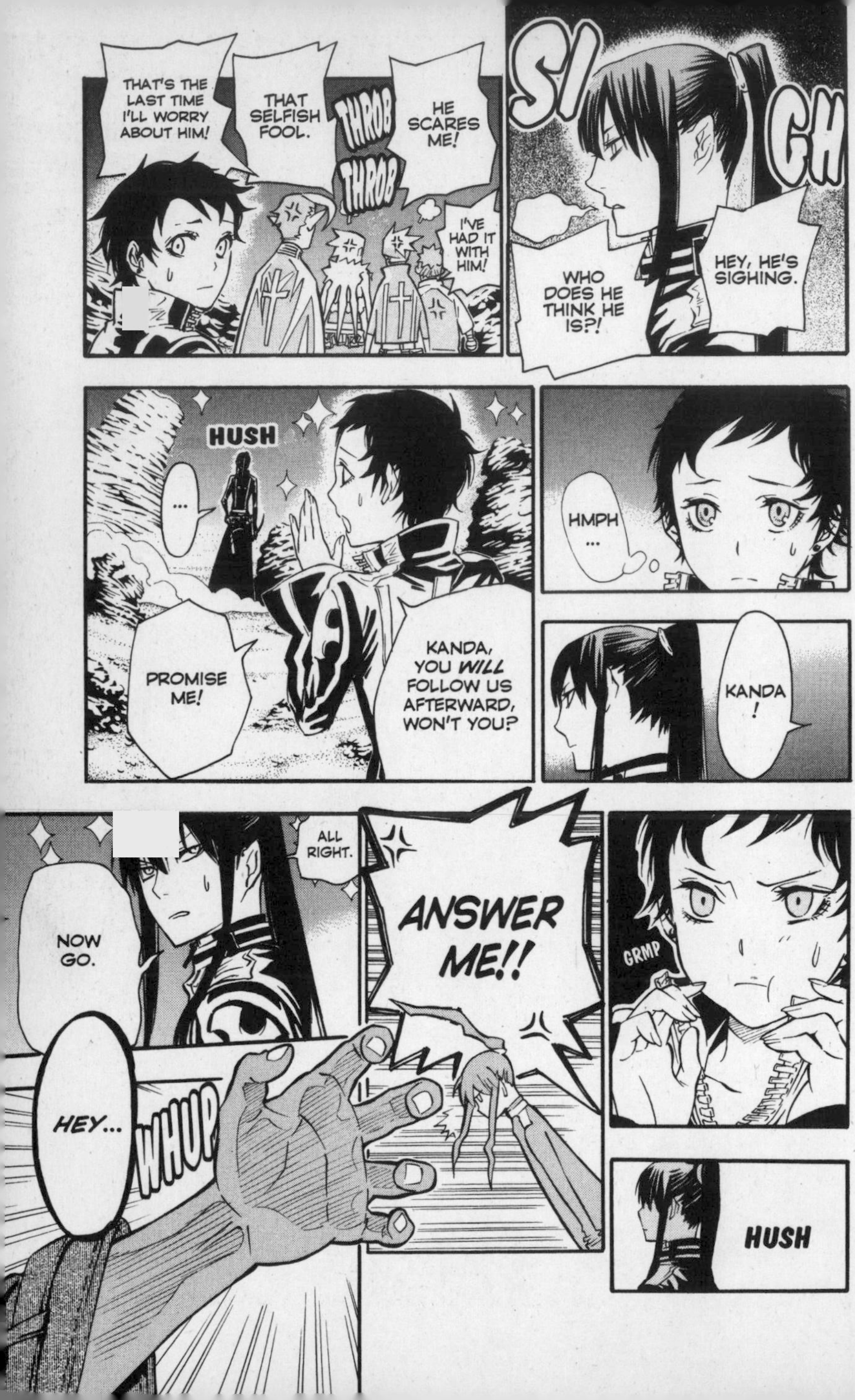
SI
CH
HEY, HE'S SIGHING.
WHO DOES HE THINK HE IS?!
HE SCARES ME!
THROB
THROB
THAT SELFISH FOOL.
I'VE HAD IT WITH HIM!
THAT'S THE LAST TIME I'LL WORRY ABOUT HIM!
HMPH ...
KANDA !
HUSH
...
KANDA, YOU *WILL* FOLLOW US AFTERWARD, WON'T YOU?
PROMISE ME!
GRMP
HUSH
ANSWER ME!!
ALL RIGHT.
NOW GO.
HEY...
WHUP

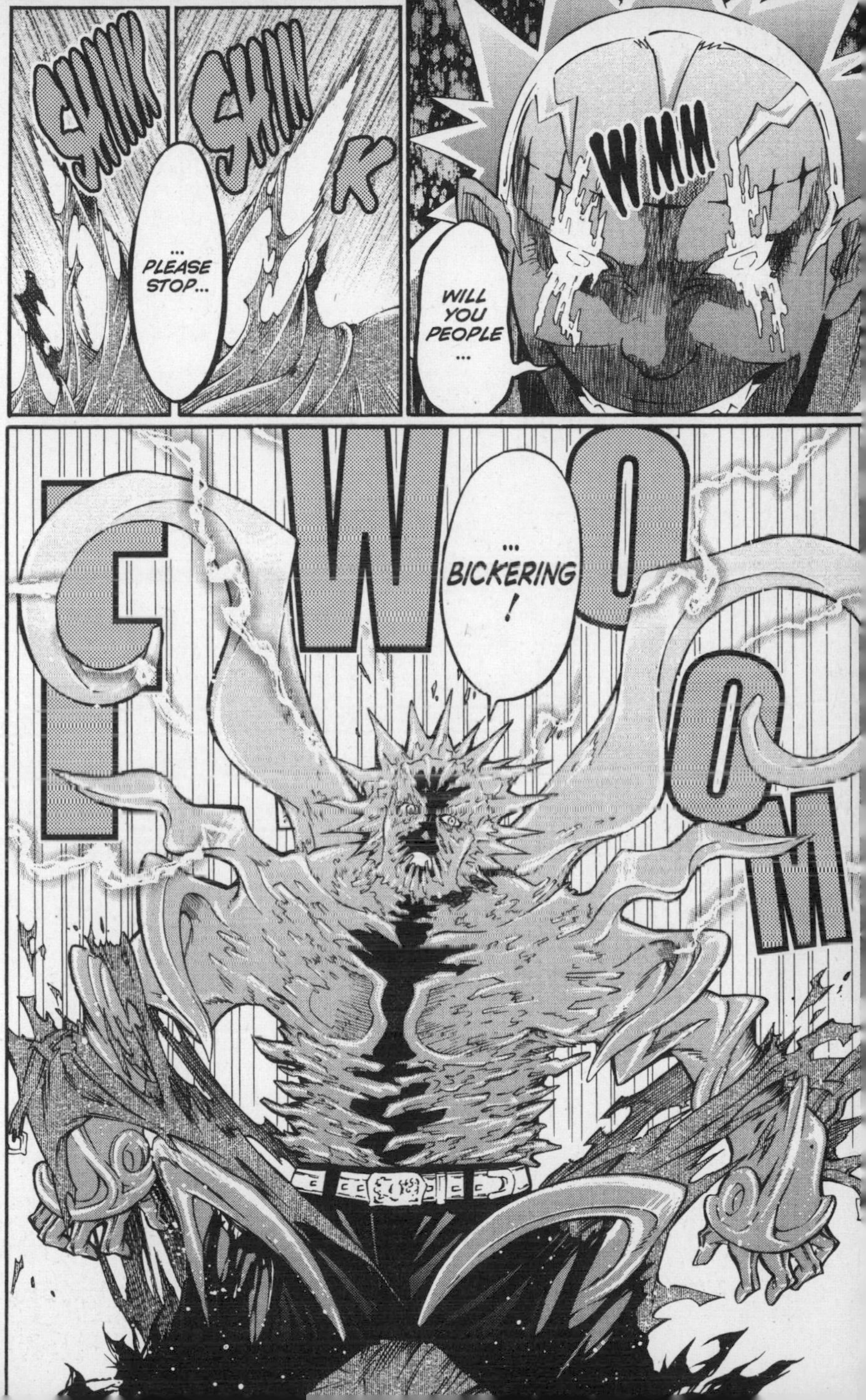
WMM
WILL YOU PEOPLE ...
SHIN K
SHINK
... PLEASE STOP...
FWOOM
... BICKERING !

READ THIS WAY

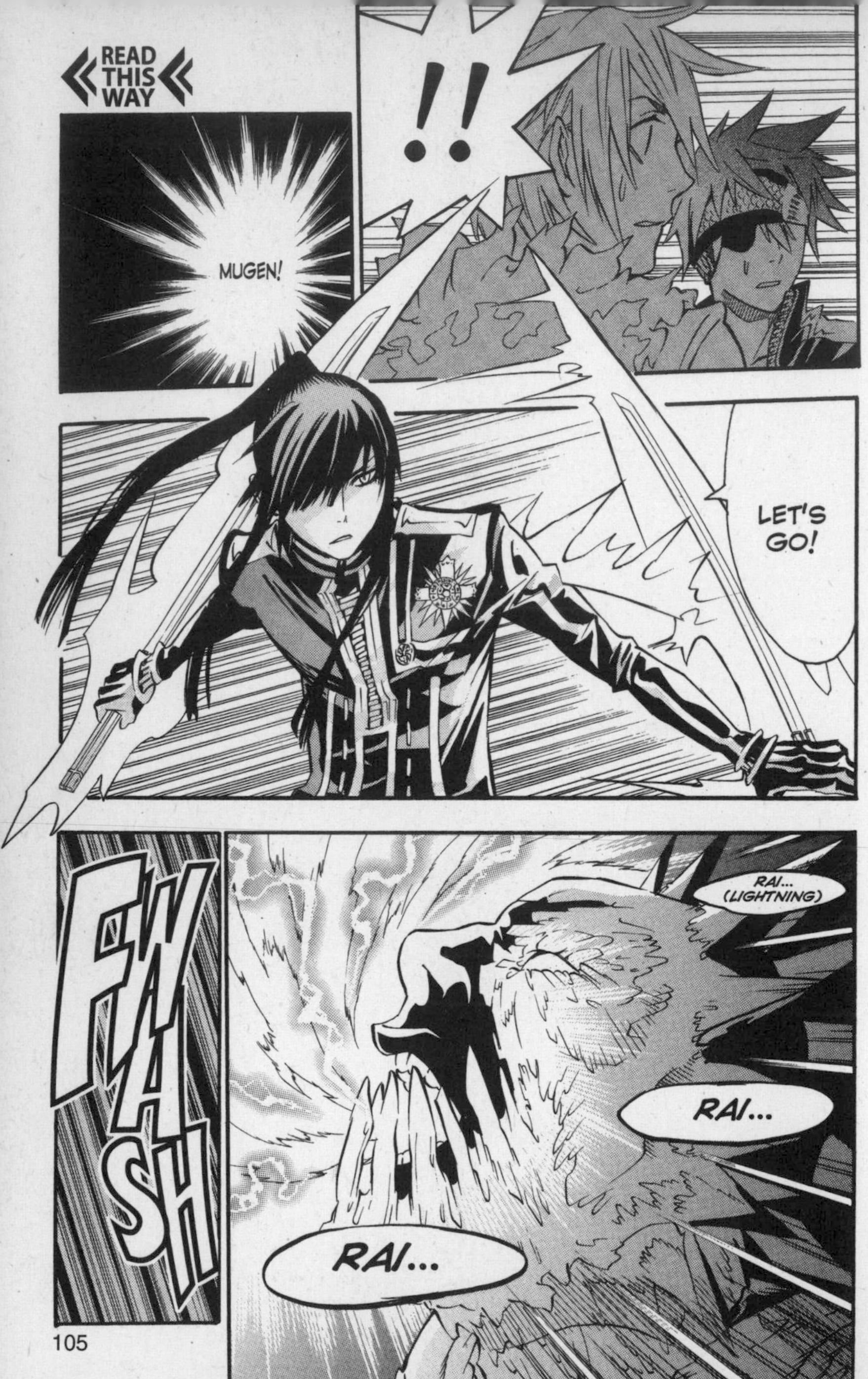
!!
MUGEN!
LET'S GO!
RAI... (LIGHTNING)
RAI...
RAI...
FLASH

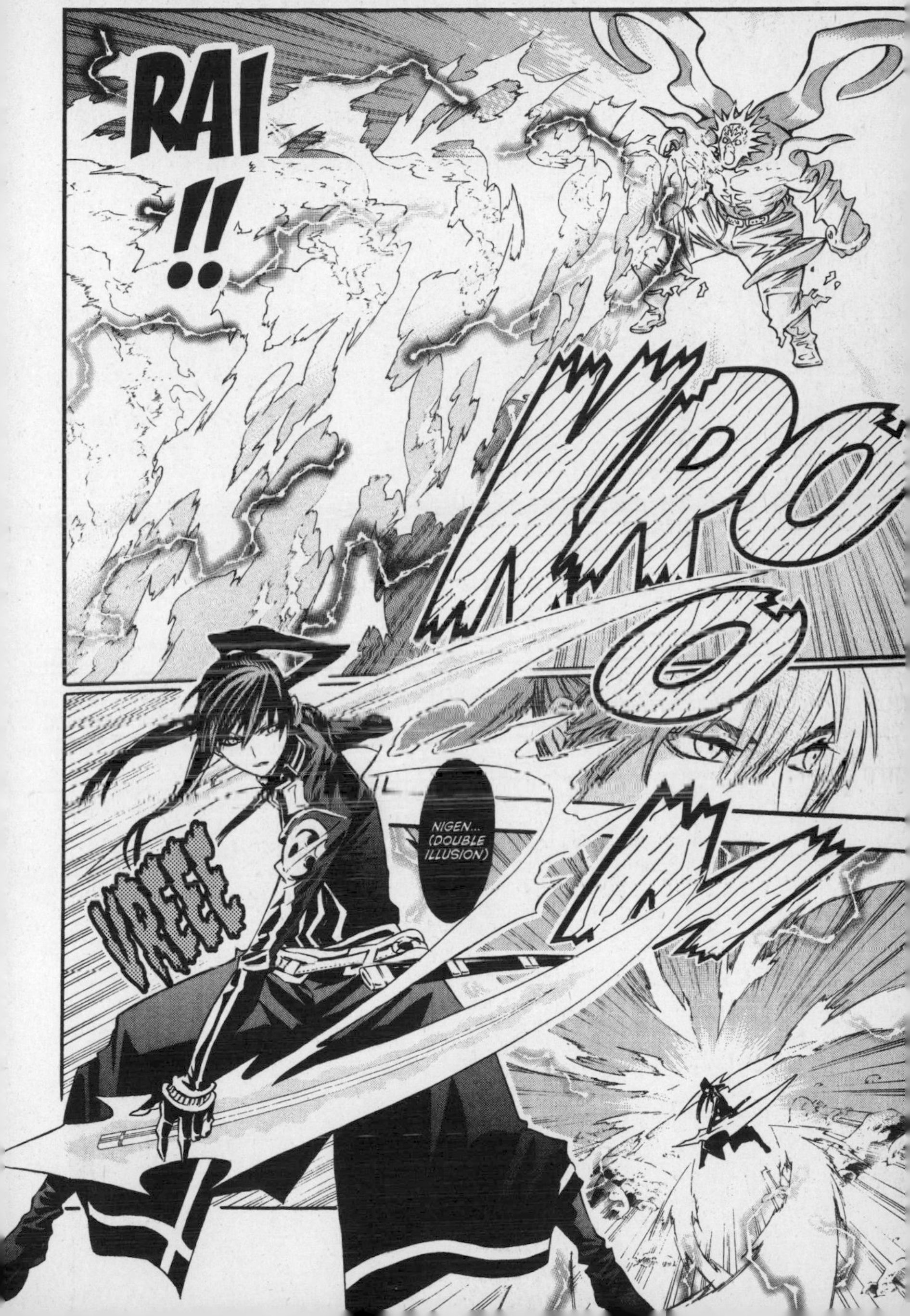
RAI!!
VROOM
NIGEN... (DOUBLE ILLUSION)
VREEE

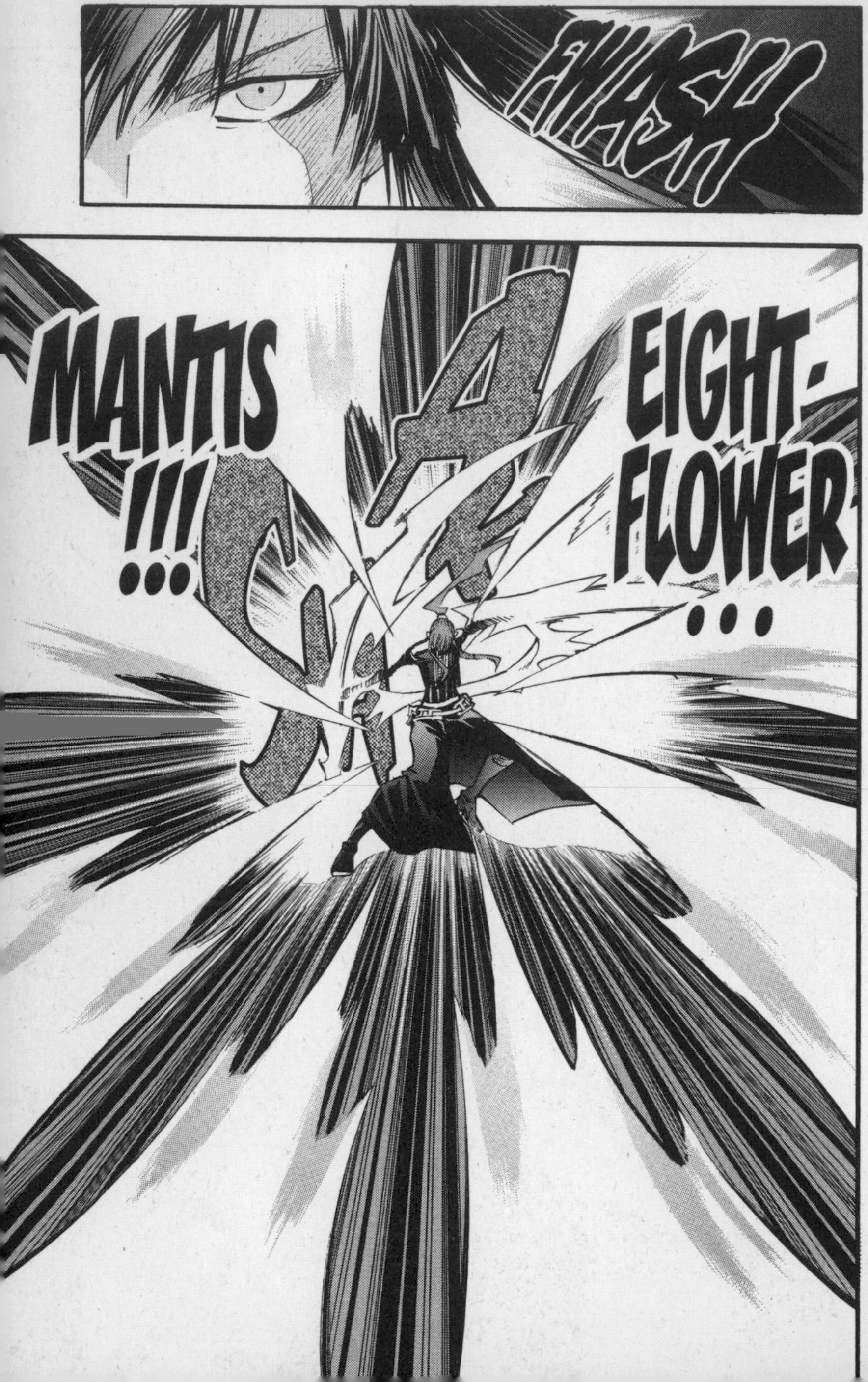
FWASH
EIGHT-FLOWER-...
MANTIS!!!...

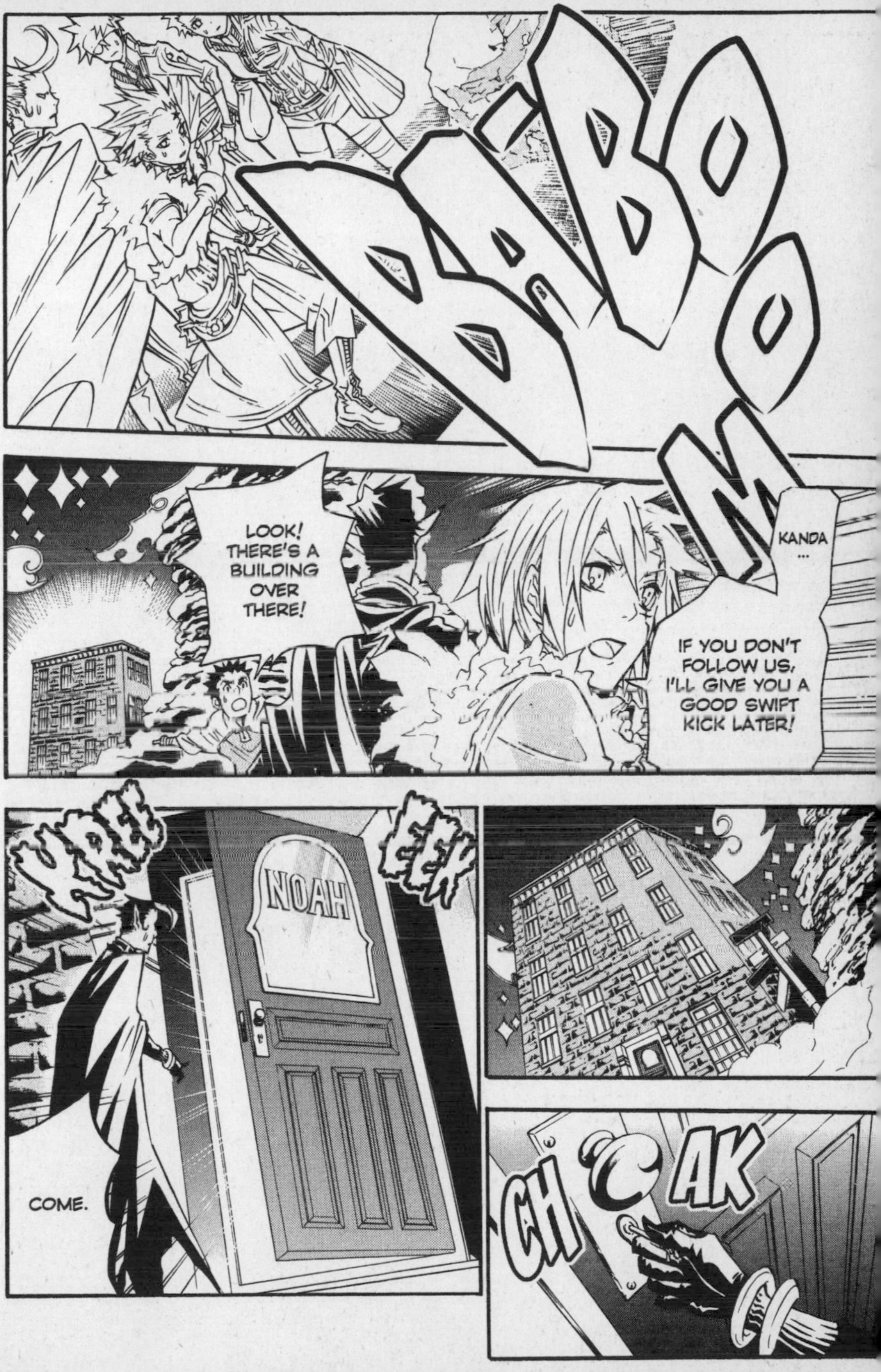
BABOOM
KANDA ...
IF YOU DON'T FOLLOW US, I'LL GIVE YOU A GOOD SWIFT KICK LATER!
LOOK! THERE'S A BUILDING OVER THERE!
CHCAK
CREEEK
NOAH
COME.

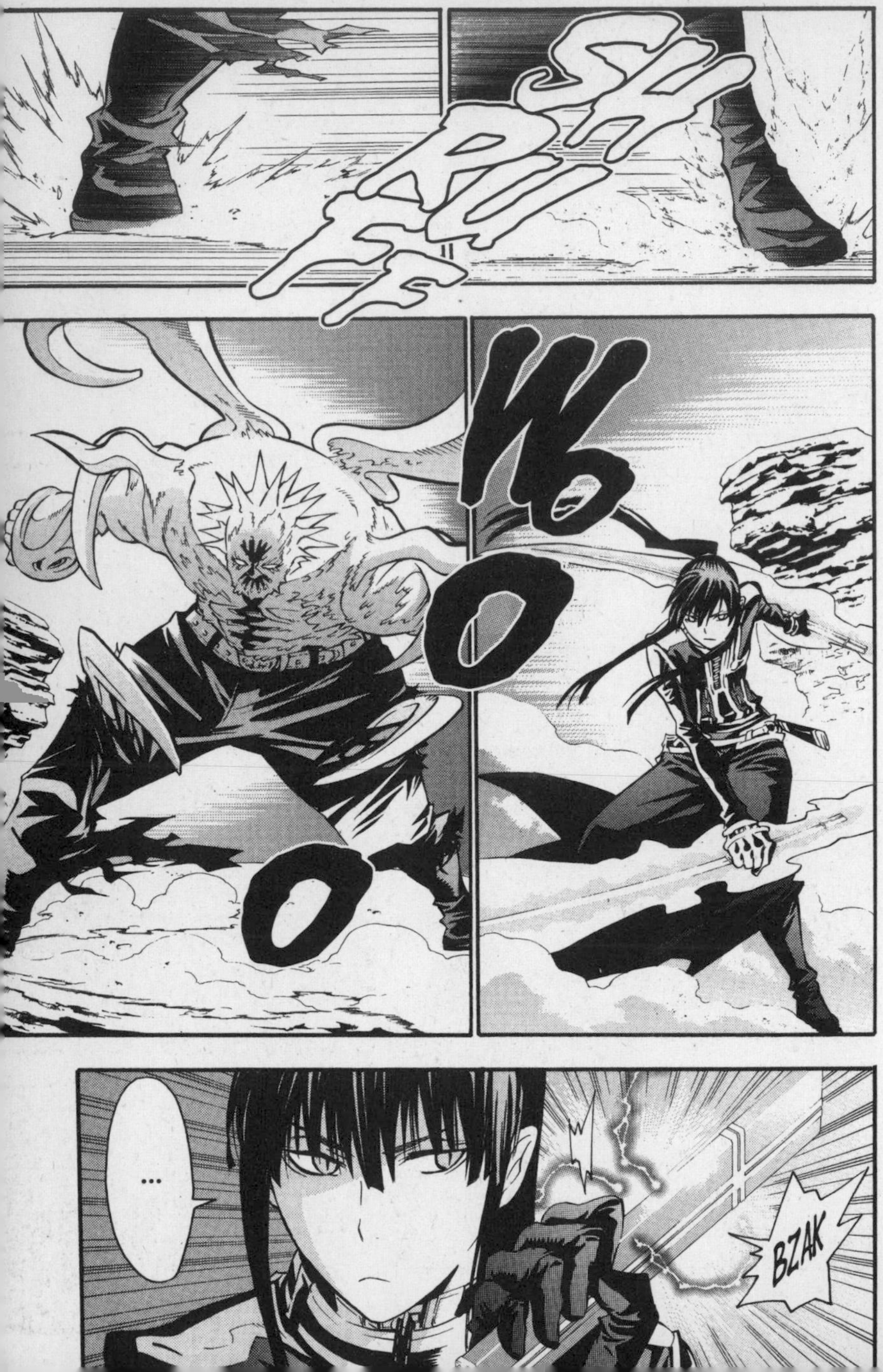
SHRUFF
WOOO
BZAK
...

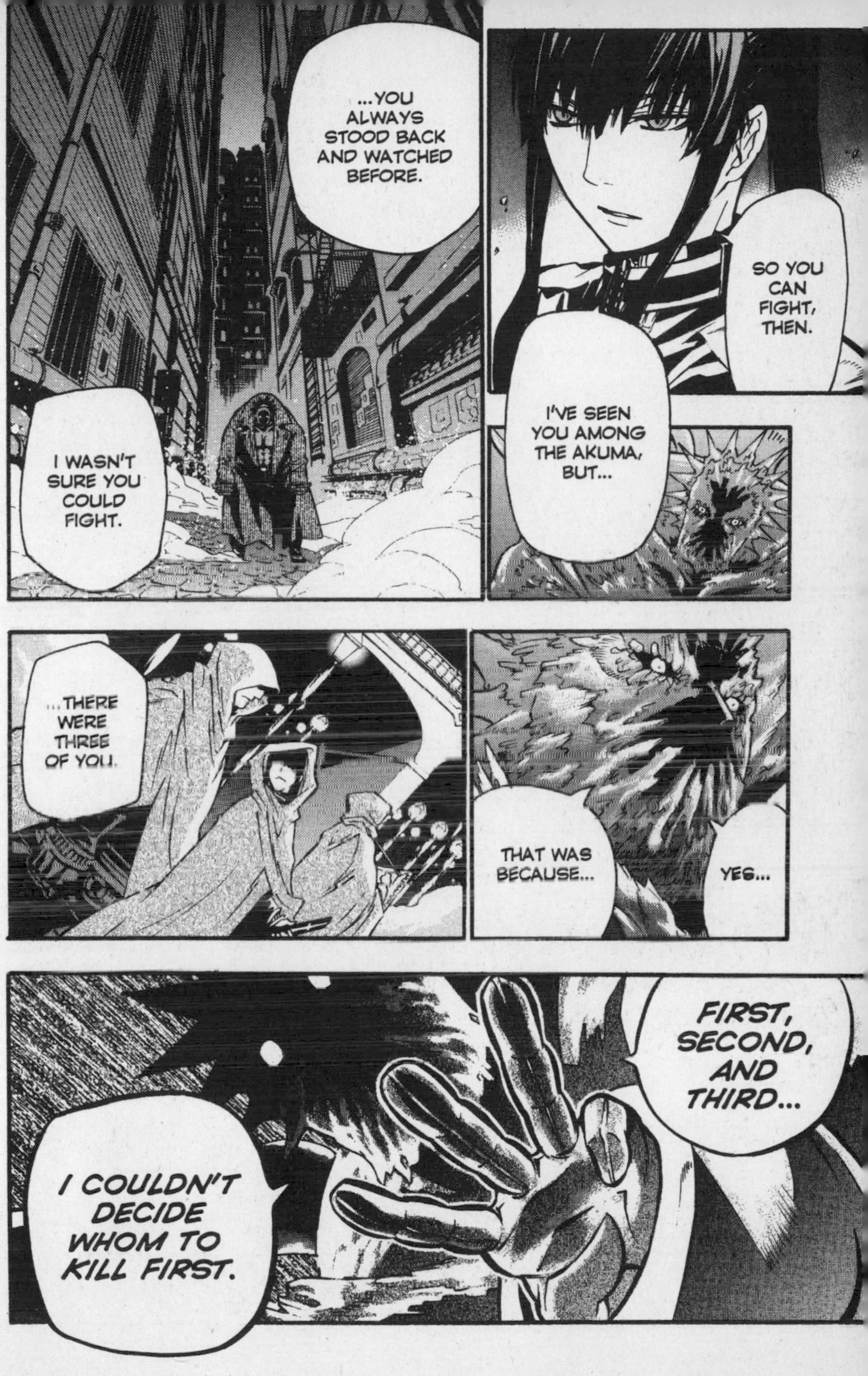
SO YOU CAN FIGHT, THEN.
I'VE SEEN YOU AMONG THE AKUMA, BUT...
...YOU ALWAYS STOOD BACK AND WATCHED BEFORE.
I WASN'T SURE YOU COULD FIGHT.
YES...
THAT WAS BECAUSE...
...THERE WERE THREE OF YOU.
FIRST, SECOND, AND THIRD...
I COULDN'T DECIDE WHOM TO KILL FIRST.

READ THIS WAY

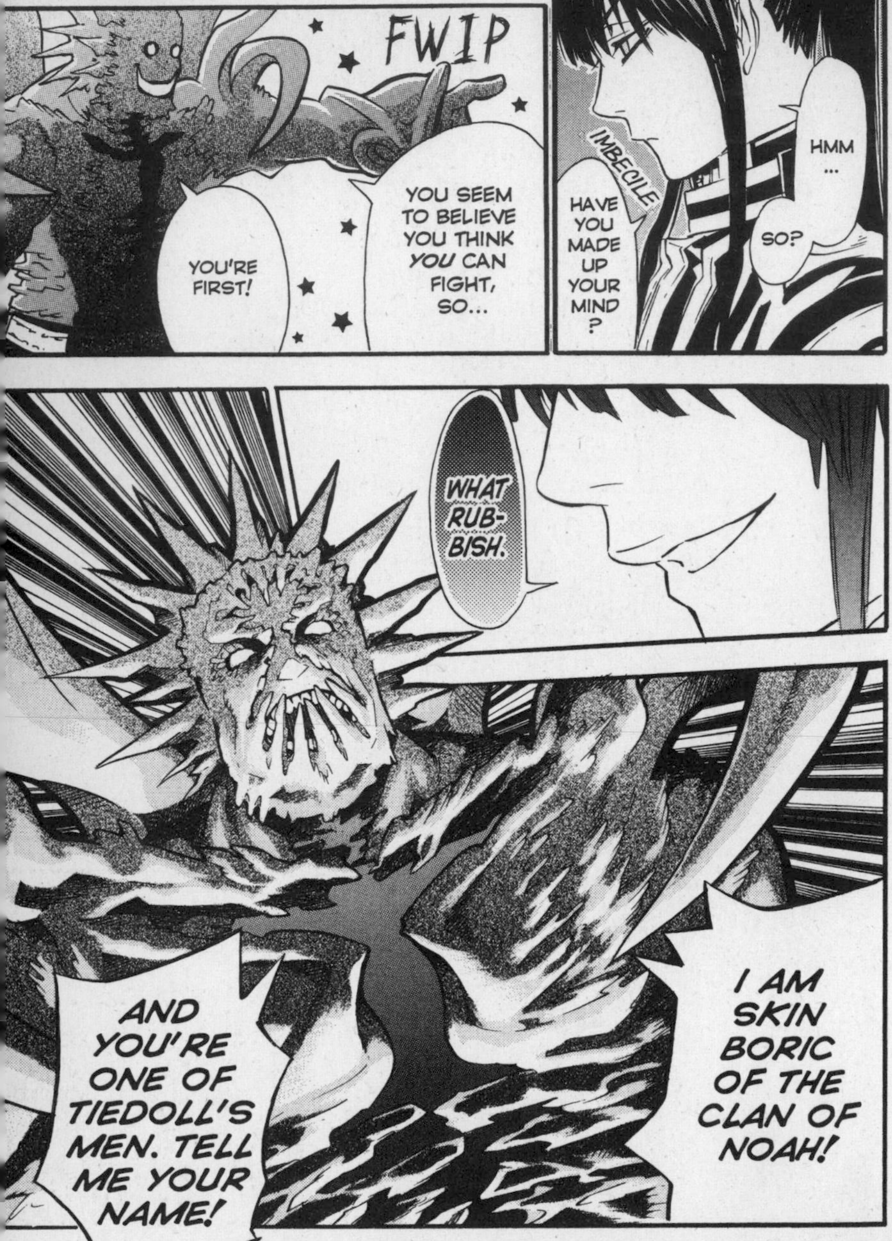
HMM ...
SO?
HAVE YOU MADE UP YOUR MIND?
IMBECILE
FWIP
YOU SEEM TO BELIEVE YOU THINK *YOU* CAN FIGHT, SO...
YOU'RE FIRST!
WHAT RUB-BISH.
I AM SKIN BORIC OF THE CLAN OF NOAH!
AND YOU'RE ONE OF TIEDOLL'S MEN. TELL ME YOUR NAME!

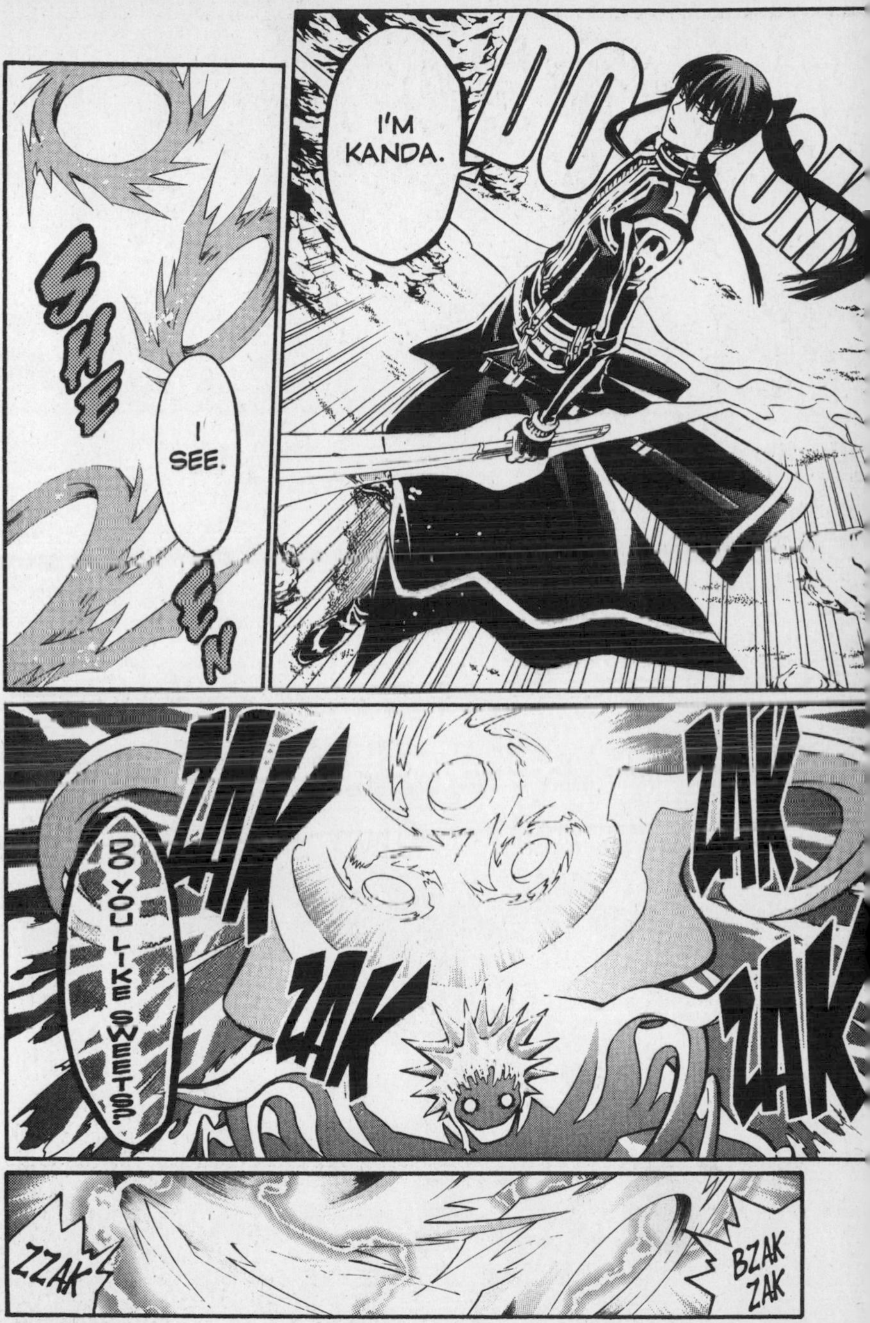
DO
I'M KANDA.
SHEEN
I SEE.
ZAK
ZAK
ZAK
ZAK
DO YOU LIKE SWEETS?
BZAK ZAK
ZZAK

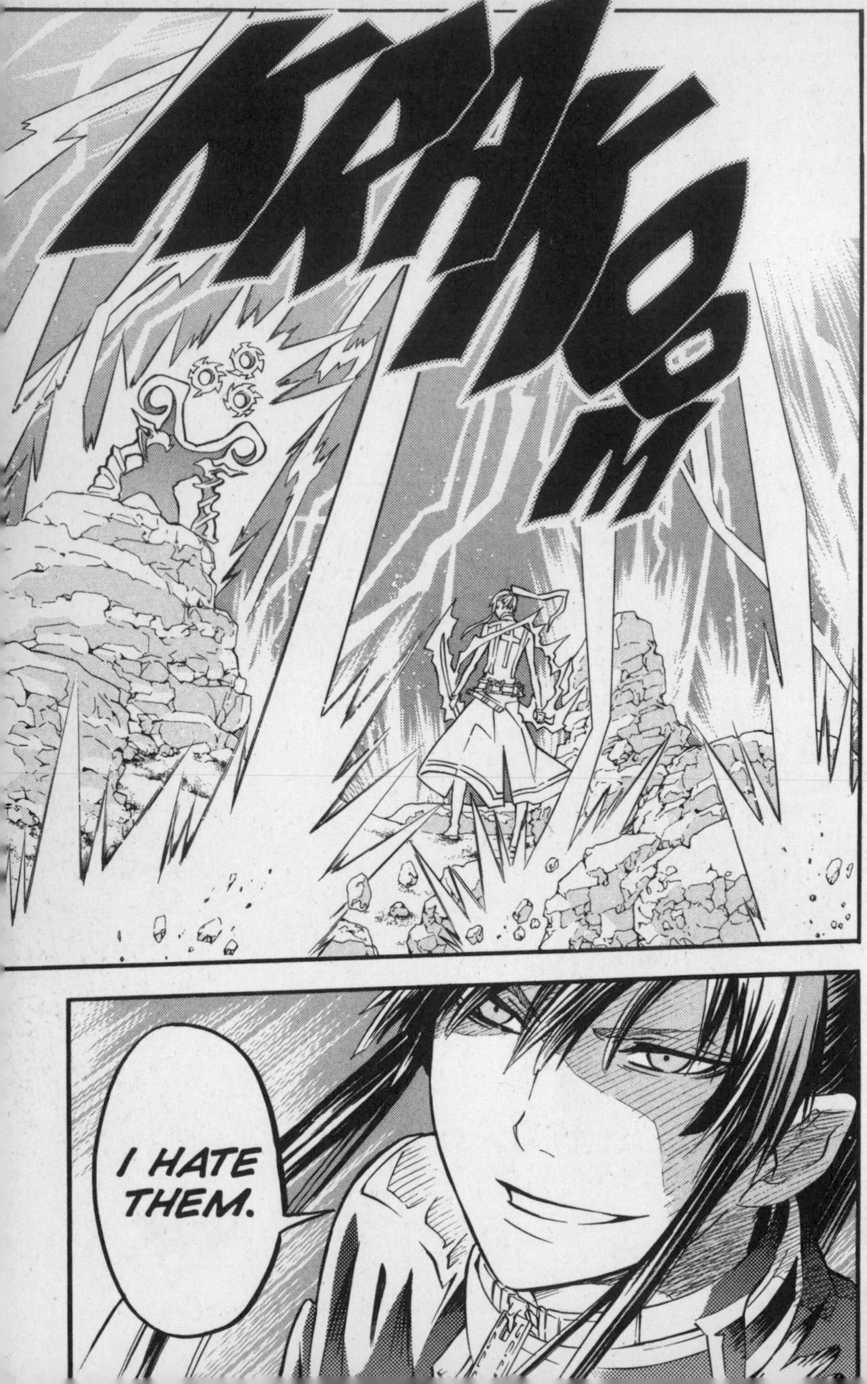
KRAKOOM
I HATE THEM.

KOMUI'S DISCUSSION ROOM, VOL. 3

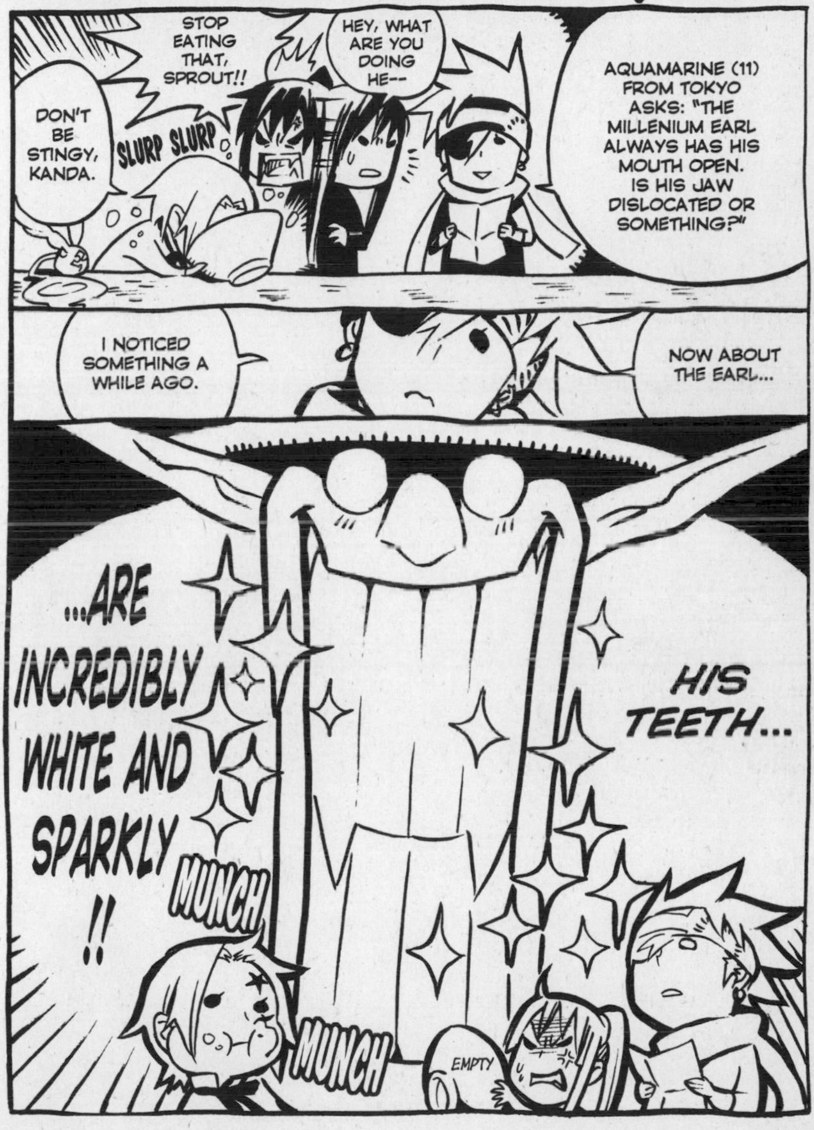
AQUAMARINE (11) FROM TOKYO ASKS: "THE MILLENIUM EARL ALWAYS HAS HIS MOUTH OPEN. IS HIS JAW DISLOCATED OR SOMETHING?"
HEY, WHAT ARE YOU DOING HE--
STOP EATING THAT, SPROUT!!
SLURP SLURP
DON'T BE STINGY, KANDA.
NOW ABOUT THE EARL...
I NOTICED SOMETHING A WHILE AGO.
HIS TEETH...
...ARE INCREDIBLY WHITE AND SPARKLY!!
MUNCH
MUNCH
EMPTY

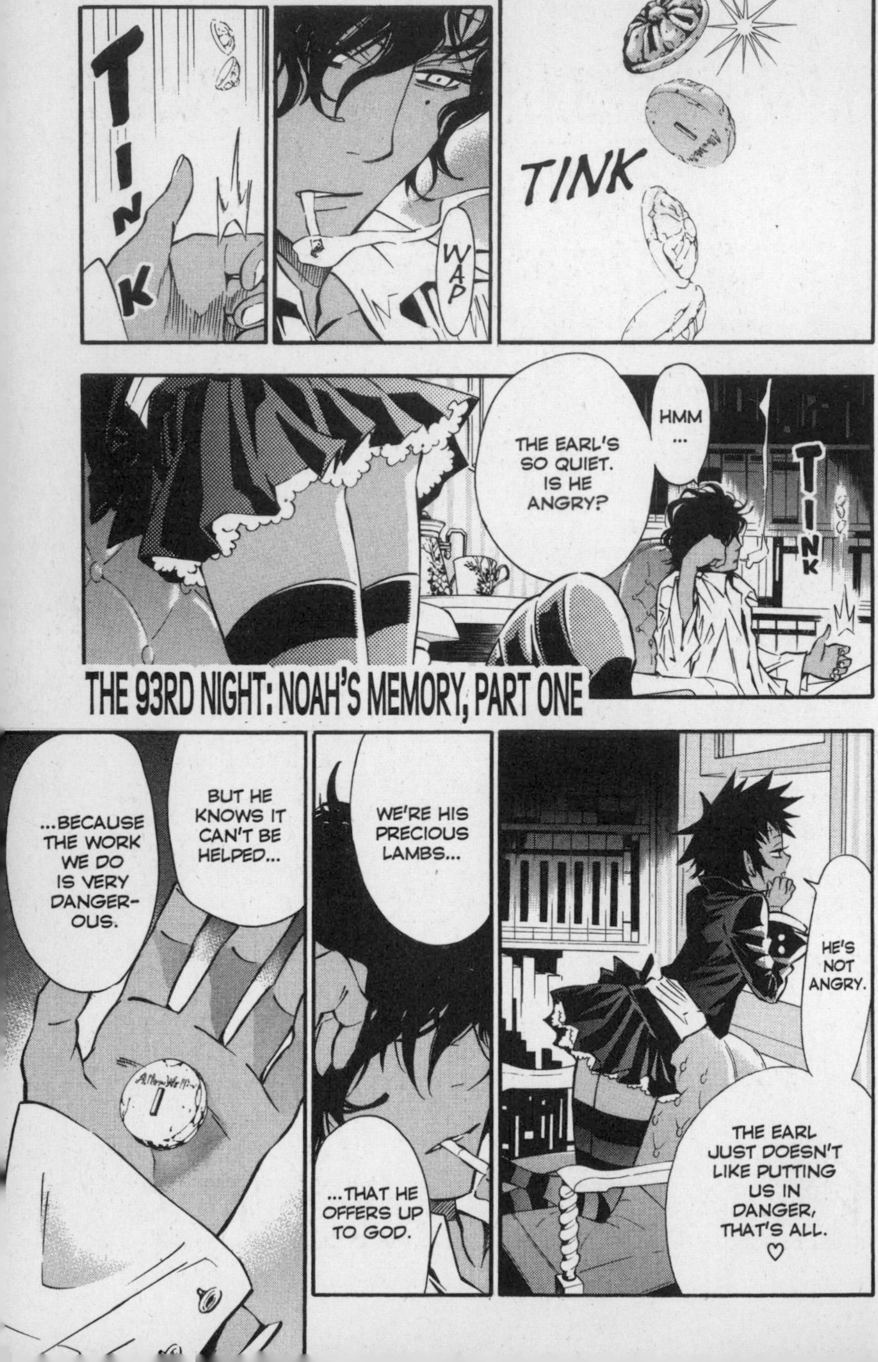
TINK
WAP
TINK
HMM ...
THE EARL'S SO QUIET. IS HE ANGRY?
TINK
THE 93RD NIGHT: NOAH'S MEMORY, PART ONE
HE'S NOT ANGRY.
THE EARL JUST DOESN'T LIKE PUTTING US IN DANGER, THAT'S ALL. ♡
WE'RE HIS PRECIOUS LAMBS...
...THAT HE OFFERS UP TO GOD.
BUT HE KNOWS IT CAN'T BE HELPED...
...BECAUSE THE WORK WE DO IS VERY DANGER-OUS.

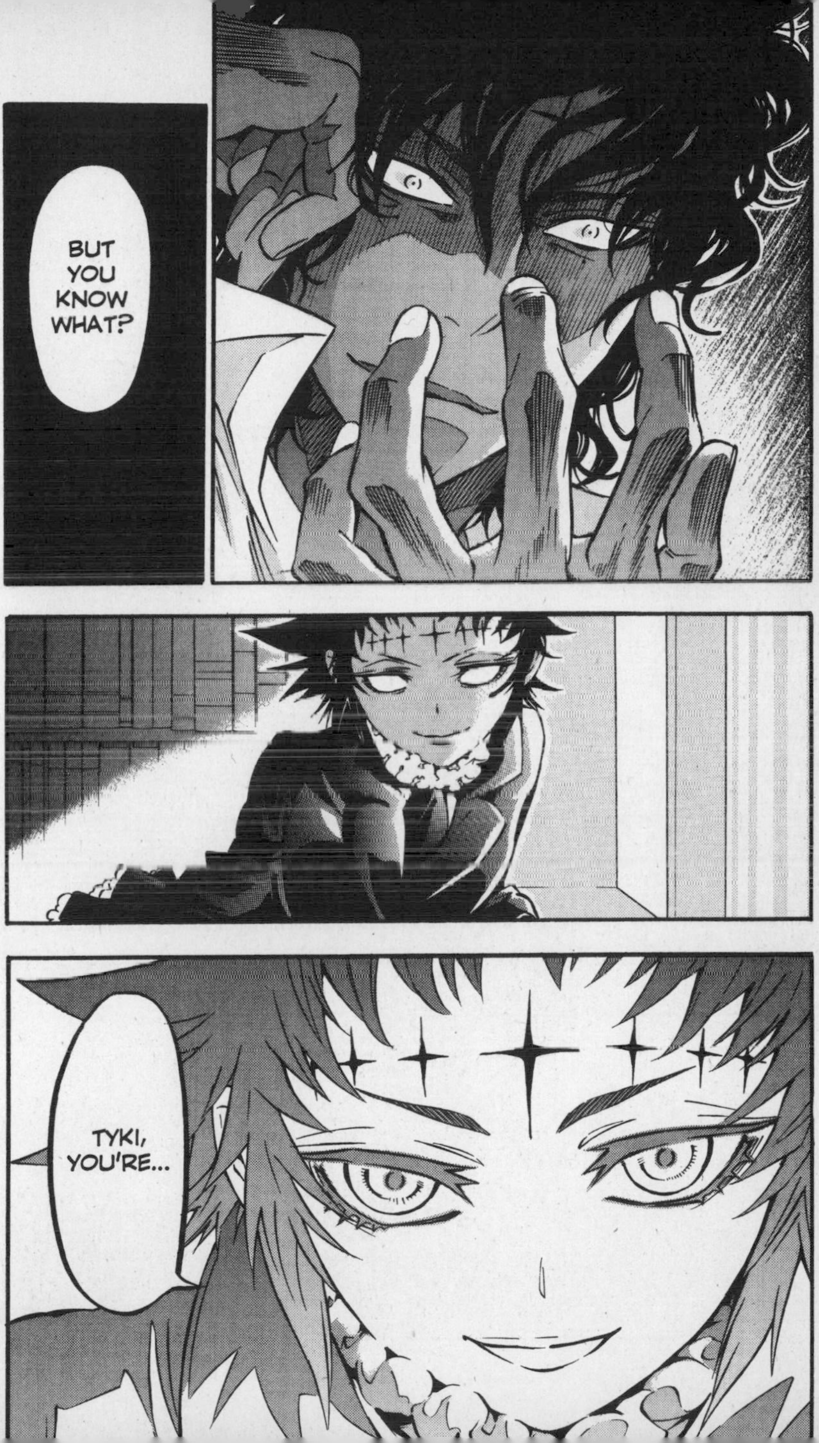
BUT YOU KNOW WHAT?
TYKI, YOU'RE...

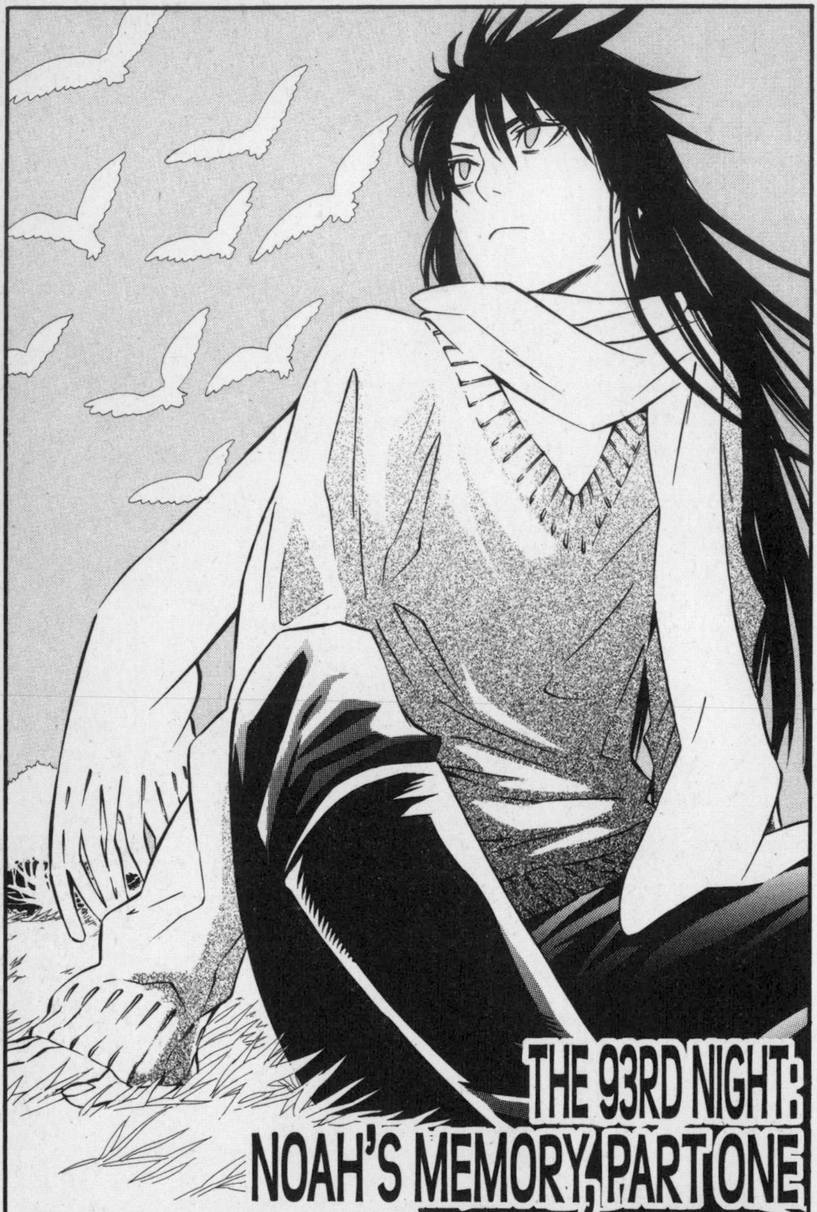
THE 93RD NIGHT:
NOAH'S MEMORY, PART ONE

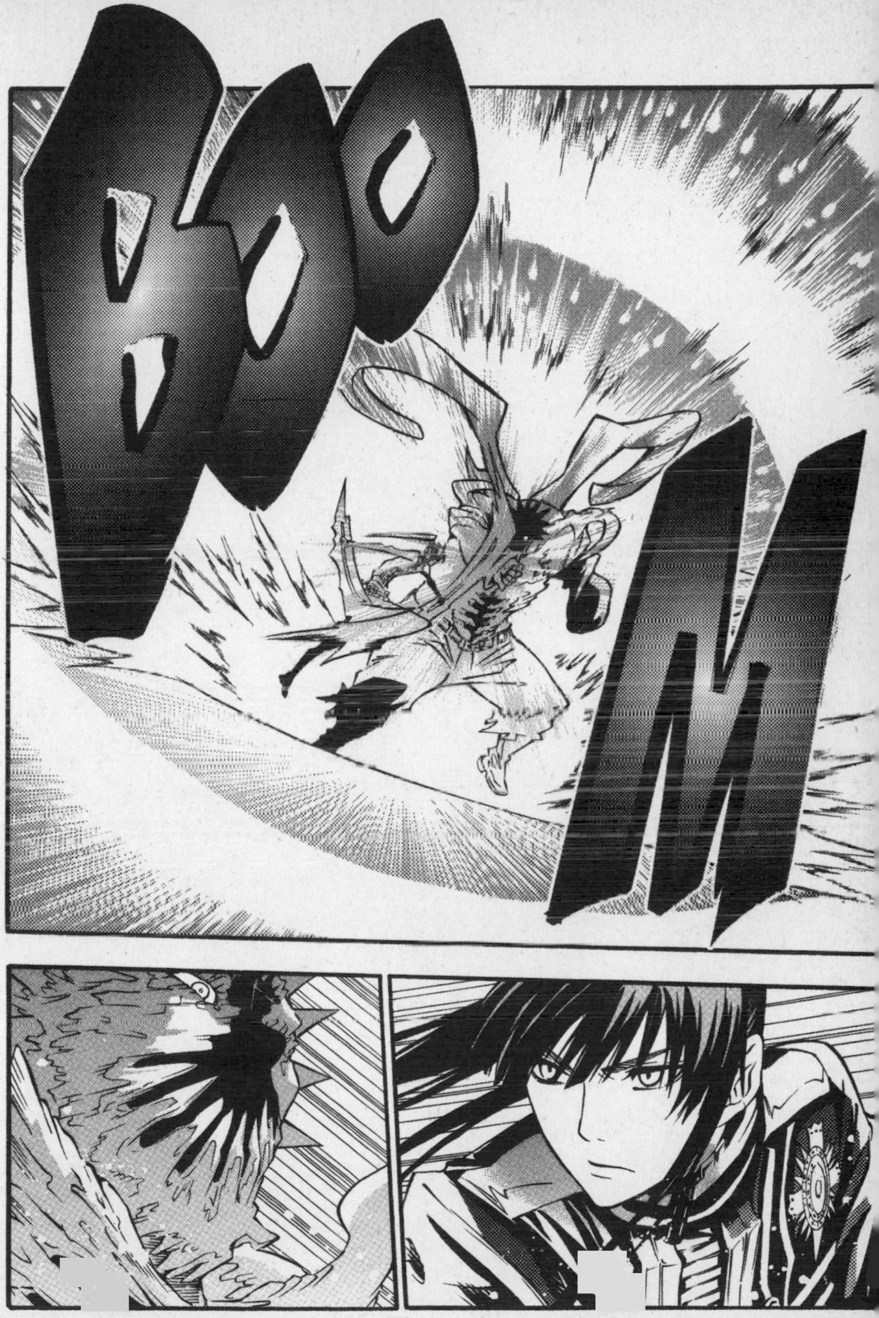
BOOOM

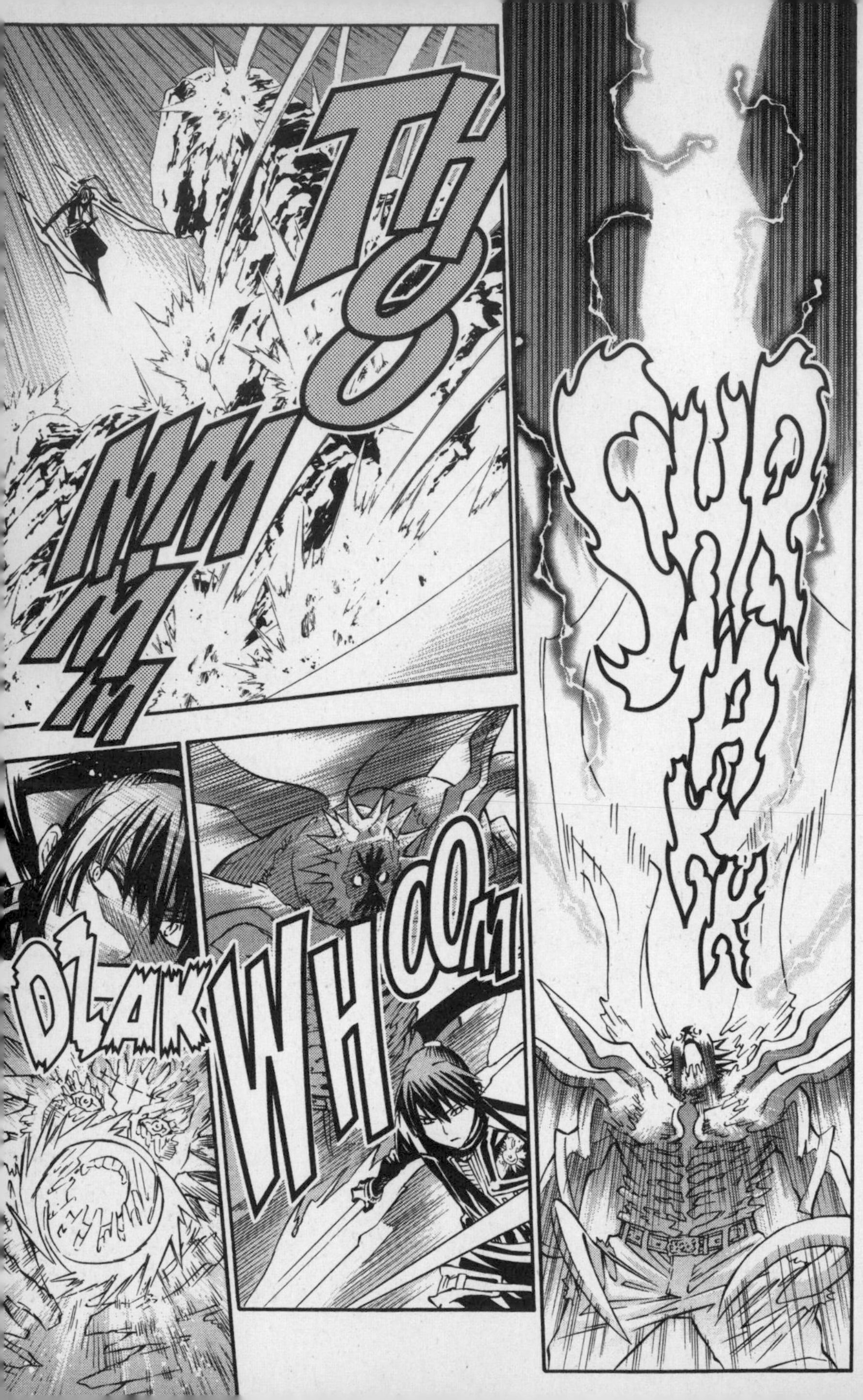
THOOMMM
WHOOM

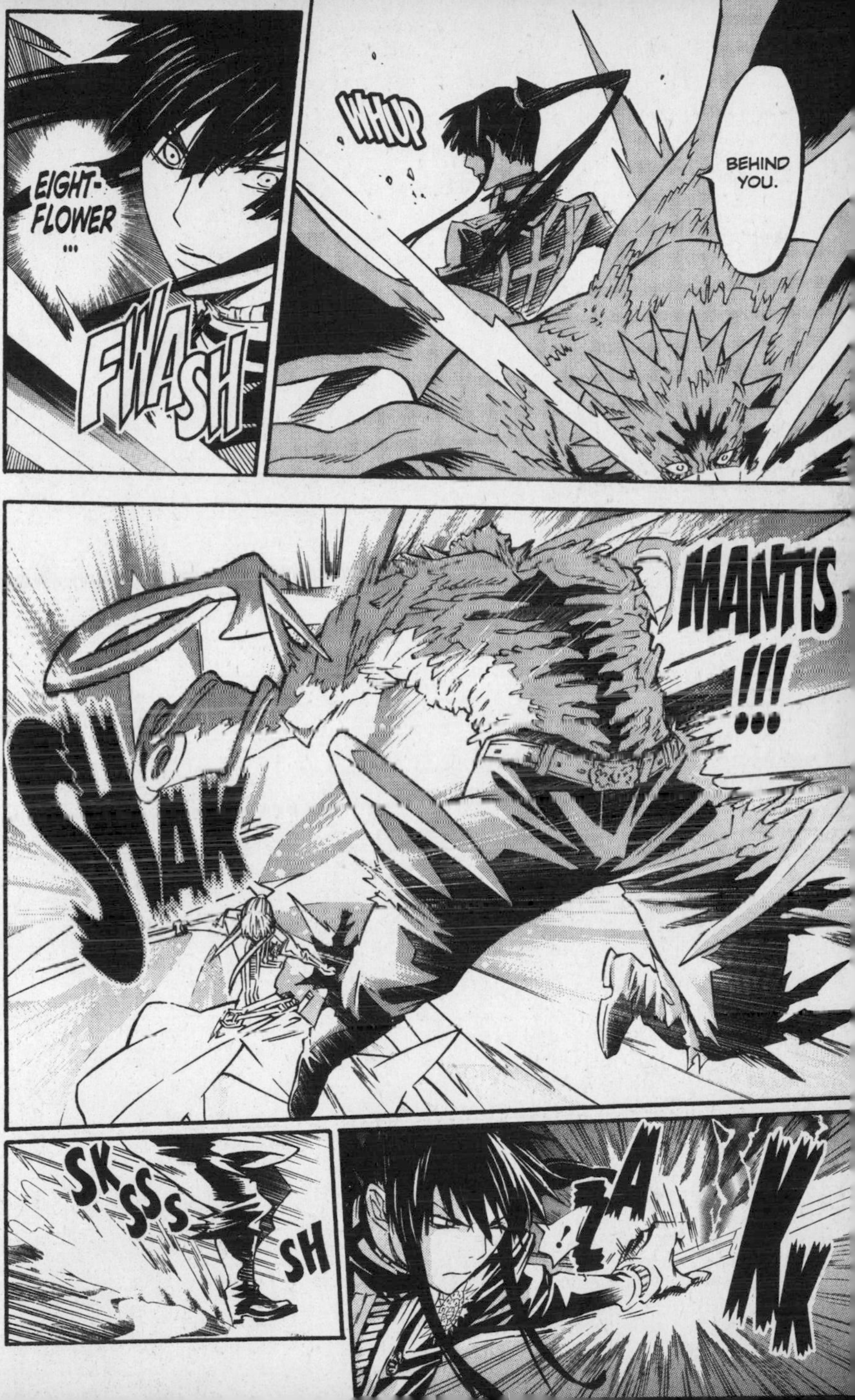
BEHIND YOU.
WHUP
EIGHT-FLOWER ...
FWASH
MANTIS!!!
SHAK
ZAK
SKSSS
SH

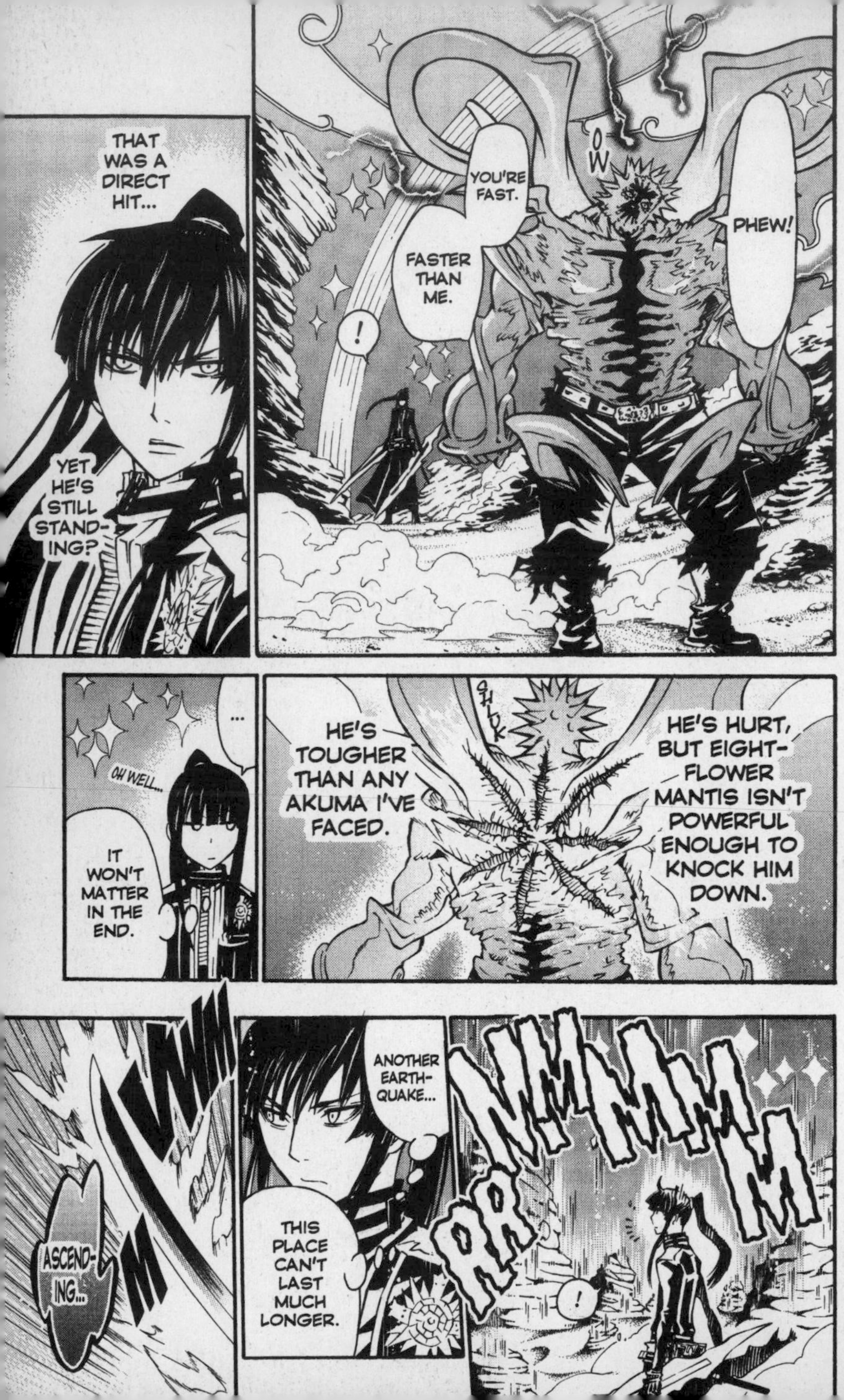
PHEW!
OW
YOU'RE FAST.
FASTER THAN ME.
!
THAT WAS A DIRECT HIT...
YET HE'S STILL STAND-ING?
SHLUK
HE'S HURT, BUT EIGHT-FLOWER MANTIS ISN'T POWERFUL ENOUGH TO KNOCK HIM DOWN.
HE'S TOUGHER THAN ANY AKUMA I'VE FACED.
...
OH WELL...
IT WON'T MATTER IN THE END.
RRMMMMMM
!
ANOTHER EARTH-QUAKE...
THIS PLACE CAN'T LAST MUCH LONGER.
ASCEND-ING...

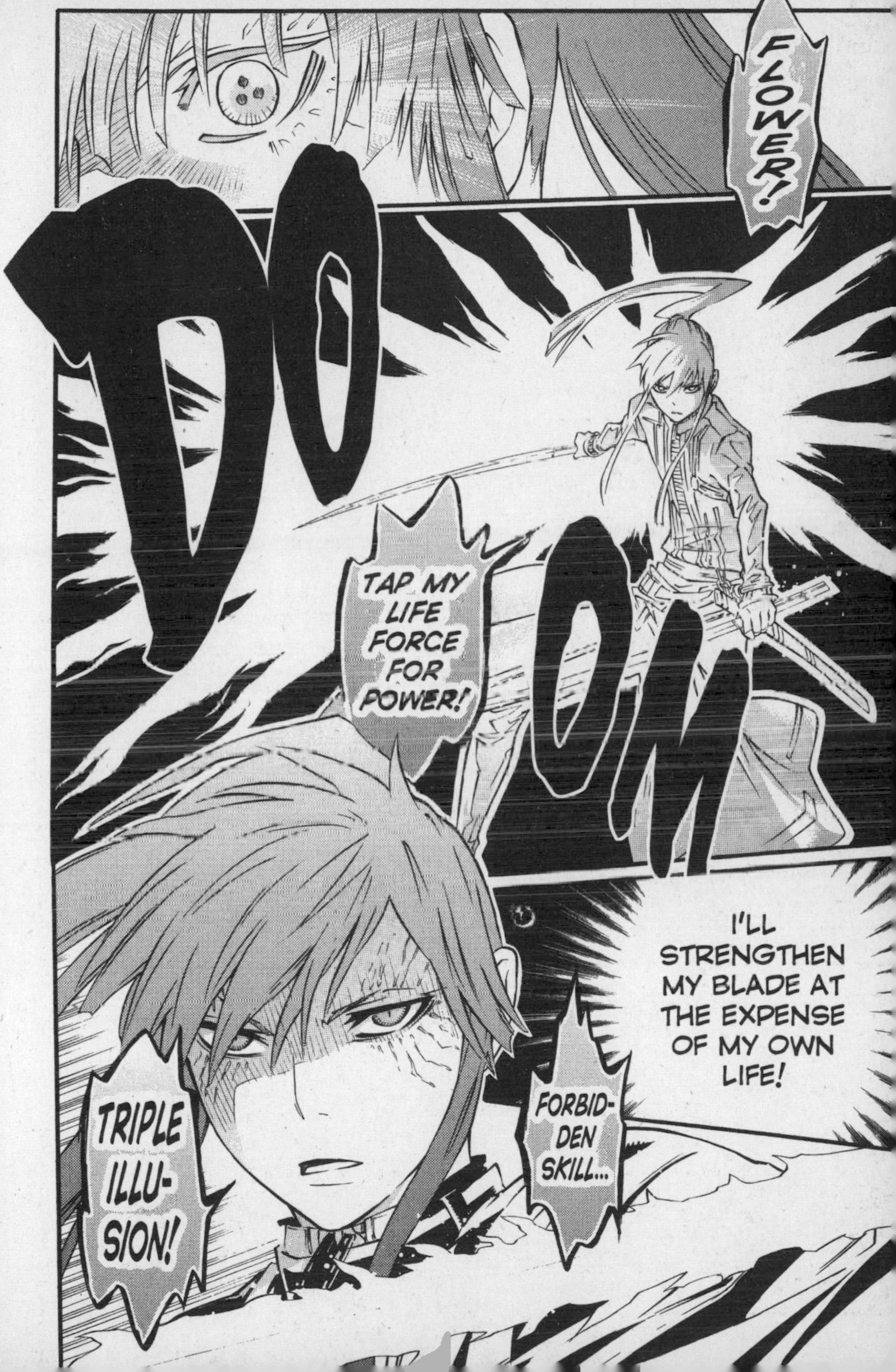
FLOWER!
DOOM
TAP MY LIFE FORCE FOR POWER!
I'LL STRENGTHEN MY BLADE AT THE EXPENSE OF MY OWN LIFE!
FORBID-DEN SKILL...
TRIPLE ILLU-SION!

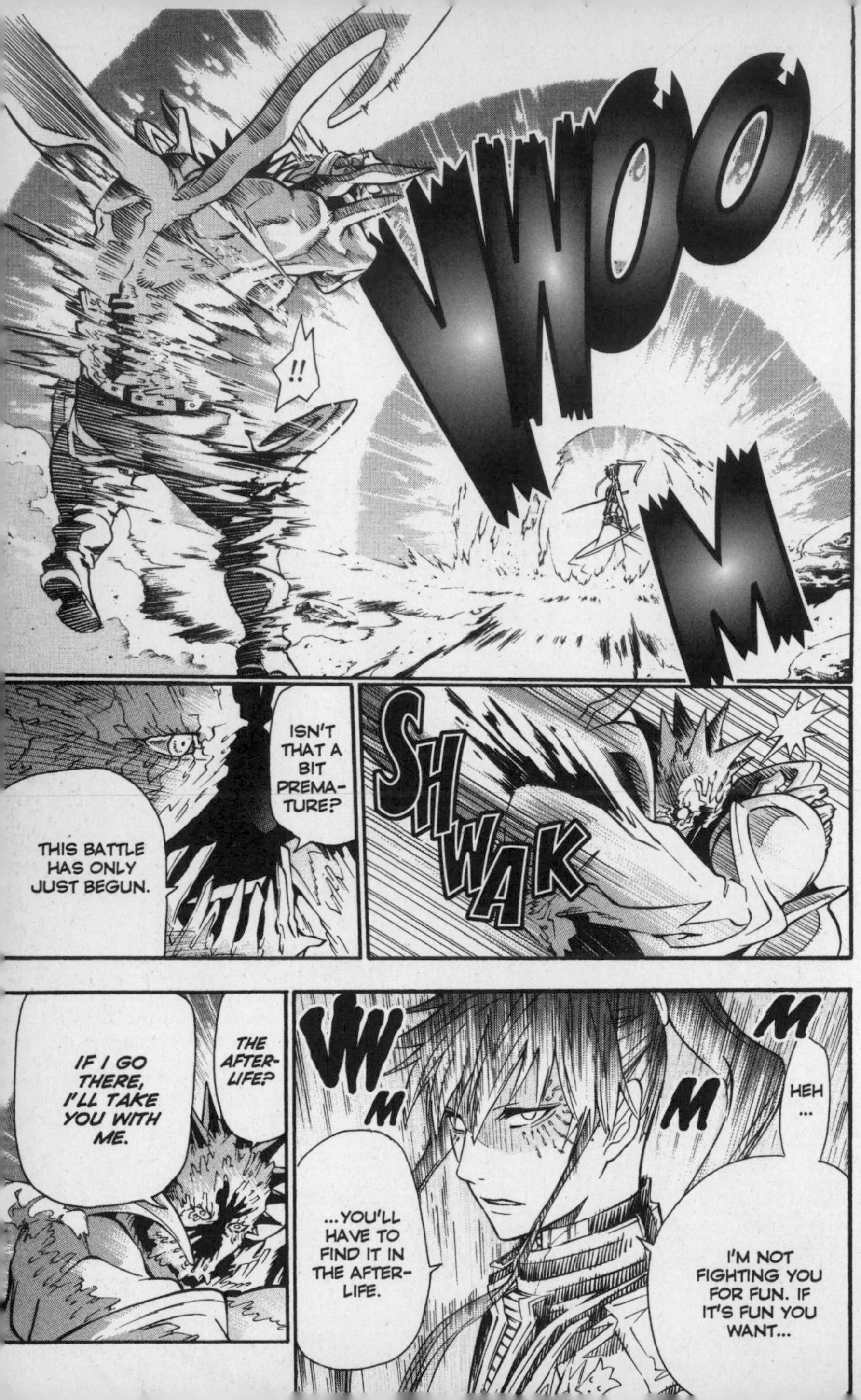
WHOOOM
!!
SHWAK
ISN'T THAT A BIT PREMATURE?
THIS BATTLE HAS ONLY JUST BEGUN.
WMMMM
HEH ...
I'M NOT FIGHTING YOU FOR FUN. IF IT'S FUN YOU WANT...
...YOU'LL HAVE TO FIND IT IN THE AFTER-LIFE.
THE AFTER-LIFE?
IF I GO THERE, I'LL TAKE YOU WITH ME.

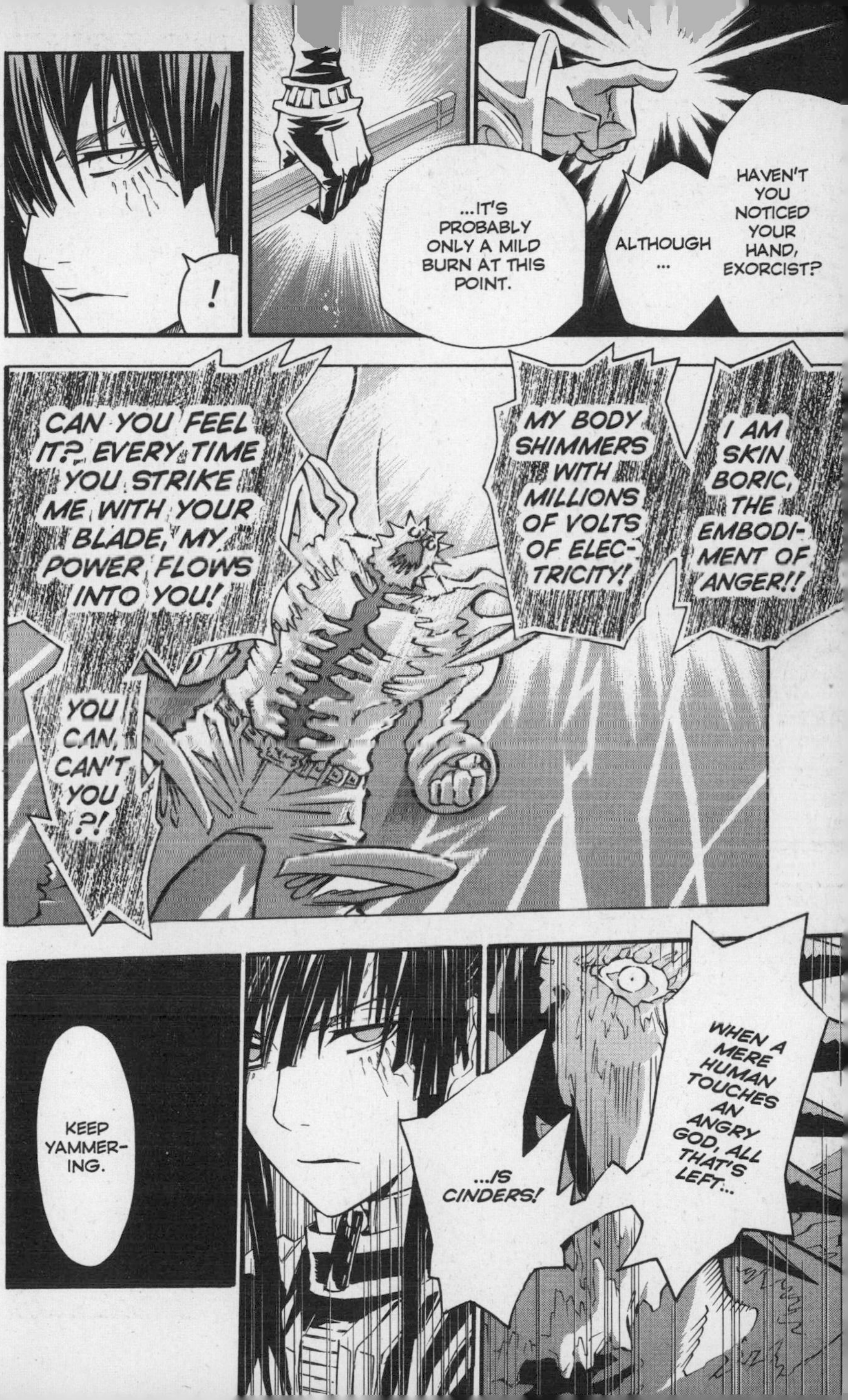
HAVEN'T YOU NOTICED YOUR HAND, EXORCIST?
ALTHOUGH ...
...IT'S PROBABLY ONLY A MILD BURN AT THIS POINT.
!
I AM SKIN BORIC, THE EMBODIMENT OF ANGER!!
MY BODY SHIMMERS WITH MILLIONS OF VOLTS OF ELECTRICITY!
CAN YOU FEEL IT?! EVERY TIME YOU STRIKE ME WITH YOUR BLADE, MY POWER FLOWS INTO YOU!
YOU CAN, CAN'T YOU ?!
WHEN A MERE HUMAN TOUCHES AN ANGRY GOD, ALL THAT'S LEFT...
...IS CINDERS!
KEEP YAMMERING.

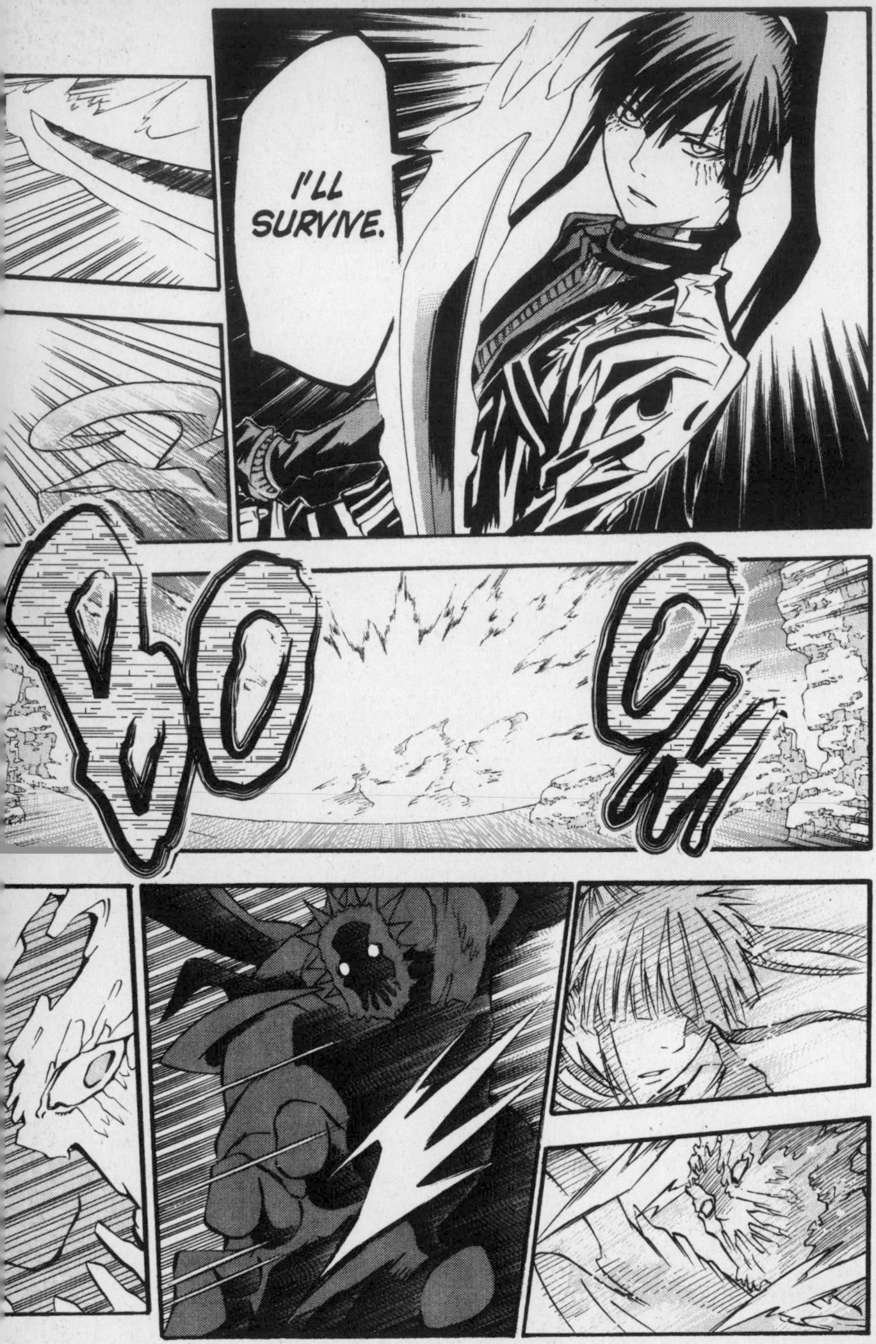
I'LL SURVIVE.
VOOOM

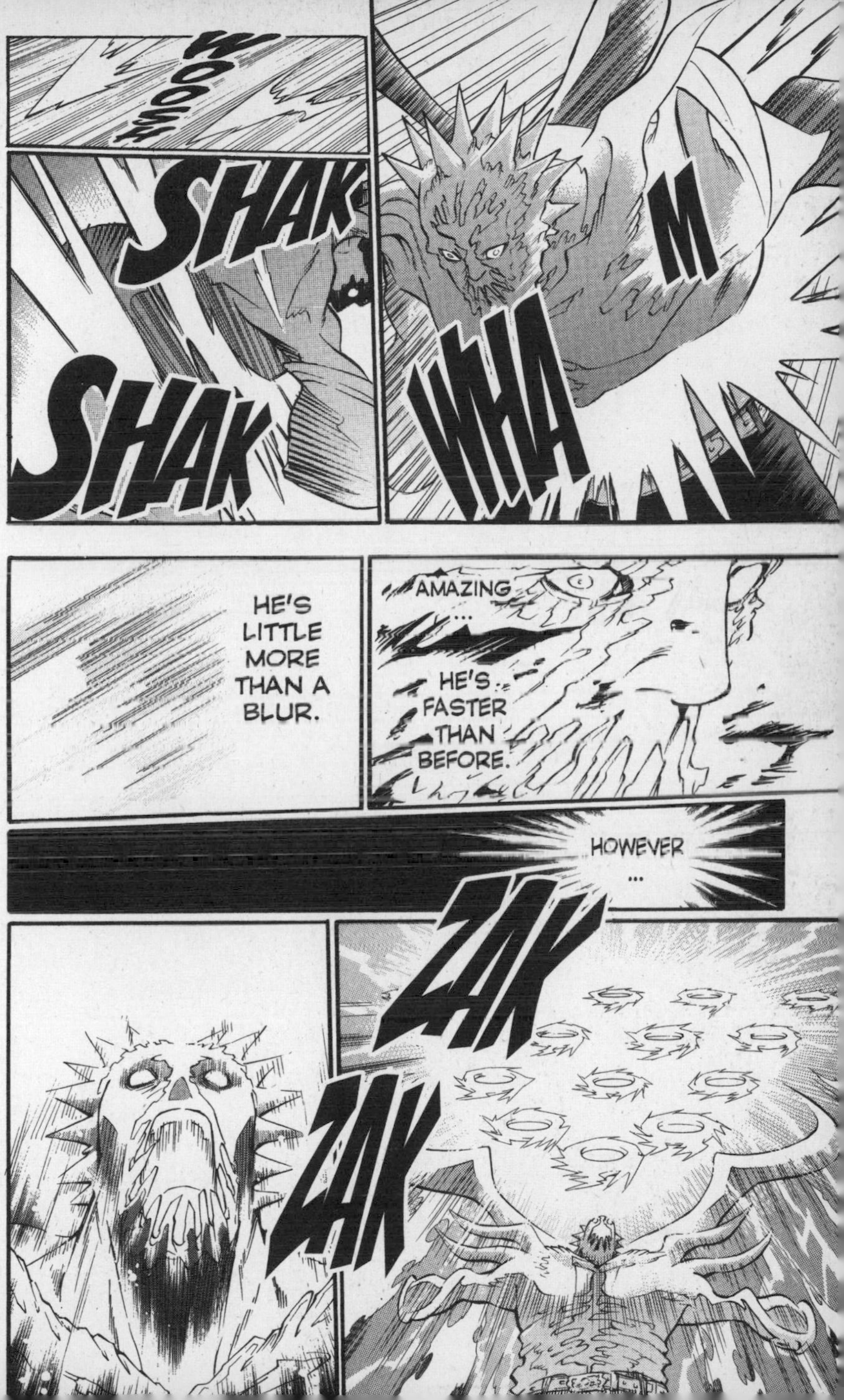
WHAM
WOOSH
SHAK
SHAK
AMAZING...
HE'S FASTER THAN BEFORE.
HE'S LITTLE MORE THAN A BLUR.
HOWEVER...
ZAK
ZAK

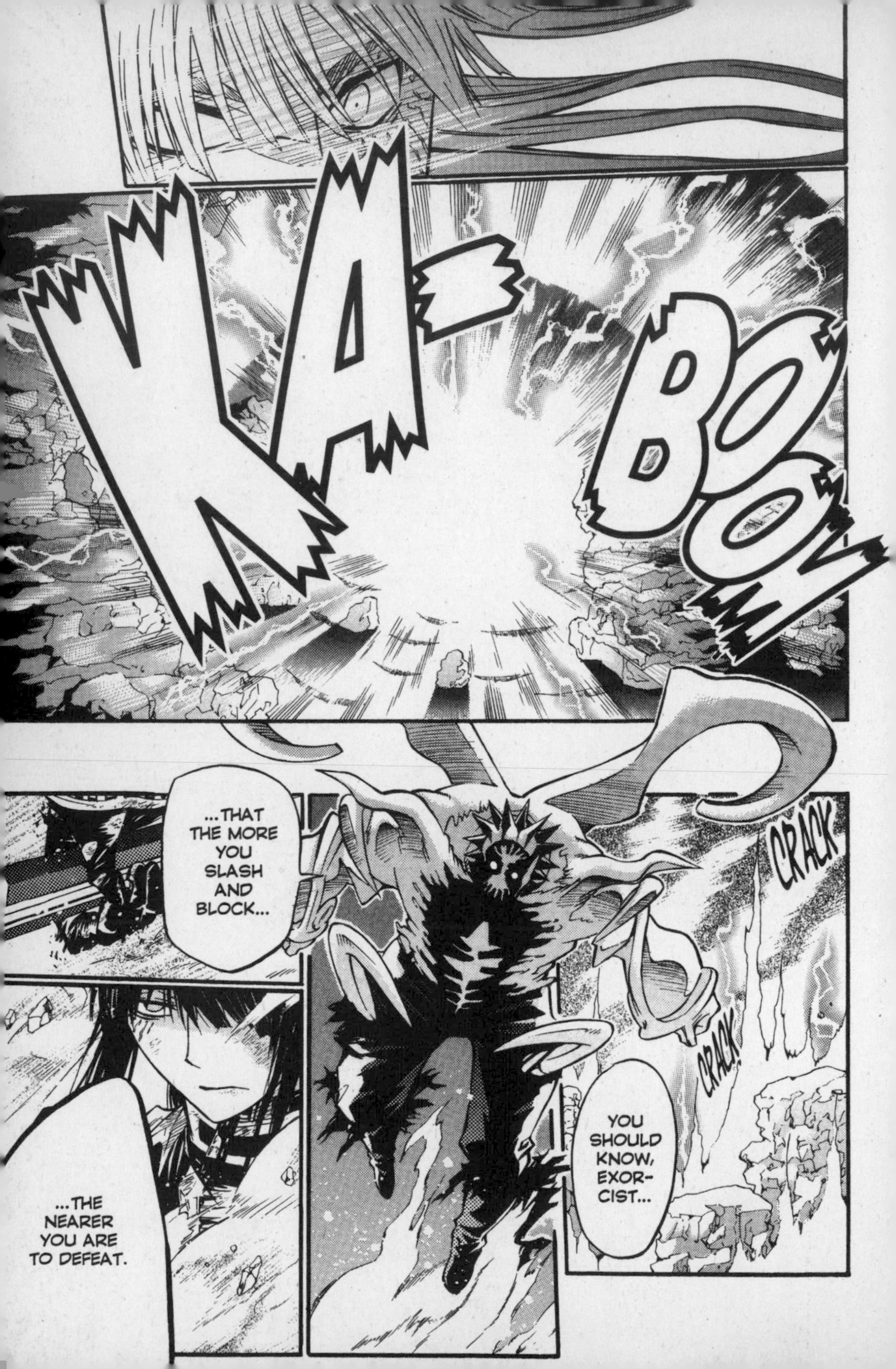
KA-BOOM
CRACK
CRACK
YOU SHOULD KNOW, EXORCIST...
...THAT THE MORE YOU SLASH AND BLOCK...
...THE NEARER YOU ARE TO DEFEAT.

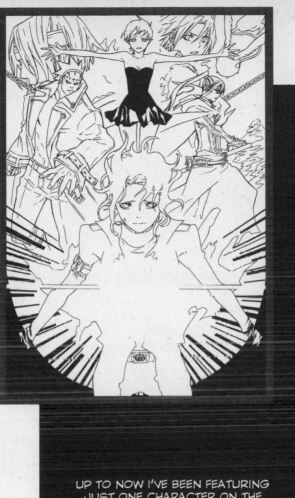

UP TO NOW I'VE BEEN FEATURING
JUST ONE CHARACTER ON THE
COVER OF EACH VOLUME. BUT
DUE TO CERTAIN UNFORESEEN
EVENTS, THE COVER OF VOLUME
9 WAS DIFFERENT. SO I'M
CONSIDERING DOING THEM
LIKE THIS FROM NOW ON. ☆

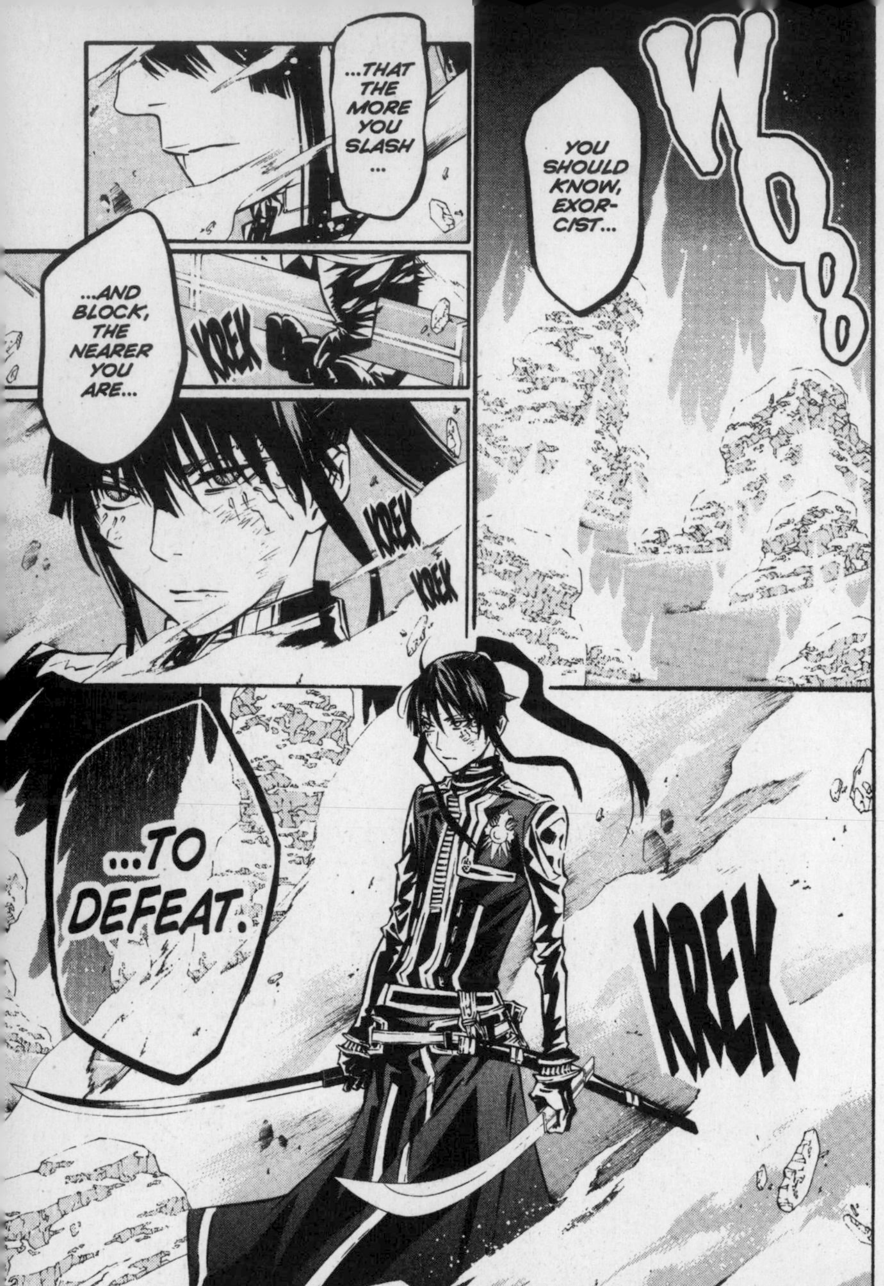
WOOB
YOU SHOULD KNOW, EXORCIST...
...THAT THE MORE YOU SLASH ...
...AND BLOCK, THE NEARER YOU ARE...
KREK
KREK
KREK
...TO DEFEAT.
KREK
THE 94TH NIGHT: NOAH'S MEMORY, PART TWO

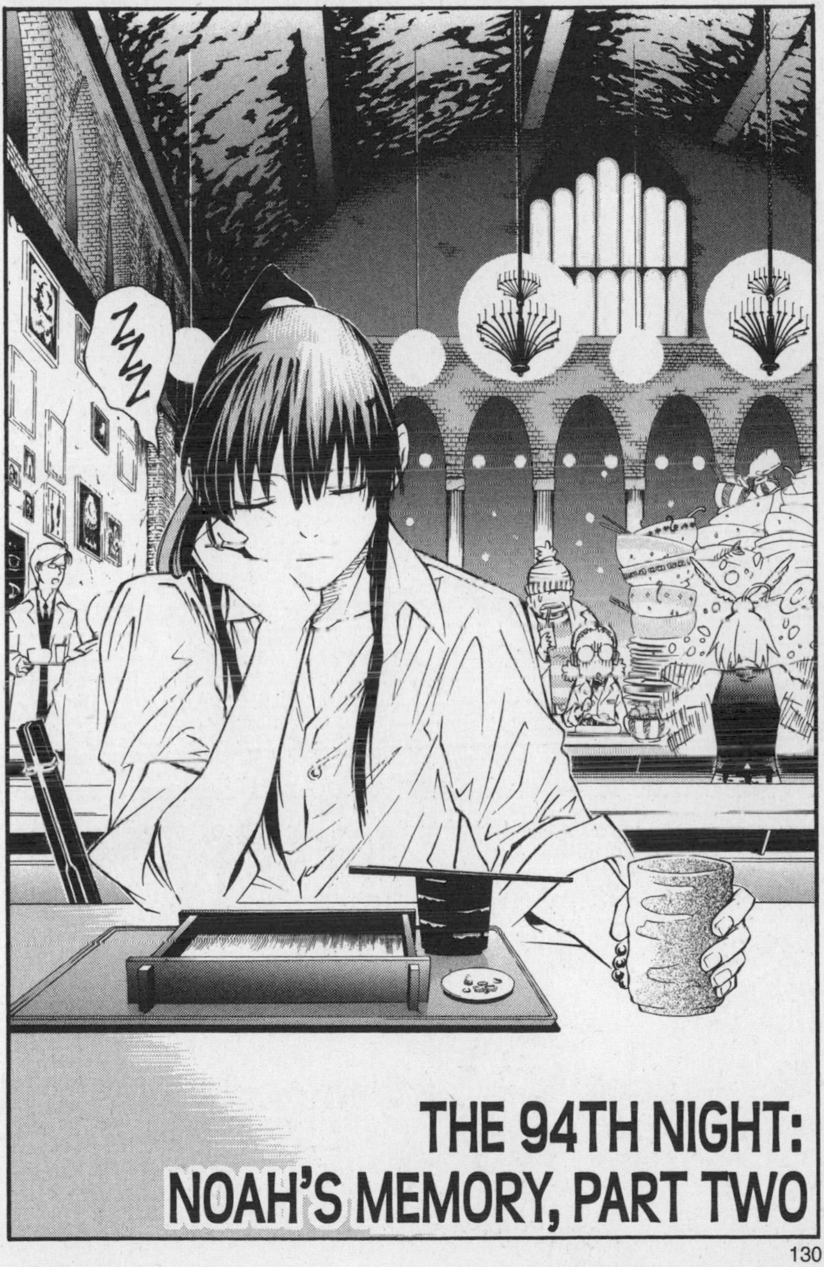
ZZZ

THE 94TH NIGHT:
NOAH'S MEMORY, PART TWO

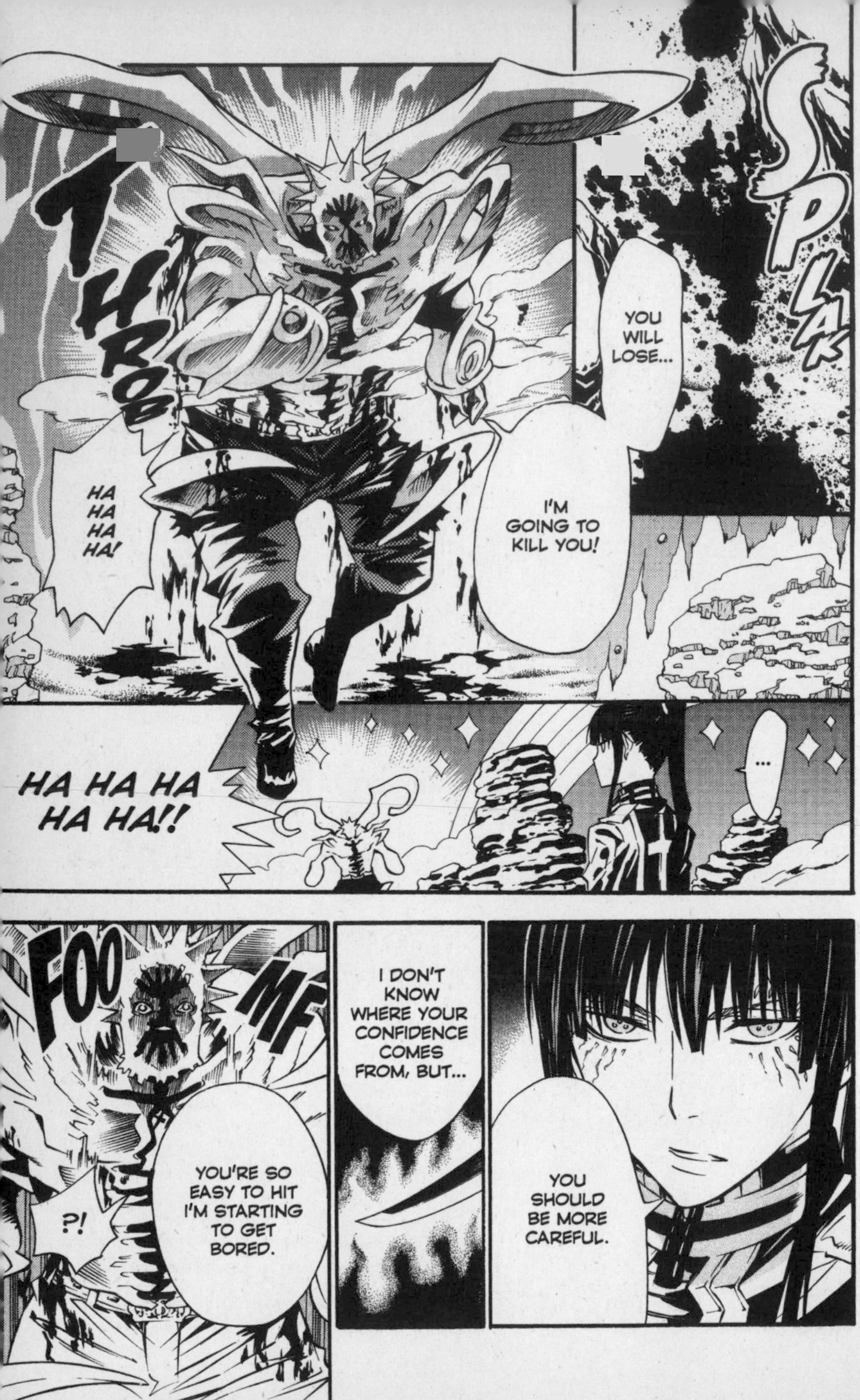
SPLAK
YOU WILL LOSE...
I'M GOING TO KILL YOU!
THROB
HA HA HA HA!
...
HA HA HA HA HA!!
YOU SHOULD BE MORE CAREFUL.
I DON'T KNOW WHERE YOUR CONFIDENCE COMES FROM, BUT...
FOOMF
?!
YOU'RE SO EASY TO HIT I'M STARTING TO GET BORED.

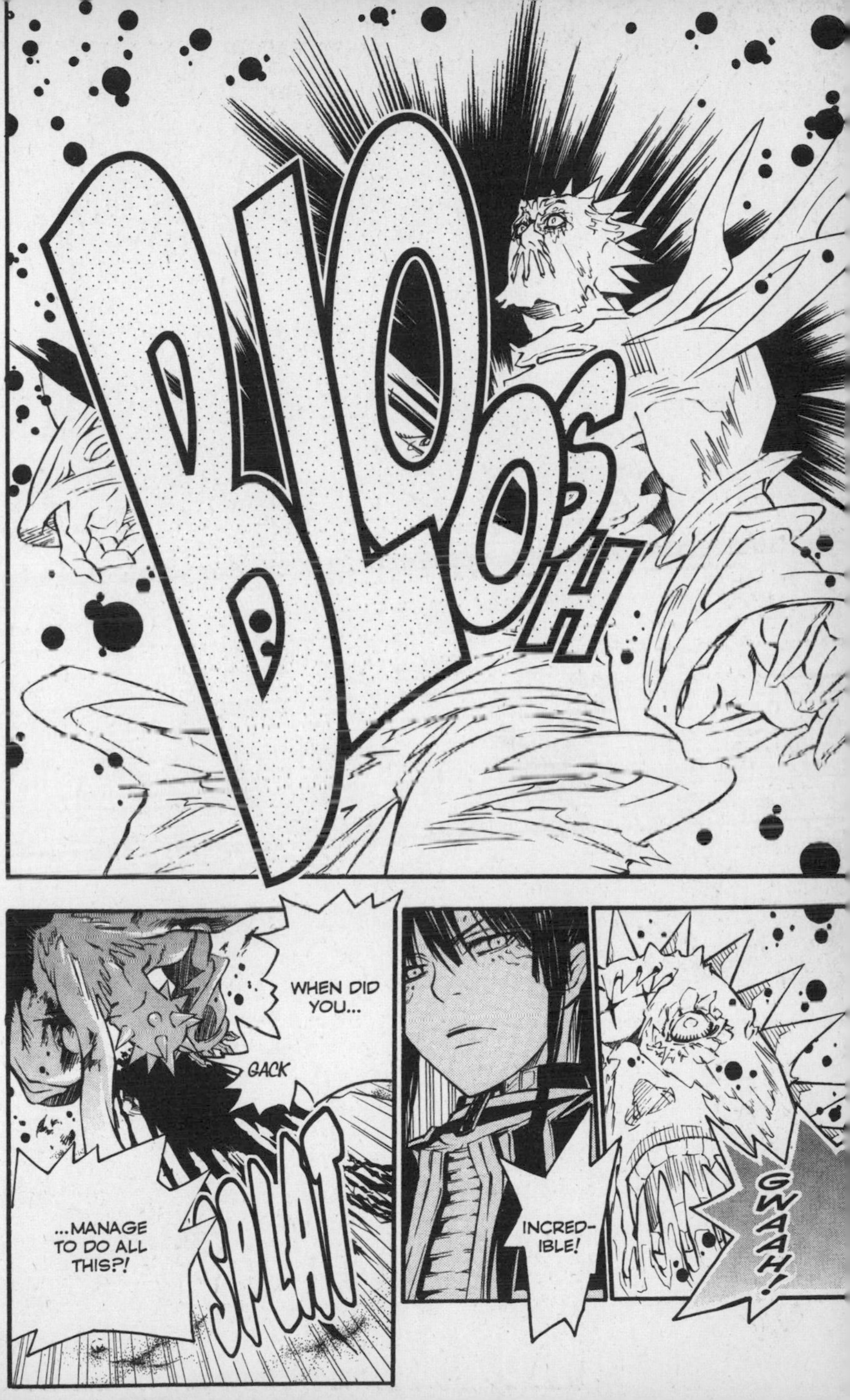
BLOOSH
GWAAH!
INCRED-
IBLE!
WHEN DID YOU...
GACK
SPLAT
...MANAGE TO DO ALL THIS?!

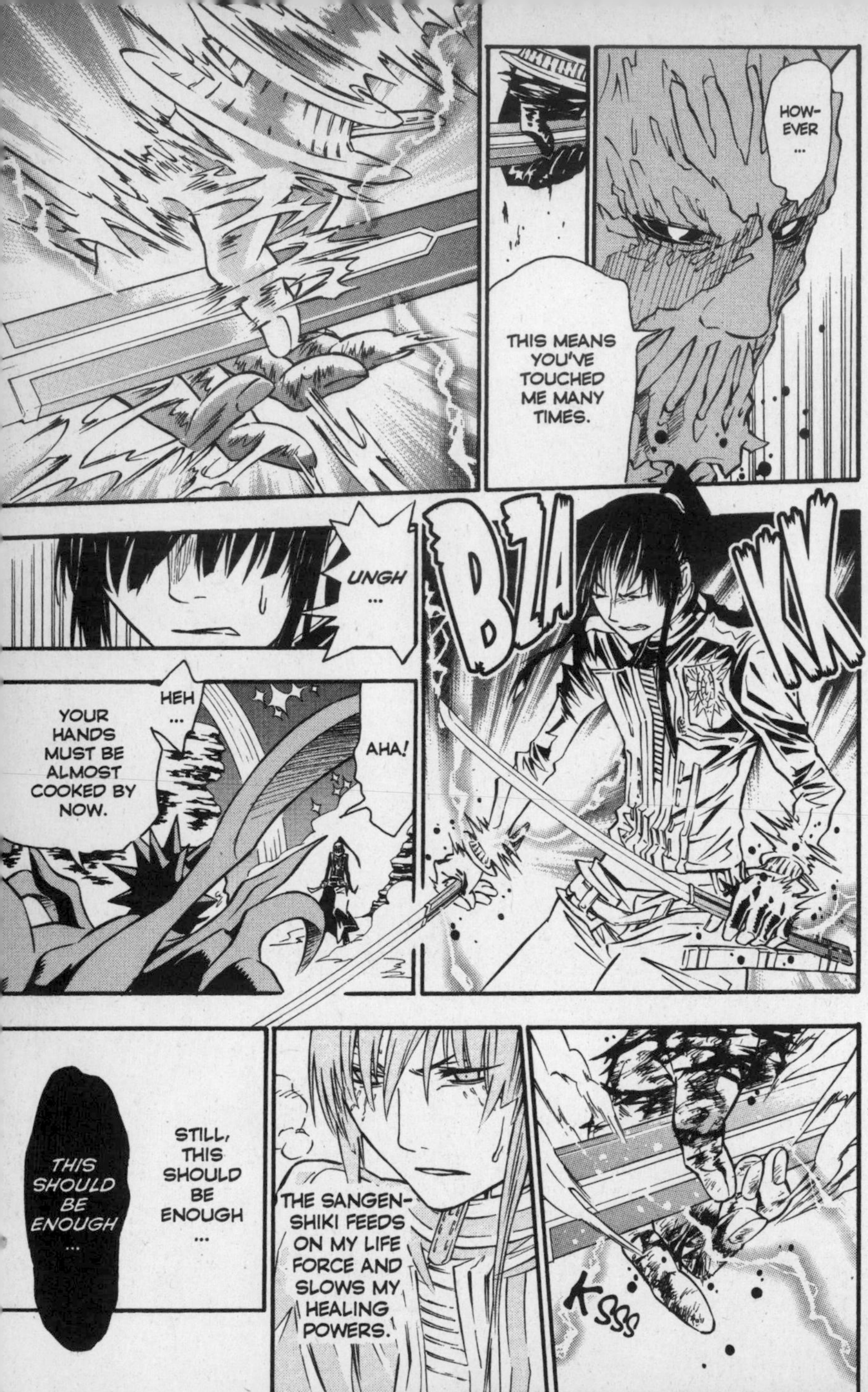
HOW-EVER ...
THIS MEANS YOU'VE TOUCHED ME MANY TIMES.
BZANK
UNGH ...
HEH ...
YOUR HANDS MUST BE ALMOST COOKED BY NOW.
AHA!
KSSS
THE SANGEN-SHIKI FEEDS ON MY LIFE FORCE AND SLOWS MY HEALING POWERS.
STILL, THIS SHOULD BE ENOUGH ...
THIS SHOULD BE ENOUGH ...

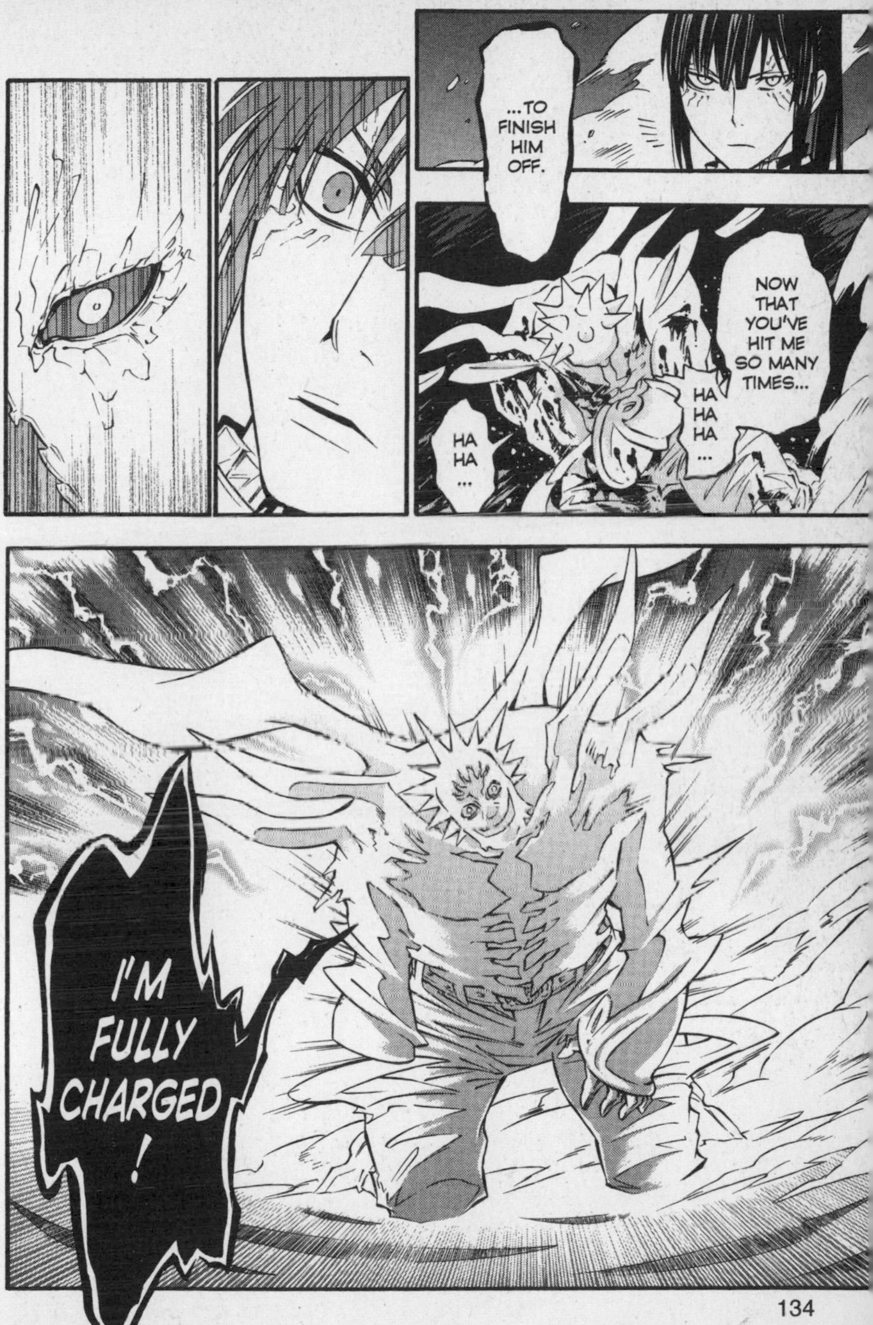
...TO FINISH HIM OFF.
NOW THAT YOU'VE HIT ME SO MANY TIMES...
HA HA HA ...
HA HA ...
I'M FULLY CHARGED!

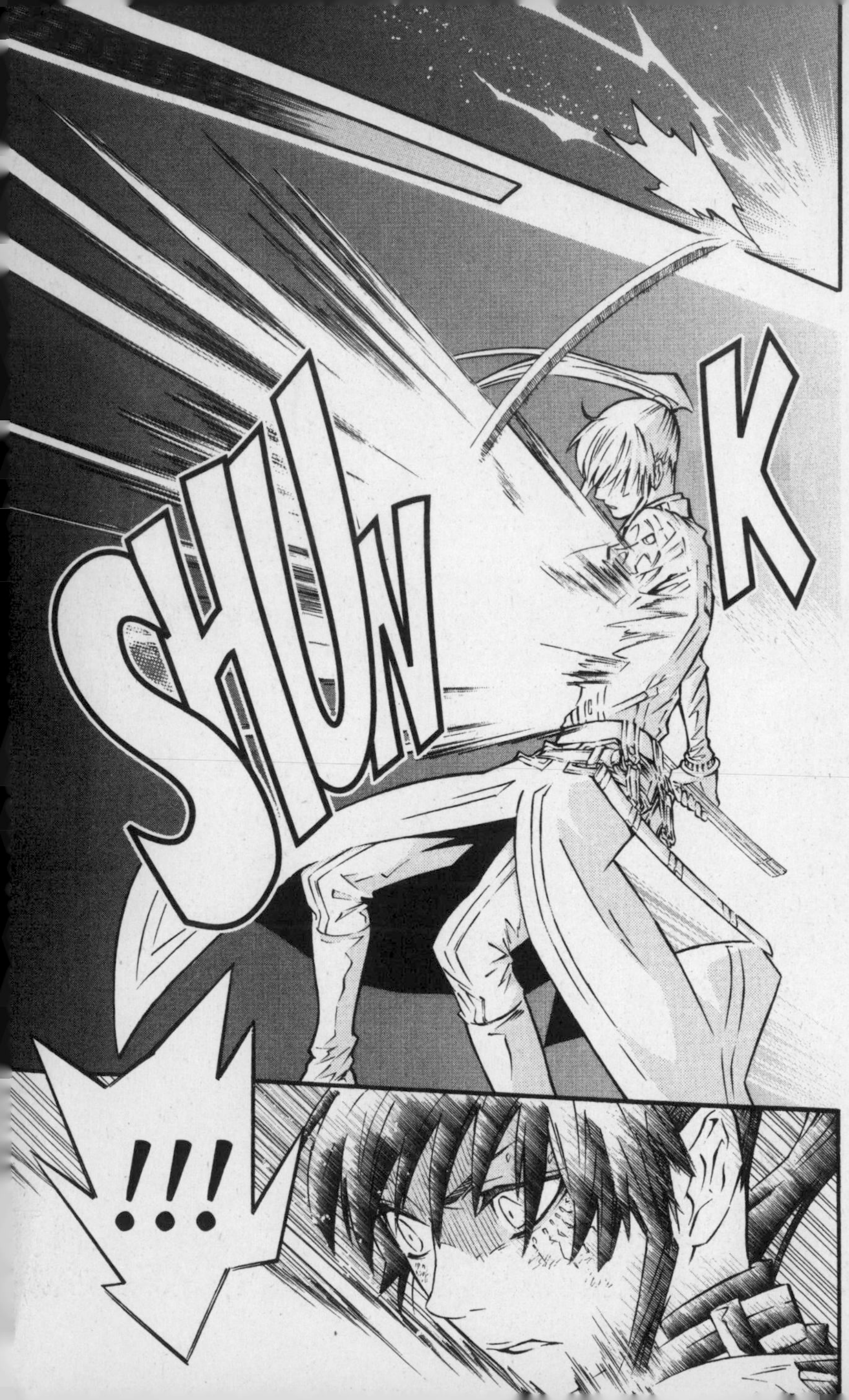
SHUNK
!!!

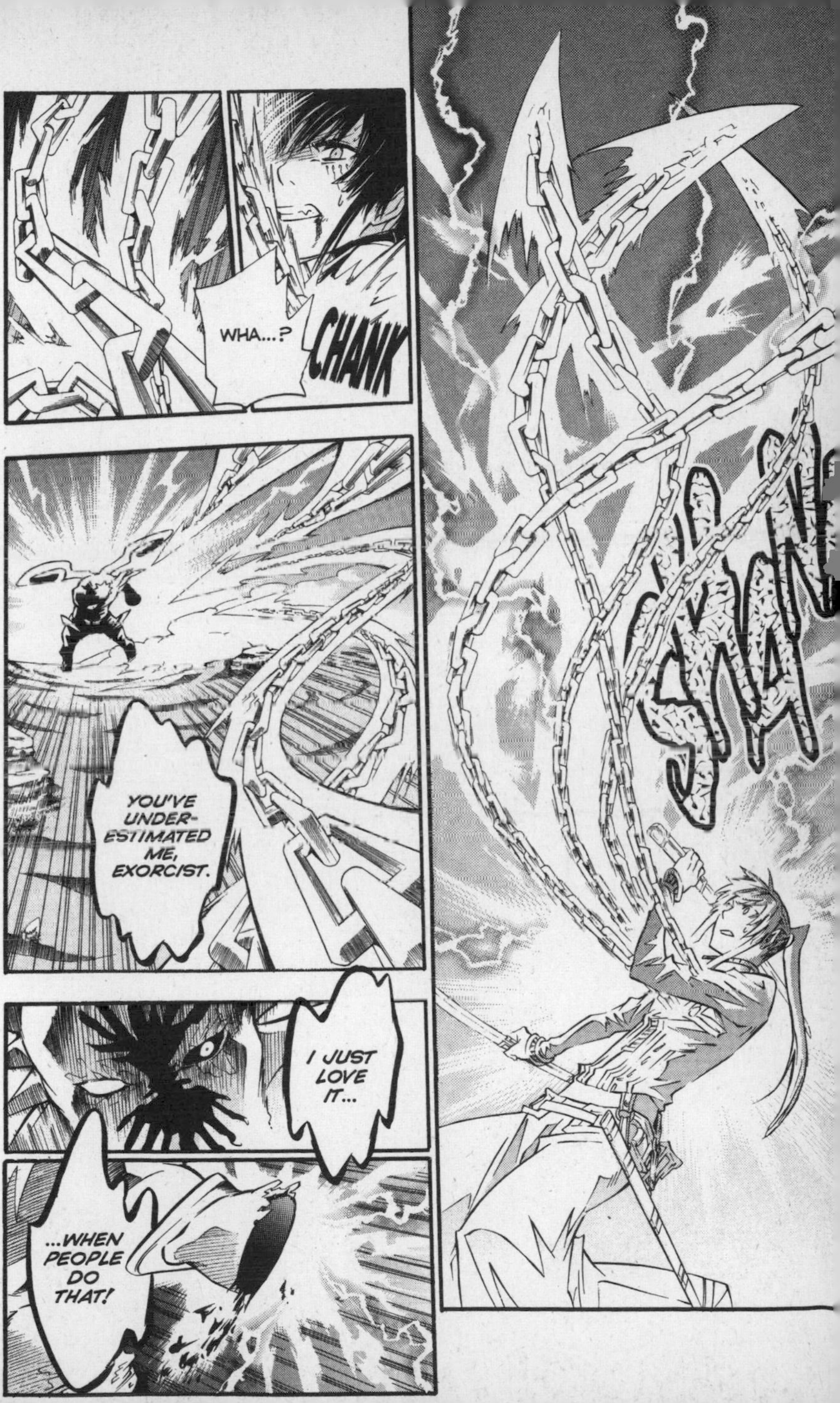

CHANK
WHA...?
YOU'VE UNDER-ESTIMATED ME, EXORCIST.
I JUST LOVE IT...
...WHEN PEOPLE DO THAT!

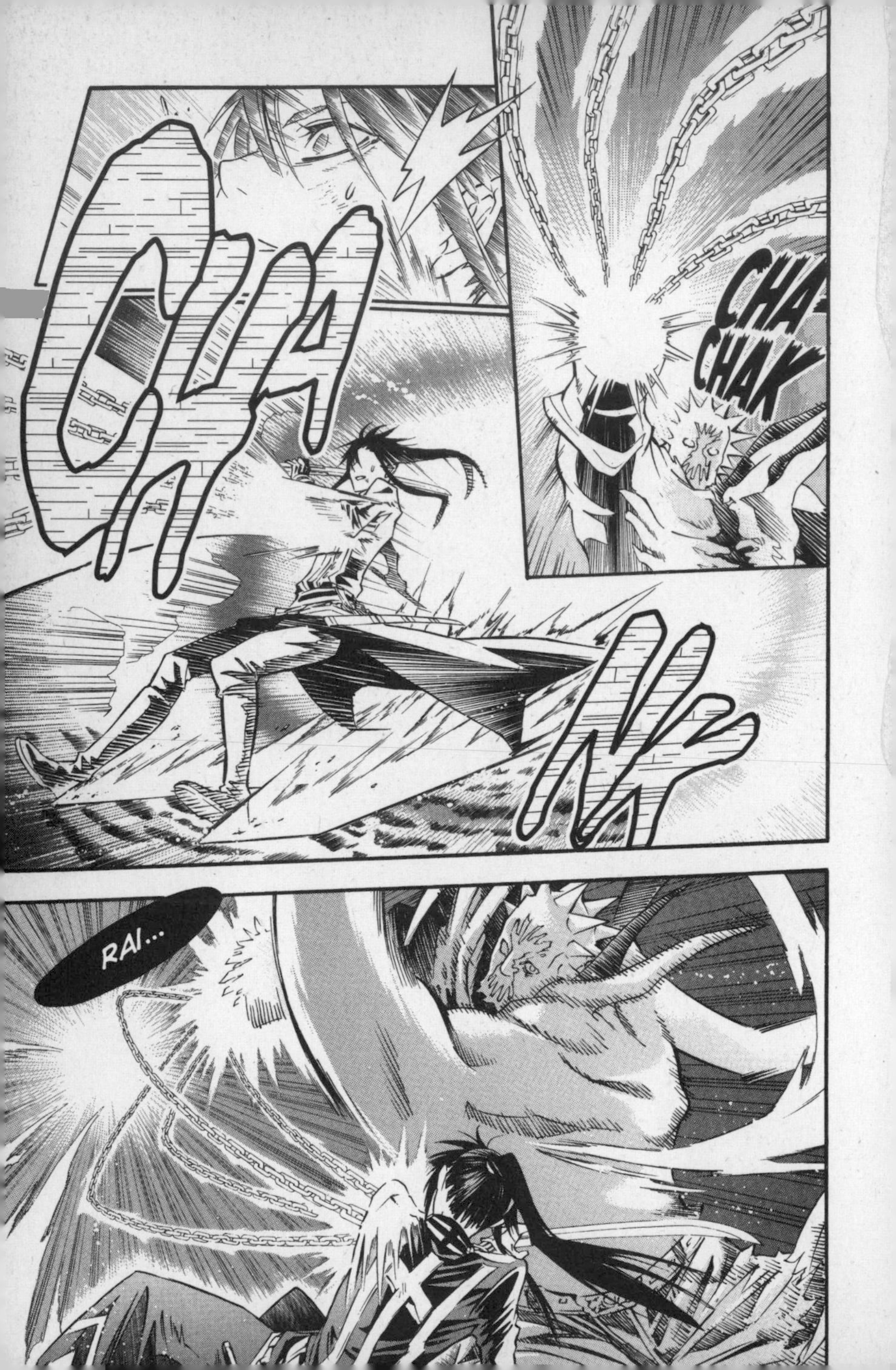
CHA-
CHAK
CHA
NK
RAI...

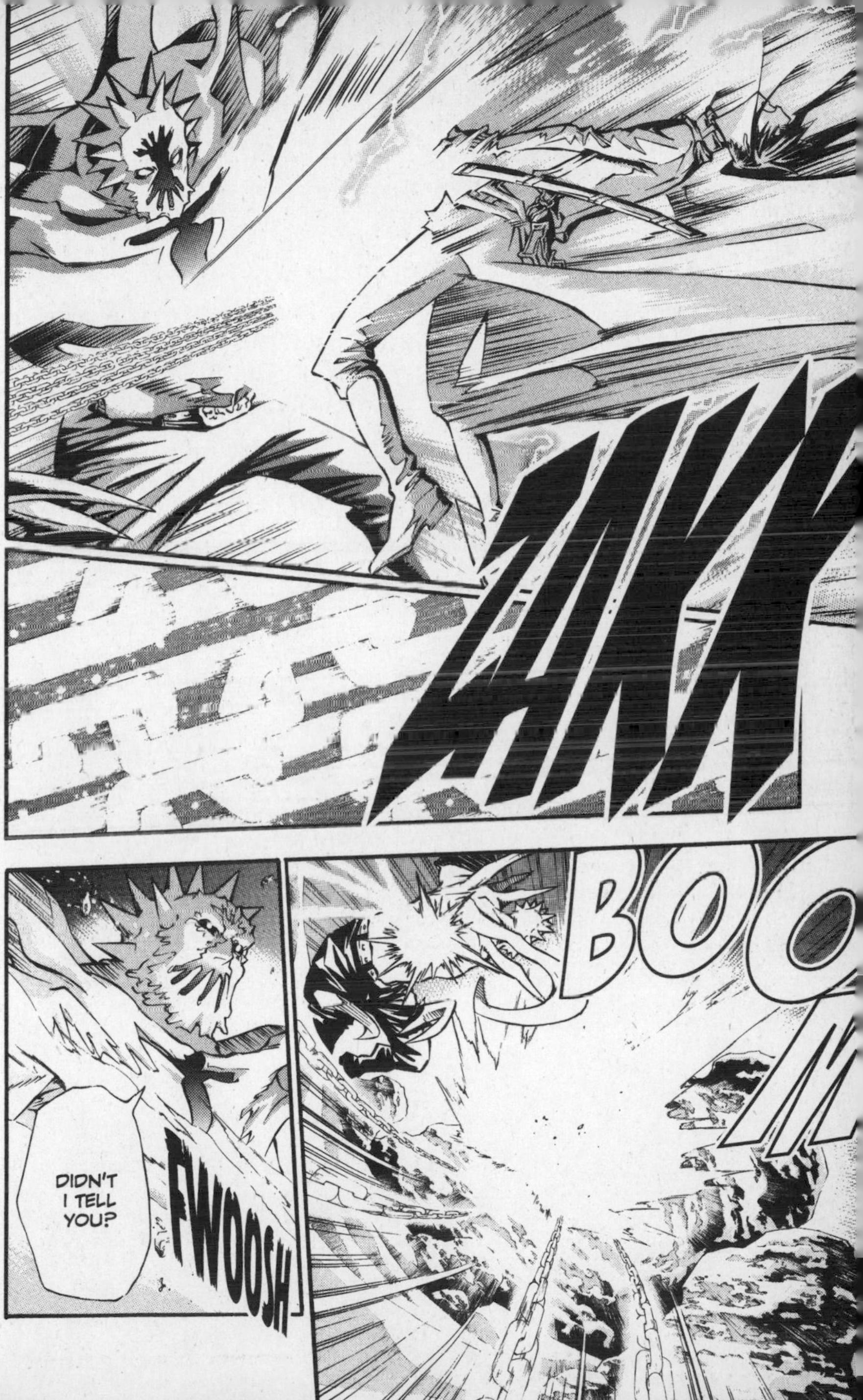
FWOOSH
DIDN'T I TELL YOU?

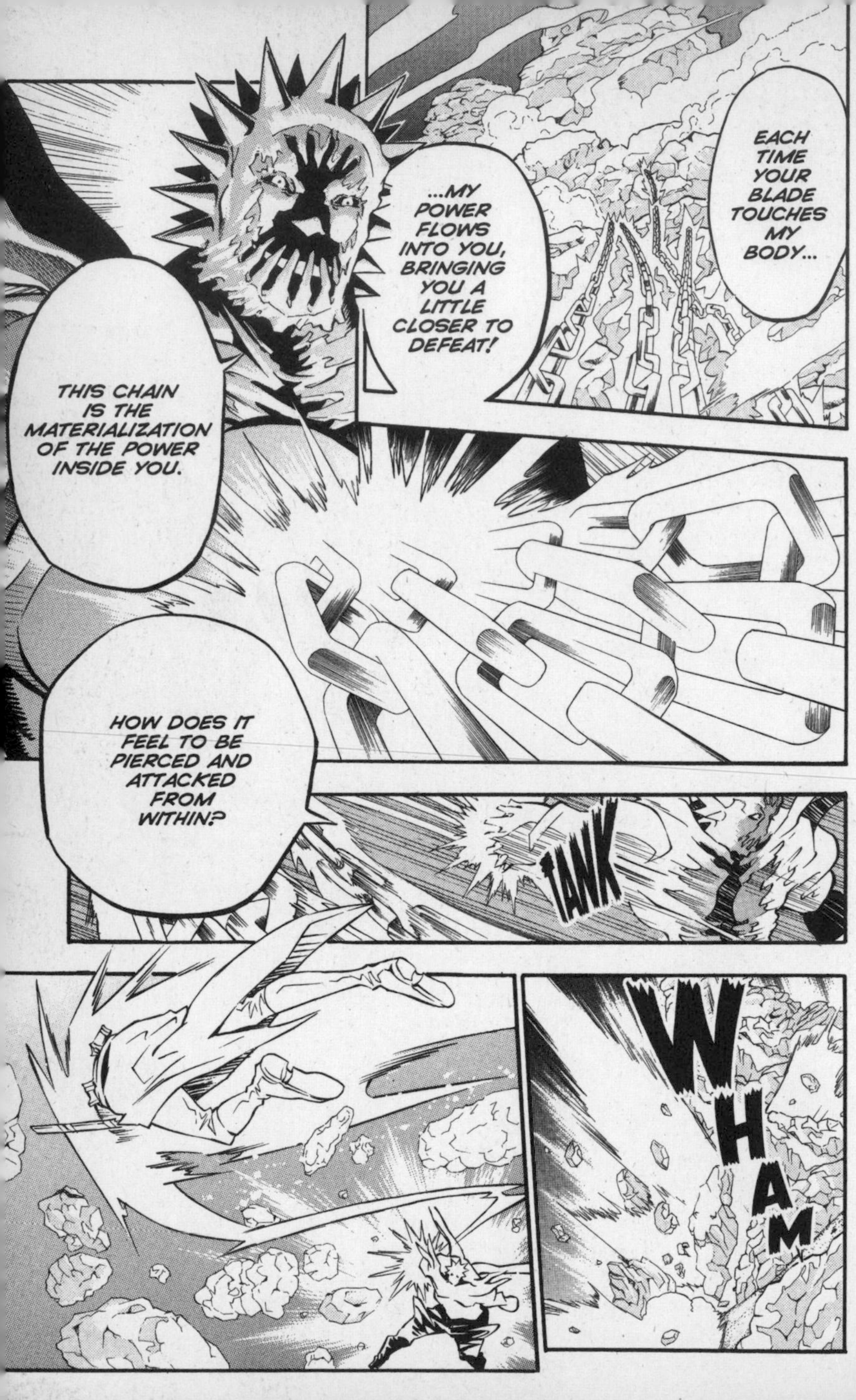
EACH TIME YOUR BLADE TOUCHES MY BODY...
...MY POWER FLOWS INTO YOU, BRINGING YOU A LITTLE CLOSER TO DEFEAT!
THIS CHAIN IS THE MATERIALIZATION OF THE POWER INSIDE YOU.
HOW DOES IT FEEL TO BE PIERCED AND ATTACKED FROM WITHIN?
TANK
WHAM

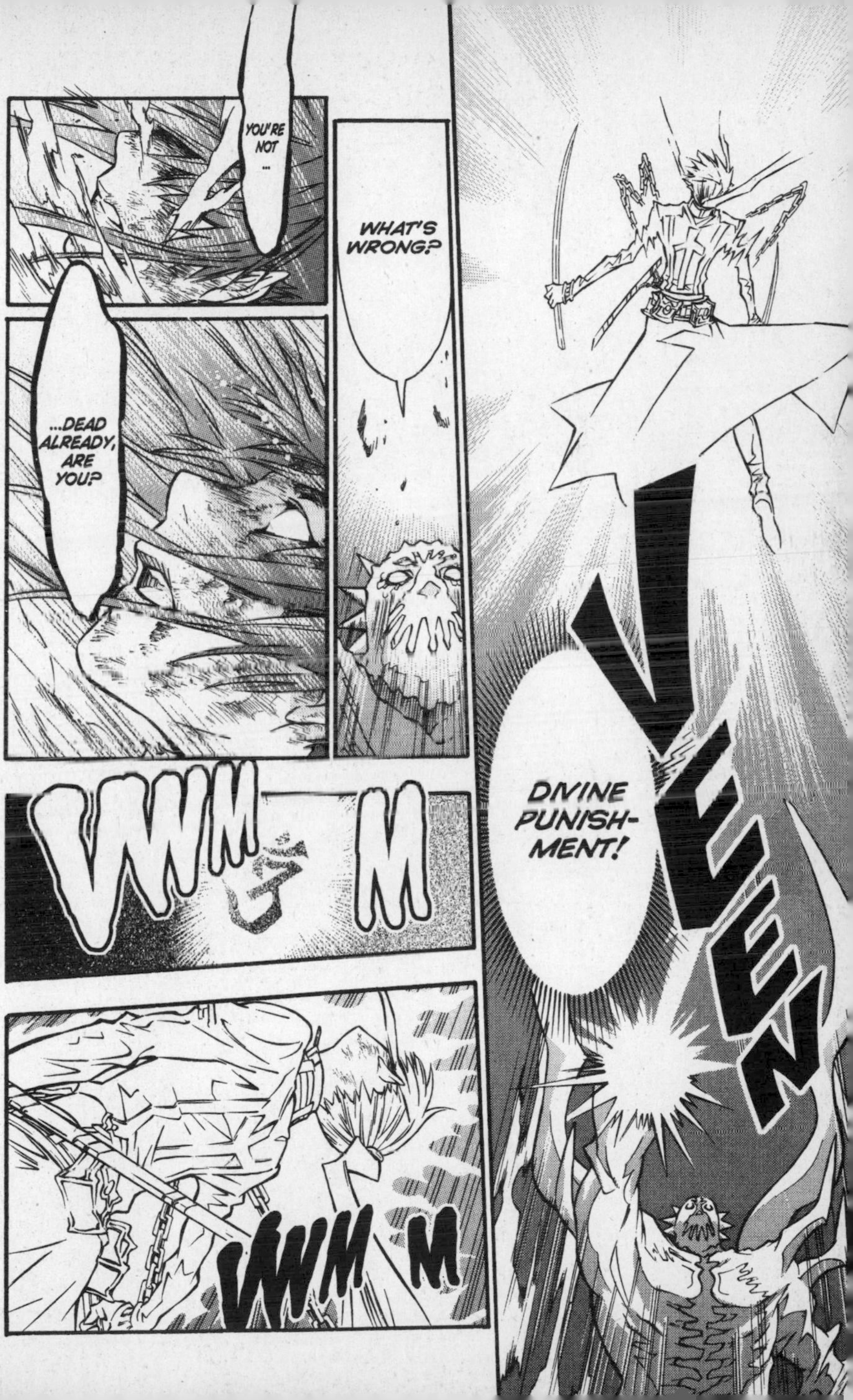
DIVINE PUNISHMENT!
WHAT'S WRONG?
YOU'RE NOT ...
...DEAD ALREADY, ARE YOU?
VWM M
VWM M

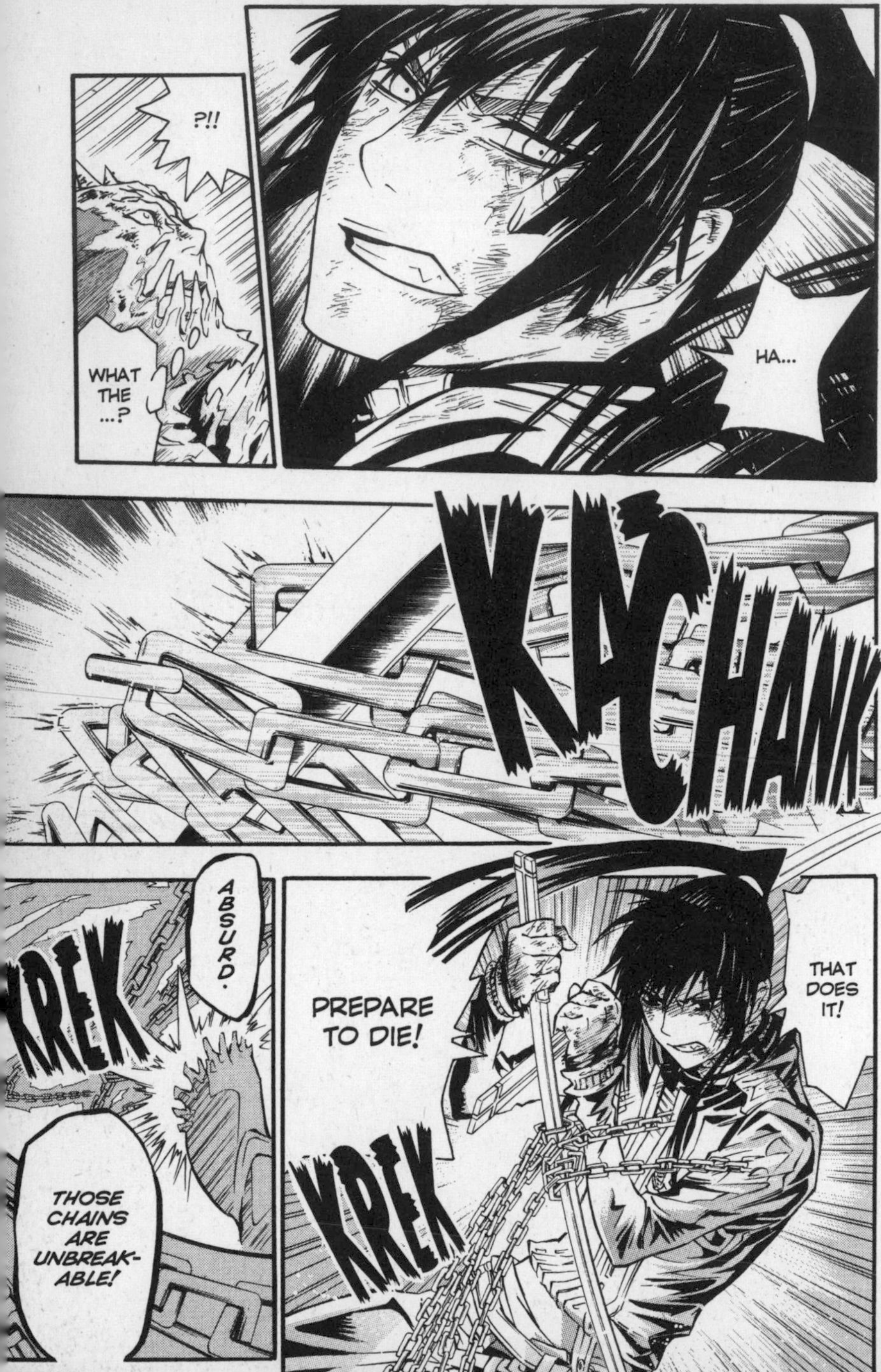
HA...
?!!
WHAT THE ...?
KACHANK
THAT DOES IT!
PREPARE TO DIE!
KREK
ABSURD.
KREK
THOSE CHAINS ARE UNBREAK-ABLE!

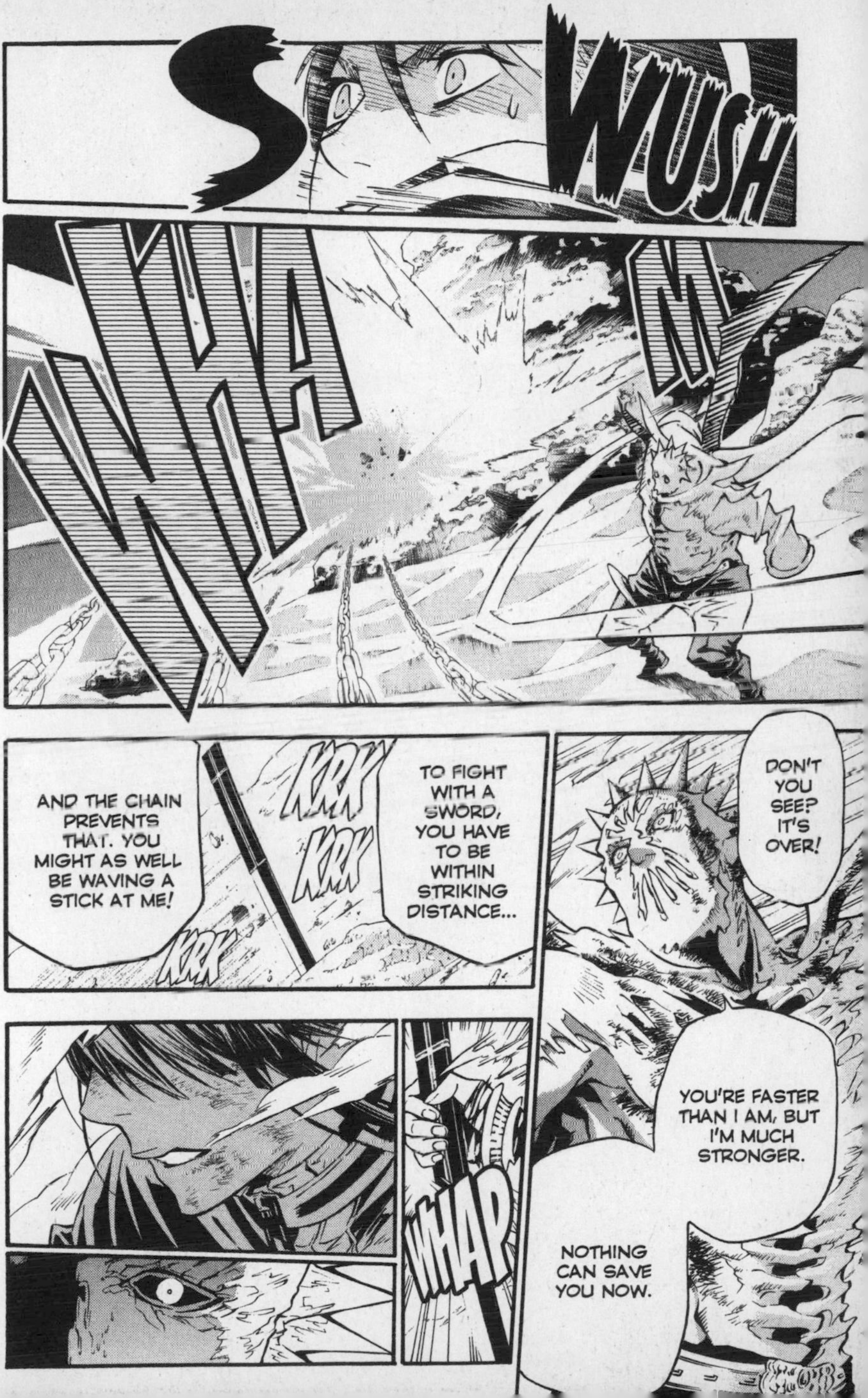
SWUSH
WHAM
DON'T YOU SEE? IT'S OVER!
YOU'RE FASTER THAN I AM, BUT I'M MUCH STRONGER.
NOTHING CAN SAVE YOU NOW.
TO FIGHT WITH A SWORD, YOU HAVE TO BE WITHIN STRIKING DISTANCE...
KRK
KRK
AND THE CHAIN PREVENTS THAT. YOU MIGHT AS WELL BE WAVING A STICK AT ME!
KRK
WHAP

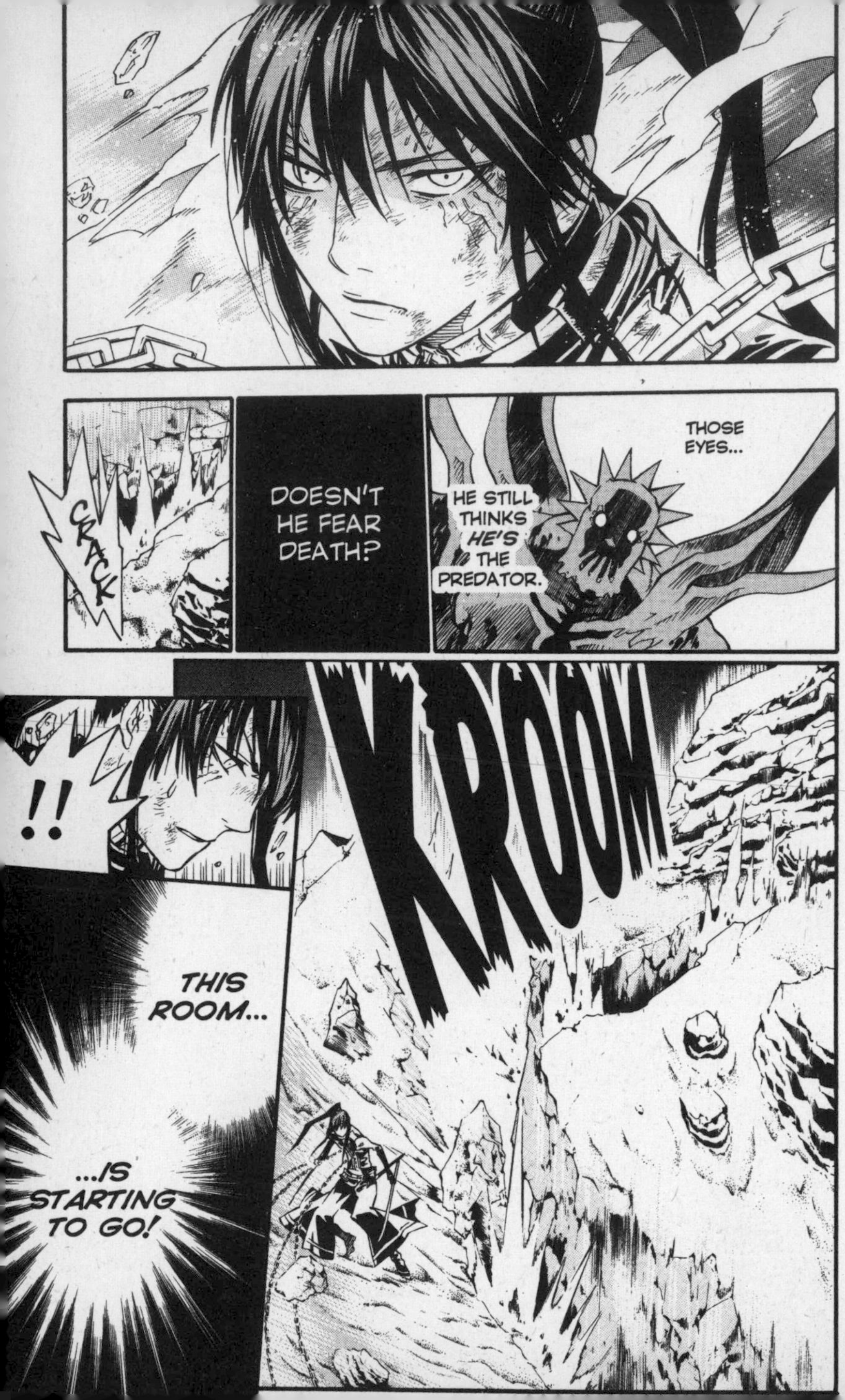
THOSE EYES...
HE STILL THINKS *HE'S* THE PREDATOR.
DOESN'T HE FEAR DEATH?
CRACK
KROOM
!!
THIS ROOM...
...IS STARTING TO GO!

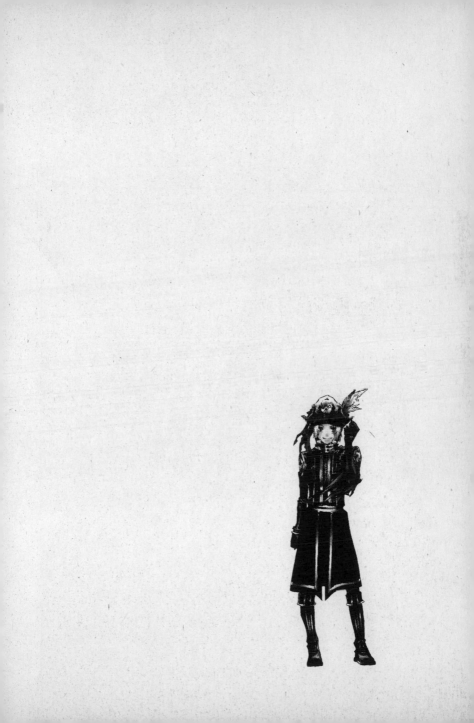

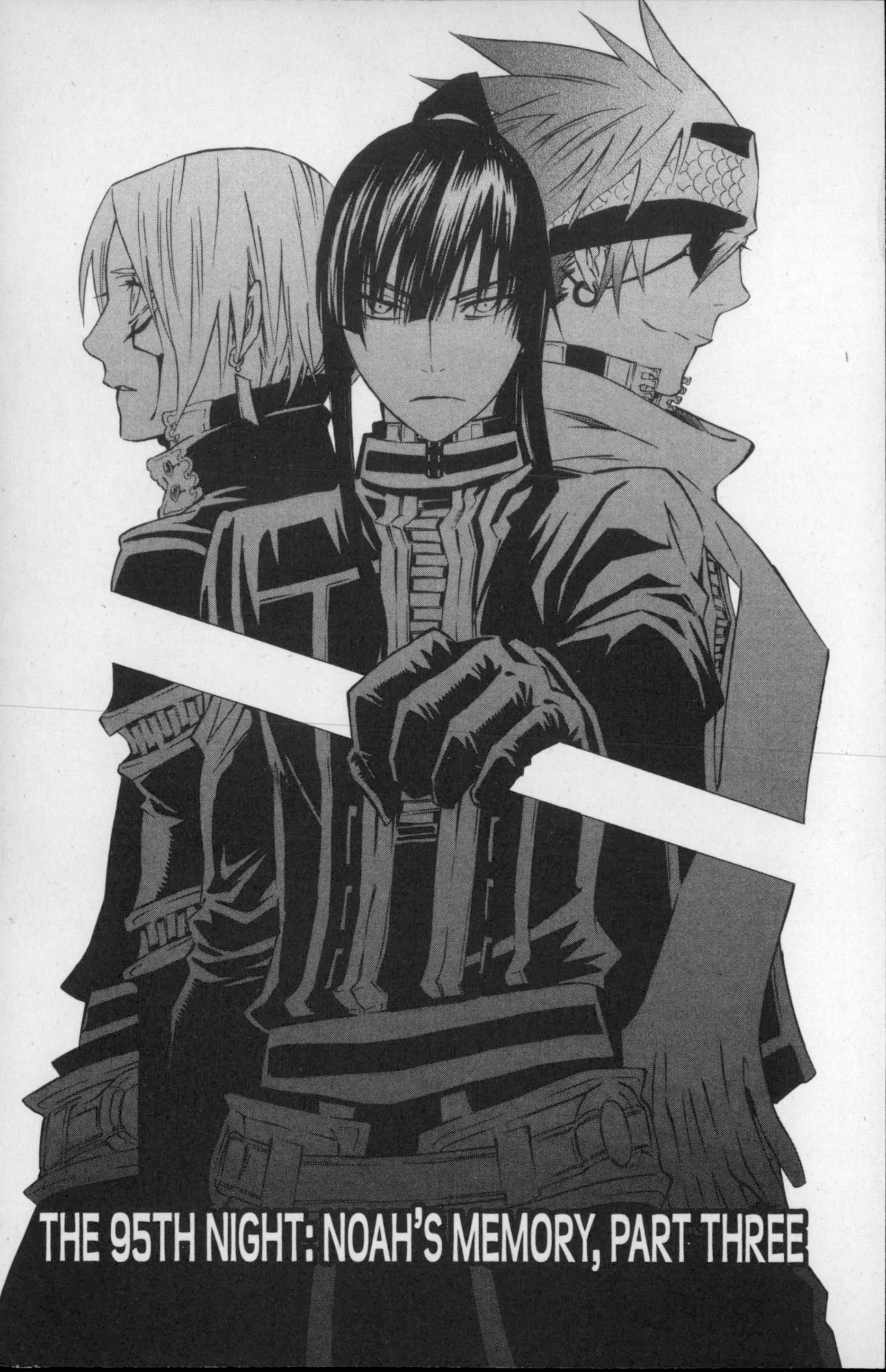

THE 95TH NIGHT: NOAH'S MEMORY, PART THREE

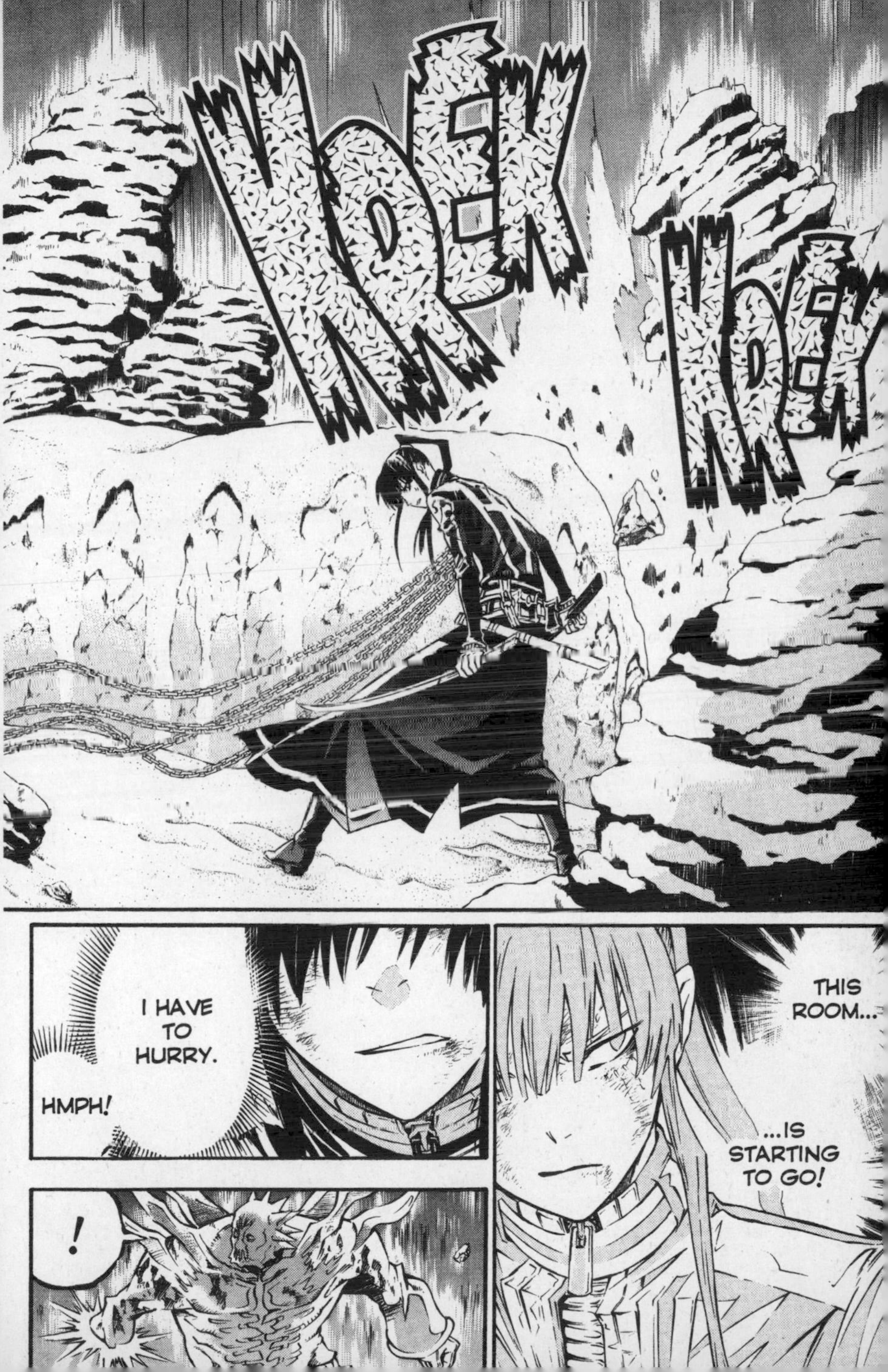
THIS ROOM...
...IS STARTING TO GO!
I HAVE TO HURRY.
HMPH!
!

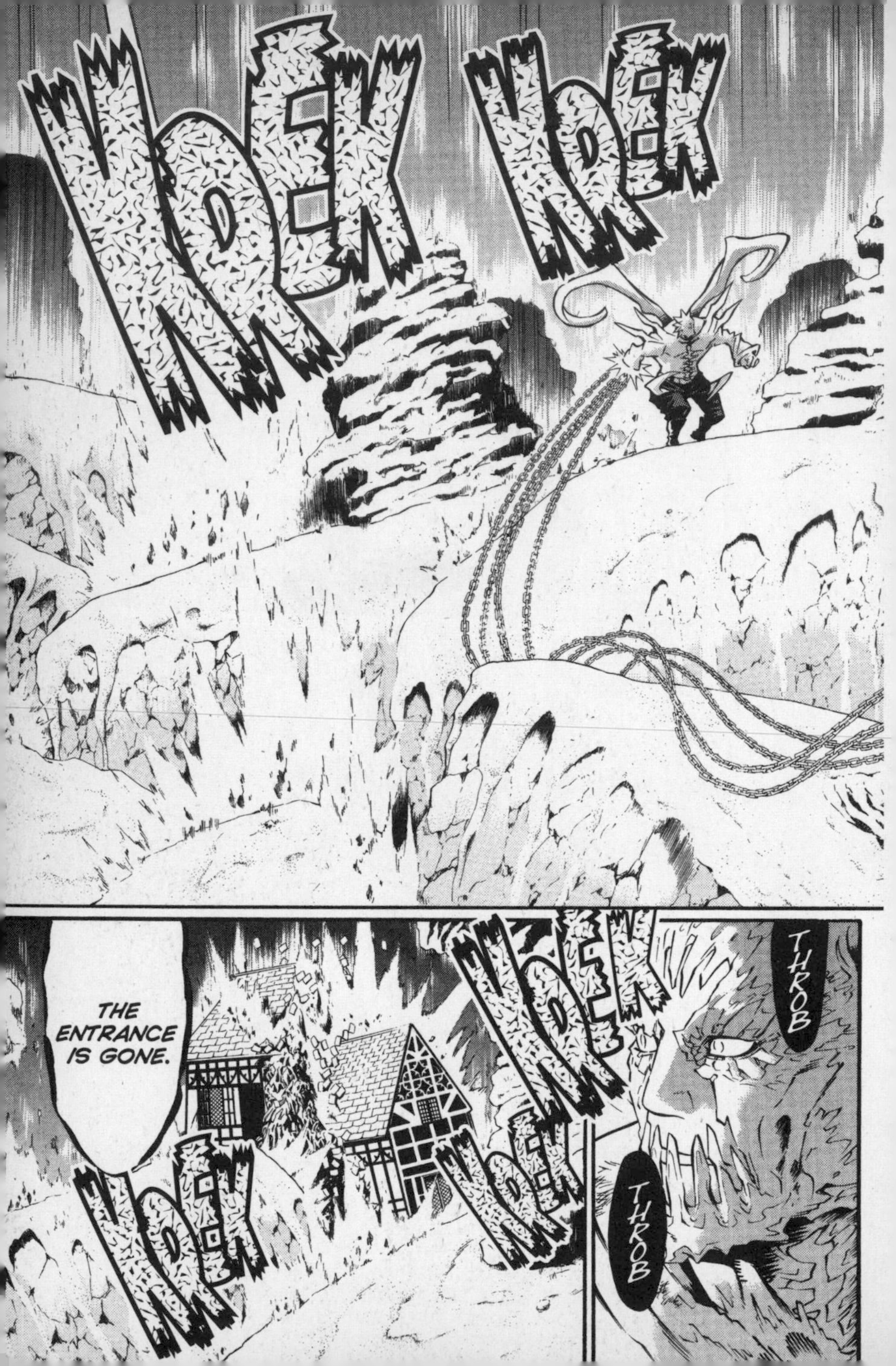
THROB
THROB
THE ENTRANCE IS GONE.

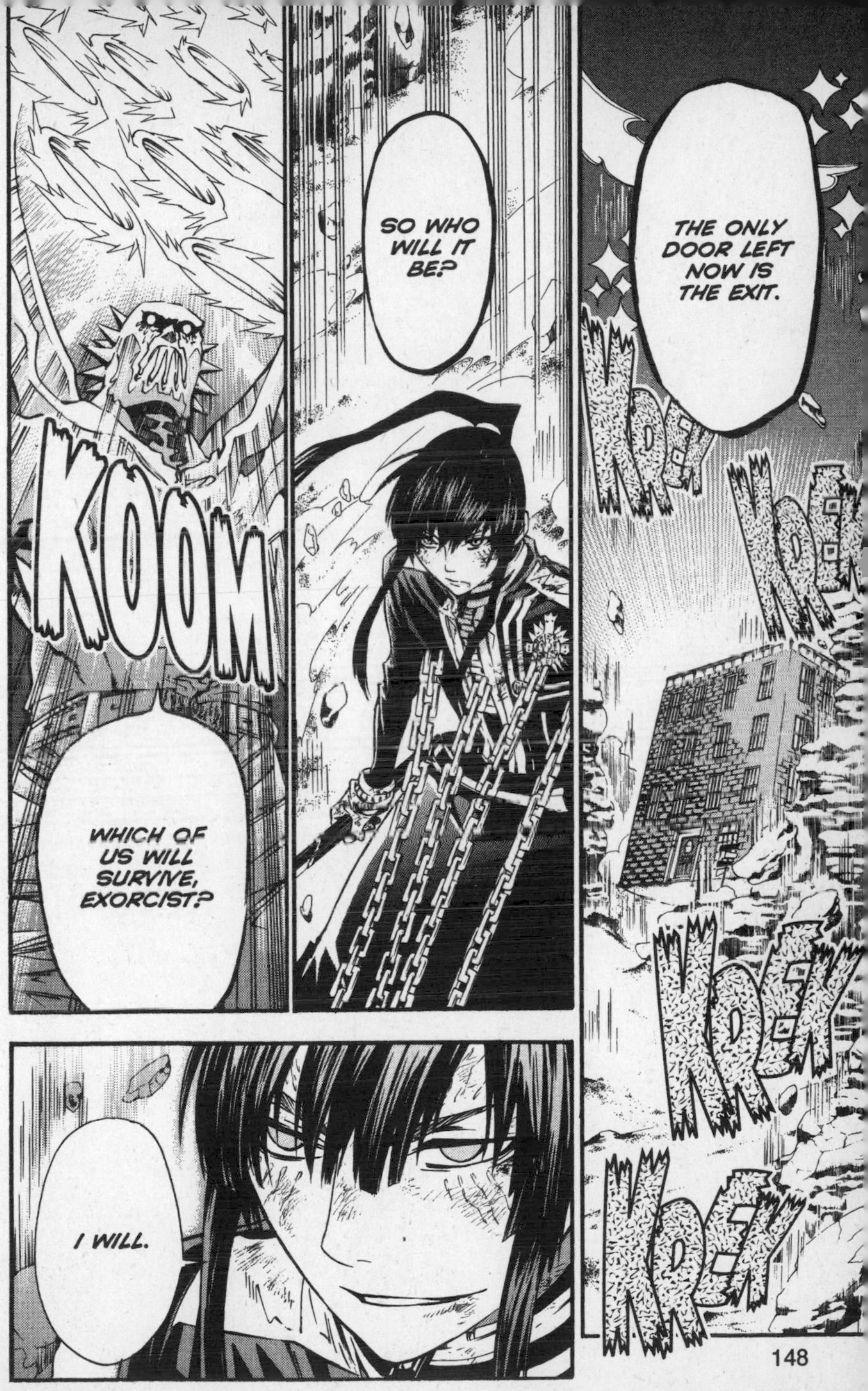
THE ONLY DOOR LEFT NOW IS THE EXIT.
KRAK
KRAK
KRAK
KRAK
SO WHO WILL IT BE?
KOOM
WHICH OF US WILL SURVIVE, EXORCIST?
I WILL.

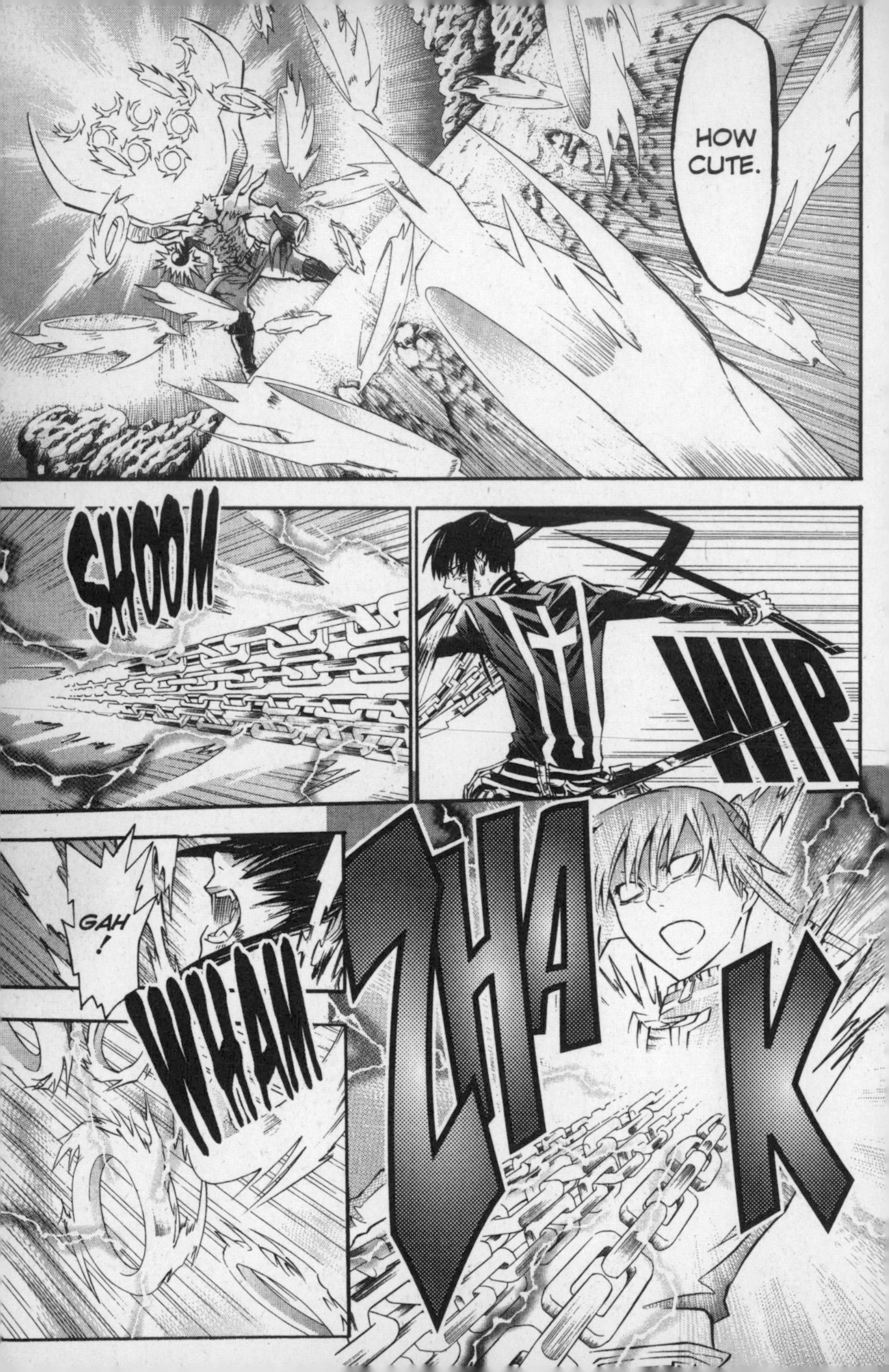
HOW CUTE.
WIP
SHOOM
ZHAK
GAH!
WHAM

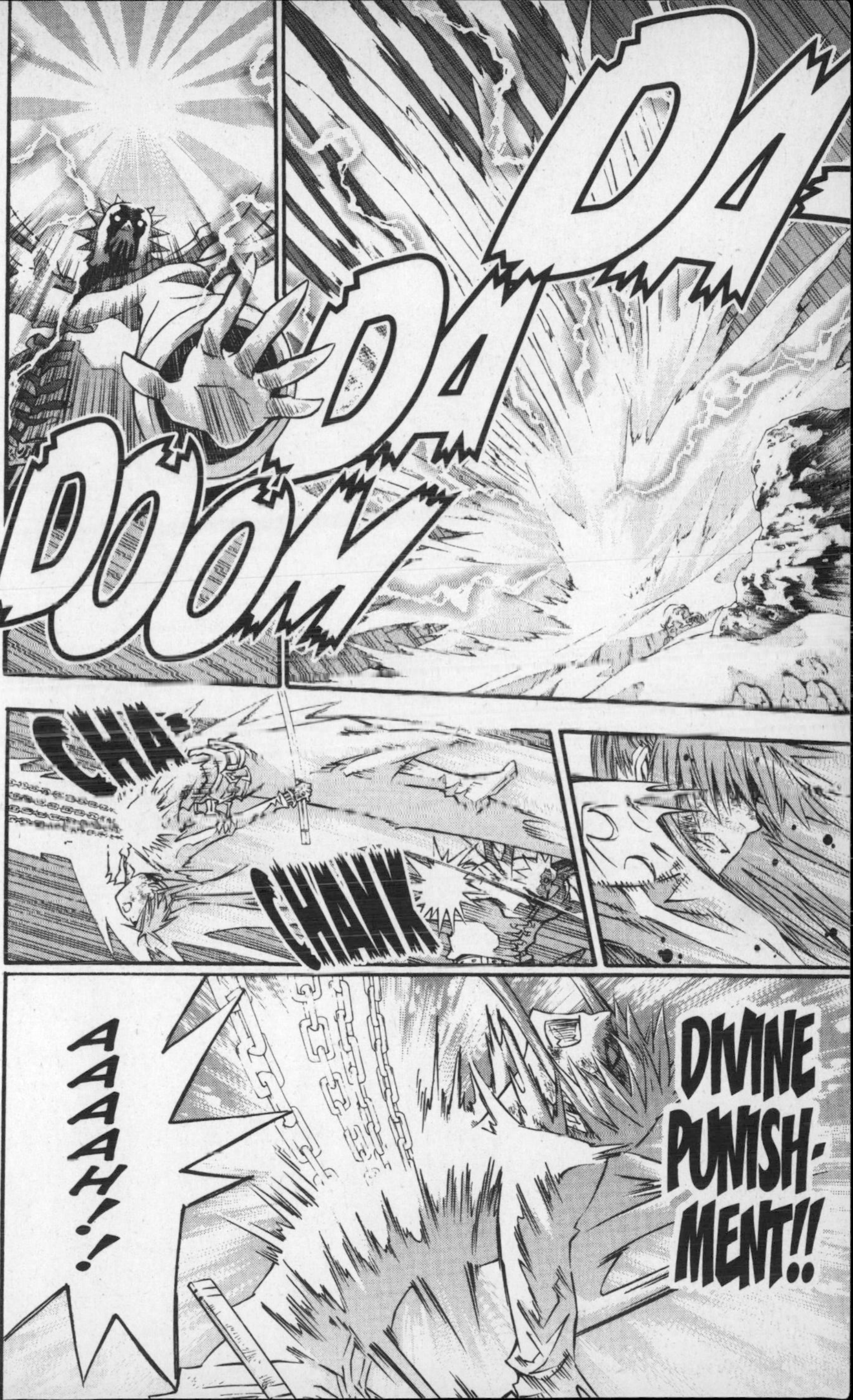
DA
DA
DOOM
CHA
CHANK
DIVINE PUNISH-MENT!!
AAAAH!!

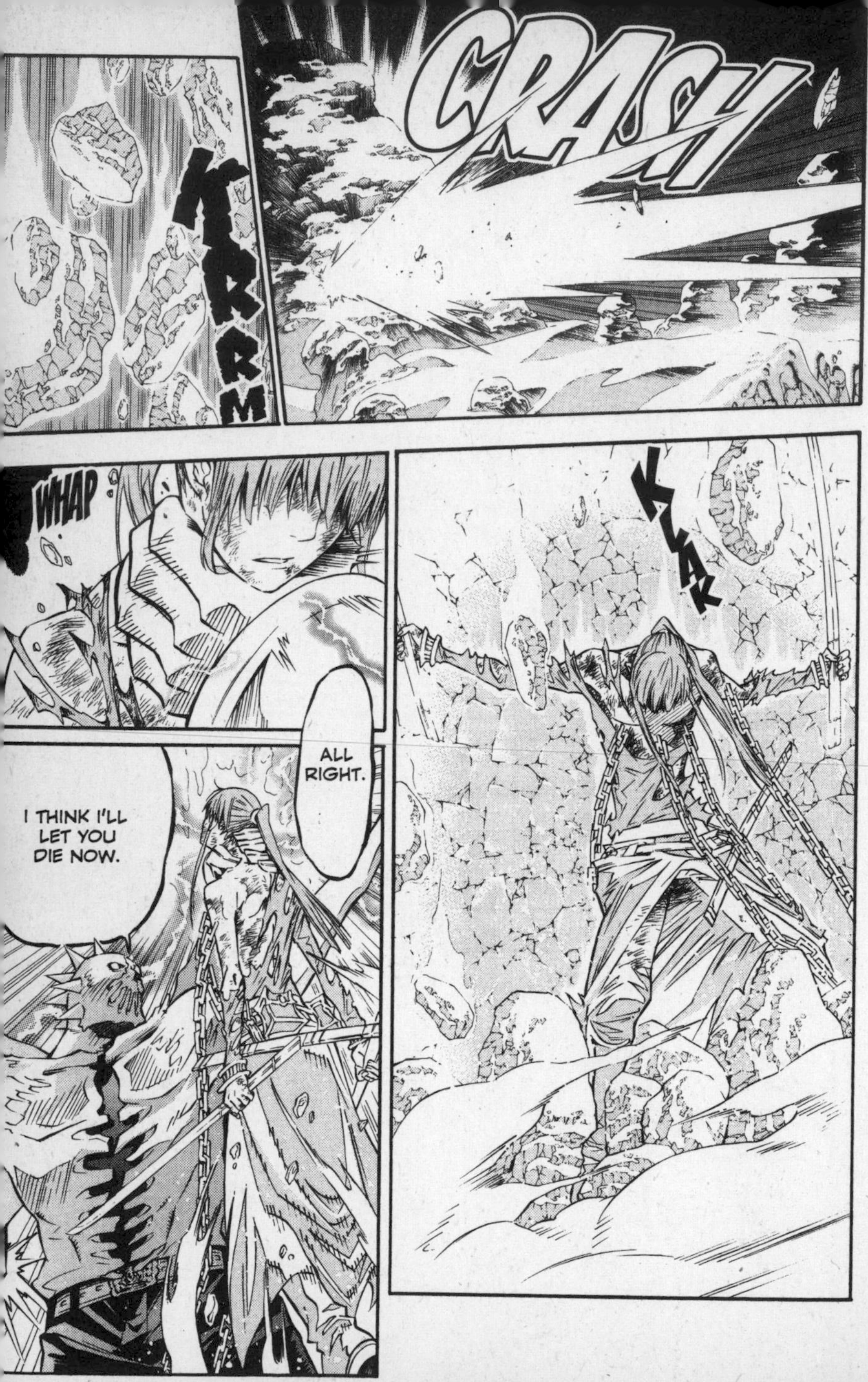
CRASH
KRRM
KWAR
WHAP
ALL RIGHT.
I THINK I'LL LET YOU DIE NOW.

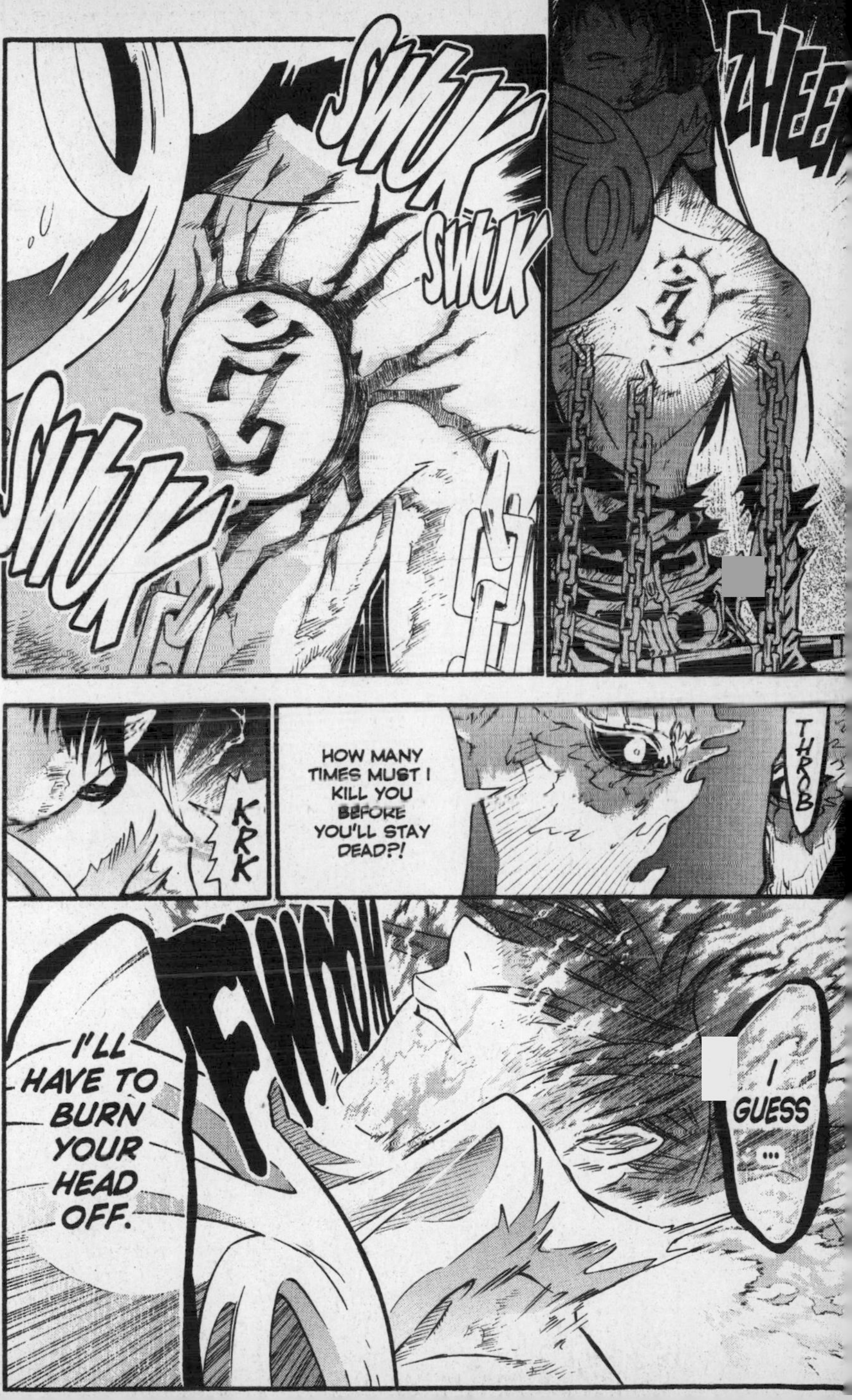
ZHEE
SWUK
SWUK
SWUK
THROB
HOW MANY TIMES MUST I KILL YOU BEFORE YOU'LL STAY DEAD?!
KRK
I GUESS ...
FWOOM
I'LL HAVE TO BURN YOUR HEAD OFF.

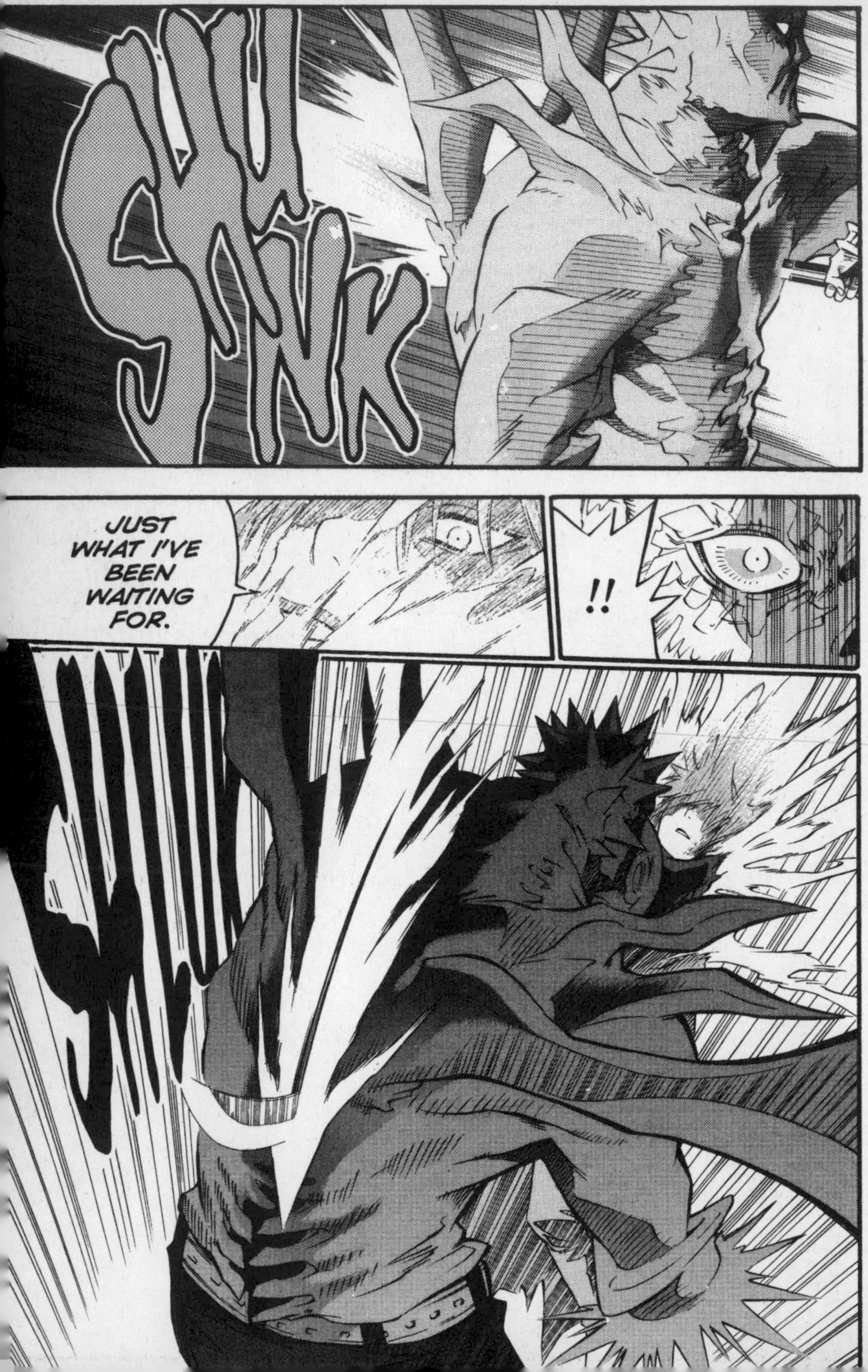
SHINK
!!
JUST WHAT I'VE BEEN WAITING FOR.

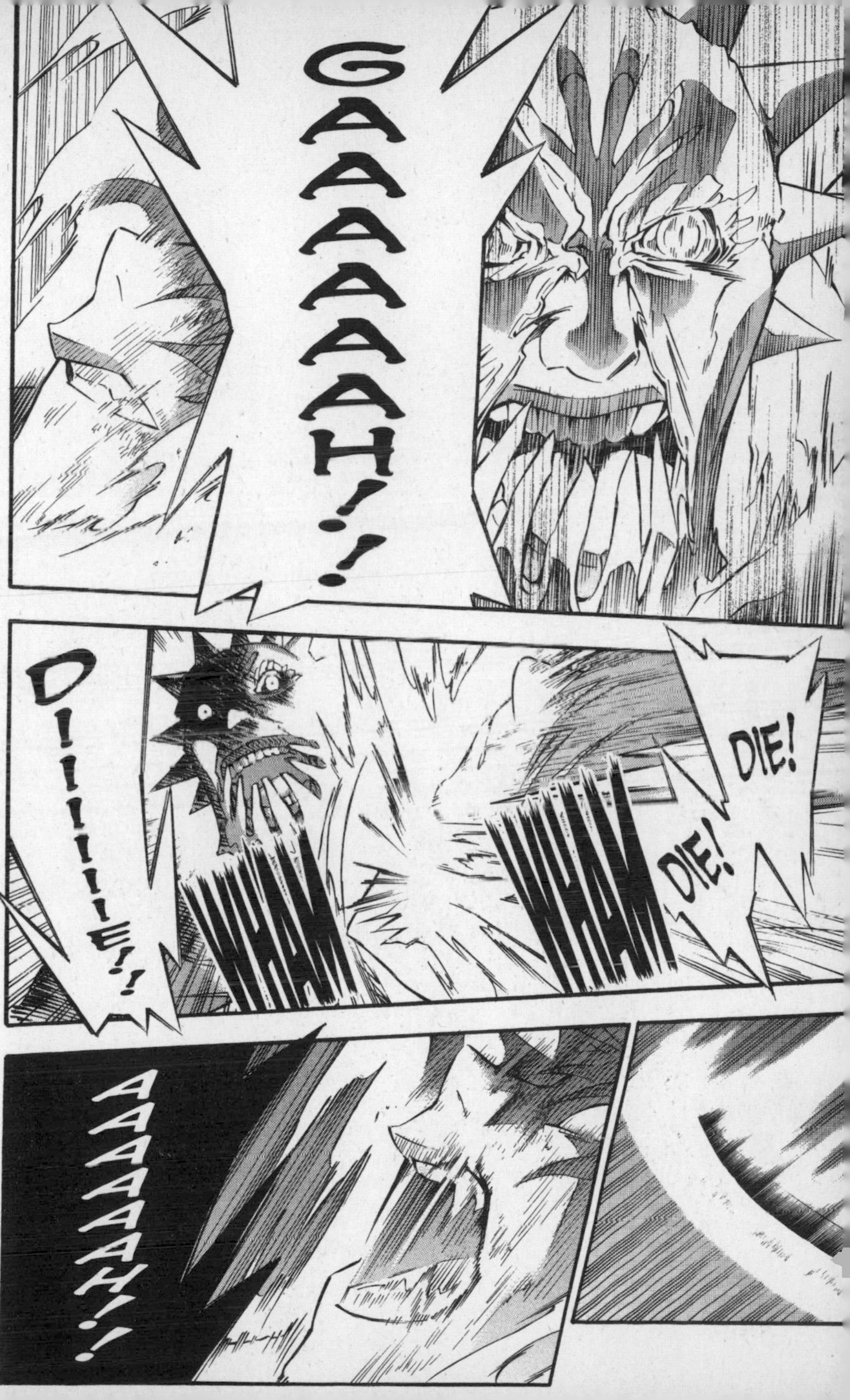
GAAAAAH!!
DIE!
DIE!
WHAM
WHAM
DIIIIIIE!!
AAAAAAH!!

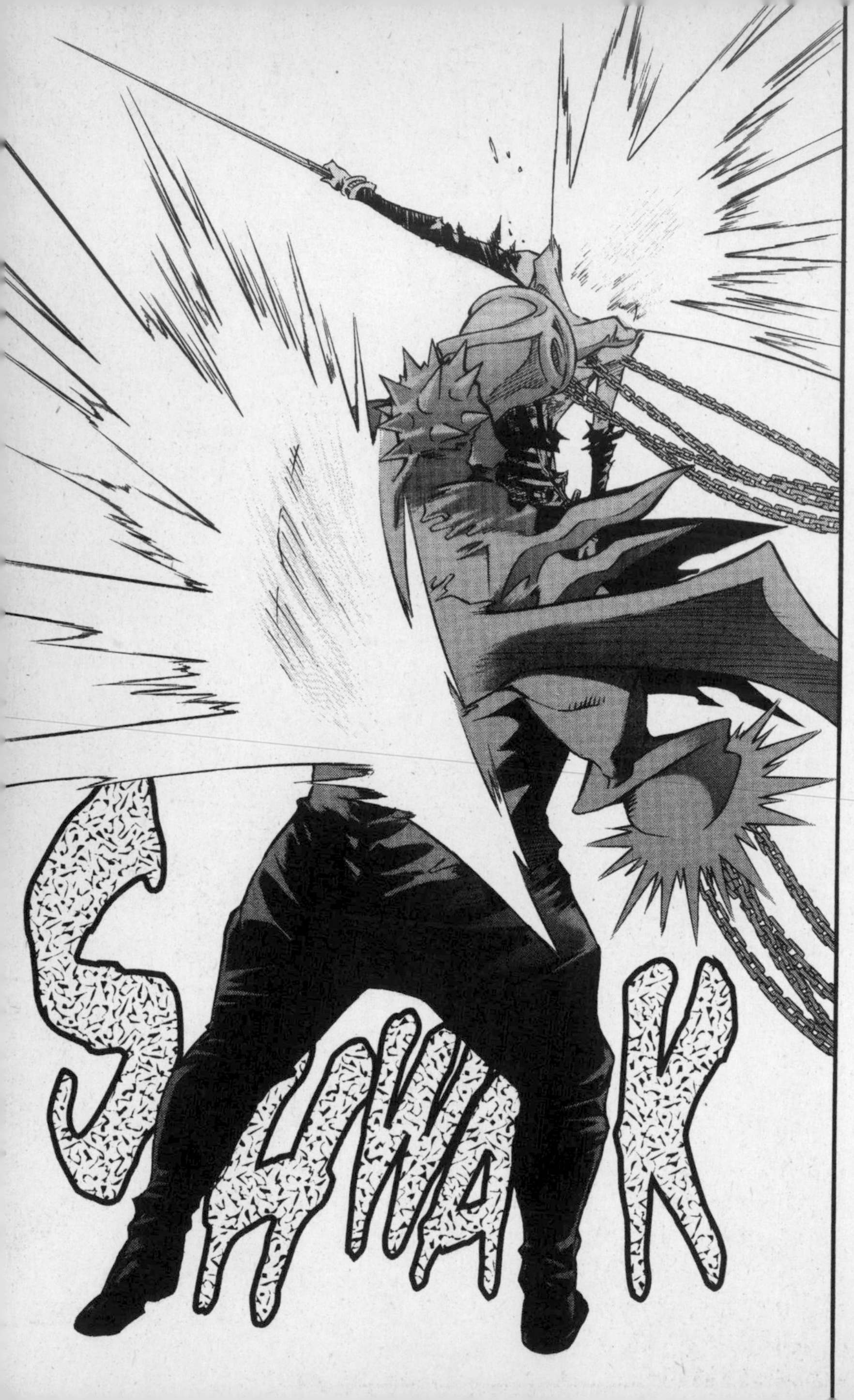
SMAK

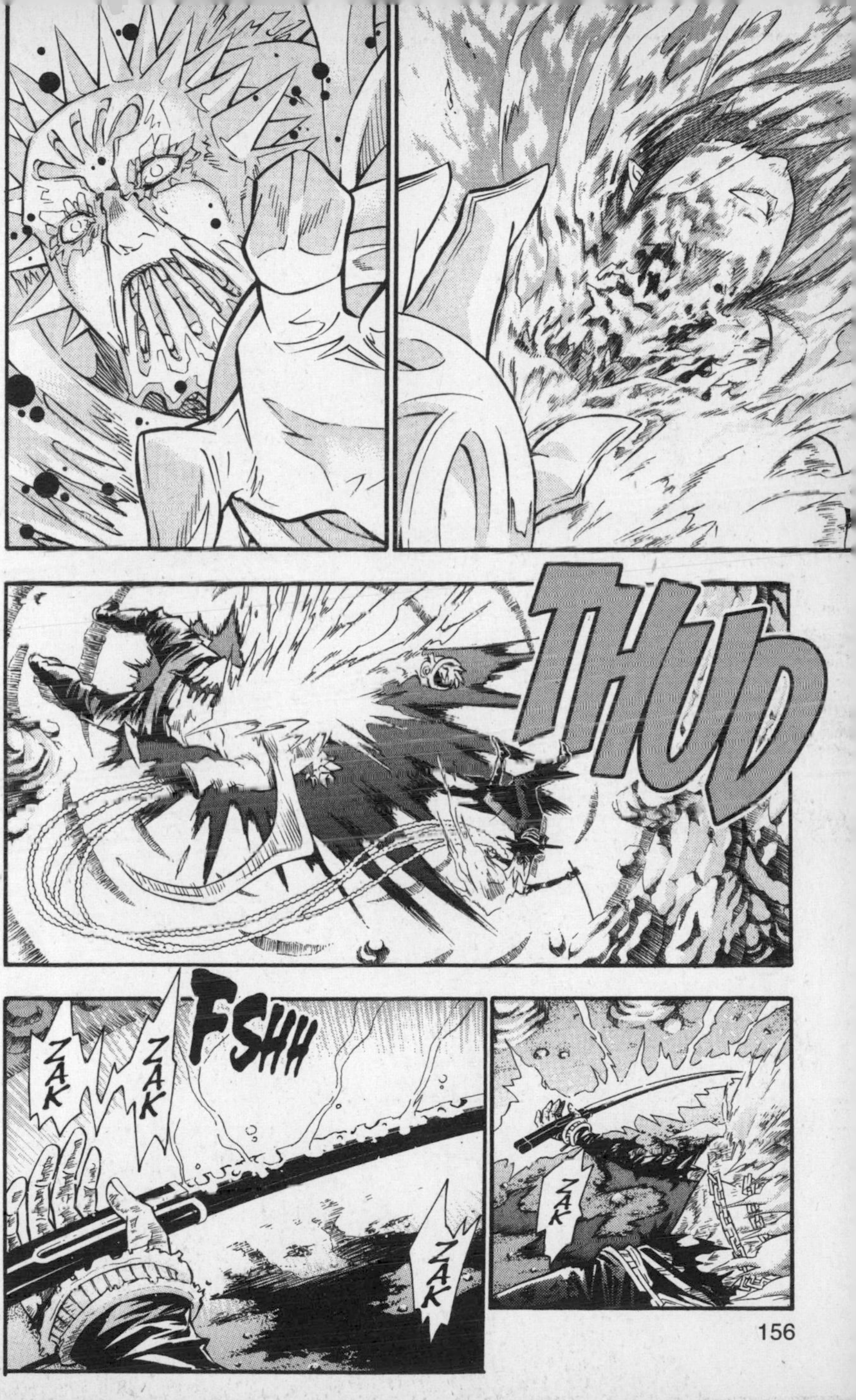
THUD
ZAK
FSHH
ZAK
ZAK
ZAK

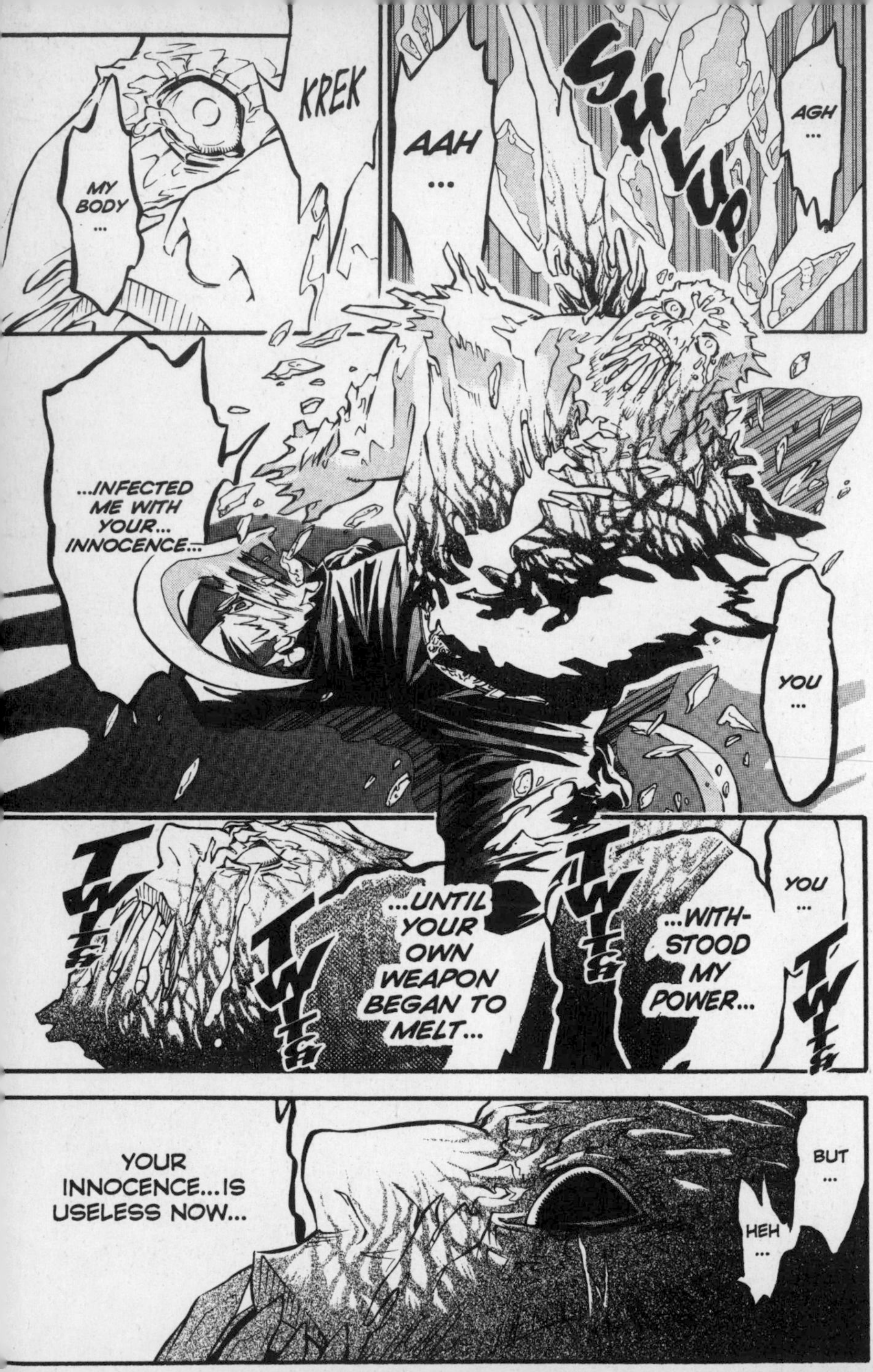
AGH ...
SHLUP
AAH ...
KREK
MY BODY ...
YOU ...
...INFECTED ME WITH YOUR... INNOCENCE...
YOU ...
...WITH-STOOD MY POWER...
...UNTIL YOUR OWN WEAPON BEGAN TO MELT...
BUT ...
HEH ...
YOUR INNOCENCE...IS USELESS NOW...

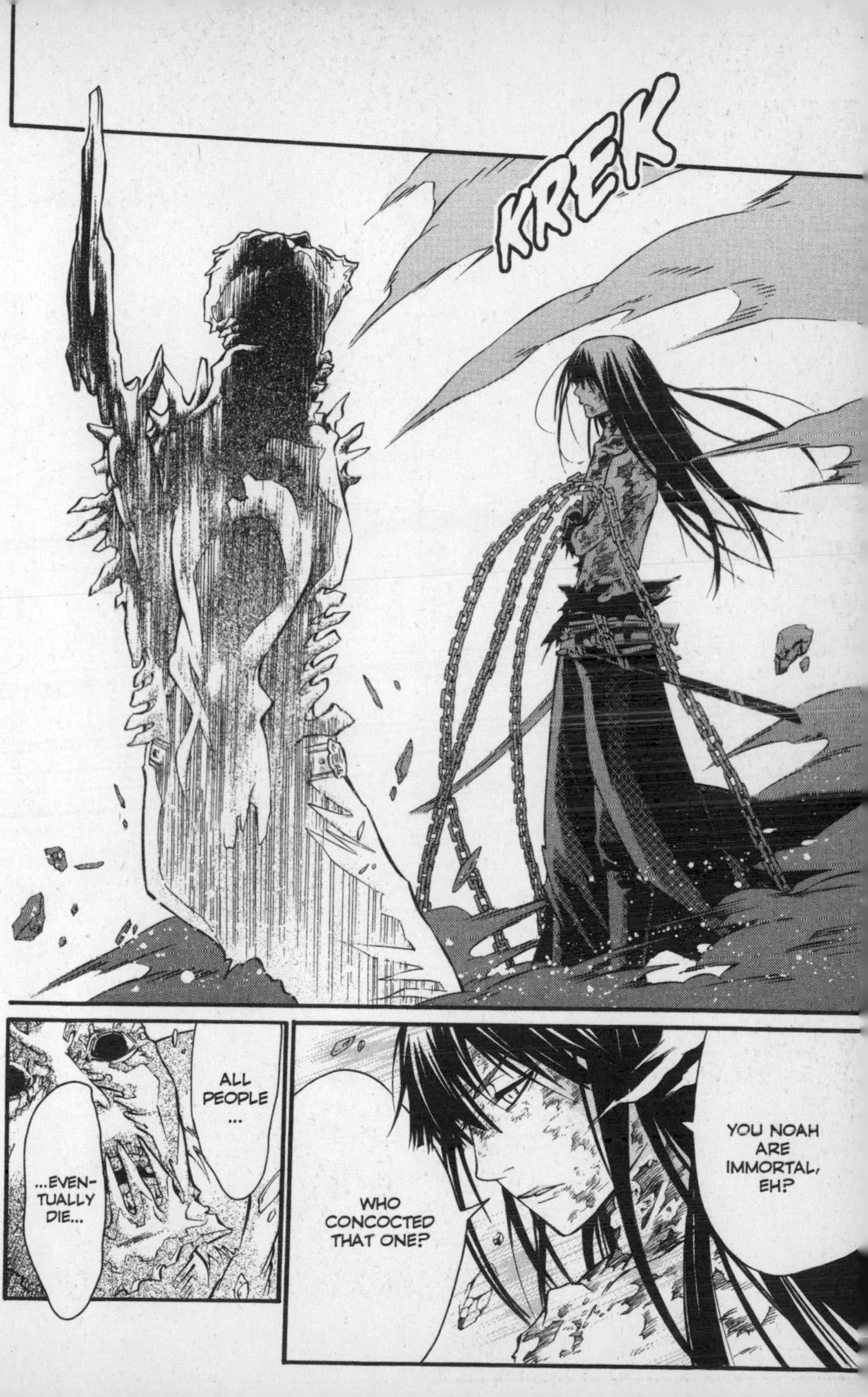
KREK
YOU NOAH ARE IMMORTAL, EH?
WHO CONCOCTED THAT ONE?
ALL PEOPLE ...
...EVEN- TUALLY DIE...

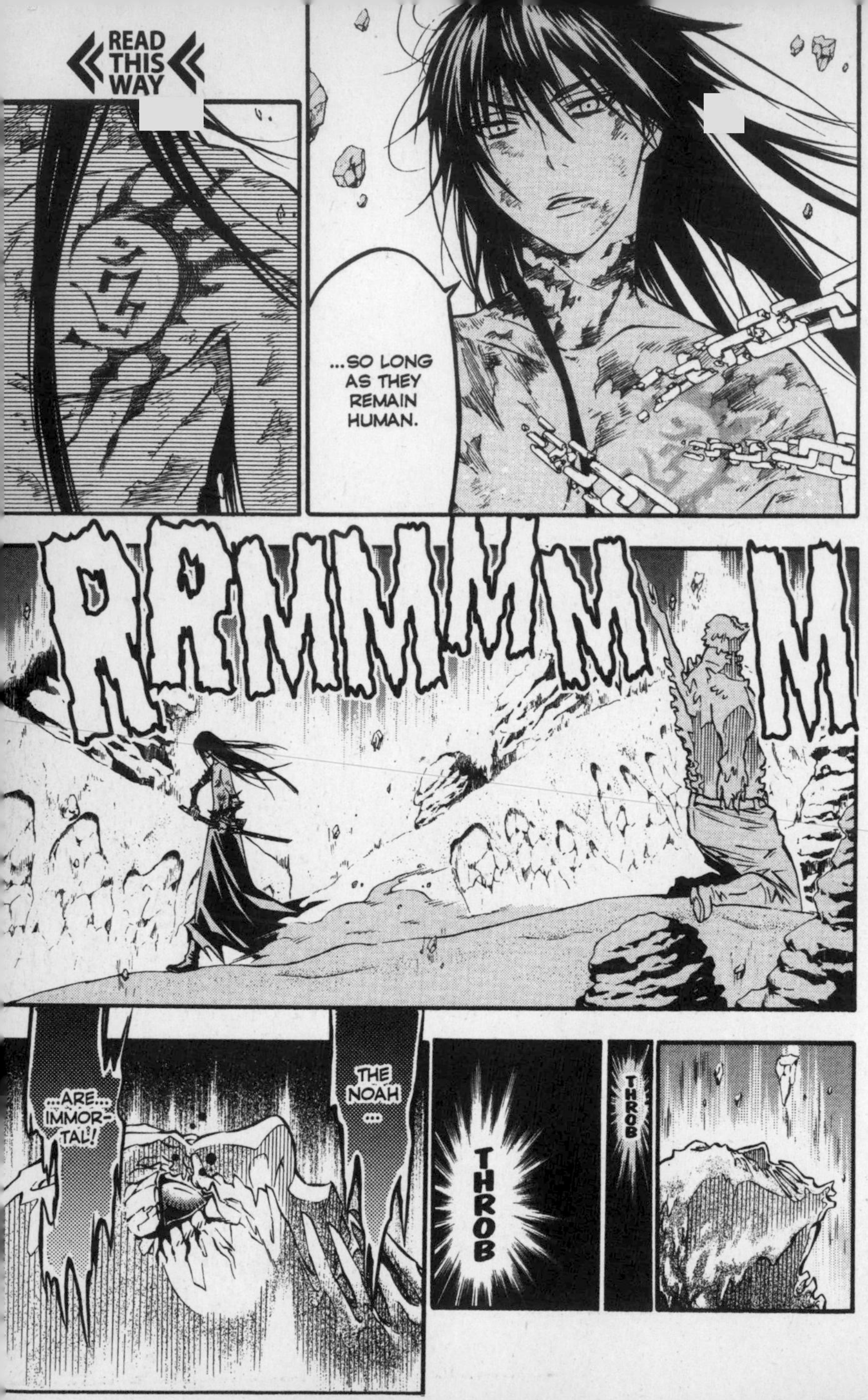
READ THIS WAY
...SO LONG AS THEY REMAIN HUMAN.
RAMMMMM
THROB
THROB
THE NOAH ...
...ARE... IMMOR-TAL!

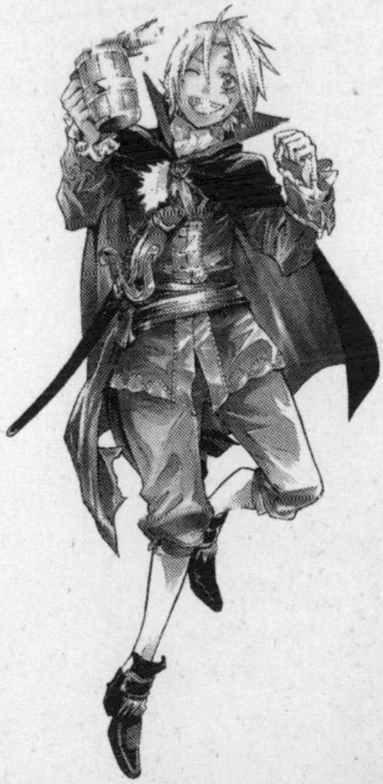

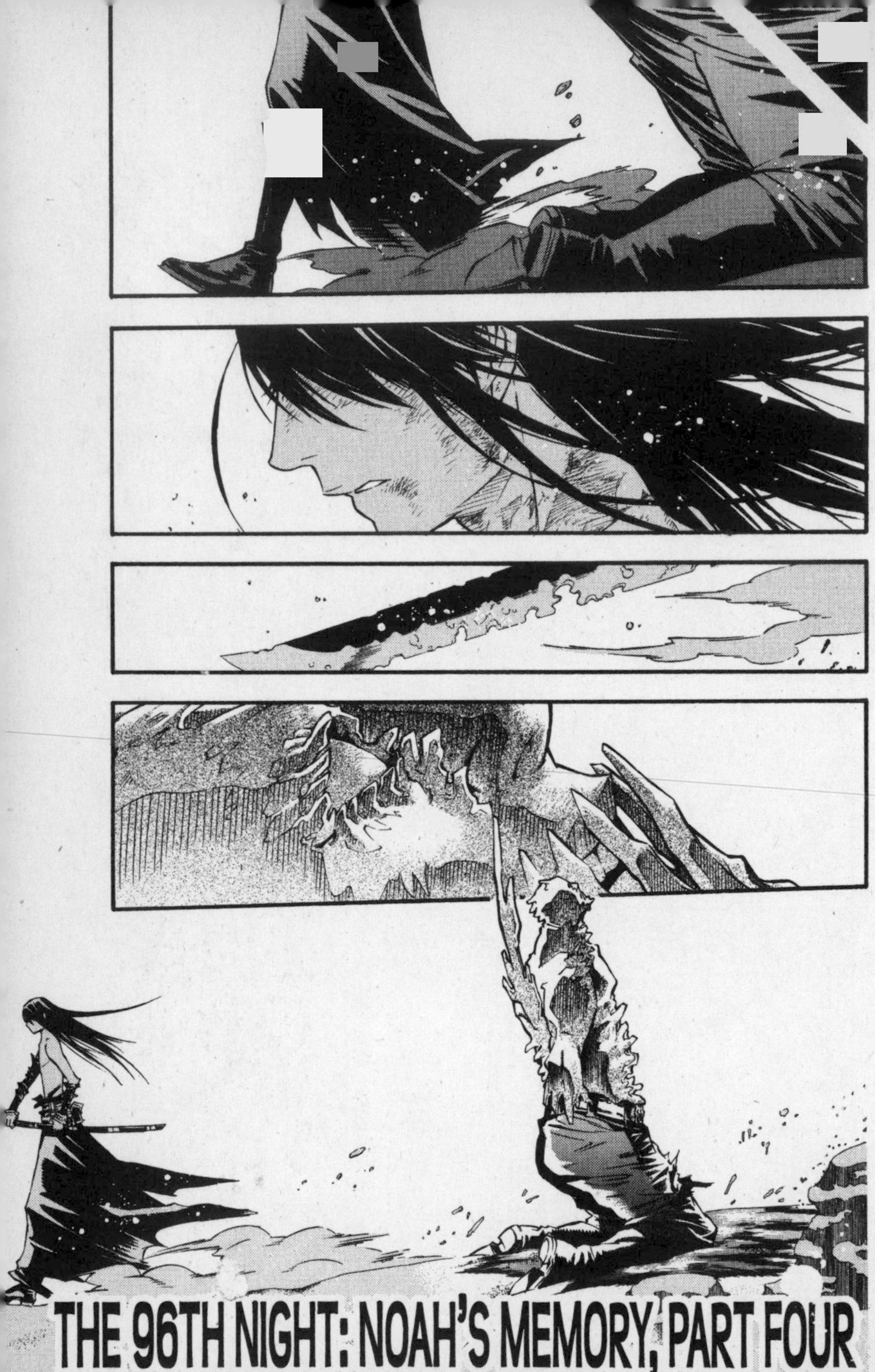

THE 96TH NIGHT: NOAH'S MEMORY, PART FOUR

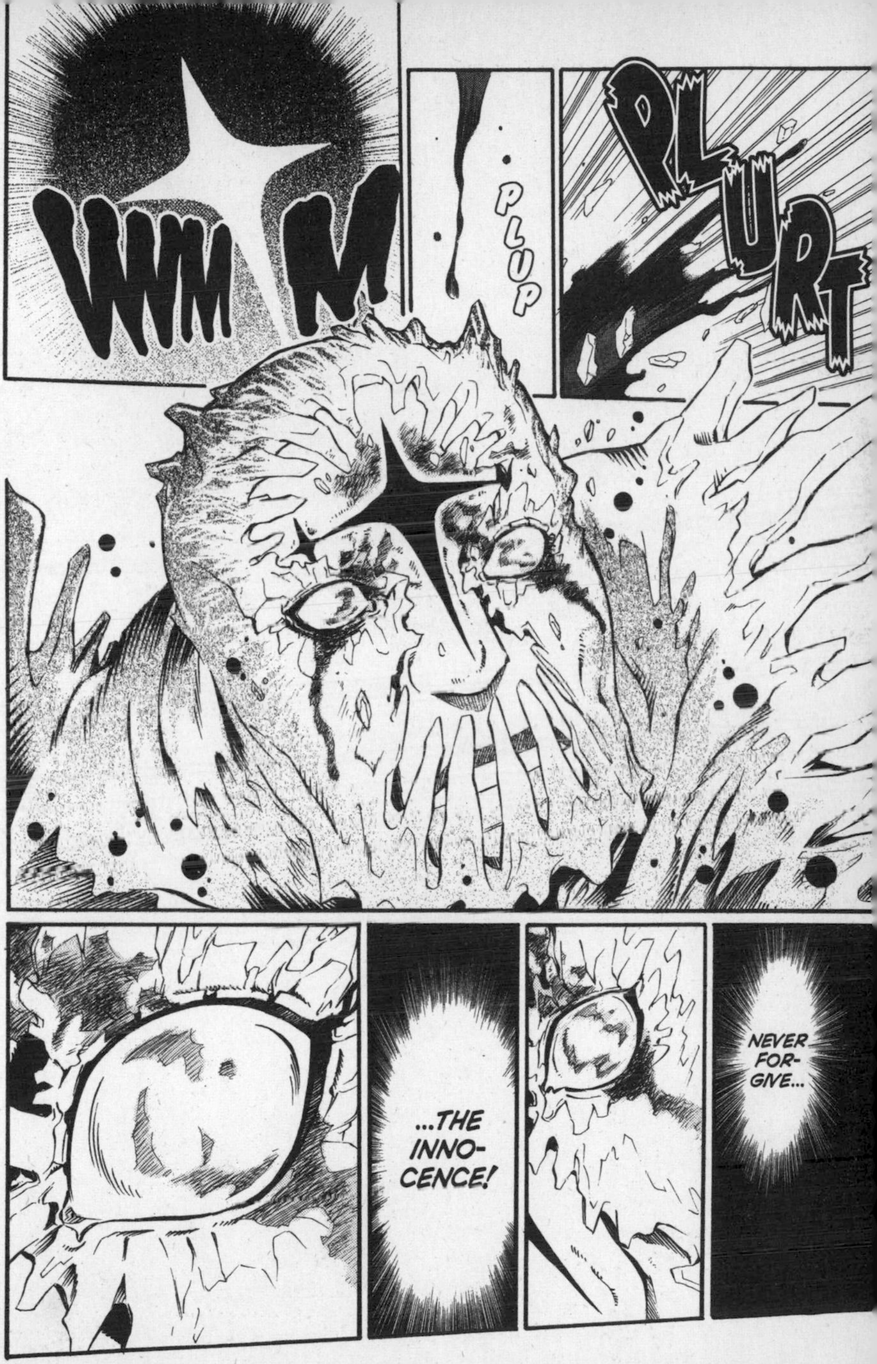
PLURT
PLUP
WMM
NEVER FOR-GIVE...
...THE INNO-CENCE!

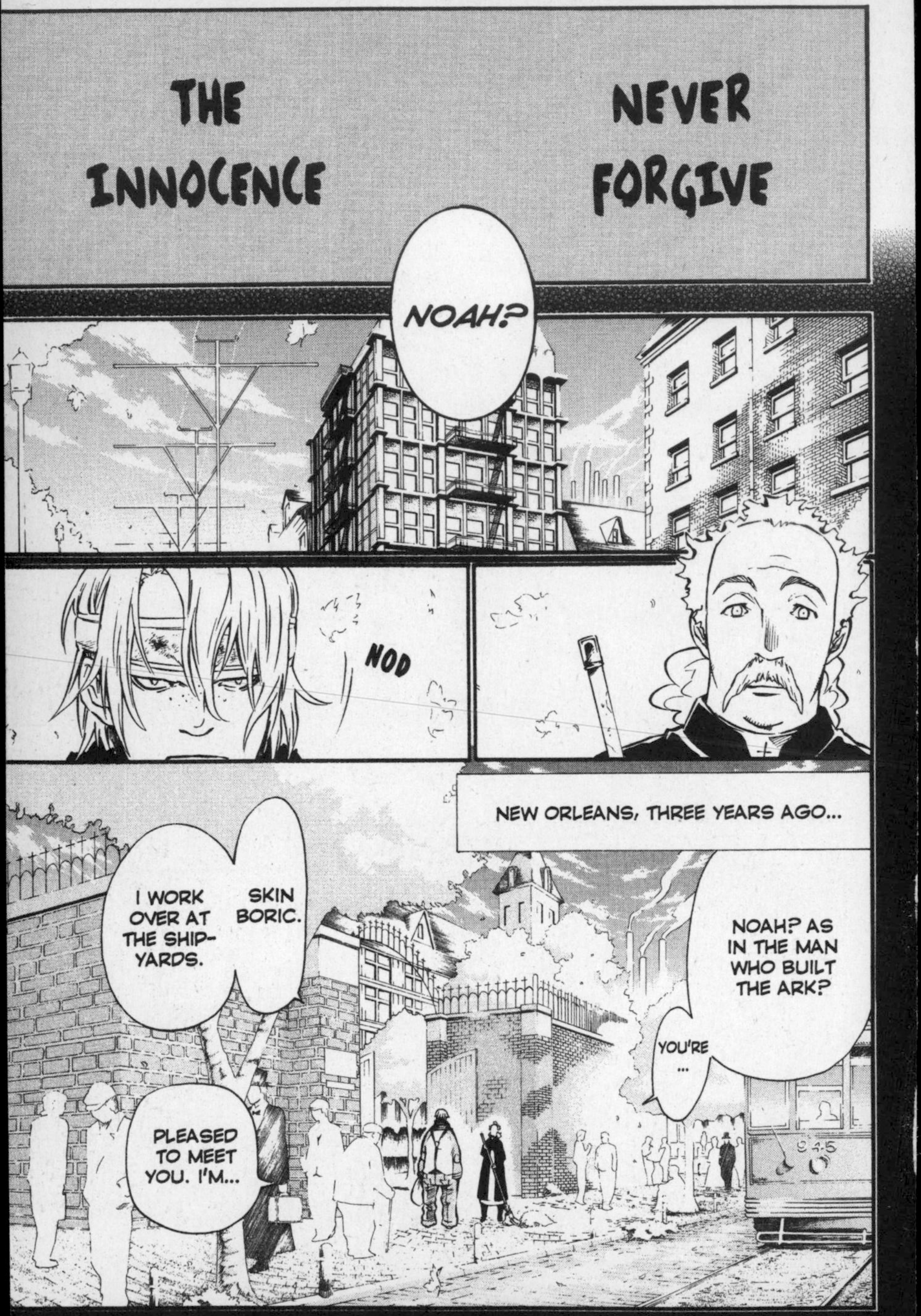
THE INNOCENCE NEVER FORGIVE
NOAH?
NOD
NEW ORLEANS, THREE YEARS AGO...
NOAH? AS IN THE MAN WHO BUILT THE ARK?
YOU'RE ...
SKIN BORIC.
I WORK OVER AT THE SHIP-YARDS.
PLEASED TO MEET YOU. I'M...

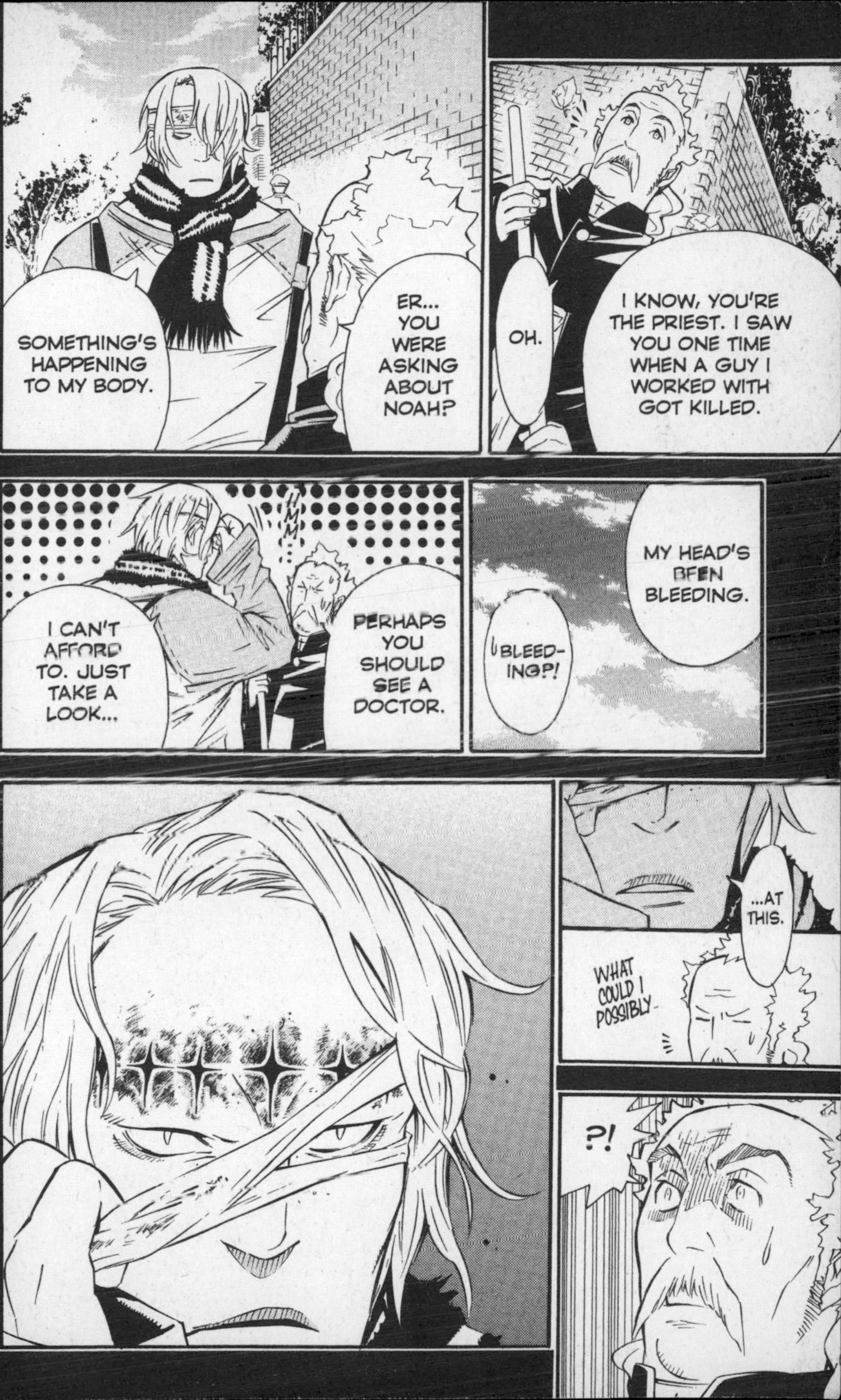
I KNOW, YOU'RE THE PRIEST. I SAW YOU ONE TIME WHEN A GUY I WORKED WITH GOT KILLED.
OH.
ER... YOU WERE ASKING ABOUT NOAH?
SOMETHING'S HAPPENING TO MY BODY.
MY HEAD'S BEEN BLEEDING.
BLEEDING?!
PERHAPS YOU SHOULD SEE A DOCTOR.
I CAN'T AFFORD TO. JUST TAKE A LOOK...
...AT THIS.
WHAT COULD I POSSIBLY
?!

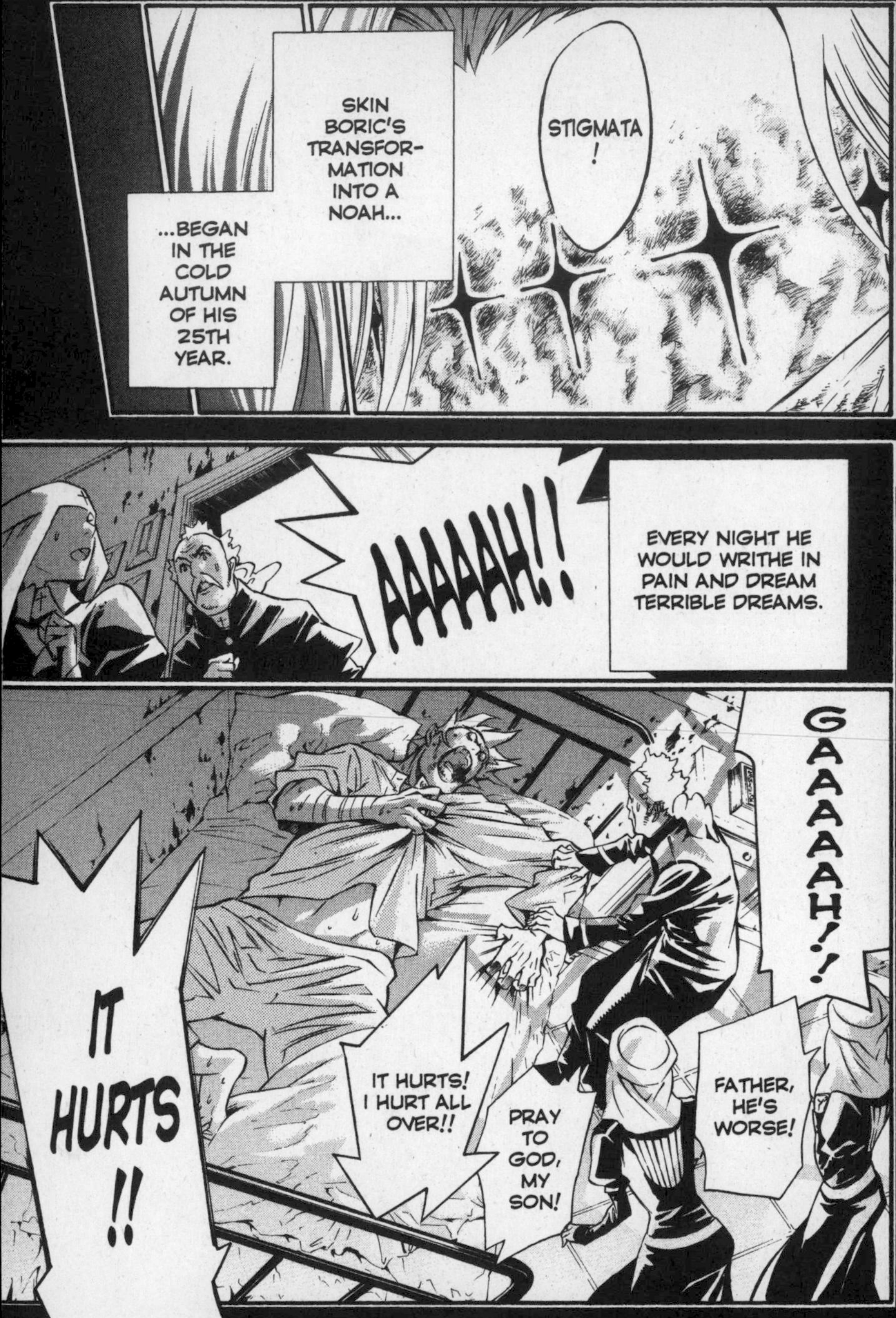
STIGMATA!
SKIN BORIC'S TRANSFOR-MATION INTO A NOAH...
...BEGAN IN THE COLD AUTUMN OF HIS 25TH YEAR.
EVERY NIGHT HE WOULD WRITHE IN PAIN AND DREAM TERRIBLE DREAMS.
AAAAAH!!
GAAAAAH!!
FATHER, HE'S WORSE!
PRAY TO GOD, MY SON!
IT HURTS! I HURT ALL OVER!!
IT HURTS!!

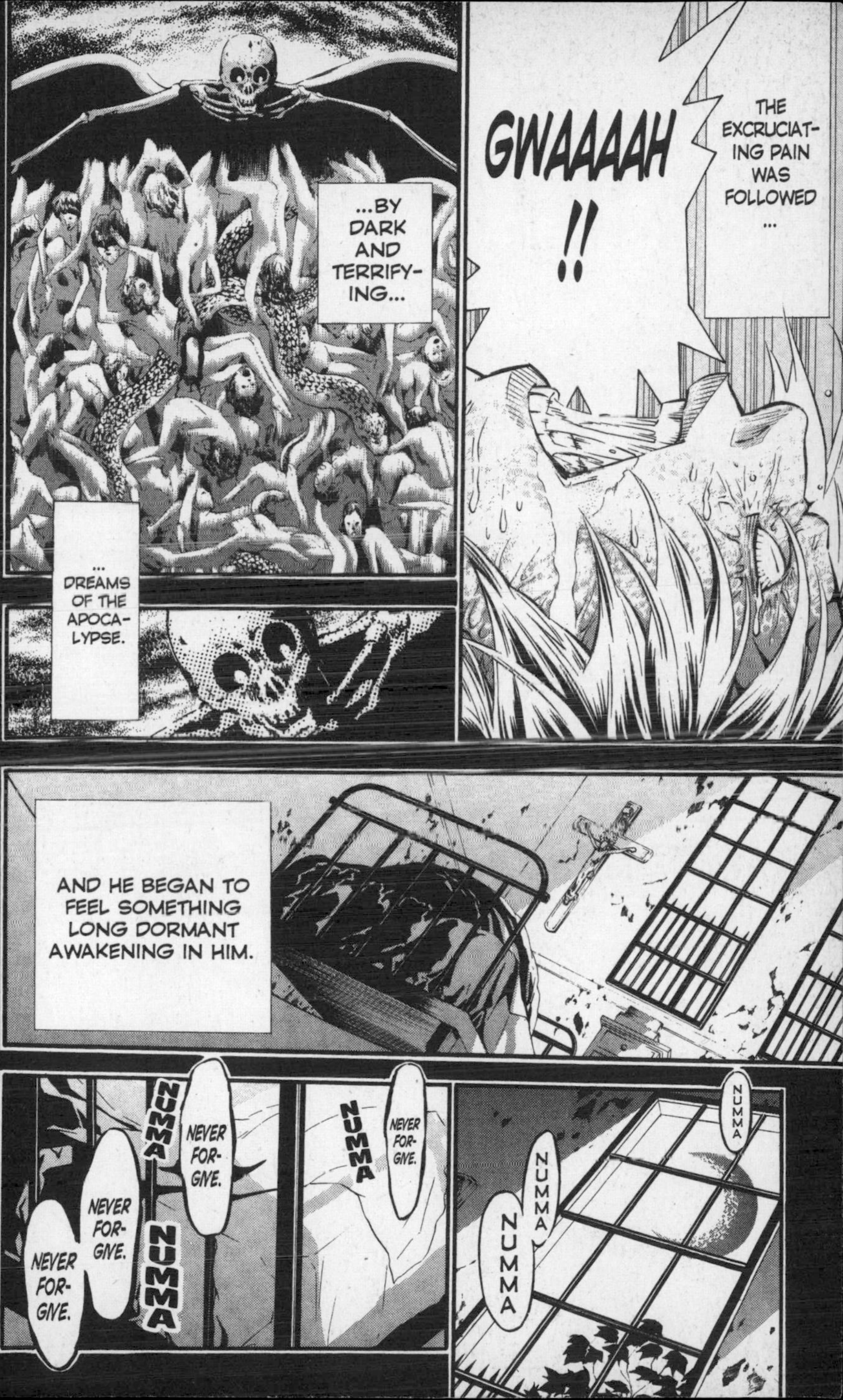
GWAAAAH !!
THE EXCRUCIATING PAIN WAS FOLLOWED ...
...BY DARK AND TERRIFYING...
... DREAMS OF THE APOCALYPSE.
AND HE BEGAN TO FEEL SOMETHING LONG DORMANT AWAKENING IN HIM.
NUMMA
NUMMA
NUMMA
NEVER FORGIVE.
NUMMA
NUMMA
NEVER FORGIVE.
NEVER FORGIVE.
NEVER FORGIVE.
NUMMA

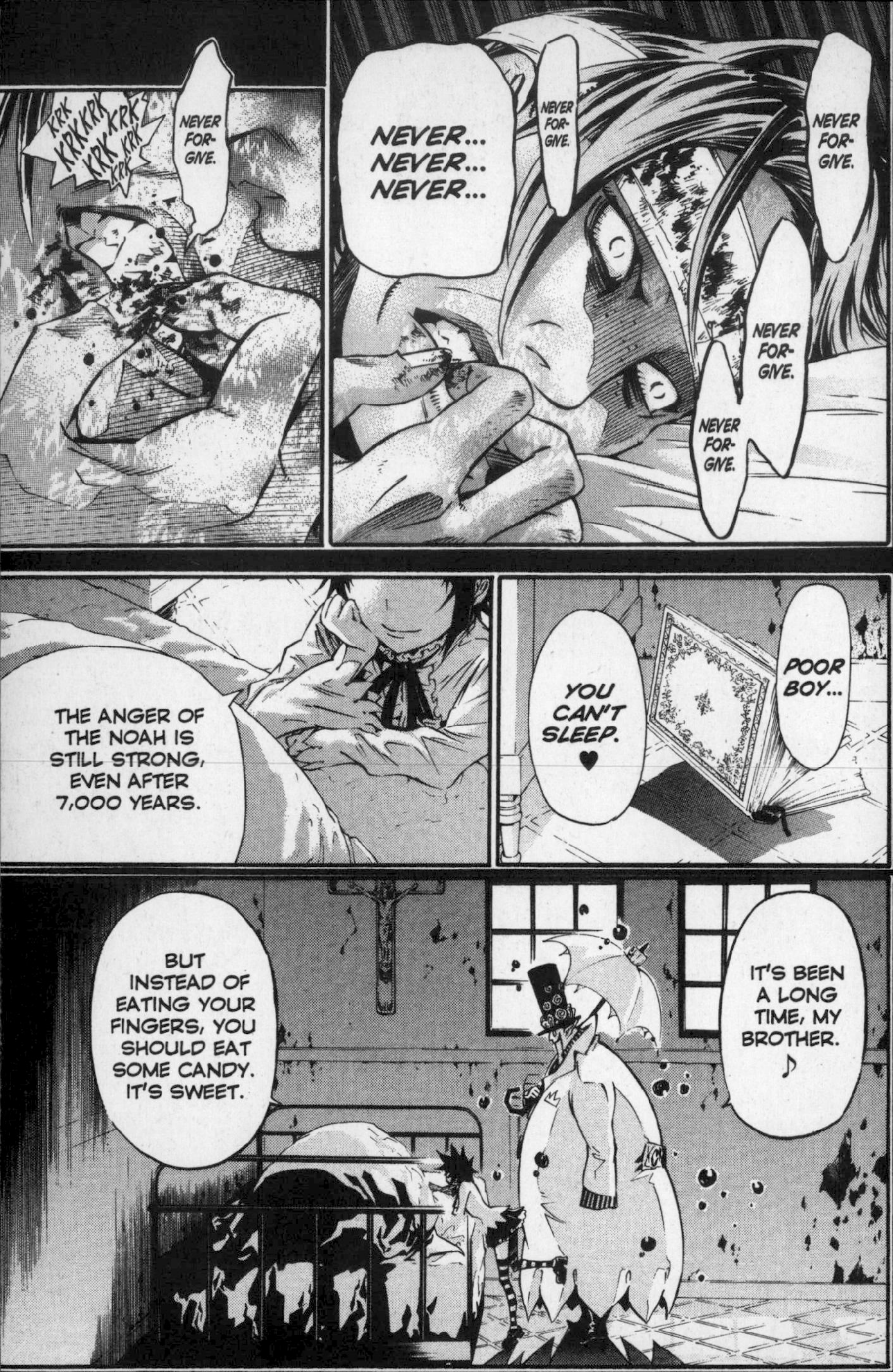
NEVER FOR- GIVE.
NEVER FOR- GIVE.
NEVER... NEVER... NEVER...
NEVER FOR- GIVE.
NEVER FOR- GIVE.
NEVER FOR- GIVE.
KRK KRKKRK KRK KRK KRK KRK
POOR BOY...
YOU CAN'T SLEEP. ♥
THE ANGER OF THE NOAH IS STILL STRONG, EVEN AFTER 7,000 YEARS.
IT'S BEEN A LONG TIME, MY BROTHER. ♪
BUT INSTEAD OF EATING YOUR FINGERS, YOU SHOULD EAT SOME CANDY. IT'S SWEET.

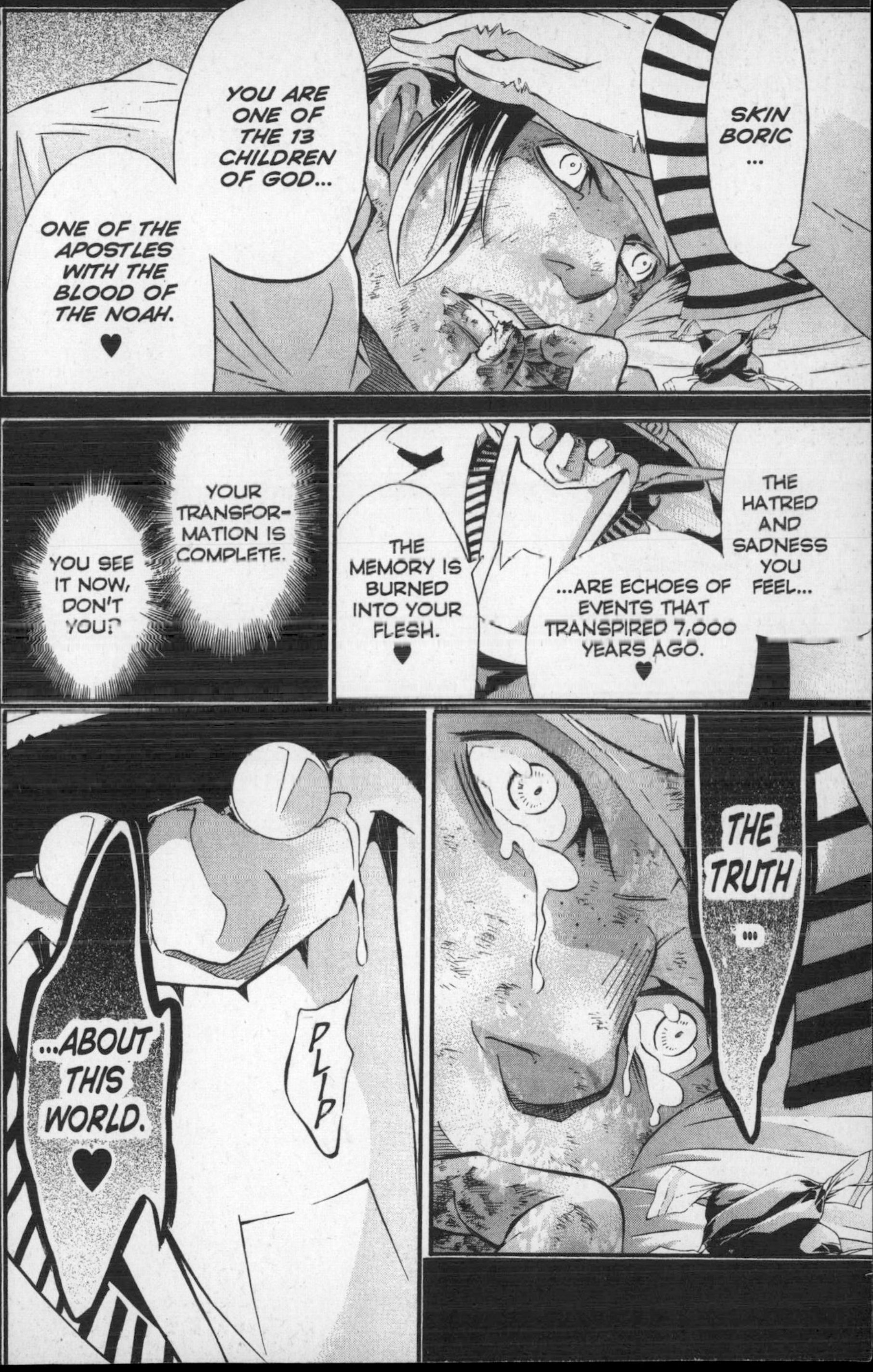
SKIN BORIC ...
YOU ARE ONE OF THE 13 CHILDREN OF GOD...
ONE OF THE APOSTLES WITH THE BLOOD OF THE NOAH. ♥
THE HATRED AND SADNESS YOU FEEL...
...ARE ECHOES OF EVENTS THAT TRANSPIRED 7,000 YEARS AGO. ♥
THE MEMORY IS BURNED INTO YOUR FLESH. ♥
YOUR TRANSFORMATION IS COMPLETE.
YOU SEE IT NOW, DON'T YOU?
THE TRUTH ...
PLIP
...ABOUT THIS WORLD. ♥

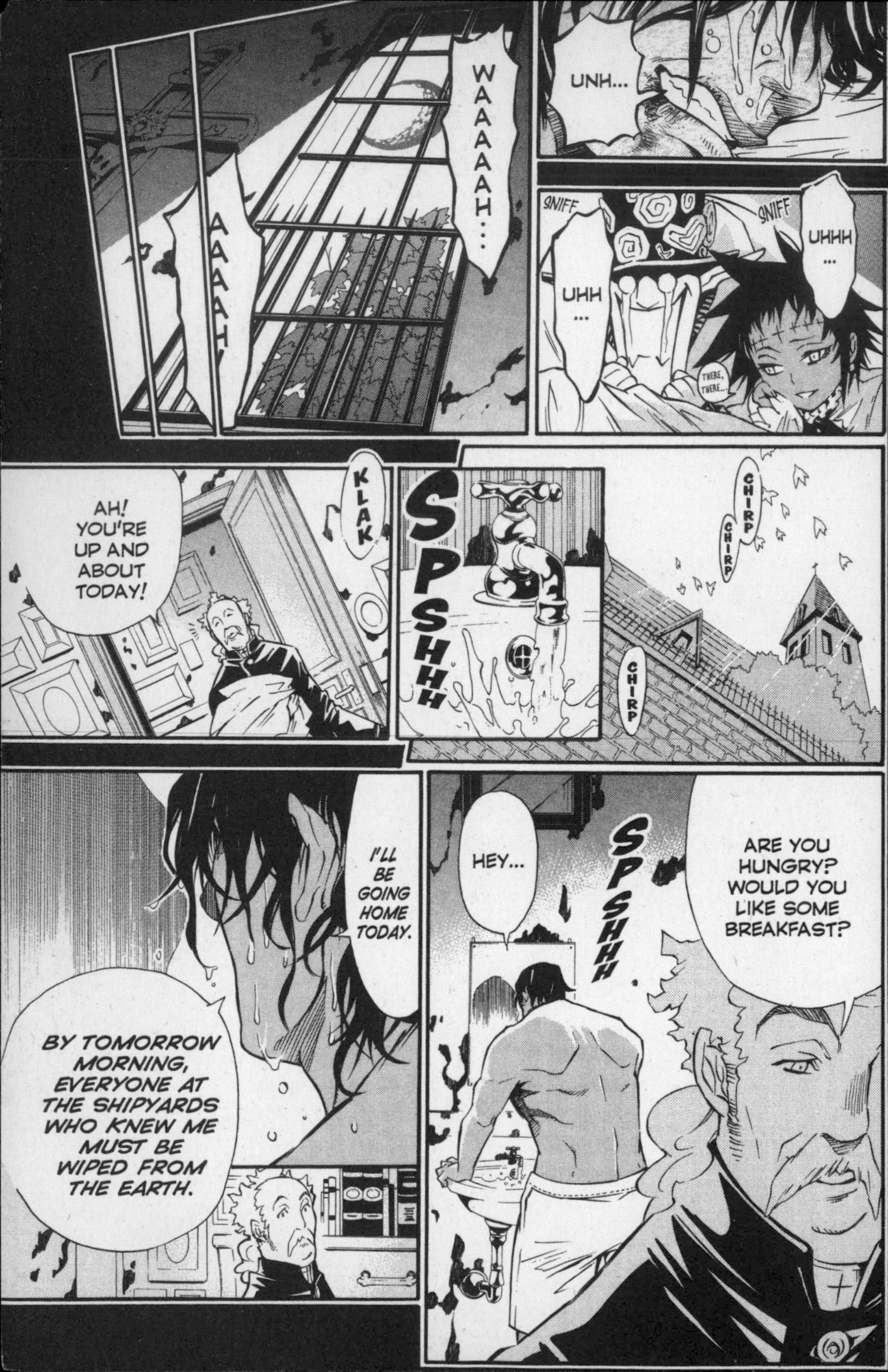
UNH...
SNIFF
UHHH ...
SNIFF
UHH ...
THERE, THERE...
WAAAAAAH...
AAAAAH
CHIRP
CHIRP
CHIRP
SPSHHH
KLAK
AH! YOU'RE UP AND ABOUT TODAY!
ARE YOU HUNGRY? WOULD YOU LIKE SOME BREAKFAST?
SPSHHH
HEY...
I'LL BE GOING HOME TODAY.
BY TOMORROW MORNING, EVERYONE AT THE SHIPYARDS WHO KNEW ME MUST BE WIPED FROM THE EARTH.

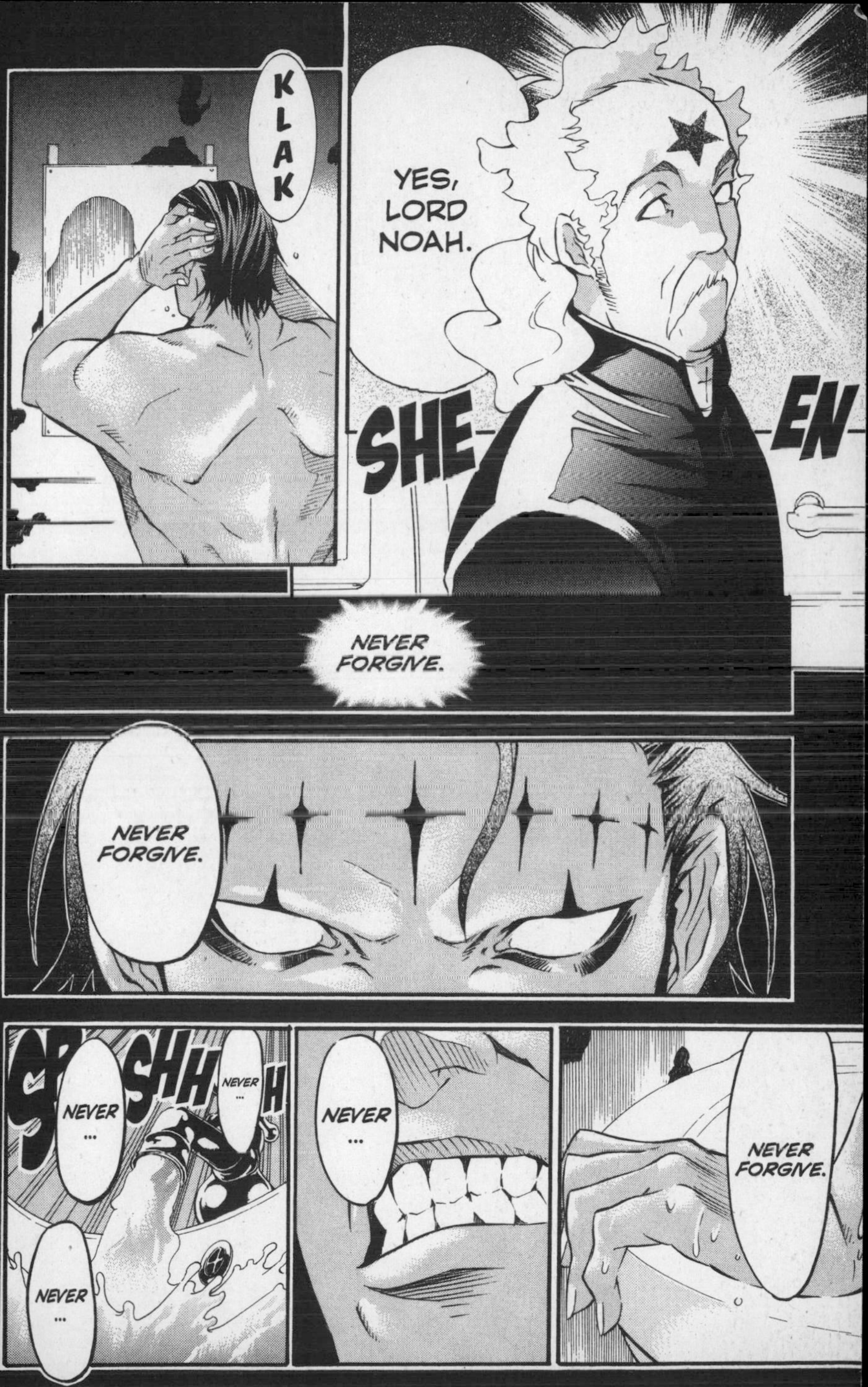
YES, LORD NOAH.
SHE—EN
KLAK
NEVER FORGIVE.
NEVER FORGIVE.
NEVER FORGIVE.
NEVER ...
NEVER ...
SHHH
NEVER ...
NEVER ...

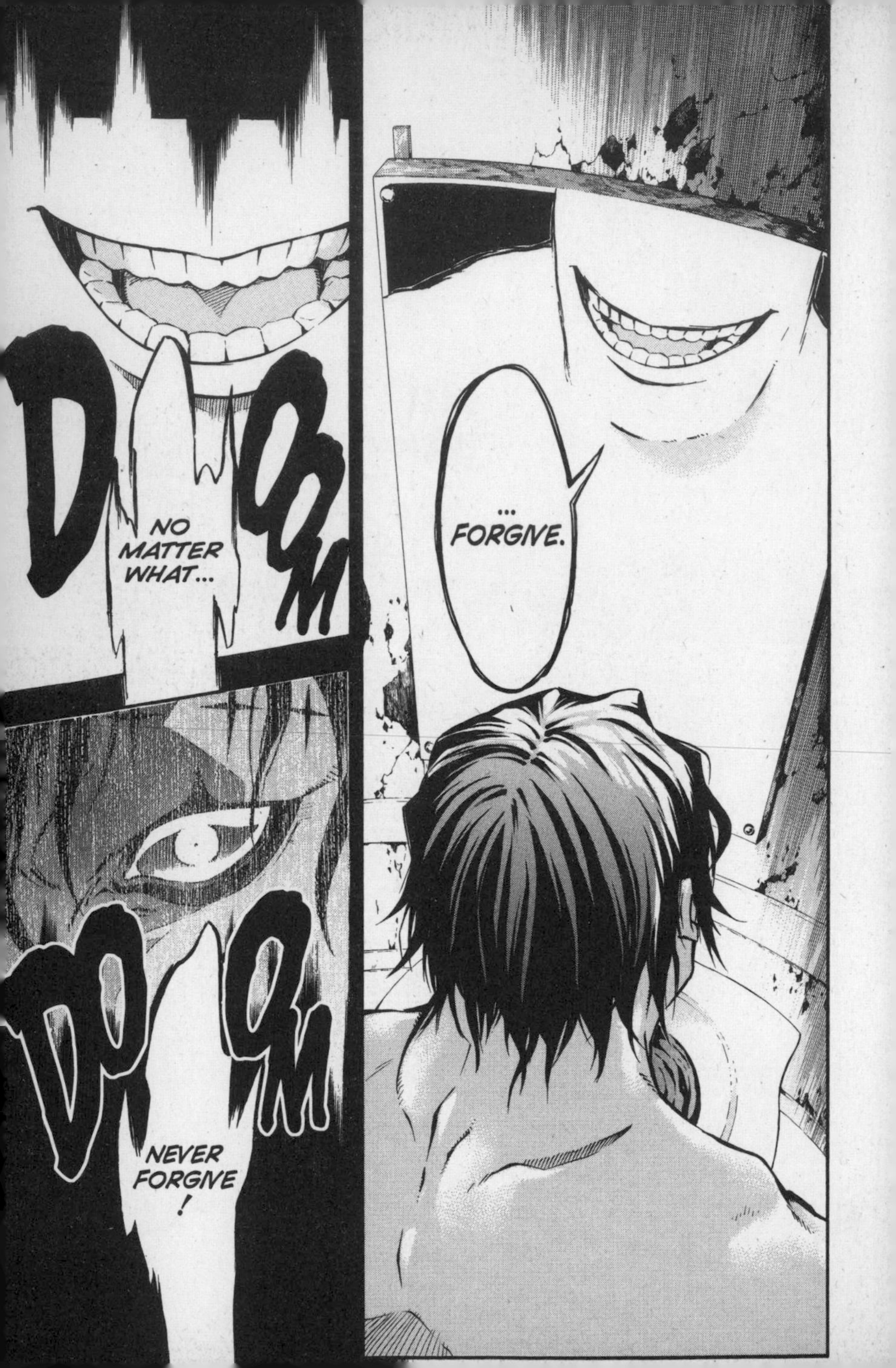

... FORGIVE.
DOOM
NO MATTER WHAT...
DOOM
NEVER FORGIVE!

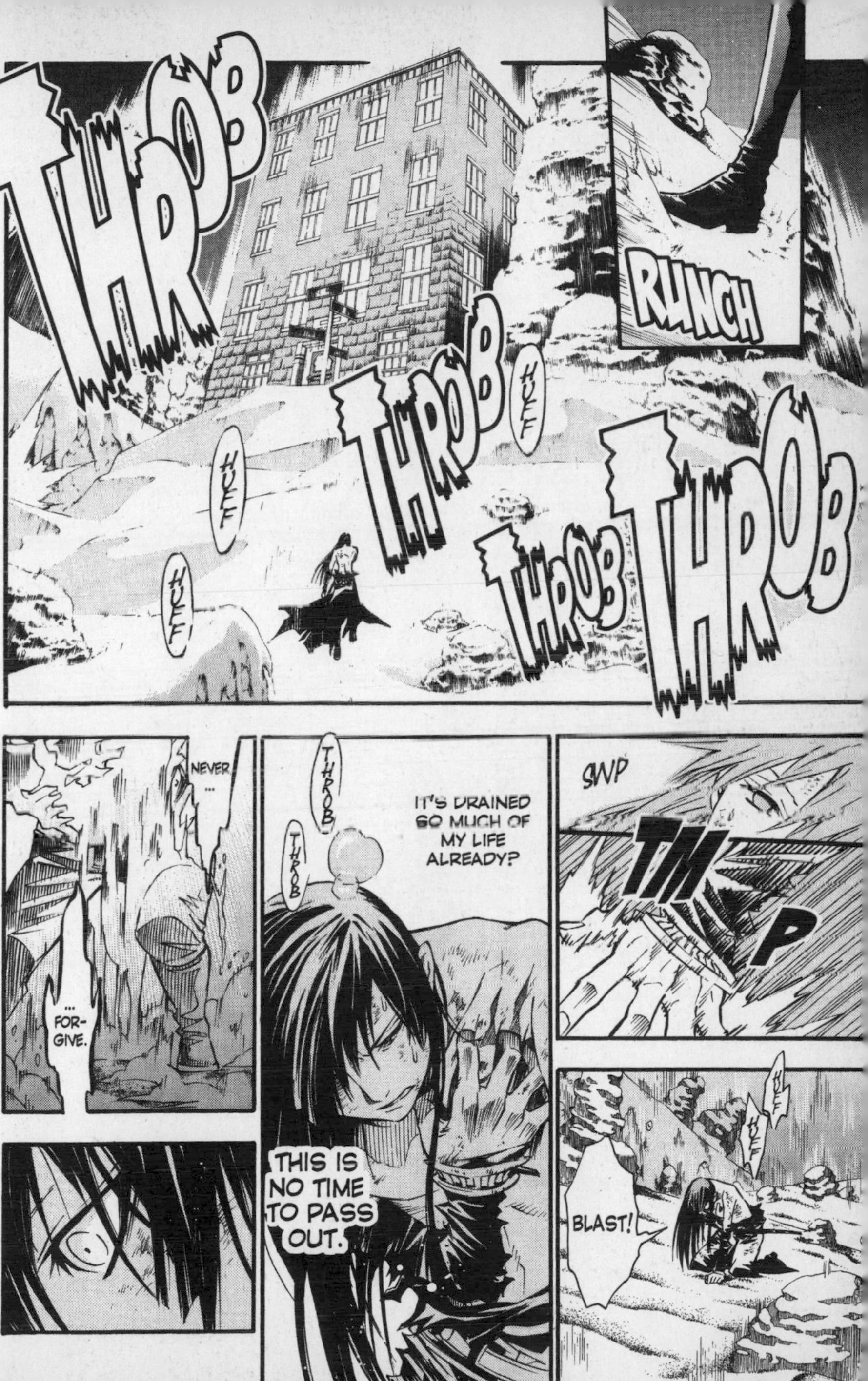
RUNCH
THROB
THROB
THROB
HUFF
THROB
HUFF
HUFF
THROB
SWP
TMP
HUFF
HUFF
BLAST!
THROB
THROB
IT'S DRAINED SO MUCH OF MY LIFE ALREADY?
THIS IS NO TIME TO PASS OUT.
NEVER...
...FOR-GIVE.

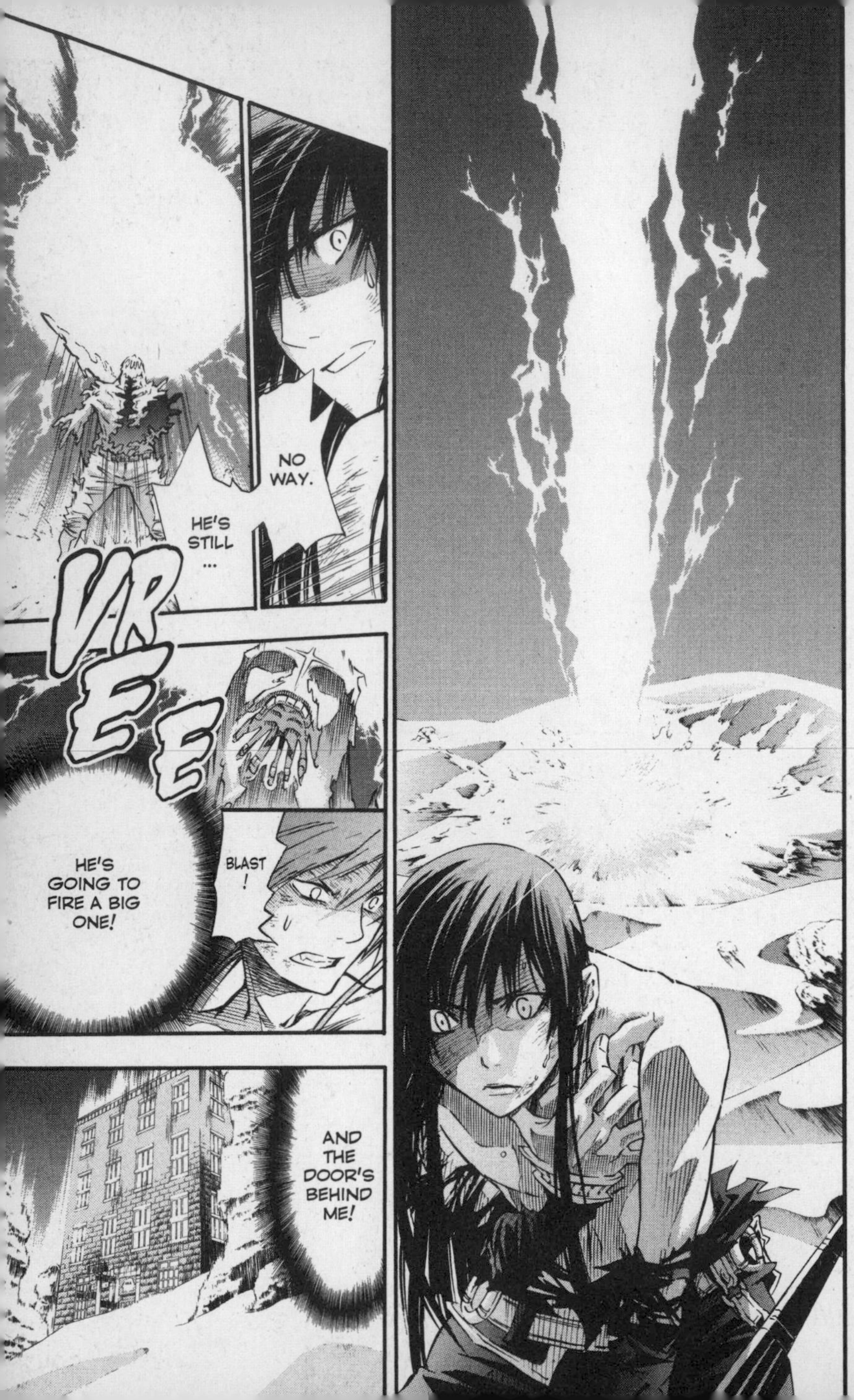
NO WAY.
HE'S STILL ...
VREEE
BLAST!
HE'S GOING TO FIRE A BIG ONE!
AND THE DOOR'S BEHIND ME!

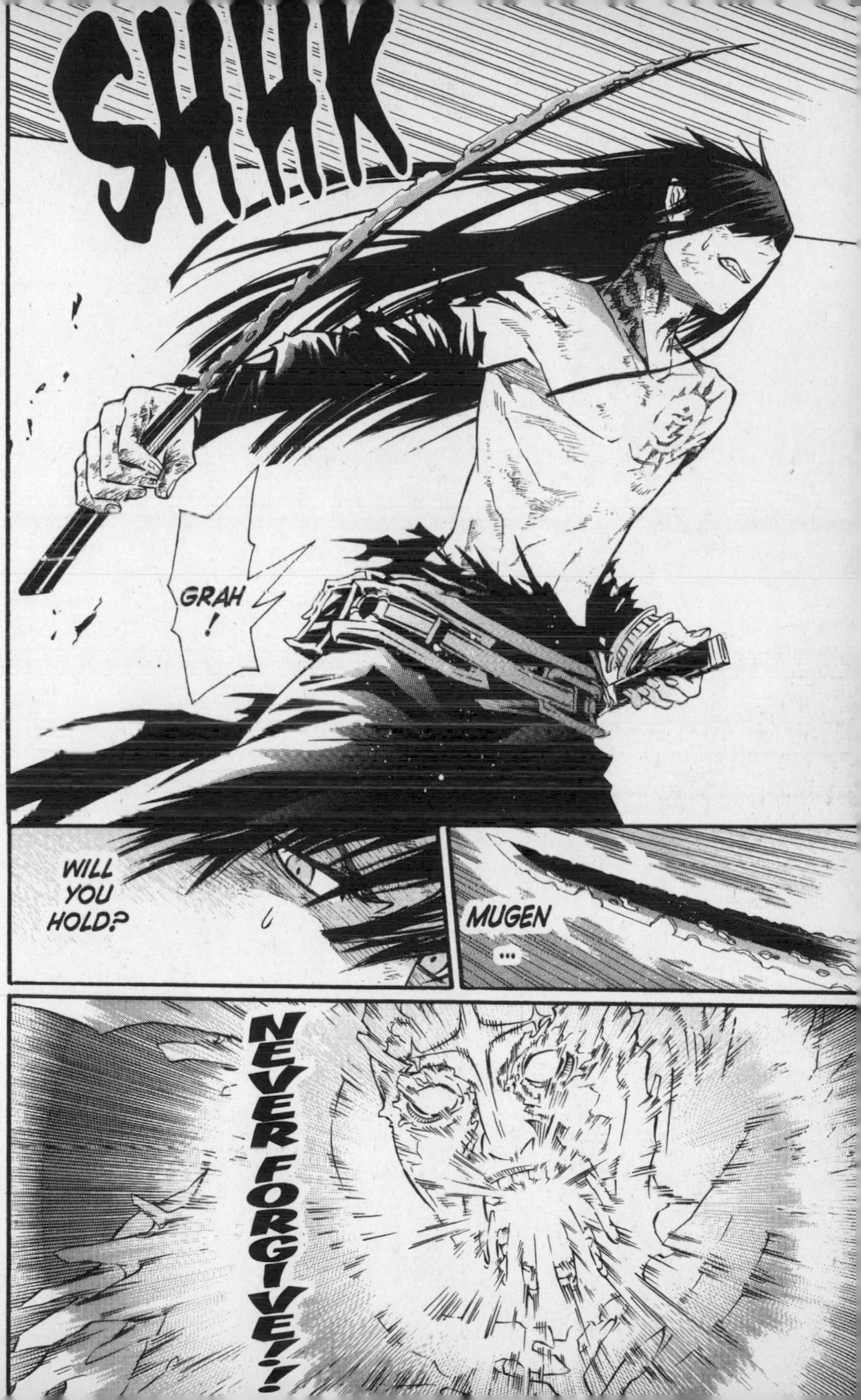
SHHK
GRAH!
MUGEN...
WILL YOU HOLD?
NEVER FORGIVE!!

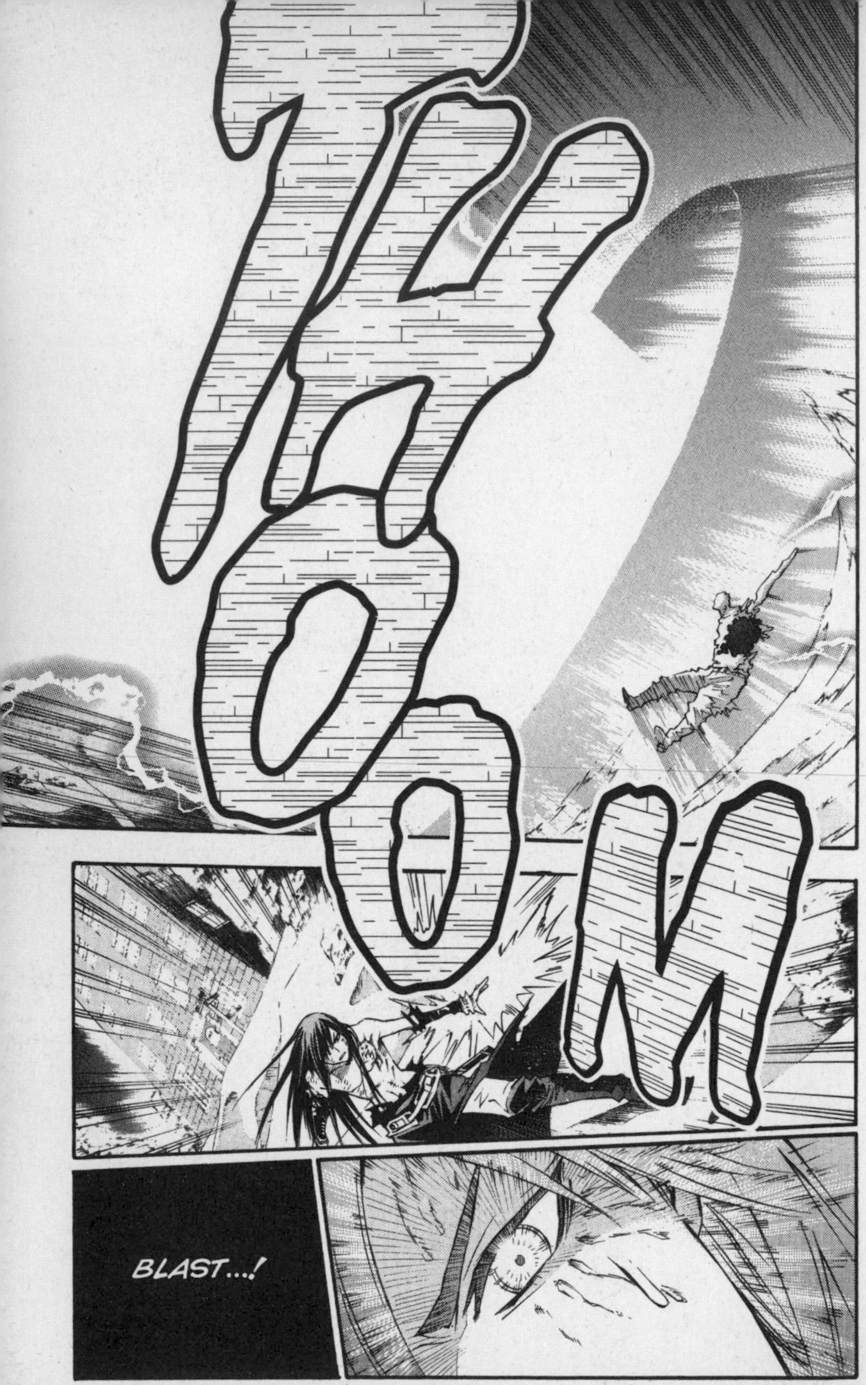
BLAST...!

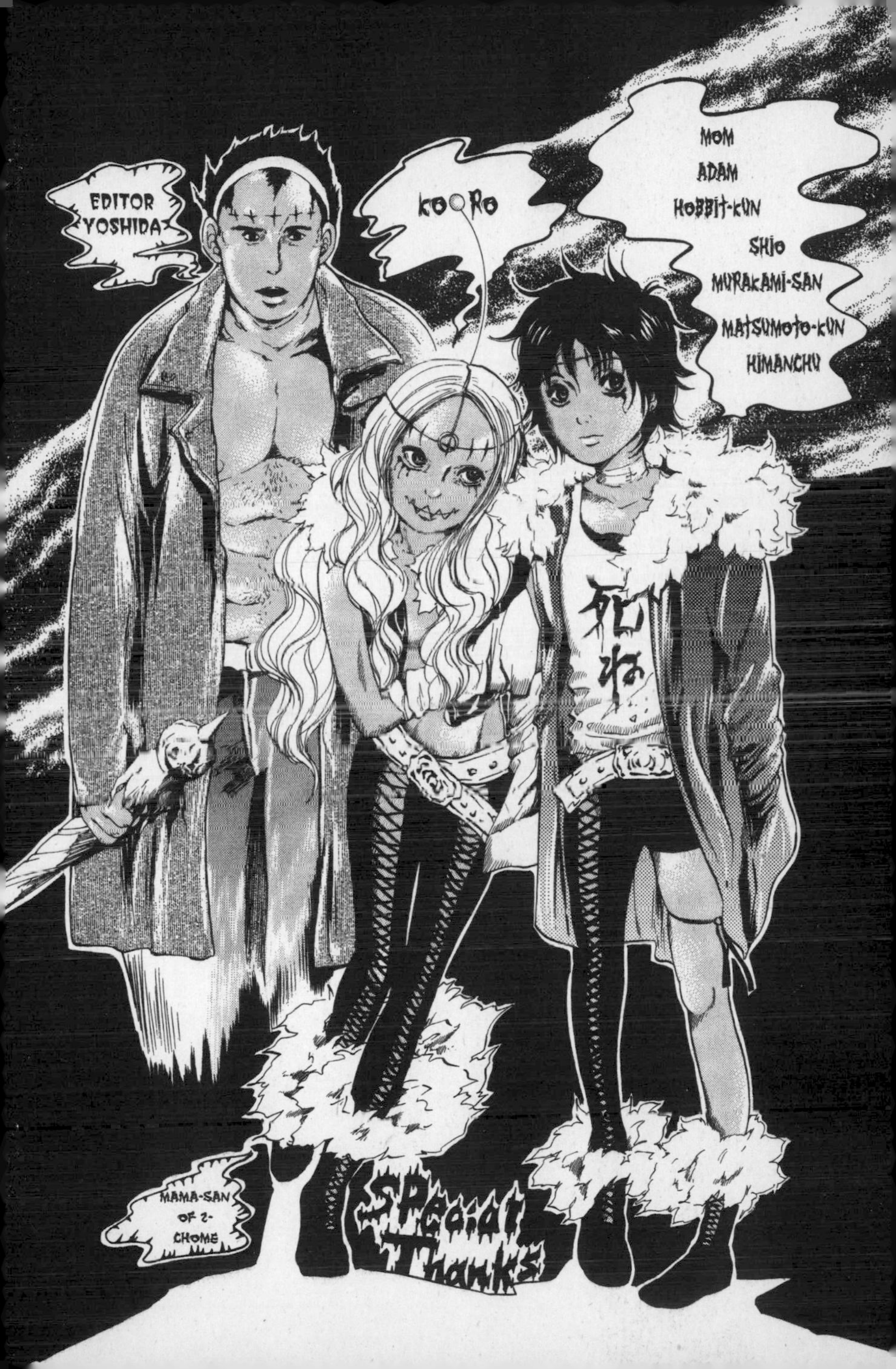
MOM
ADAM
HOBBIT-KUN
SHIO
MURAKAMI-SAN
MATSUMOTO-KUN
HIMANCHU
KO○RO
EDITOR YOSHIDA
SPecial Thanks
MAMA-SAN OF 2-CHOME

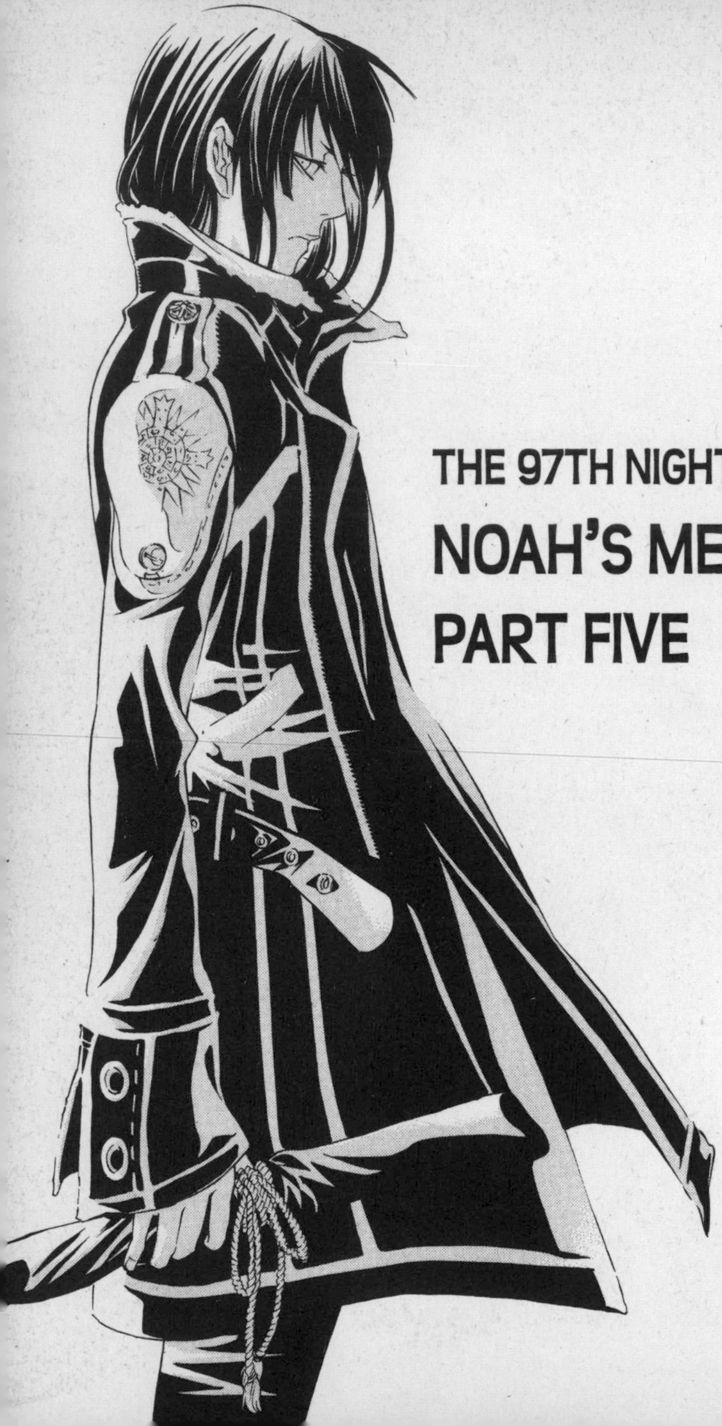

THE 97TH NIGHT:
NOAH'S MEMORY, PART FIVE

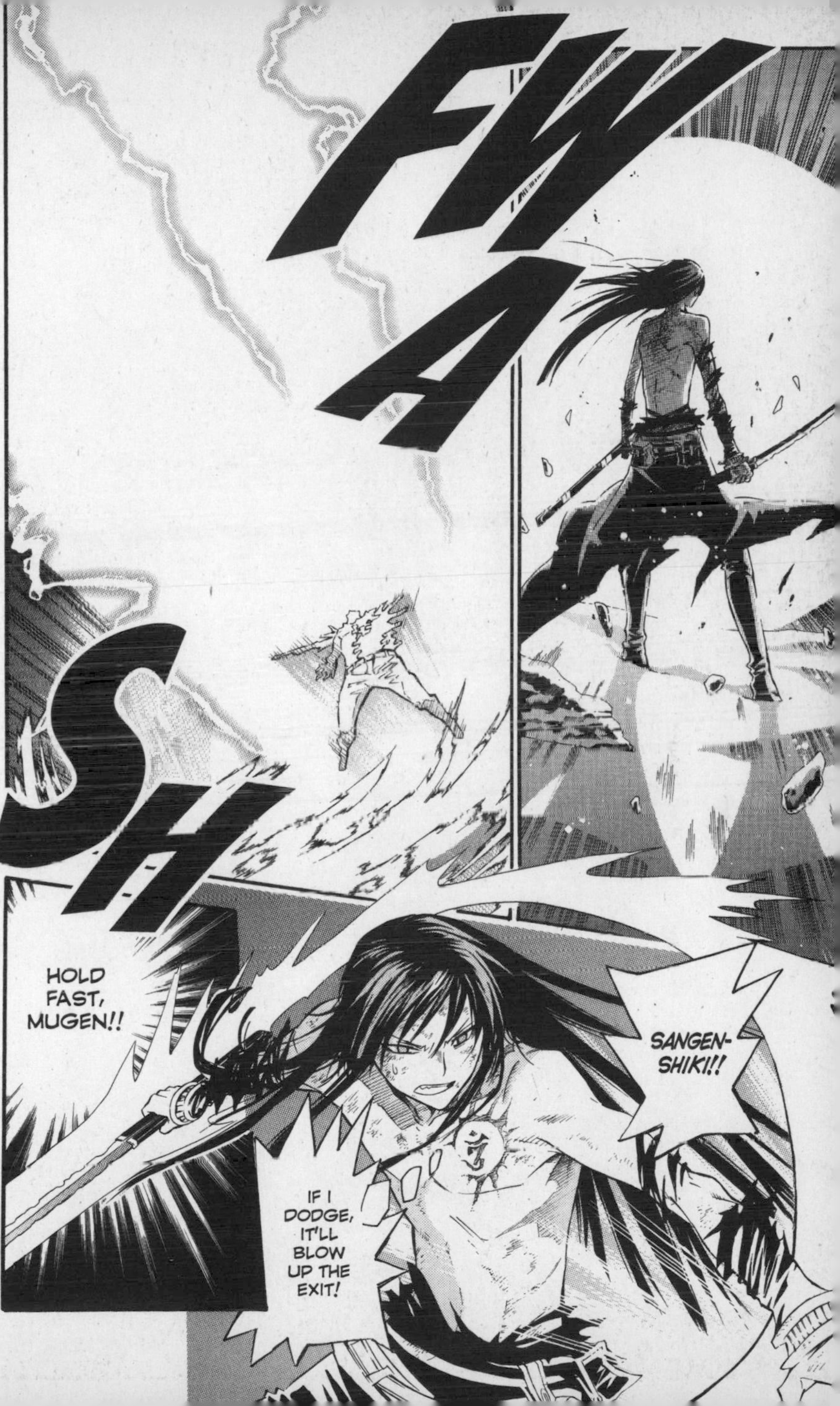
FWA
SH
SANGEN-SHIKI!!
HOLD FAST, MUGEN!!
IF I DODGE, IT'LL BLOW UP THE EXIT!

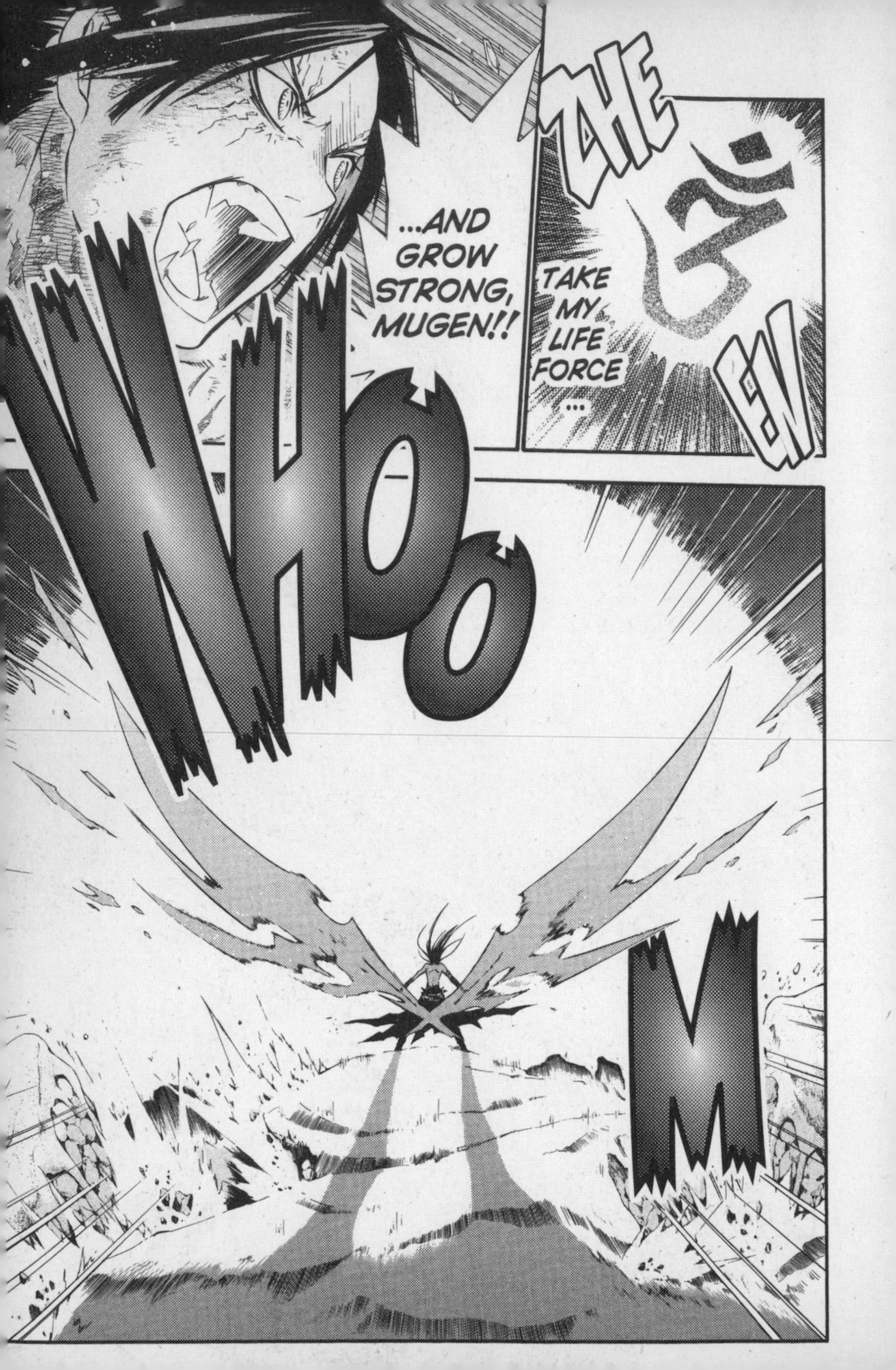
ZHE
TAKE MY LIFE FORCE ...
...AND GROW STRONG, MUGEN!!
WHOOM

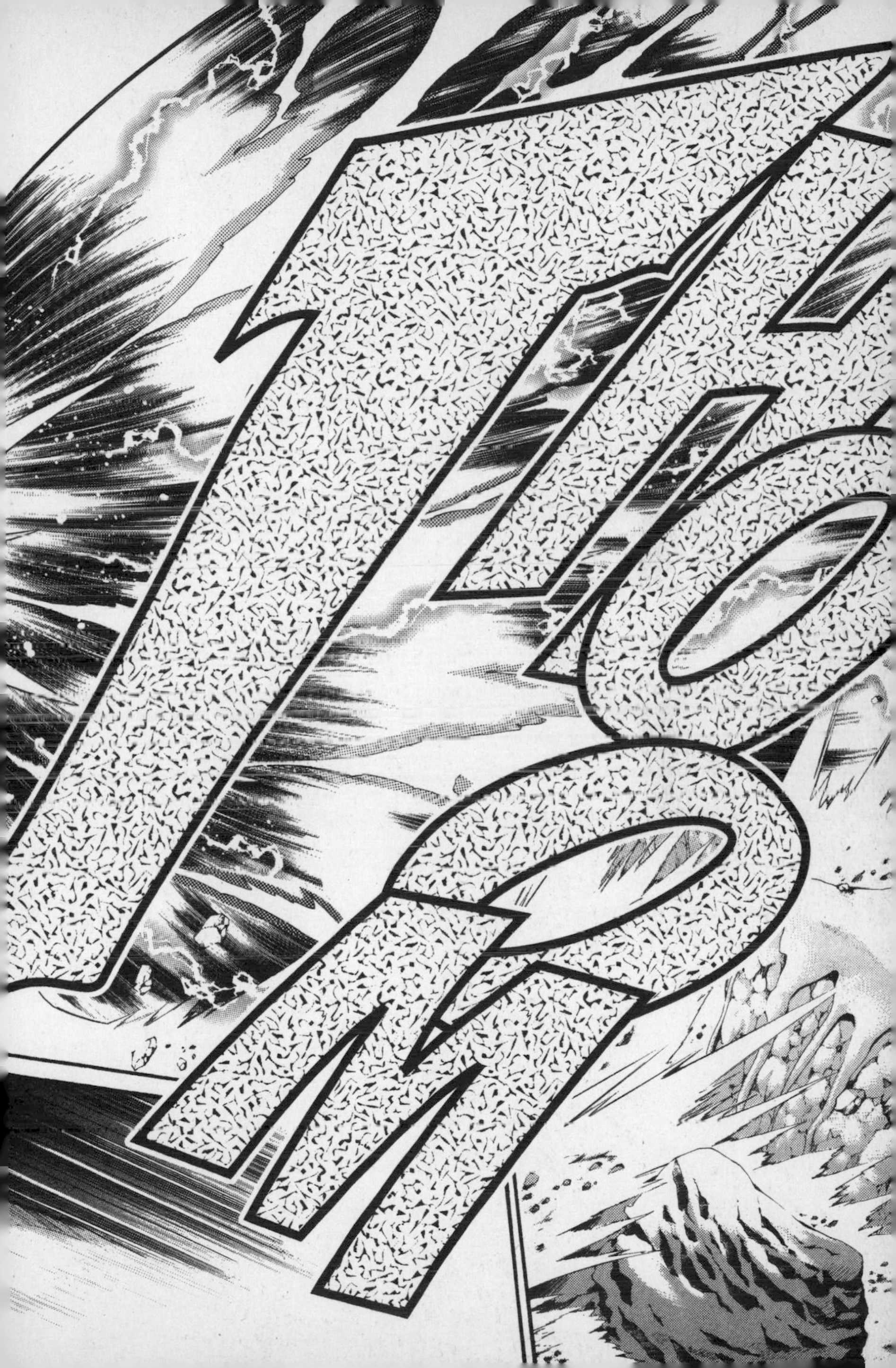

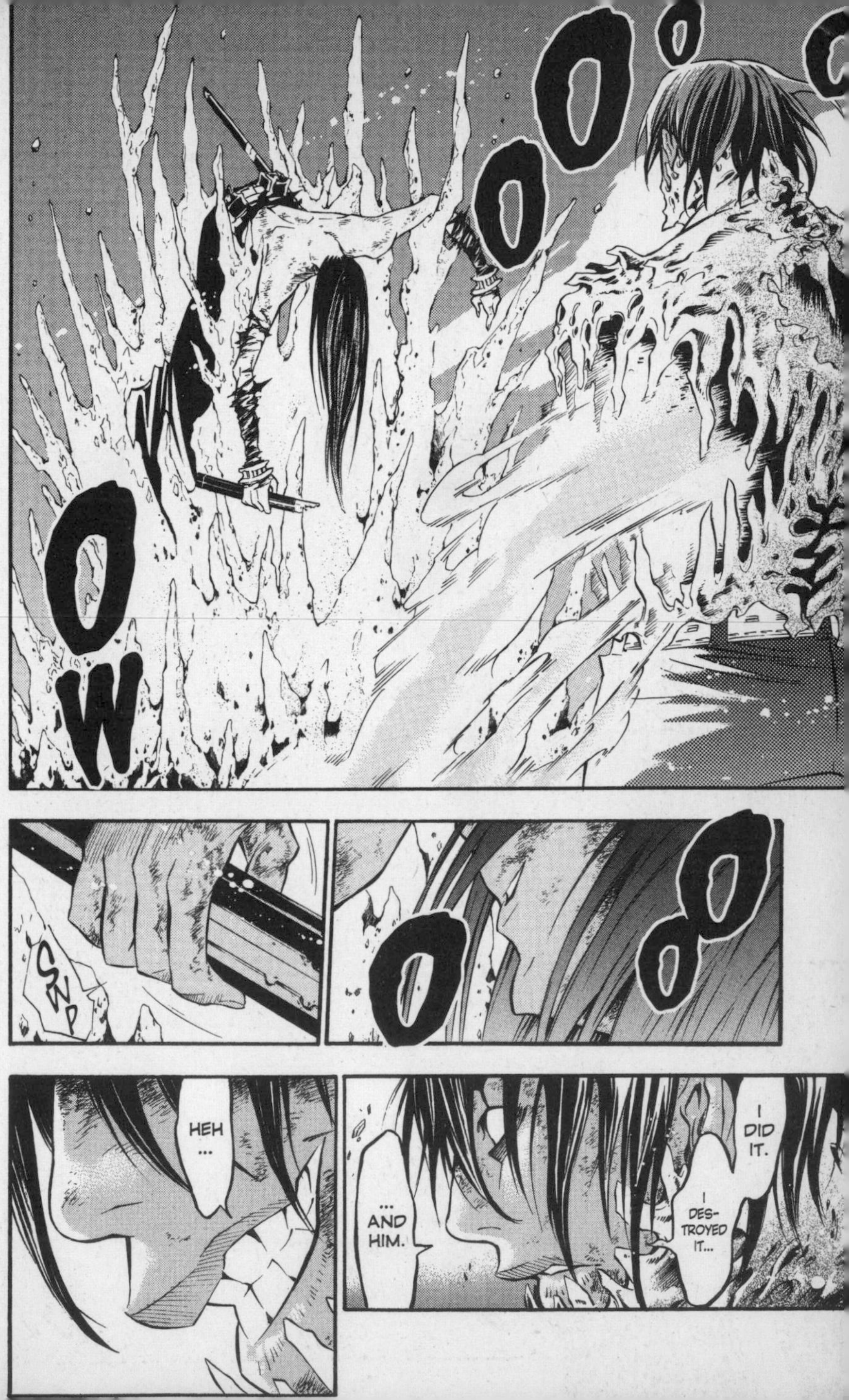

OOOOOOW
OOO
SWP
I DID IT.
I DES-TROYED IT...
...AND HIM.
HEH ...

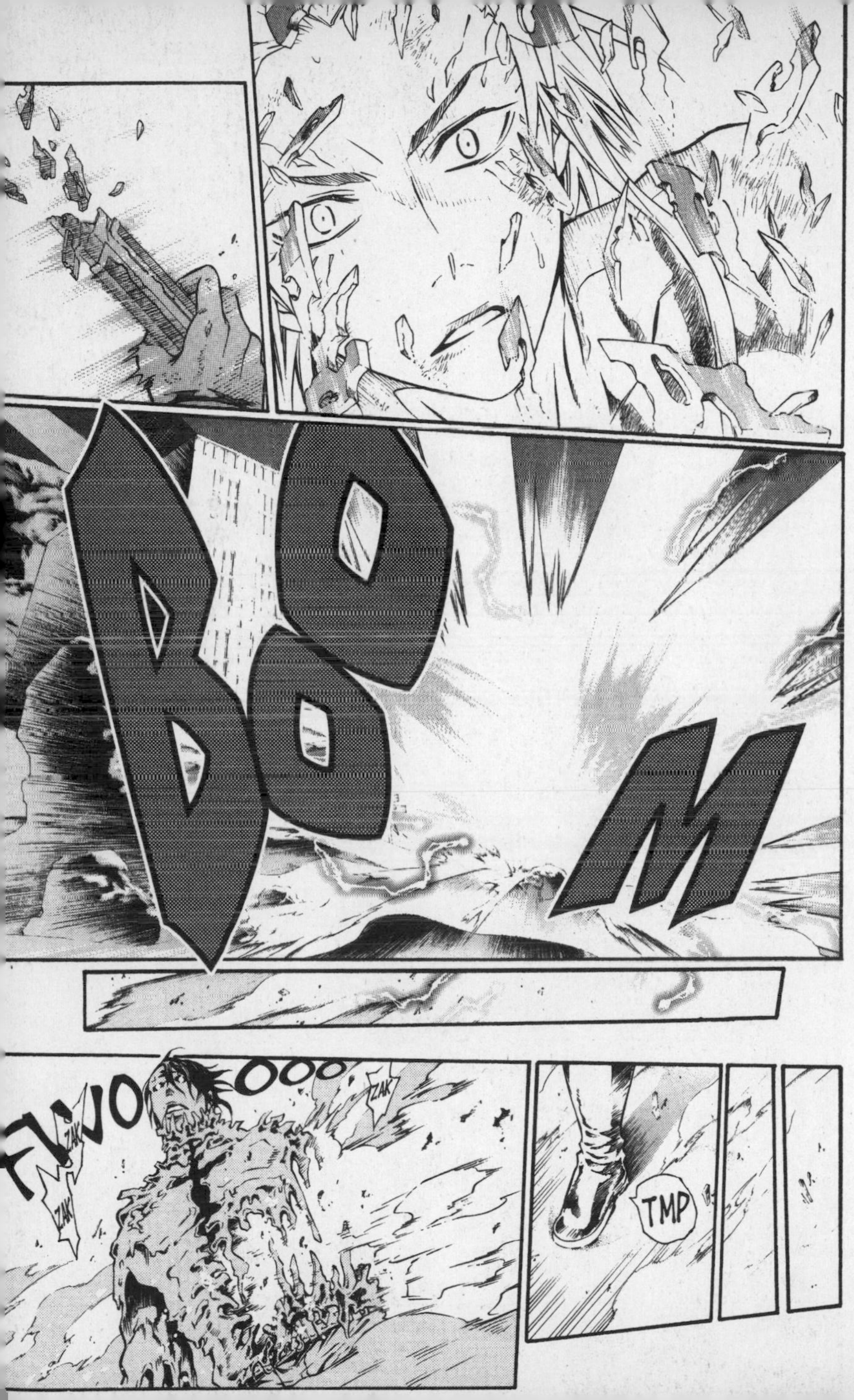
BOOM
TMP
FWOOOO
ZAK
ZAK
ZAK

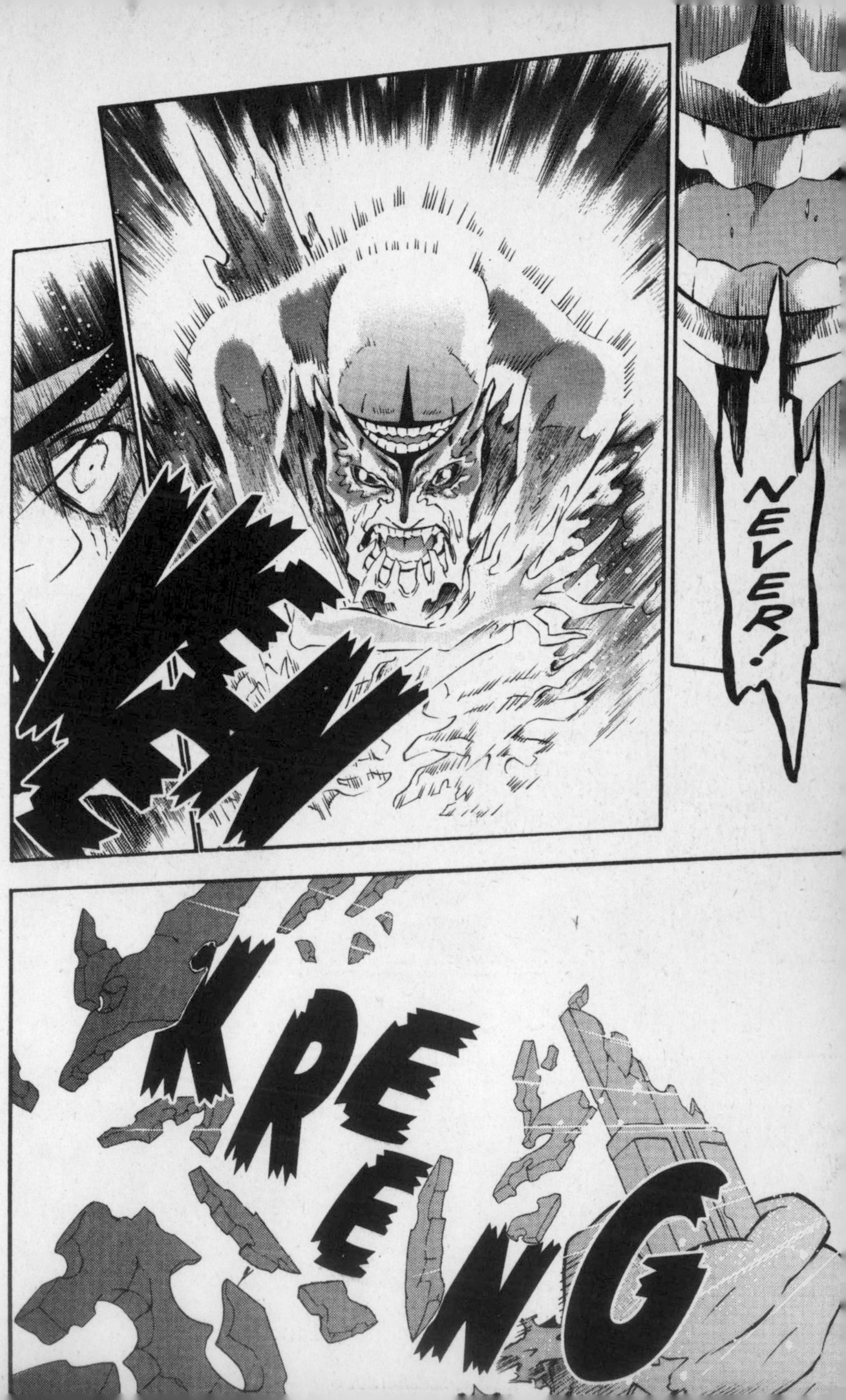
NEVER!
KREENG

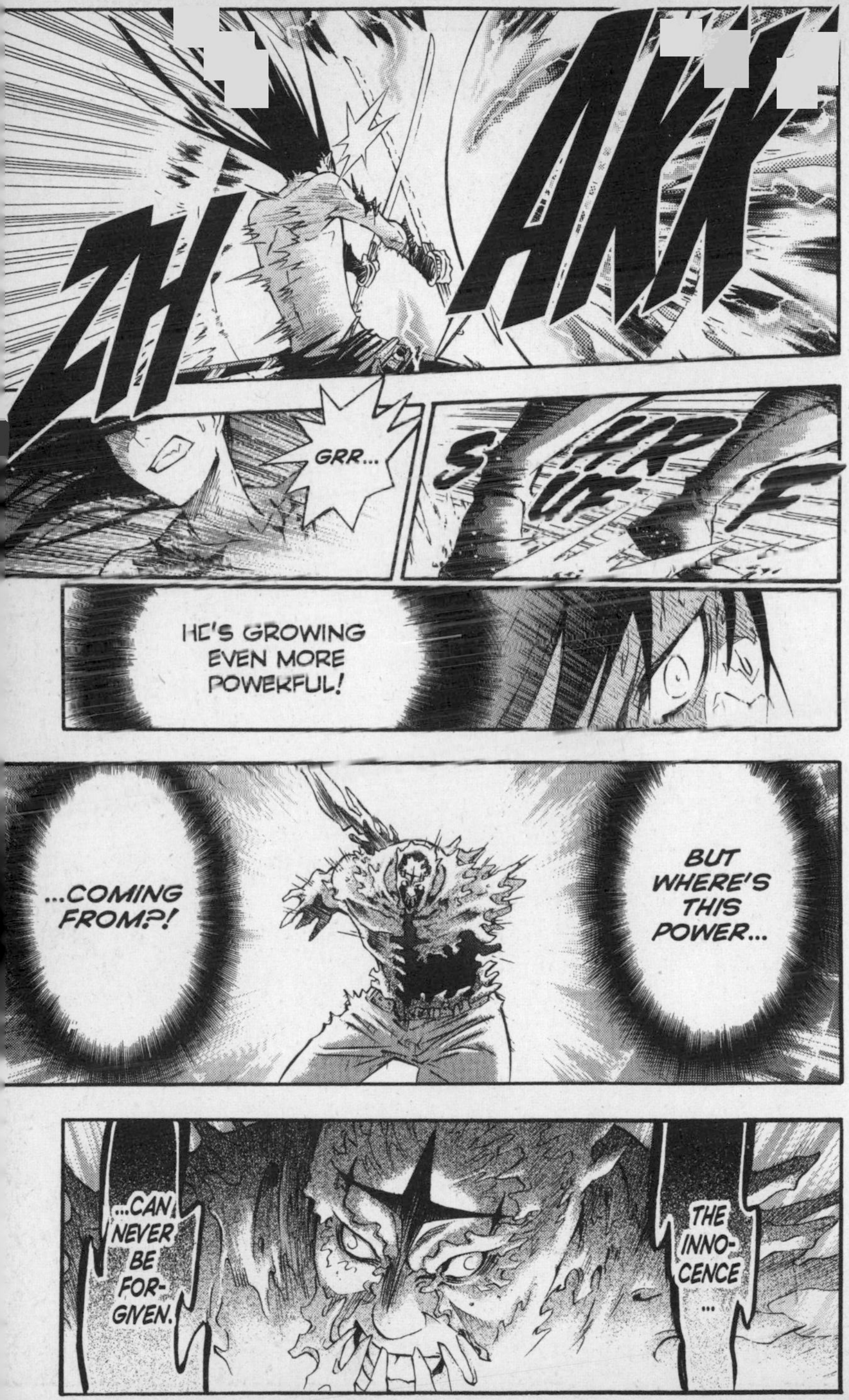
ZHANK
GRR...
HE'S GROWING EVEN MORE POWERFUL!
BUT WHERE'S THIS POWER...
...COMING FROM?!
THE INNO-CENCE...
...CAN NEVER BE FOR-GIVEN.

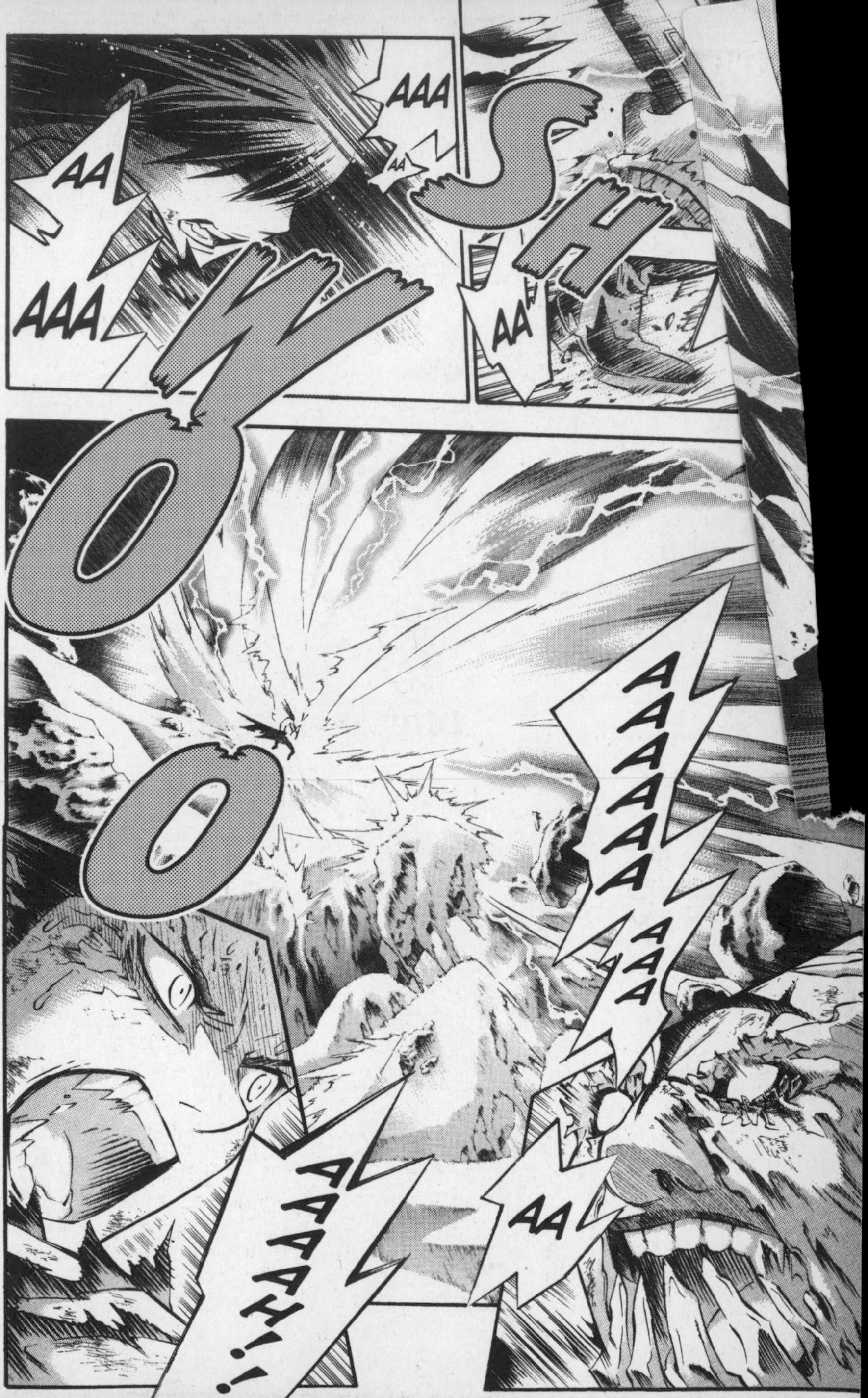
AA
SHWOOO
AAA
AA
AA
AAA
AAAAAAAAAA
AA
AAAAAH!!

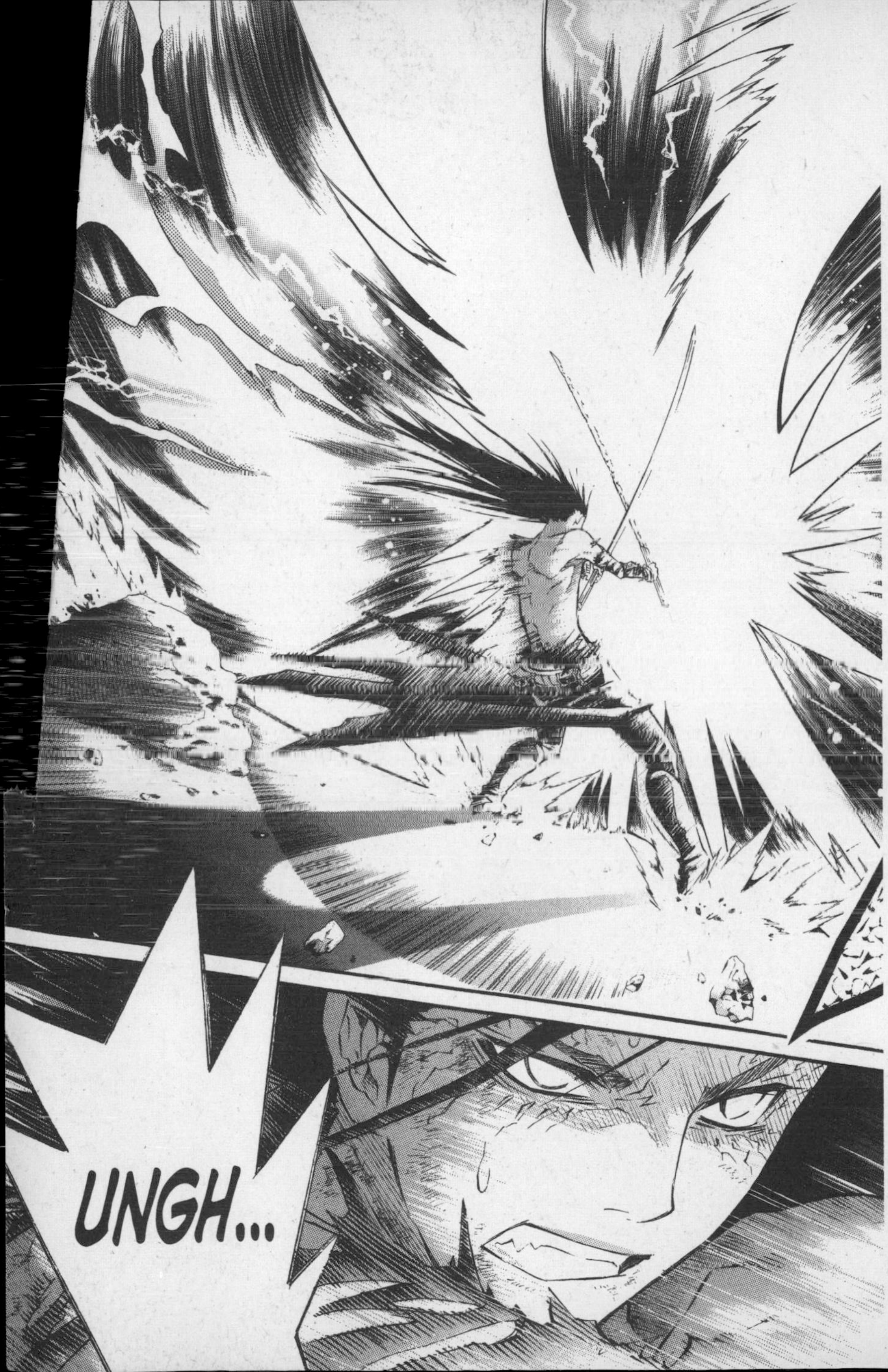
UNGH...

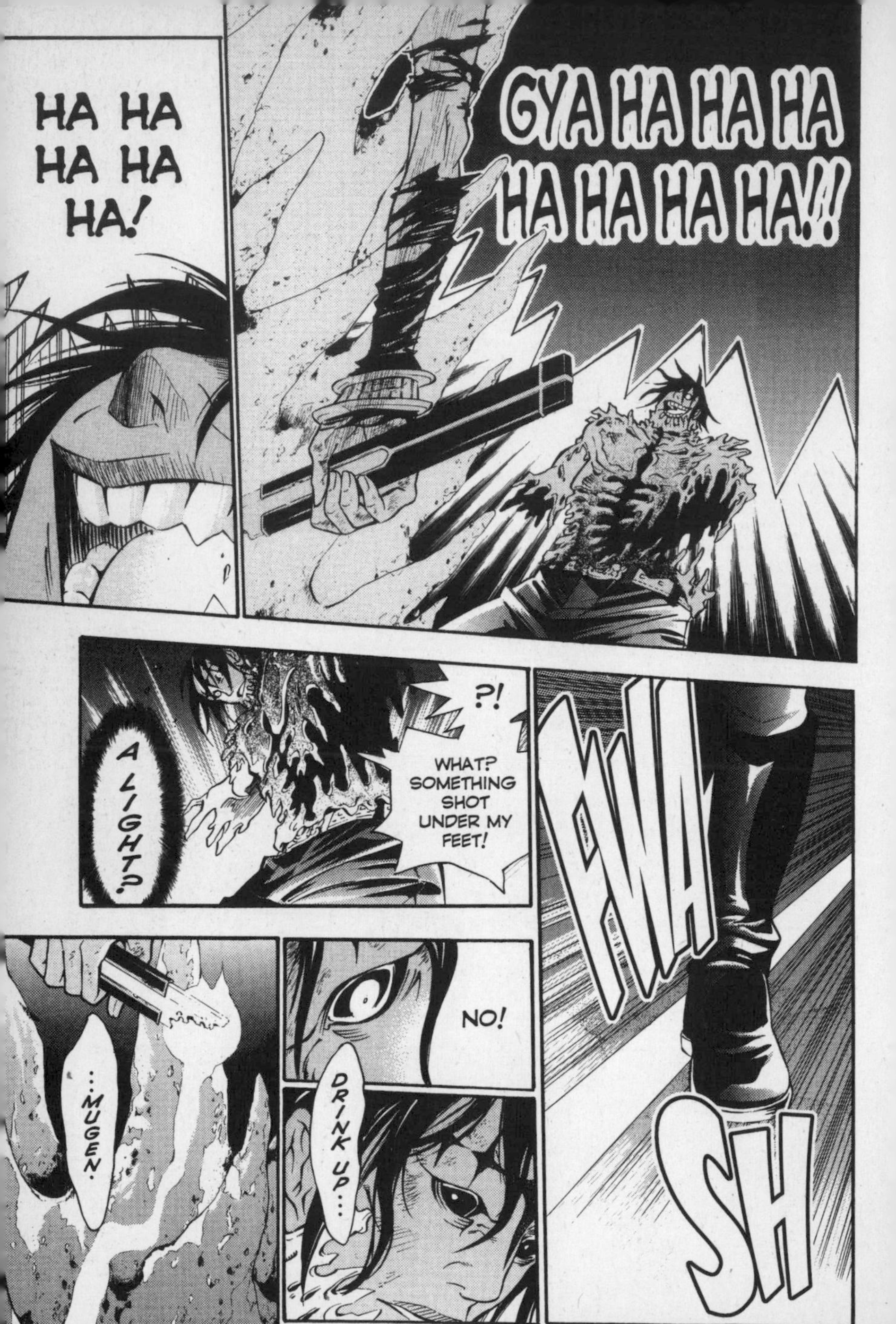
GYA HA HA HA HA HA HA HA!!
HA HA HA HA HA!
FWA
SH
?!
WHAT? SOMETHING SHOT UNDER MY FEET!
A LIGHT?
NO!
DRINK UP...
...MUGEN.

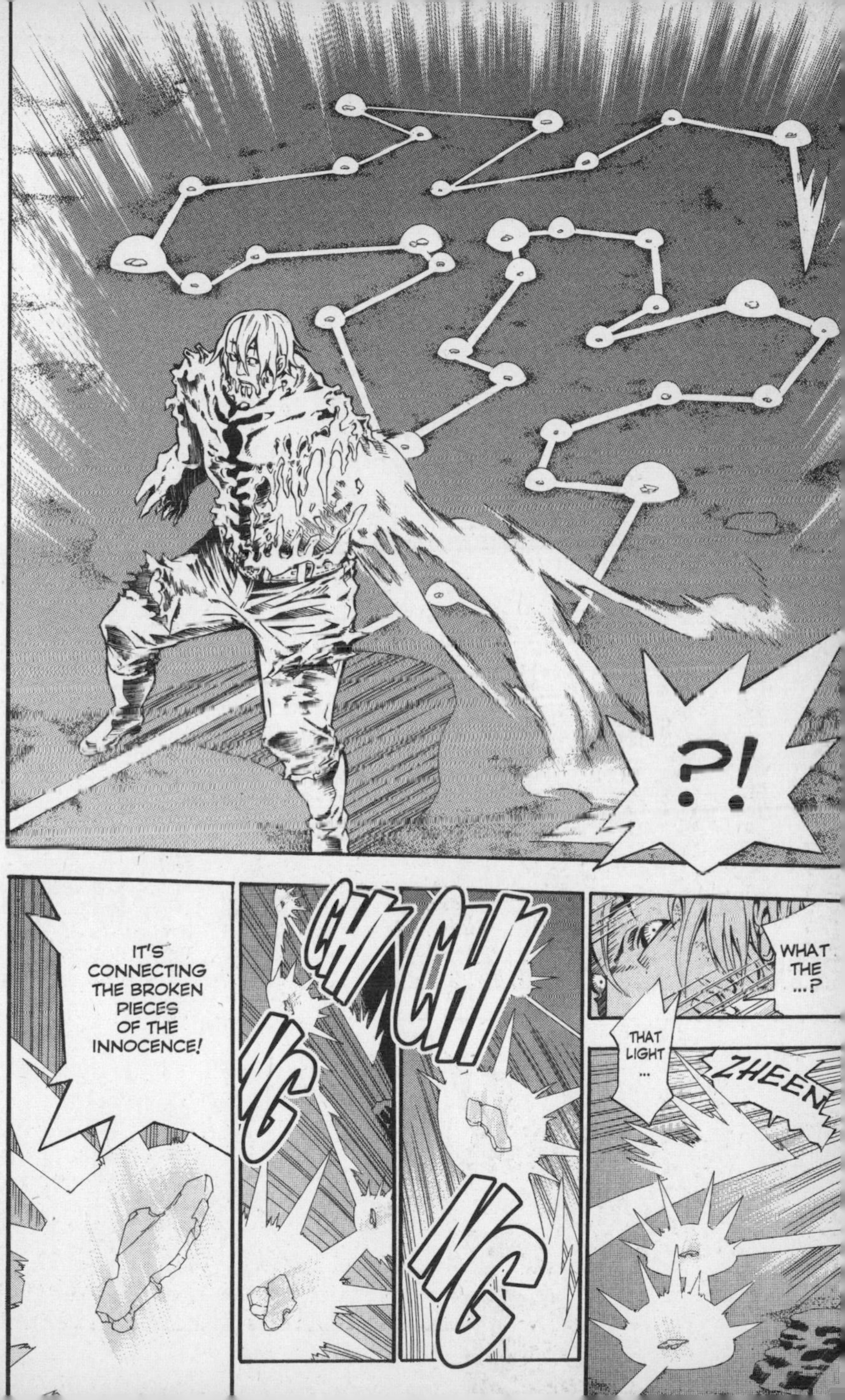
?!
WHAT THE ...?
THAT LIGHT ...
ZHEEN
CHING
CHING
IT'S CONNECTING THE BROKEN PIECES OF THE INNOCENCE!

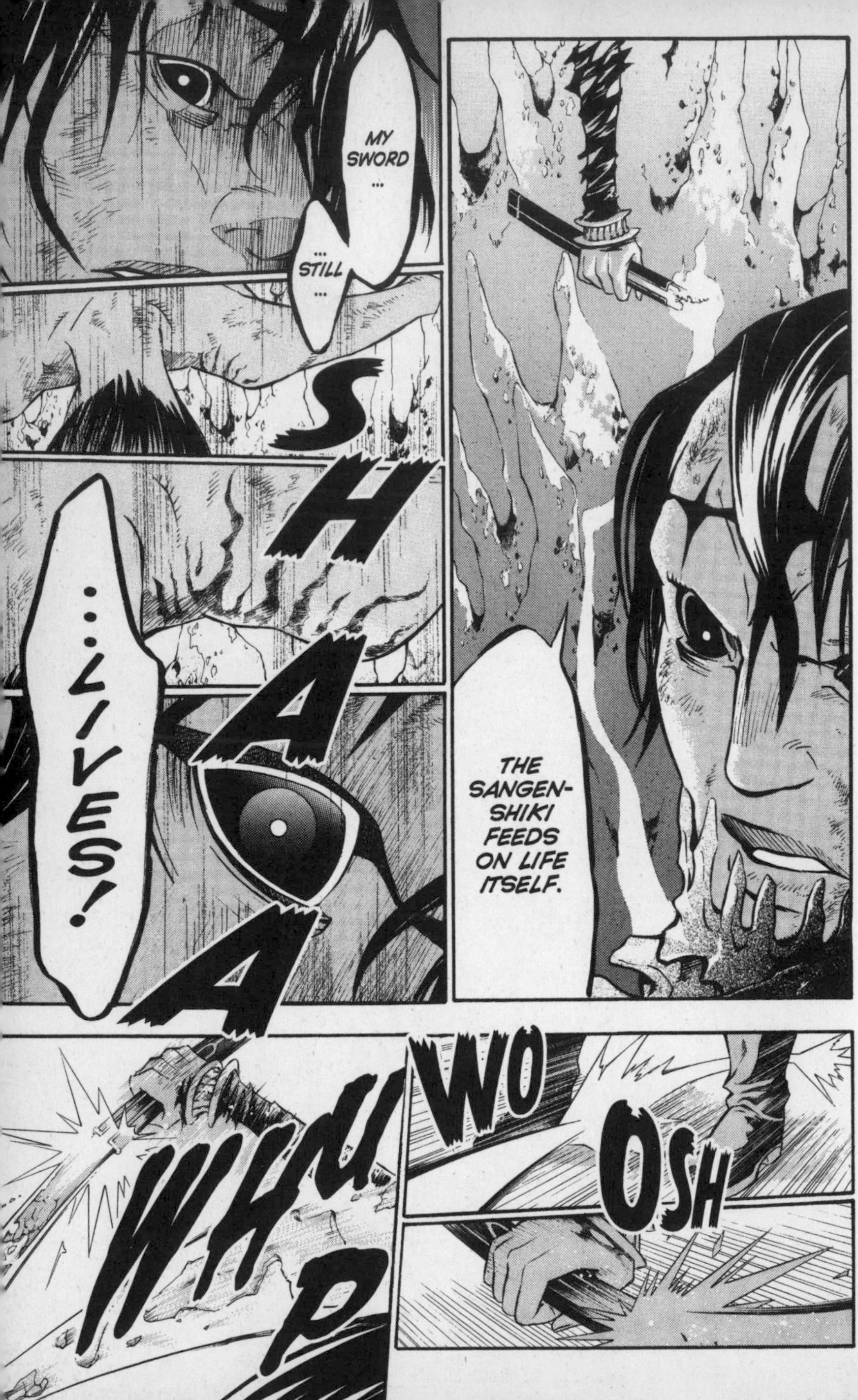
THE SANGEN-SHIKI FEEDS ON LIFE ITSELF.
MY SWORD ...
... STILL ...
SHAAA
...LIVES!
WOOSH
WHUMP

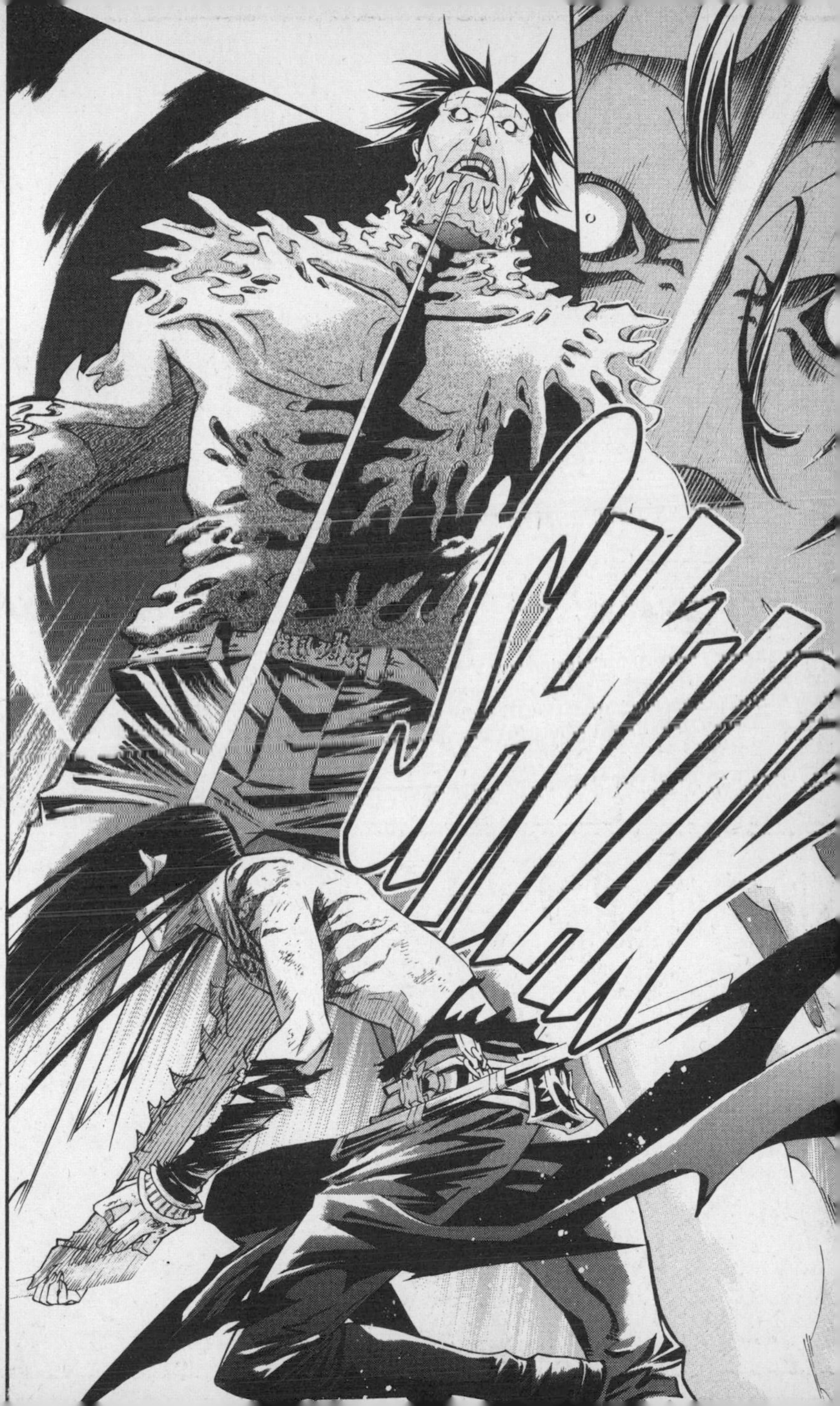

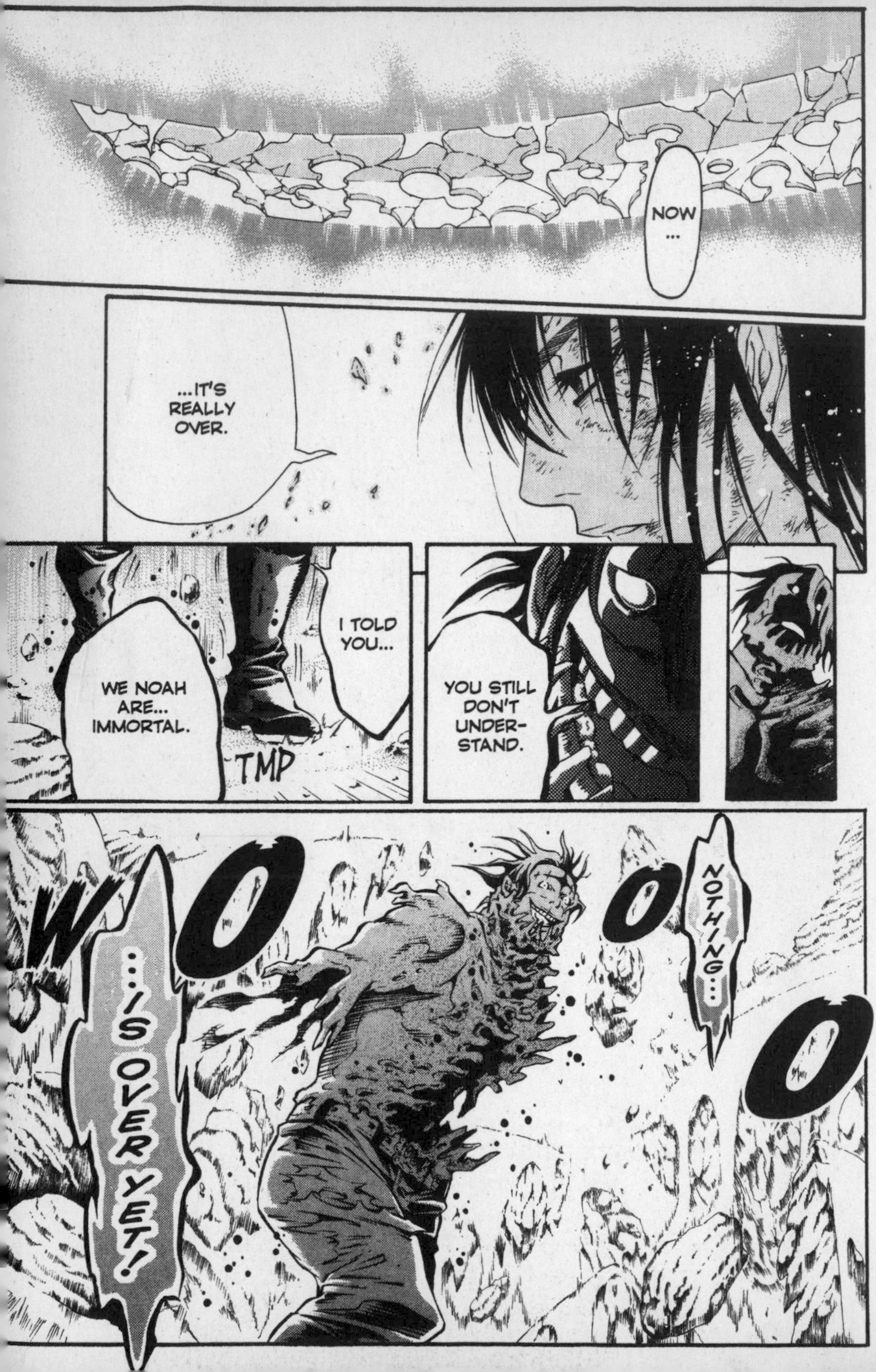
NOW...
...IT'S REALLY OVER.
YOU STILL DON'T UNDER-STAND.
I TOLD YOU...
WE NOAH ARE... IMMORTAL.
TMP
NOTHING...
...IS OVER YET!
WOOOO

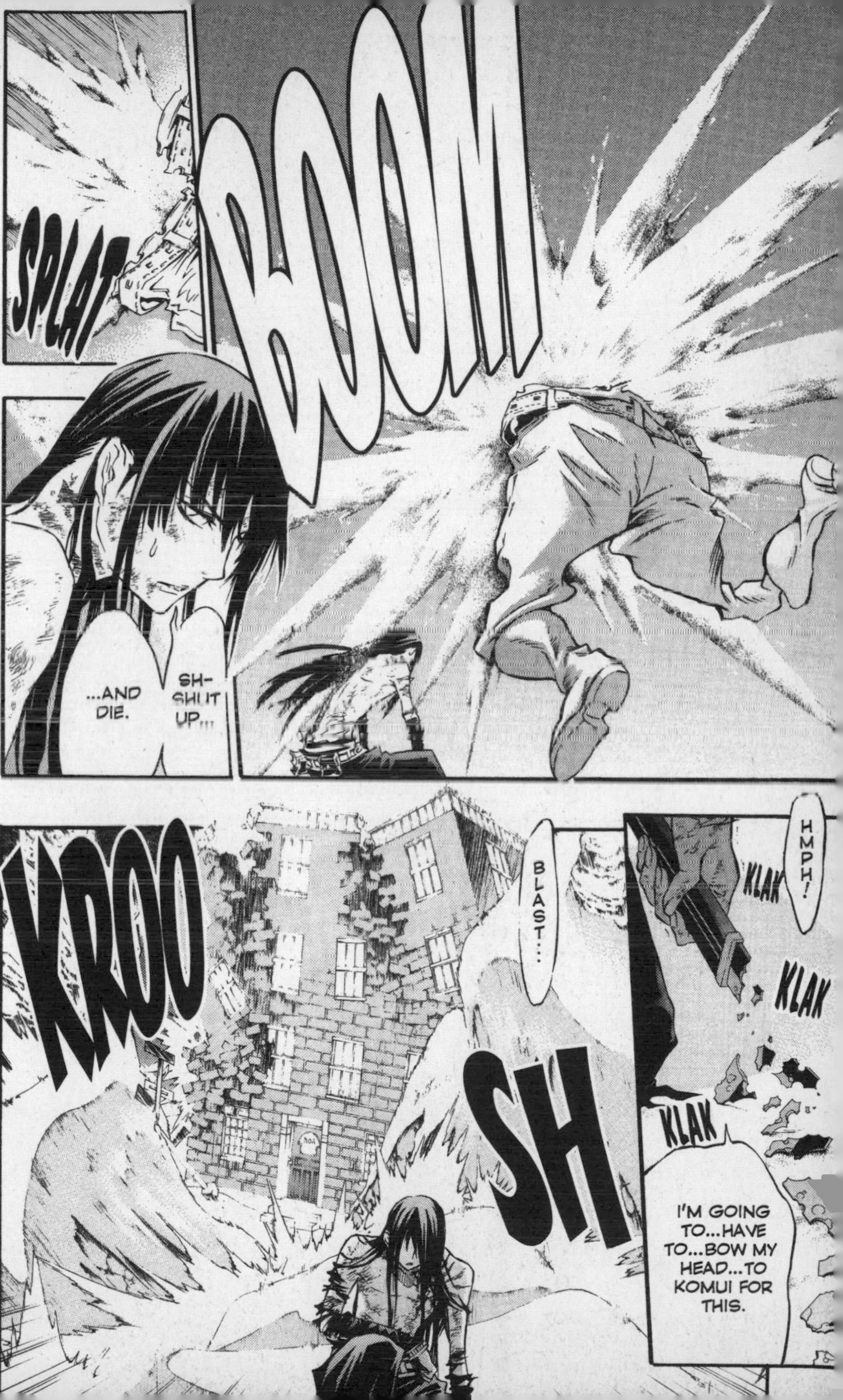
BOOM
SPLAT
SH-SHUT UP...
...AND DIE.
HMPH!
KLAK
KLAK
KLAK
I'M GOING TO...HAVE TO...BOW MY HEAD...TO KOMUI FOR THIS.
BLAST...
KROO
SH

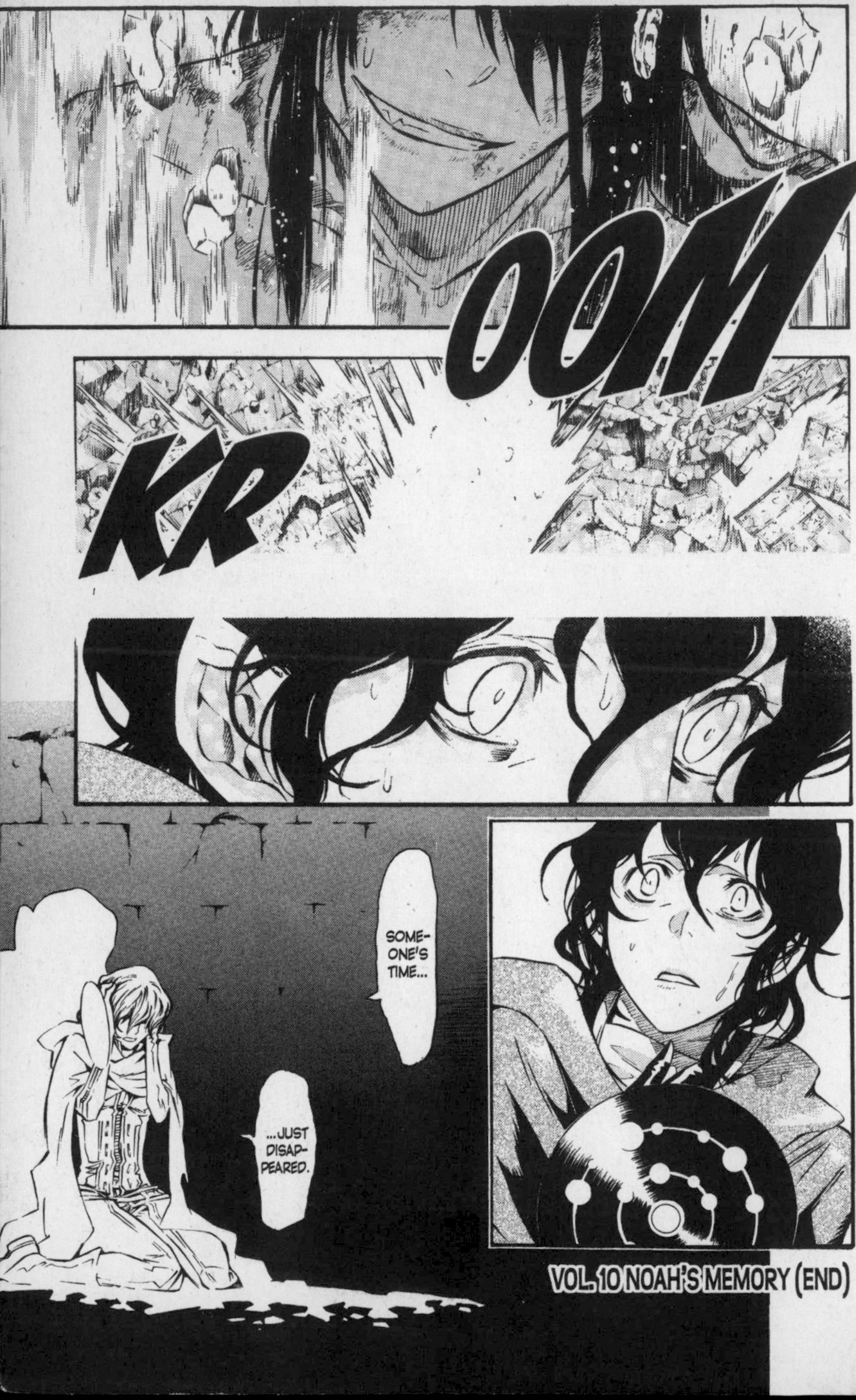
KR
OOM
SOME-ONE'S TIME...
...JUST DISAP-PEARED.
VOL. 10 NOAH'S MEMORY (END)

D.GRAY THEATER

STORY BY KATSURA HOSHINO
ART BY RANDOM ASSISTANT

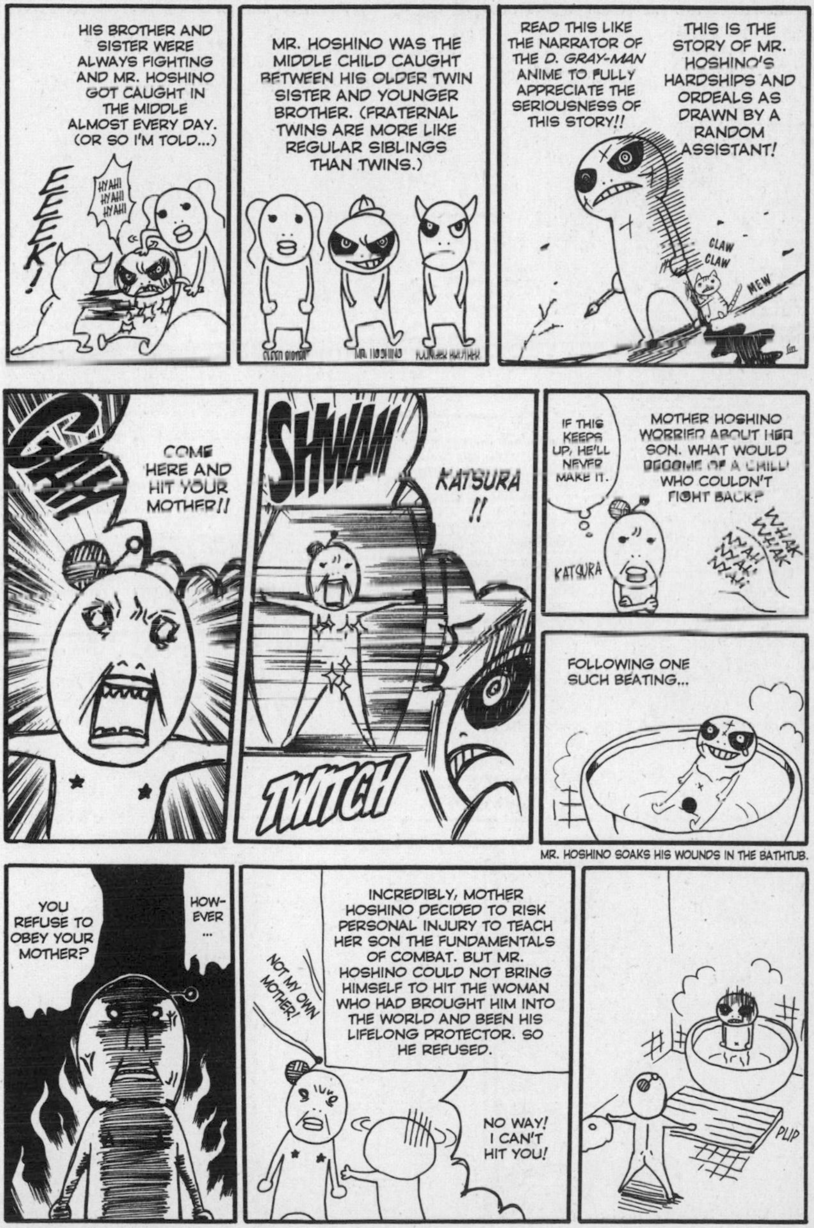
THIS IS THE STORY OF MR. HOSHINO'S HARDSHIPS AND ORDEALS AS DRAWN BY A RANDOM ASSISTANT!
READ THIS LIKE THE NARRATOR OF THE *D. GRAY-MAN* ANIME TO FULLY APPRECIATE THE SERIOUSNESS OF THIS STORY!!
CLAW CLAW
MEW
MR. HOSHINO WAS THE MIDDLE CHILD CAUGHT BETWEEN HIS OLDER TWIN SISTER AND YOUNGER BROTHER. (FRATERNAL TWINS ARE MORE LIKE REGULAR SIBLINGS THAN TWINS.)
HIS BROTHER AND SISTER WERE ALWAYS FIGHTING AND MR. HOSHINO GOT CAUGHT IN THE MIDDLE ALMOST EVERY DAY. (OR SO I'M TOLD...)
HYAH! HYAH! HYAH!
EEEEK!
MOTHER HOSHINO WORRIED ABOUT HER SON. WHAT WOULD BECOME OF A CHILD WHO COULDN'T FIGHT BACK?
IF THIS KEEPS UP, HE'LL NEVER MAKE IT.
WHAK WHAK
NYAH! NYAH! NYAH!
KATSURA
FOLLOWING ONE SUCH BEATING...
MR. HOSHINO SOAKS HIS WOUNDS IN THE BATHTUB.
SHWAM
KATSURA!!
TWITCH
GAH
COME HERE AND HIT YOUR MOTHER!!
PLIP
INCREDIBLY, MOTHER HOSHINO DECIDED TO RISK PERSONAL INJURY TO TEACH HER SON THE FUNDAMENTALS OF COMBAT. BUT MR. HOSHINO COULD NOT BRING HIMSELF TO HIT THE WOMAN WHO HAD BROUGHT HIM INTO THE WORLD AND BEEN HIS LIFELONG PROTECTOR. SO HE REFUSED.
NOT MY OWN MOTHER!
NO WAY! I CAN'T HIT YOU!
HOW-EVER...
YOU REFUSE TO OBEY YOUR MOTHER?

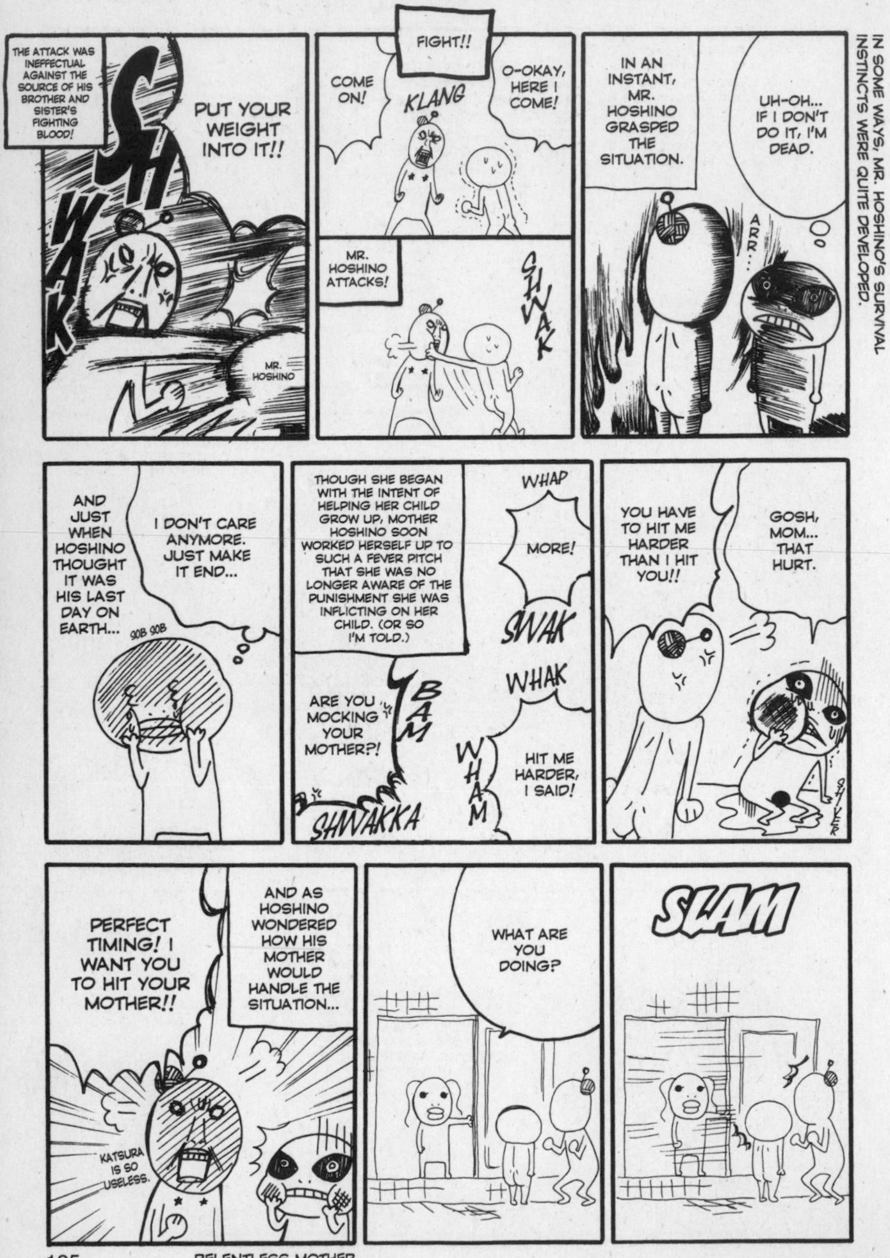
IN SOME WAYS, MR. HOSHINO'S SURVIVAL INSTINCTS WERE QUITE DEVELOPED.
UH-OH... IF I DON'T DO IT, I'M DEAD.
IN AN INSTANT, MR. HOSHINO GRASPED THE SITUATION.
ARR...
FIGHT!!
O-OKAY, HERE I COME!
KLANG
COME ON!
SHWAK
MR. HOSHINO ATTACKS!
PUT YOUR WEIGHT INTO IT!!
SHWAK
THE ATTACK WAS INEFFECTUAL AGAINST THE SOURCE OF HIS BROTHER AND SISTER'S FIGHTING BLOOD!
MR. HOSHINO
GOSH, MOM... THAT HURT.
YOU HAVE TO HIT ME HARDER THAN I HIT YOU!!
SHIVER
WHAP
MORE!
SWAK
WHAK
HIT ME HARDER, I SAID!
WHAM
BAM
THOUGH SHE BEGAN WITH THE INTENT OF HELPING HER CHILD GROW UP, MOTHER HOSHINO SOON WORKED HERSELF UP TO SUCH A FEVER PITCH THAT SHE WAS NO LONGER AWARE OF THE PUNISHMENT SHE WAS INFLICTING ON HER CHILD. (OR SO I'M TOLD.)
ARE YOU MOCKING YOUR MOTHER?!
SHWAKKA
I DON'T CARE ANYMORE. JUST MAKE IT END...
AND JUST WHEN HOSHINO THOUGHT IT WAS HIS LAST DAY ON EARTH...
SOB SOB
SLAM
WHAT ARE YOU DOING?
AND AS HOSHINO WONDERED HOW HIS MOTHER WOULD HANDLE THE SITUATION...
PERFECT TIMING! I WANT YOU TO HIT YOUR MOTHER!!
KATSURA IS SO USELESS.

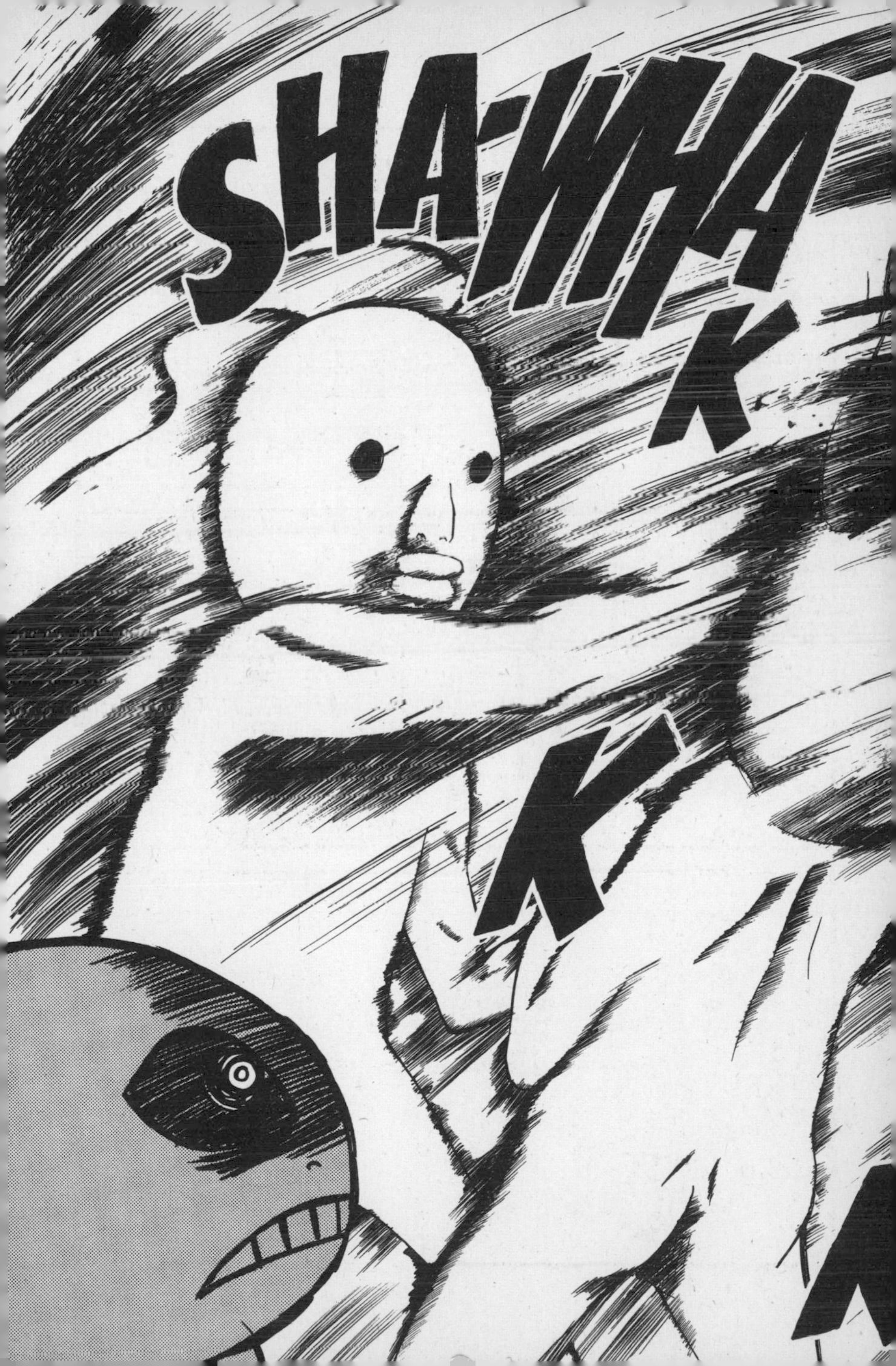
SHA-WHAKK

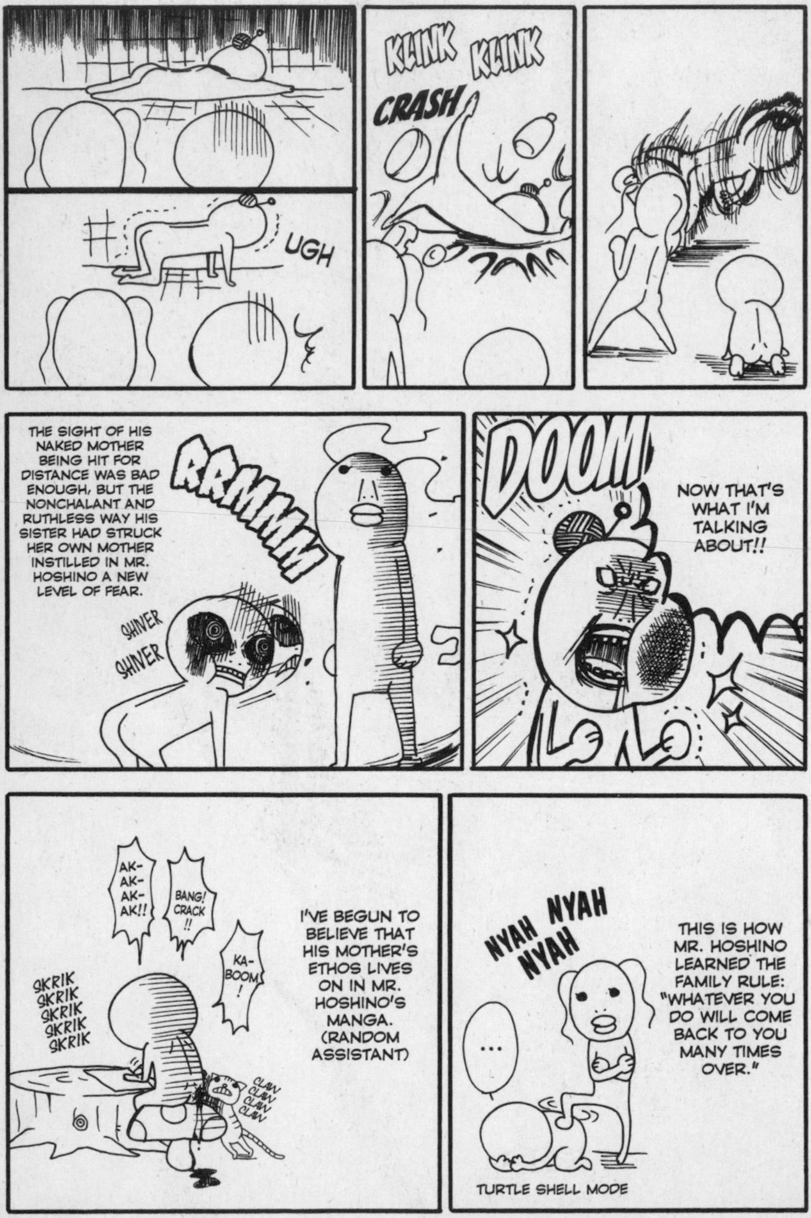
KLINK
KLINK
CRASH
UGH
DOOM
NOW THAT'S WHAT I'M TALKING ABOUT!!
THE SIGHT OF HIS NAKED MOTHER BEING HIT FOR DISTANCE WAS BAD ENOUGH, BUT THE NONCHALANT AND RUTHLESS WAY HIS SISTER HAD STRUCK HER OWN MOTHER INSTILLED IN MR. HOSHINO A NEW LEVEL OF FEAR.
RRMMMM
SHIVER
SHIVER
NYAH NYAH
NYAH NYAH
...
THIS IS HOW MR. HOSHINO LEARNED THE FAMILY RULE: "WHATEVER YOU DO WILL COME BACK TO YOU MANY TIMES OVER."
TURTLE SHELL MODE
AK-AK-AK-AK!!
BANG! CRACK!!
KA-BOOM!
I'VE BEGUN TO BELIEVE THAT HIS MOTHER'S ETHOS LIVES ON IN MR. HOSHINO'S MANGA. (RANDOM ASSISTANT)
SKRIK SKRIK SKRIK SKRIK SKRIK
CLAW CLAW CLAW CLAW

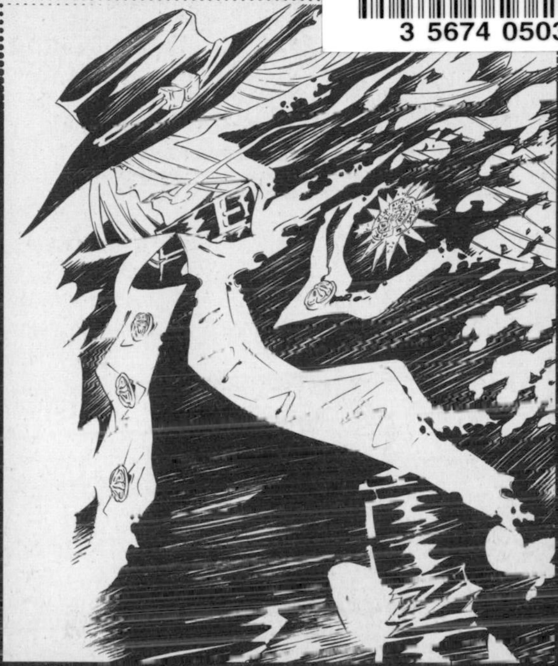

IN THE NEXT VOLUME...

Allen Walker has rejoined his fellow Exorcists, and together they enter the Ark of Noah. They're opposed by two young Noah who seem less interested in the grand plans of the Millennium Earl than in collecting on yet another of the seemingly endless debts Allen's master, General Cross, has left in his wake. That, however, doesn't make the Noah any less lethal!

Available Now!

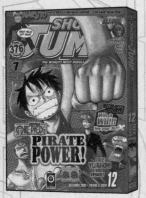
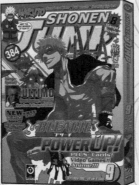
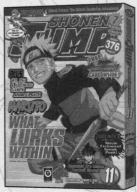